Virginia Woolf

Virginia Woolf

The Impact of
Childhood Sexual Abuse
on Her Life and Work

LOUISE DeSALVO

BEACON PRESS
Boston

BEACON PRESS
25 Beacon Street
Boston, Massachusetts 02108

Beacon Press books
are published under the auspices of
the Unitarian Universalist Association of Congregations.

96 95 94 93 92 91 90 89   1 2 3 4 5 6 7 8

Text design by Joanna Steinkeller

Library of Congress Cataloging-in-Publication Data
DeSalvo, Louise A.
Virginia Woolf : the impact of childhood
sexual abuse on her life and work.
Bibliography: p. 343.
Includes index.
1. Woolf, Virginia, 1882–1941.   2. Novelists,
English—20th century—Biography.   3. Sexually
abused children—Great Britain—Biography.
4. Incest victims—Great Britain—Biography.
5. Psychoanalysis and literature.   6. Children
in literature.   7. Family in literature.
I. Title.
PR6045.072Z613   1989   823'.912 [B] 88-47657
ISBN 0-8070-6326-6

"What awful lives children live!"
"Yes . . . And they can't tell anybody."
Martin and Rose in Virginia Woolf, *The Years*

I believe the only hope for the world is
to put all children of all countries
together on an island and let them start
fresh without knowing what a hideous
system we have invented here.
Virginia Woolf, in a letter
to Margaret Llewelyn Davies
Wednesday, 2 January 1918

For Robert S. Berlin
who taught me to pay attention
to the words of children

For Jane Marcus
who taught me how to read
Virginia Woolf in a new way

For Ernest J. DeSalvo
who once again helped it happen

and for
Jason DeSalvo and Justin DeSalvo
who, I hope, will have many good things
to remember

Contents

List of Illustrations

Preface

In 1962, while I was a student of Carol Smith at Douglass College, I first became interested in Virginia Woolf's portraits of children in *To the Lighthouse*. I was twenty years old at the time, and fascinated by the figure of Cam Ramsay, the young alter ego of her creator, Virginia Woolf. While other students concerned themselves with the grownups in the novel, with the compelling figures of Mrs. Ramsay and Mr. Ramsay, and Lily Briscoe, and the big issues that the novel takes up—the passage of time, the meaning of art, whether or not nature is indifferent to human beings—my own focus stayed firmly fixed on Cam and on the other Ramsay children.[1] In the inside cover of the copy of the novel which I used at the time, and to which I still refer, I listed the names of the Ramsay brood, as if to fix them as individuals in my mind: Prue, Nancy, Rose, James, Cam, Jasper, Andrew, Roger.

Some twenty-five years later, I turned again to these young inhabitants of Woolf's novels, and to Woolf's own childhood, adolescence, and young adulthood. This study is the culmination of fifteen years of work on Virginia Woolf, during which I traced the composition of her first novel, *The Voyage Out* (in which the central figure is the young adult Rachel Vinrace), edited an early version of that novel, called *Melymbrosia*, charted her friendship with Vita Sackville-West, co-edited Vita's letters to Virginia, and began an exploration of Woolf's adolescence which I continue here.[2]

Although I had always been interested in Woolf's younger characters, this interest quickened as a result of an essay I wrote on Djuna Barnes's play *The Antiphon*, on rape, incest, and child abuse in that work.[3] I noticed almost immediately that Barnes used images about the instability of the world and about the dangers of living that were extremely similar to those used by Woolf—Mrs. Dalloway, in the novel which bears her name, has a persistent feeling that "something awful was about to happen."[4] In Barnes, these feelings are accounted for by the incestuous experience of the central character Miranda, by the fact that she was raped by her father Titus.

As I worked out what was most confusing and compelling about Barnes's use of language (how images are used to simultaneously explore yet withhold information about what happened to Miranda), something clicked, and I knew that I wanted to again work on Woolf, not only on her own childhood, but also on the world as it is experienced through the eyes of Woolf's young characters. I suspected that, in her characters, Woolf, like Barnes, might be tracing how life felt to her as a child who had been sexually abused, an aspect of her work to which I had not paid sufficient attention. In Woolf's case, the abuse was by her half brothers Gerald and George Duckworth; it began, according to her own testimony, when she was about six years old.

Virginia Woolf's and Djuna Barnes's experiences, as we now know, were not extraordinary but are representative of the great number of women who have been victims of sexual abuse and violence in childhood.[5] They are but two of the multitudes of children who have been forced to endure what the psychoanalyst Alice Miller in *Thou Shalt Not Be Aware* refers to as "society's betrayal of the child"—the child's endurance of extreme psychological and physical cruelty from the very people from whom they expect care.[6]

Even though I had read some of Woolf's novels more than a dozen times before I began this study, in my maturity I had stopped seeing the children in Woolf's work. But once I shifted my focus to the world of the young, I saw that there are scores of young people in Woolf's work and that she also explores the effect of Victorian modes of child rearing in many of her nonfictional works, such as in her biography of Roger Fry. She has a great deal to say about that institution, the nursery, about education, and about gender- and class-determined patterns of enculturation. So what I had originally conceived as a study which would explore Woolf's treatment of sexual abuse as an example of society's betrayal of the child became a study which also included the effect of Victorian child-rearing practices which, in their own more covert way, also involved a betrayal of the child—a topic that Woolf describes and treats in some detail.

The intent of this book is not to try to find culprits, or to fix blame for what happened to Woolf, for what happened to the other children in her family, or for what happens to the young characters in her works. Nor is it to demonstrate how maladjusted Virginia Woolf was because of what happened to her as a youngster. Rather, I have explored, through Woolf's life, through the experience of the other members of her family, through her creations, through her nonfiction, and through the work of contemporary researchers into the history of the family, sexual abuse, and patterns of child rearing, what the effect and experiences were of a childhood like hers. I believe that they are relevant for understanding the consequences of child-rearing practices which are still to some degree being practiced today.

I had two intentions in writing this book. First, to use Virginia Woolf's work to form a portrait of the world of the child and adolescent as she understood it. Second, to form a portrait of how Virginia Woolf perceived and described herself and her experiences as a child and adolescent by using both works that she wrote during these time periods, and works that she wrote in her maturity describing them. Two other issues emerged as I worked: to describe the climate of the Stephen family household during Woolf's infancy—a period that is documented in scores of letters and memoirs of other members of her family, a period which contemporary researchers believe is especially significant in the formulation of human personality, and about which she herself has something to say; to explore the experiences of the other girls in the Stephen family household, her half sister Laura Stephen, her half sister Stella Duckworth, and her sister Vanessa Stephen Bell, to determine the extent to which Virginia's life was part of a family pattern.

I record here how Virginia Woolf viewed and interpreted the experience of growing—how she perceived the movement from infancy through childhood and young adulthood. She presents a cogent and coherent analysis about the impact of child rearing on personality development that locates the causative factors in human personality in how one is treated as a child. Like many other survivors of sexual abuse, she described the deleterious and permanent impact of those experiences upon her psyche, but she did it without the supportive environment of the contemporary movement to "speak out" about violence. She also understood that the possibilities for children to realize their fullest potential are complicated by one's class, and race, as well as one's gender and that world events impinge upon the experience of childhood.

An introduction recounts attitudes of several of her biographers about the incest she experienced as a child, and describes the consequences of sexual abuse and Victorian child-rearing practices.

I then turn my attention, in part 1, "A Family Pattern," to the experiences of two of Woolf's half-sisters, Laura Stephen and Stella Duckworth, and her sister Vanessa Bell, all of whose treatment illuminates Woolf's own. Taken together, their experiences provide an important glimpse into the climate in the home of the Stephen family. This section dramatically revises the commonly held notion that Woolf's infancy was spent in a secure and serene household and that what happened to her within the Stephen household was somehow anomalous.

Part 2, "Childhood," examines Virginia Woolf's interpretation of her own childhood and its effects on her later life, examines a juvenile work which depicts family life, written before her mother's death, during a period that has been described as idyllic, and describes the portraits of selected children in the novels of her maturity. Chapter 4, "A Daughter Remembers," describes Woolf's recollections of her late Victorian childhood and her experiences as a sexually abused child and discusses their impact. Chapter 5, "In the House of the Paterfamilias," treats the juvenile novel that Virginia Woolf wrote, A *Cockney's Farming Experiences* and its sequel *The Experiences of a Pater-familias,* both of which have been virtually ignored or misrepresented by biographers of Woolf as a hilarious young attempt at fiction. Yet, like the juvenilia of the Brontës, they explore, in graphic detail, Woolf's early perception that the child was severely mistreated within the patriarchal family. Chapter 6, "'In the Beginning There Was the Nursery,'" examines the significant portraits of many of the children in Woolf's published novels and the statements that she made about childhood in selected works of nonfiction.

In part 3, I discuss the most well-documented year of Woolf's adolescence, her adolescent writings, and her portraits of adolescents and her analysis of the impact of education upon young people in the work of her maturity. Chapter 7, "1897, Virginia Woolf at Fifteen," recreates the life of Virginia Woolf as an adolescent primarily through her 1897 diary. Chapter 8, "As Miss Jan Says," traces the creation of Woolf's fictional writing persona, Miss Jan, speculates about a long work that she wrote, "The Eternal Miss Jan," about the existence of a god, and a "news story," "Terrible Tragedy in a Duckpond"—a work which documents Woolf's early preoccupation with death by drowning, the method of suicide which she chose for herself in 1941. Chapter 9, "Changing Lives," describes certain of those superb portraits of adolescents in the Woolf canon: Cam and James in *To the Lighthouse*, the young people of several generations of the Pargiter family in *The Years*, as well as Woolf's analysis of education in adolescence. I describe as well Woolf's nonfictional explorations of the issue of education for young women and their treatment within the Victorian family.

This book is not strictly biographical; nor is it strictly a work of literary criticism. Rather, it is a work which makes use of Virginia Woolf's youthful experiences, and her own writing in and about childhood, adolescence, and young adulthood for exploring and understanding "society's betrayal of the child." And as we shall see, Virginia Woolf has a great deal to say about this issue. I believe that her point of view was visionary, anticipating by more than half a century the insights that researchers are arriving at today about the prevalence of sexual violence and its impact upon personality.

When we focus upon the experience of the child in a family, we must discuss the sometimes damaging consequences of parental behavior. But we must also understand why parents act as they do—we must remember that parents, in fact, have had parents, who also have had parents—all of whom have performed the difficult and complex task of parenting within a social structure which proscribes very clearly, if sometimes very indirectly, how children must be raised and what the role of the mother and father should be.

I explain the parenting Woolf received as a consequence of social roles, of personal and political history, of the institutions that had developed (the patriarchal family, the nursery) to raise children, rather than as an example of the personal virtue or pathology of her parents. I believe that the experience of Woolf's life is an example of the negative consequences of a system which largely excludes the father from nurturing or from the work attending child rearing; which overworks the mother; which uses poorly paid working-class girls for child care; and which invites the father, because of his powerful position within the household, to co-opt any and all nurturing within the family if he chooses to; and which expects parents to be unbounded sources of love, security, and affection, when they themselves have often been severely mistreated or deprived. In describing maternal and paternal behavior as a consequence of personal and political history within a given class and society, I believe that we can discuss the ill effect of parental treatment without falling into the trap of blaming mothers or fathers for how they have raised children.

My thinking on Woolf has changed over the course of these years largely as a result of the insights from the disciplines of feminist inquiry, the history of the family, Victorian studies, and the changes in psychoanalytic theory that stress personal history rather than internal drives as causative factors in neurosis. These disciplines now make it possible to understand Virginia Woolf's life in the widest possible context, in the context of the history of women, of how children were raised in Victorian England, of the consequences of the kind of child rearing that the Victorian middle and upper classes adopted for the rearing of their children, of how doctors treated children whom the family believed to have problems, of the impact of childhood incest upon personality development. I do not now believe, although I once did, that the behavior which Woolf manifested later in her life can be accounted for by any single cause, and surely not by an inherent madness. Any view which explains Virginia Woolf's behavior as madness is archaic: too much is now known about the behavior of victims of childhood abuse to support such a description. Rather I now believe that her life, as indeed any life, can be seen as a complex and creative response to many significant conditions of the time in which she grew up, and the family into which she was born, and the special experiences she had to endure, and the damaging behavior that was directed at her.

Surely, as in any life, some of these factors were far more significant than others—the fact of her abuse, for example. But that abuse occurred within the context of a family in which there were many other problems, some indigenous to that particular family, some the product of the times. And the very structure of the Victorian family, and their very attitudes towards sexuality, both contributed to the fact of Woolf's abuse, and made it impossible to dilute, through good care, the impact of that abuse once it had occurred. Indeed, there is every indication that it was made worse.

Woolf's depictions of the world of the child, of the adolescent, and the young adult afford us valuable insights because of her willingness to discuss her own abuse, to explore her relationships with her mother, father, and several siblings, and her own position in society as "the daughter of an educated man." She describes the effect on her psyche of being raised as a girl within a late Victorian family, which gave preferential treatment to its sons. She illuminates these issues in many of her novels and she treats them in her nonfictional works such as *A Room of One's Own* and *Three Guineas*. She was an important pioneer critic of the inequity in the different ways that girls and boys were raised and educated, and she was a severe critic of the elitist function of the educational system within her society. Her insights are as striking and as relevant today as they were when she first began to publish them, nearly three-quarters of a century ago.

Acknowledgments

This book is dedicated to five people who helped me immeasurably: Robert S. Berlin, who was my teacher at New York University, with whom I studied adolescence in literature; Ernest J. DeSalvo, who, once again, listened to every version of every chapter, and who insisted that I not obfuscate; Jason DeSalvo and Justin DeSalvo, who provided daily reminders about the concerns of adolescents, their continuing need for care, and who provided, as well, views about young people that were illuminating; and Jane Marcus, who prompted the writing of many of my essays, who saw to it that I met virtually every major Woolf scholar working in the United States, and whose own work exemplified the best of Woolf scholarship for more than a decade.

I have had the supreme good fortune to know many of the finest Virginia Woolf scholars, biographers, editors, and critics of our time, in addition to those working on other members of the family, and to have profited from their work, often well before publication, and from innumerable conversations, letters, and telephone calls with them: Elizabeth Abel, Morris Beja, Quentin Bell, Maxine Berry, John W. Bicknell, Margaret Comstock, Blanche Wiesen Cook, Maria Di-Battista, Kathleen Dobie, David V. Erdman, Alice Fox, Ralph Freedman, Angelica Garnett, Sandra M. Gilbert, Diane F. Gillespie, Laura Moss Gottlieb, John Graham, Susan Gubar, Jean Guiguet, Ellen Hawkes, Carolyn G. Heilbrun, Elizabeth Heine, Suzette A. Henke, Mark Hussey, Angela Ingram, Judith L. Johnston, Mitchell A. Leaska, Thomas S. W. Lewis, Jane Lilienfeld, Judy Little, Carol Hanbery MacKay, Madeline Moore, Roger Poole, Grace Radin, Sara Ruddick, Sonya Rudikoff, Lucio P. Ruotolo, Josephine O'Brien Schaefer, Beverly Schlack-Randles, Brenda Silver, Mark Spilka, Claire Sprague, Elizabeth Steele, Martine Stemmerick, Susan Merrill Squier, Lola L. Szladits, Ruth Z. Temple, Joanne Trautmann, Stephen Trombley, J. J. Wilson, Elizabeth Wood, Alex Zwerdling.

I owe James M. Haule a special debt: our long-distance phone calls and a voluminous correspondence through the years has been a special source of inspiration; his own work on a concordance to Virginia Woolf's work makes it possible to locate passages that stick in the mind. Nigel Nicolson graciously provided a copy of his typescript listing all references to Virginia Woolf in Vita Sackville-West's diaries and correspondence. Catherine F. Smith generously shared her knowledge of Woolf's Greece/Italy diary. Judith Walkowitz provided information and insights from her book-in-progress on Jack the Ripper. Blanche Cook insisted that I read Alice Miller, as did Harriet Field: to them I am immensely grateful.

The burden of this work has been eased considerably by many friends, family members, and colleagues at Fairleigh Dickinson University, where I began this work, and at Hunter College of the City University of New York, where I finished it: Carol Ascher, Dan Balaban, Richard Barickman, Allan Brick, the late Jilda Calabrese, Nancy Dean, Frances DeSalvo, the late Radames DeSalvo, Janet Emig, David Gordon, Dorothy O. Helly, Alan Holder, Harriet Johnson, Wendell Johnson, David Leverenz, Nick Lyons, Frank McLaughlin, Phyllis Moe, Charles Persky, Ann Raimes, Louise M. Rosenblatt, Mildred and Louis Sciacchetano, Donna Shalala, and Susan Shapiro. I owe a special debt of gratitude to my editor Joanne Wyckoff, who kept me happy and working and whose meticulous care with regard to this manuscript helped me immeasurably; to Ann Waters, who read my manuscript and gave invaluable suggestions; to Thomas Fischer, who made this a better book; to three anonymous readers; to Amy Ellis, for a great deal of hard work; to T. Walter Herbert's work on Nathaniel Hawthorne's family, which has enabled me to think through similar issues in relationship to Woolf; to Katherine Probst for nearly daily telephone conversations which helped me sort through many ideas.

I would like to thank everyone who invited me to speak about my work-in-progress, which allowed me to refine my ideas by subjecting them to public discourse: the organizers of the 1975 "Birth of Women" Conference at the State University of New York, at New Paltz, where I presented my work on *The Voyage Out* for the first time; David V. Erdman, who organized a panel at the 1979 Modern Language Association Convention in San Francisco, where I spoke on the creation of *Melymbrosia*; Susan M. Squier, who organized another panel at that convention; the organizers of the National Council of Teachers of English Convention in Omaha, Nebraska in 1980, where I discussed Woolf's work; the Wednesday Seminars at Fairleigh Dickinson University, for inviting me to talk about Woolf's transformation of her personal experiences into her art in 1980; Jane Lilienfeld, for convening a session at the 1980 MLA Convention in Houston, where I presented my work on Vanessa Bell for the first time; Jane Marcus, who also organized a panel for that convention, where I presented my work on Woolf's intellectual development for the first time; organizers of the "How Right We Write Conference" sponsored by the New Jersey Council of Teachers of English, held at Paramus High School in 1981, for asking me to talk about Woolf as a young woman; Jane Marcus, for organizing a panel for the MLA in New York in 1981, where I discussed the 1897 diary for the first time; the Center for the Psychological Study of the Arts, for inviting me to address the Plenary Session of the Sixth Annual Symposium in Literature and Psychology, SUNY, Buffalo, 1982, where I discussed "The Myth of Sexual Hysteria"; Jane Marcus, who organized the Virginia Woolf Centenary Symposia at the University of Texas at Austin, 1982, who invited me to lecture on Woolf's fifteenth year, where I gave "'As Miss Jan Says'"; Thomas S. W. Lewis, who invited me to Skidmore College to lecture on "Virginia Woolf's Diaries and Their Readers: A Study in Biography, Sexuality, and Sexism" in 1982; Douglass College, "Virginia Woolf: A Centenary Conference," 1982, for inviting me to give "'Children Never Forget'"; Hofstra University, the Twentieth-Century Women Writers' International Conference, in 1982, where I gave "Virginia, Virginius, Virginity," which became a part of the chapter on Woolf's childhood; Gay Tuchman, for inviting me to respond to Blanche Cook's paper at the Columbia Women's Studies Seminar in 1983, where I gave "Overt and Covert Methods of Censoring and Distorting

Women's Biographies" and who invited me again, in 1985, to discuss the writing of women's biography; the organizers of the Campus Seminars, Fairleigh Dickinson University, for inviting me to lecture on all of Woolf's early diaries in 1983; Phyllis Mannocchi, for inviting me to address the "Feminist Fortnight" at Colby College in 1983, where I gave "Virginia Woolf's Early Diaries: A Study in Biography, Sexuality, and Sexism"; the Center for the Psychological Study of the Arts, SUNY, Buffalo, for inviting me in 1983 to give "Literary Allusion as Self-Disclosure"; the organizers of the National Women's Studies Association Convention, Columbus, Ohio, 1983, for inviting me to speak on Woolf's early diaries; and, finally, Dorothy O. Helly, for inviting me to speak at the Berkshire Conference, 1987, in Wellesley, on the issue of writing the biographical sections of this work.

Many of these ideas were discussed, as well, with the four classes on Virginia Woolf and her works that I have held over the years at Hunter College of the City University of New York. I would like to thank the present chair, Allan Brick, and the past chairs, Charles Persky and Phyllis Moe, for always encouraging me and enabling me to teach courses which coincided with my current research interests; I would of course like to thank my students—well over a hundred and fifty of them—in those classes where I first aired my readings of the young people in Woolf's work. Their ideas greatly stimulated my own; their questioning forced me to refine my views.

I would like to thank the editors of journals and books in which early versions of some of these chapters first appeared. The section of the chapter on Vanessa Bell, describing Angelica Garnett's memoir, appeared in different form, under the title "Bloomsbury Born and Bred" in the *Women's Review of Books*, August 1985, and I would like to thank the editor, Linda Gardiner. The chapter "Virginia Woolf at Fifteen" was first written for Jane Marcus's edition, *Virginia Woolf: A Feminist Slant,* published by the University of Nebraska Press; I would like to thank Willis G. Regier, editor, and T. M. Farmiloe, of Macmillan, London. "As Miss Jan Says" appears in an earlier form in Jane Marcus, ed., *Virginia Woolf and Bloomsbury: A Centenary Celebration*, published by the Macmillan Press; I would like to thank T. M. Farmiloe of the press. The version which appears in that collection deals only with the creation of Woolf's writing persona and her religious essay. The chapter was presented at the Women's Studies Seminar at Hunter College, organized by Dorothy O. Helly, and I am extremely grateful to the participants in the forum, particularly Joan Tronto, for questions causing me to substantially revise my views presented in that part of the chapter dealing with the application of Carol Gilligan's ideas.

My work on the manuscript now referred to as "The Journal of Mistress Joan Martyn" began many years ago when I was checking early Woolf fictions. Lucio Ruotolo was assembling a team of scholars to edit some manuscript material for a special issue of *Twentieth Century Literature*, which appeared in Fall/Winter 1979, edited by William McBrien, and Susan Squier had been chosen to edit the story. She generously allowed me to co-edit the work with her; I wrote "Shakespeare's Other Sister" based on the story, for Jane Marcus's edition *New Feminist Essays on Virginia Woolf*, published by Macmillan, London, and the University of Nebraska Press.

The staffs of the various libraries where I worked were extremely helpful: Lola L. Szladits, curator of the Berg Collection at the New York Public Library has been a source of inspiration through the years, and so has Brian McInerney; the staff at the library at Drew University; Mrs. McMahon and the staff at the Fairleigh Dickinson University Library; the staff at the library at Hunter College; the staff at the library at Ramapo College; John Burt at the University of Sussex Library; the staff at the British Library, to name those where I spent most of my time.

Thanks are also due to the Virginia Woolf Estate for permission to quote from her published and unpublished work, and the other unpublished work included in this volume, as well as for permission to reproduce the photographs. I should like to thank Frances Spalding, Quentin Bell, Angelica Garnett, Diane F. Gillespie, and Jennifer Booth for their help in locating photographs, and Lola L. Szladits for her help in reproducing photographs.

Introduction

Virginia Woolf was a sexually abused child; she was an incest survivor.

Adeline Virginia Stephen was born on 25 January 1882 into the family of Julia and Leslie Stephen which already contained six other children. Each of her parents had been married before; each had survived the death of a spouse. Julia's first husband, Herbert Duckworth, had died in 1870; Leslie's wife Minny Thackeray had died in 1875. Julia and Leslie married in 1878 and settled at 22 Hyde Park Gate in London. In their combined household there was Laura, from Leslie's first marriage to Minny Thackeray, who was twelve at the time of Virginia's birth. There were Gerald, Stella, and George Duckworth, from Julia's first marriage to Herbert Duckworth, who were twelve, thirteen, and fourteen when Virginia was born. Then there were Vanessa and Thoby, the children born to Leslie and Julia, who were two and three. In 1883, when Virginia was one, her younger brother Adrian was born. The Stephen household then contained eight children.

Virginia Stephen was raised in a household in which incest, sexual violence, and abusive behavior were a common, rather than a singular or rare occurrence, a family in which there is evidence that virtually all were involved in either incest or violence or both, a family in which each parent had lived through childhood trauma. The evidence which has survived presents a frightening picture of a family in the most desperate disarray, with its children at supreme risk and adversely affected for a lifetime by the events that will be examined in this volume.

In Virginia Woolf's *To the Lighthouse*, Mrs. Ramsay, brooding about her children, thinks to herself that "children never forget" their childhood, never forget what happened to them, good or bad, for all their lives. In the year before she committed suicide, Virginia Woolf was rewriting a memoir, "A Sketch of the Past," indicating that she had not forgotten what had happened to her as a child. In it, she described the past as "an avenue lying behind; a long ribbon of scenes, emotions"; "at the end of the avenue, still, are the garden and the nursery."[1] She described the violence that erupted in the Stephen household in the form of overt sexual assault, temper tantrums, physical violence, sexually threatening behavior, bullying, abductions, and probably even rape.

Virtually every male member of the Stephen household was engaged in this behavior; without exception, all of the women within the family were the victims of abuse or sexual violence—Virginia herself, her sister Vanessa, her half-sisters Laura and Stella, her mother Julia. But their stories were hidden, and rationalized, revised, and recast, both in the versions which the family told themselves and each other, and in the versions of their lives that were written after their deaths.

Every event that is described within these pages has been available for some time, either as a matter of public record, or in archives open to the public. Yet the Stephen family is not ordinarily seen as a pathologically dysfunctional family and Virginia Woolf's upbringing is not usually seen as rife with the most severe and potentially damaging problems. Instead, in the words of her latest biographer, Lyndall Gordon, Virginia Woolf, as a child, was "bathed in a protective love."[2]

Tracing how Woolf's incestuous experiences are described by some of her major biographers is a disconcerting experience. Fortunately, however, there have also been important attempts to assess the impact of Woolf's incestuous experiences upon her development.

Quentin Bell, Virginia Woolf's nephew and official biographer, described her incestuous experiences in his biography which first appeared in 1972. He describes how George Duckworth's fraternal attentions turned into "a nasty erotic skirmish" after the death of Julia Stephen, Virginia's mother: there were "fondlings and fumblings in public . . . and these were carried to greater lengths—indeed I know not to what lengths—when, with the easy assurance of a fond and privileged brother, George carried his affections from the schoolroom into the night nursery."[3]

Although Bell indicates that Woolf had her first experiences with George after her mother's death, and although he includes the information, provided by Woolf herself, that George carried on until 1903 or 1904, Bell's account elides the fact that this went on for nine or ten years. And, although he records Woolf's belief that "George had spoilt her life before it had fairly begun" (44), he attributes her response to George's behavior to the fact that she was "naturally shy in sexual matters" (44), to an implicit weakness in her character. When he describes her first "breakdown," Bell states that he does not know enough about her mental illness "to say whether or not this adolescent trauma was in any way connected" (44); yet he does describe her "breakdown" as "a cancer of the mind, a corruption of the spirit striking one at the age of thirteen" (44). Bell blames Woolf's response to incest on her—on her inherent shyness in sexual matters, on the cancer of her mind, on the corruption of her spirit. Bell, therefore, blamed the victim Woolf for her response to incest.

Jean O. Love, in *Sources of Madness and Art* (1977), traced what she believed to be evidence of Woolf's early and excessive dependence to her upbringing. She stated bluntly, regarding the Duckworths, that "it cannot be determined that the alleged offenses actually took place. Nor can it be determined that they did not." According to Love, it is entirely possible that "they were imaginative elaborations of some innocent action and therefore exemplify Virginia's tendencies to extend and embroider actual events."[4] Woolf exaggerated because of a defect in her personality: "as Virginia both wanted and liked affection from George, [she] imagined that he had made erotic advances when he was merely being kind and innocently affectionate"; "[he] was trying to be a brother and not a lover" (207). Later in the volume, Love describes Woolf as "naturally" frigid (256), with a "disposition to shrink from sex" (281), who had an inherent "shame about the sexual parts of her body" (281). As with Bell's account, Love describes Woolf as simply inheriting these traits.

In *Woman of Letters: A Life of Virginia Woolf* (1978), Phyllis Rose blunts the effect of Woolf's records of her incestuous experience by referring to them as "the set of stories she made up about her own experience," "the myths she generated."[5] Regarding the Duckworth episodes, Rose remarks that "Woolf cannot resist telling a good story, or, on the next go round, telling it even better" (ix). She uses, as evidence of Woolf's story-telling propensities, a discrepancy between two "stories" which Woolf tells about incest: at the end of one, Woolf describes "how her half-brother, George Duckworth, entered her room one night to plague her with embraces. The light was out, she was almost asleep, and he told her not to turn the light on." But then, "she recalls that episode again, only now she is in bed reading Marius the Epicurean when Duckworth comes in, and he turns the light out—a trivial change, perhaps, but the effect is more sinister" (ix).

Rose does not entertain the possibility that Woolf is describing two different episodes. As Rose herself observes: they "present the leading figures and events in the myth of her youth, material which served as the basis of much of her fiction" (ix). She also believes that Woolf's memoirs are "evidence of myth rather than fact" (xi). For Rose, Woolf's memoirs were themselves fictions.

The memoirs of sexual assault confirm, for Rose, "a sexual reticence already established rather than traumatically provoking it" (7–8); Woolf's disgust at the abuse "is culturally conditioned" rather than an appropriate response to incest. Rose implies that victims are disgusted by incest because society teaches them to have such a response.

Roger Poole in *The Unknown Virginia Woolf* (1978) takes serious issue with Quentin Bell's descriptions of Woolf as "mad" or "insane." He described how Woolf's so-called breakdowns were really emotional responses to incestuous abuse: he describes how the "effect of George Duckworth's attentions was . . . to traumatise Virginia, and to provoke in her a sexual anaesthesia,"[6] a "disassociation in Virginia's sense of her own body" (112). He describes how willing Virginia Woolf's husband, Leonard, was to fall in with the prevailing Stephen family view that Woolf was mad, to treat her as "insane," and to consult doctors and family members in secret about her, without inquiring into "why his wife was showing such signs of stress" (130).

Stephen Trombley's *'All That Summer She Was Mad': Virginia Woolf and Her Doctors* describes a "crisis of truth"[7] in biographies of Virginia Woolf. Although biographers often portray Woolf as insane, Trombley believes that no biographer has really proved Woolf's madness. Trombley's book investigates what the definition of madness was for those doctors who treated Woolf, and he has discovered that her doctors, too, "can present no useful or responsible definition" (297). Trombley's most significant contribution is to argue that Virginia's anxious, "mad" behavior was a *response* to her incestuous experiences, which her doctors then used as evidence that she was mad. Once she was determined to be mad, then her doctors treated her with medications which have "side-effects . . . which correspond with the main symptoms of Virginia's breakdowns: the inability to read or concentrate; depression; feelings of dread . . . ; confusion; hallucinations; failure of appetite; 'a dry and unpleasant feeling in the throat . . . '; and loss of power within the limbs" (142). Woolf's "madness" therefore is a response to the drugs which were used to treat her.

Lyndall Gordon's most recent biography of Woolf (*Virginia Woolf: A Writer's Life*, 1984) is, in my judgment, an unfortunate throwback to the kind of view promulgated by Bell regarding Woolf's incest. It presents an appalling account of the incestuous episodes in Woolf's life. (And Gordon was writing *after* the appearance of the significant studies of the effect of incest that I shall discuss later in this chapter.) To Gordon, "It is impossible to know what truly happened."[8] But Gordon believes that Woolf enjoyed whatever *did* happen. "[H]owever uncontrolled and ill-judged" George's behavior was, it "may have been irresistible to a girl like Virginia." Why? Because George was "thought very handsome and his combination of sensual lips and considerate manners made him the pet of society ladies" (119).

Gordon's attitude displays what Louise Armstrong, in *Kiss Daddy Goodnight: A Speak-Out on Incest*, terms the two most common damaging attitudes that one can take toward incest: "we tried it, we liked it"; or "it was all a fantasy."[9] Louise Thornton in *I Never Told Anyone: Writings by Women Survivors of Child Sexual Abuse* also assails the pernicious yet all too common view, held by Gordon, that depicts the child as "an accomplice, that she enjoys being sexually abused even though she says clearly that she does not."[10]

Alice Miller, in *Thou Shalt Not Be Aware: Society's Betrayal of the Child*, uses the example of Woolf to illustrate how biographers minimize the effect of childhood abuse: "The appearance of her later delusions of persecution is without a doubt a logical consequence of this situation [her sexual abuse], and yet the connection is carefully ignored."[11] Miller remarks that although Bell reports that Woolf "felt that George had spoilt her life before it had fairly begun," "the link between this fact and her 'mysterious' psychosis remains a riddle to him" (128).

According to Miller, it is imperative not to discount reports of physical abuse or sexual abuse as fantasy; treating these reports as worthy of investigation usually leads to the discovery of early trauma. But Miller believes that many disciplines, including psychoanalysis, sociology, history, and biography, suppress the essential question of how parents or other family members "consciously, or more often unconsciously, treat their children in the first years of life" (11).

Miller's psychoanalytic position, which she applies to the life of Woolf, holds that a neurosis originates because of someone's real-life experiences, rather than because of one's wishes: "early traumatic experiences could not be articulated and *therefore* had to be repressed" (52). For Miller, the case of Virginia Woolf "shows how completely such drive interpretations can ignore the child's very real distress and loneliness" (127); Woolf's life demonstrates, as well, Miller's belief that the consequences of sexual abuse permeate one's entire life and undermine and contaminate the most fundamental of life's experiences: the formation of one's sense of integrity and worth as a human being (162).

A great deal of the suffering is caused because the trauma is inflicted upon the child by those upon whom the child is dependent for care, so that the child cannot escape, and often has bonds of love and emotional closeness with the very persons causing them pain and harm. Miller explores the complicated and conflicting responses that abused children often have to their caretakers (63); their tendency to idealize them, to make excuses for them, even to protect them. But these attitudes and practices also stand in the way of their experiencing rage and sadness. Rage, although "an appropriate reaction to cruelty" (61) is very often misinterpreted as the sign of innate mental imbalance.

In this, Miller departs from the position that Sigmund Freud came to maintain, that "a neurosis originates because a drive conflict has been repressed" (drive theory), and she goes back to the position that Freud maintained earlier in his career, his "seduction theory," which held that hysteria was the result of sexual abuse. As Freud stated in 1896: "at the bottom of every case of hysteria there are *one or more occurrences of premature sexual experiences.*"[12] Freud himself described that he abandoned the seduction theory because he could not believe that so many respectable men were involved in sexually abusing their daughters; in a letter to Wilhelm Fliess written in 1897 he wrote: "there was the astonishing thing that in every case blame was laid on perverse acts by the father . . . ; it was hardly credible that perverted acts against children were so general."[13] Instead, he concluded that his patients' reports of sexual abuse were "figments of their imaginations based on their own sexual desires."[14]

Why Freud abandoned the seduction theory and replaced it with the drive theory has been the subject of much inquiry, including Jeffrey Moussaieff Masson's controversial *The Assault on Truth: Freud's Suppression of the Seduction Theory.* According to Judith Lewis Herman, Freud was never comfortable with his discovery about the prevalence of sexual abuse and its effects "because of what it implied about the behavior of respectable family men." However, at the moment when Freud chose to deny the truth of his patients' experiences, "he forfeited his ambition to understand the female neurosis."[15] According to Diana E. H. Russell, disturbed by "his own incestuous desires toward his daughter and by suspicions of his father's incestuous wishes, Freud expressed enormous relief and even a feeling of triumph"[16] when he abandoned the seduction theory and articulated the drive theory. Thus, the drive theory can be seen as fulfilling *Freud's* needs rather than explaining the causes of his patients' behavior.

The drive theory found widespread acceptance among doctors and psychotherapists during Virginia Woolf's lifetime and throughout much of the twentieth century. As a result, children's behavioral clues about sexual violation were interpreted as evidence of an underlying neurosis; their reports of seduction were dismissed as fantasies. Virginia Woolf suffered the effects of her abuse—nervousness, irritability, outbursts, tantrums—but here too they were interpreted as evidence of her pathology, rather than as a response to what had happened to her. During the fifty-three years in which she suffered from these ill effects, she tried to understand the impact of sexual abuse by reflecting upon her own experiences. She had the support of sympathetic women like her sister Vanessa, who, the evidence suggests, tried to stop the abuse, and a friend Violet Dickinson, who offered emotional closeness. She knew that she had been adversely affected.

According to Florence Rush, there was an alarming increase in sexual assaults upon children during the Victorian era;[17] and, as many historians of childhood have discovered, it is incorrect to assume that children of the Victorian age were well cared for; there is considerable evidence indicating an institutionalized neglectfulness as the hallmark of Victorian child-rearing practices; indeed, the esteemed historian Walter E. Houghton refers to the "terrifying world of Victorian childhood."[18]

The Stephen family warrants our close and careful attention, not only because Virginia Woolf, one of the greatest writers of our century, grew up within it, but also because the record that she kept of her existence within it serves to illuminate a very shadowy area in history, the life that went on within the private enclave of the middle-class Victorian family. What happened to Woolf is far more common than had ever been imagined. And the impact of Woolf's experiences was extremely traumatic; the effect of incest on her life as a survivor exhibit many of the same features of other survivors:[19] she was first abused when young; her abuse continued for a long time; it probably involved many incidents; there was a significant disparity between her age and the ages of her half brothers; she was abused by trusted members of her family circle; she was abused by more than one family member; and another member of her family was also abused.

Judith Lewis Herman and Lisa Hirschman, in *Father–Daughter Incest*, have argued that the tendency in men toward sexually exploitative behavior, include rape and incest, can best be understood, not as a deviance from the ethics of family care, but rather as a logical outgrowth of how the patriarchal family is organized, an understanding that Woolf herself came to realize. The patriarchal family was the normative family of Victorian England, and it remains the "ideal" family of many segments of contemporary society.

Within the patriarchal family, male members exhibit a "diminished capacity for affectionate relating."[20] Incest is one outgrowth of despotic paternal rule: fathers in such families are described as "perfect patriarchs" (71) within the home, although they often present themselves as "pathetic, helpless, and confused" (76); sons have excessive privilege (73); the activities of the female members of the family are supervised, restricted, and controlled and they are isolated from the world (73); the mothers have little or no power or independence, and they are often depressed and withdrawn or overburdened with the rearing of many children (78). This pattern is typical; it is precisely the pattern of the Stephen household.

Herman has also argued that the primary motivation in incest is an enacting of "power and dominance" (87) and male privilege rather than sexual pleasure. Males in incestuous households commonly manifest assumptions regarding the father's and sons' prerogatives and the mother's and daughters' obligations. The dependency needs of the father supersede those of the children; the possibility that the father "might be expected to take on the mother's caretaking role is never entertained" (46, 87). In the patriarchal family, the father has immense powers over his wife and children—an unrestricted right of physical control, the right to control behavior, and sexual rights.

Incest enacts profound hostility to all women, but chooses girls in the family because they are least likely to retaliate: the "right to initiate and consummate sexual relations with subordinate women becomes . . . a jealously guarded male prerogative, guaranteed by the explicit or tacit consent of all men" (56). Incest, thus, can be seen as the fullest expression of misogyny.[21]

The incest survivors studied by Herman longed for their mothers to come to their aid (88); and, in their adulthood, they "lacked any internal representation of an adequate, satisfactory mother, and could only imagine either the ideal mother they wished they had had or the neglectful mother of their childhood experience" (107)—all features that we shall find when we examine Woolf's response to her experiences in detail.

In adulthood, incest survivors are far more likely to feel pity for their fathers and their fathers' shortcomings than they were of their mothers or themselves (82). One of the most terrifying consequences is the repeated feeling in adulthood of being dominated and overwhelmed, of losing one's sense of self, of losing, in fact, one's very identity: many are "haunted by the fear that beneath the facade lurked a contemptible person who would eventually be exposed or gain the upper hand" (120). As adults, incest survivors tend to give an enormous amount of power to their husbands (100); some felt it was "only natural to be completely dominated by the men they loved" (103). Many features of Virginia Woolf's adult life are understandable when viewed in the light of these findings: critics have observed that a running motif in her fiction is the "loss of the self"; others, like Roger Poole, have commented on the despotic nature of Virginia Woolf's husband, Leonard, and his "rule" over her life that included his regulating her bedtime and her social engagements.

Incest survivors often display impressive strengths; but they rarely, however, truly enjoy "the benefits of their hard labor or derived much satisfaction from their competence or strength" (107). Rather, they press themselves on to further achievements. When Woolf completed her novels, she rarely took pleasure in her accomplishments; she sometimes had insights into her power as a writer; more often, her own words filled her with despair. Only recently have researchers begun to demonstrate the extent to which sexual abuse in childhood taints the quality of the rest of the victim's life, often causing a lifetime or periods of overwhelming sorrow, mental anguish, self-destructive and self-abusive behavior, negative feelings about one's body, feelings of emotional coldness, emptiness, and detachment.

Repression is "a common protective mechanism," particularly of victims of traumatic abuse in childhood (34); memories might trickle out in bits and pieces throughout the course of their lives. This accounts for the fact that so far as we can tell Woolf did not describe her abuse by Gerald Duckworth until late in her life, although there are indications that she had a shadowy recollection of what had happened to her even earlier.

The survivor of incestuous abuse may become cautious, or phobic; she may withdraw from the world; she may become mentally ill (12); she may have nightmares or severe sleep disturbances (140); she may develop inexplicable headaches; she sometimes feels that she is choking, that she is drowning, or that she is being strangled; she may eat too much, or too little; she might eat too much and then vomit; she may develop marked seductive behavior; as an adolescent, she might run away from home (12); she might become a prostitute; if she has a daughter, she will probably be less able than other women to protect her from incestuous abuse (12). She may have generalized and sometimes inexplicable feelings of fear, anxiety, and mistrust. She always exhibits symptoms of depression (12, 139).

In the severest of cases (and we must remember that Woolf's case was severe), women who have been incestuously abused are more likely than other women to disfigure themselves; to suffer severe substance abuse; to enter into relationships in which they are repeatedly physically or sexually assaulted; to be raped; to experience suicidal tendencies; to make suicide attempts; to commit suicide. Therapists have reported that in group counseling sessions it is difficult if not impossible to get incest survivors to react aggressively; they "passively continued taking whatever was given."[22]

Incest forces the survivor into abandoning the belief in her own personal worth, the possibility of her own personal safety, the belief that the world is a meaningful and comprehensible place. To have been incestuously abused means that someone who should have given you care, and should have protected you, saw you as being fit for abuse. Florence Rush has stated that a growing child gains self-esteem and confidence "from the value placed upon her by adults whom she trusts and upon whom she must depend"; if that trust is violated by incestuous abuse, it is virtually impossible for her to develop a positive self-identity. Incest survivors' self-esteem has been so severely damaged that they do not know how to give themselves "their own loving self-protection";[23] they have been repeatedly taught that they are not worth protecting. To Judith Herman, incest is "as destructive to women as genital mutilation or the binding of feet."[24]

The negative consequences of incestuous abuse are severe and long-lasting, although sometimes they do not emerge for many years, and the victim of sexual abuse in childhood does not always connect, even in therapy, her bad feelings with the fact that she has been abused. Incest survivors often do not report their abuse; nor do therapists always connect a patient's symptoms with the possibility of sexual abuse. Woolf realized that she had been adversely affected. But, like many incest survivors, she had no idea that so many of the symptoms of her supposed illnesses were in all likelihood manifestations of the extreme and severe trauma that she had endured.

Many women survivors report responses, feelings, images, dreams that are identical to those of Virginia Woolf. One survivor reports that her memories of her abuse were blocked until her adulthood, when "a rush of memories—flashes of scenes, disconnected and disconcerting" came to her. She realized that the memories existed in this form precisely because she had been asleep or half asleep when her abuse had occurred. She, like Woolf, was terrified of going to sleep.[25] Survivors report a blocking of feeling, because they have needed to steel themselves against feeling to tolerate the fact that they were being abused.

Feelings of profound and utter powerlessness accompanied the survivor's inability to stop the abuse, and many of them tried. Feelings of profound betrayal and rage at other members of the household also existed; many times they remained unexpressed; as some of the survivors reported, they believed that if they told anyone, they would be responsible for the entire edifice of the family falling to pieces. Nobody had protected them; yet they had to protect the family, which often involved dealing with their feelings, their terrors, their fears by themselves.

Like Woolf, who felt that she had been tainted, other survivors describe feeling "unclean," "dirty," "guilty" (105); One woman believed that the world was a terribly unsafe place, that "the entire earth is cracked, not just the main fault lines" (119). Woolf uses a comparable image: the surface of the earth covers a subterranean network of potentially deadly veins containing a poisonous substance that, at any moment, and without warning, might leach into the ground and devastate everything. Another survivor describes a terrifying dream in which the only thing present "is a pair of hands that never stops moving and an unrecognizable face" (162). Woolf describes a "malicious arm" unconnected to any body, that is "coarsely haired," and that tortures its victims.[26]

Woolf's torturous revision process has been the subject of much critical scrutiny; this sense of shame at the product of one's efforts is evidenced in the statements of many survivors of incestuous abuse. Other survivors describe their apparently uncalled-for "rages" and constant "depressions"; some describe, like Woolf, their inability to "look at myself in a mirror without diverting my eyes"[27]—Woolf called it her "looking-glass complex" and it is undoubtedly related to her feelings of shame about her incest.[28] One woman described a recurring feeling, probably the result of forced oral sex, that she was being gagged,[29] that interfered with her ability to eat; Leonard Woolf described how long it could take for Woolf to eat a meal.

Virginia Woolf was surely traumatized by the events and experience she had been subjected to within her family. Her reports of illness, disorientation, and feelings of worthlessness coincide with those of other incest survivors; her suicide is surely linked to it. But her story, like that of so many other women, is also one of survival and achievement against all odds. Although she suffered, she also experienced great joy, and her life is one of monumental achievement.

Virginia Woolf wrote about her sexual abuse in order to understand why it had happened and how it had affected her. She wrote about it in her fiction, in her essays; she wrote about it in her memoirs and in her letters. She did so before the support groups of today which encourage survivors of sexual abuse to speak out in a protected environment. Virginia Woolf had the courage to go it alone. Her writing was her own particular life insurance, her own ticket to survival, even though it often caused her great pain.

She left, at her death, diaries, memoirs, letters, notebooks, notes, which document the trauma that she endured as a child and how she coped with it, reacted to it, and understood it. Especially significant are Woolf's early diaries—one which was begun in 1897, when she was an adolescent, and which continue through 1909, after she had begun her first novel.[30] Significant too are stories that she wrote in childhood and in adolescence that record the traumatic effect of the sexual assaults. She also left behind her published work, as well as the drafts of her novels which demonstrate how she transformed that childhood trauma into an art that portrayed, very directly, the mistreatment of children in families.

Every one of her novels describes a child abandoned, a child ignored, a child at risk, a child abused, a child betrayed. To be sure, there are also moments of closeness and of pleasure for these children in Woolf's work, but they tend to be few and fleeting, as if to underscore how rare these moments are in childhood. Because these extraordinary portraits of traumatized children are embedded in populated novels, these children and their stories are often overlooked or ignored by readers, who fix their focus upon the grownups, just as abused children are often overlooked, or ignored, or left to fend for themselves.

These children appear on the page for a moment—as the baby in the carriage of the nanny who sits next to Peter Walsh in *Mrs. Dalloway*, as the children that Daisy, Peter Walsh's lover, will lose if she divorces her husband and marries him. Or their development is traced in the course of an entire novel, as Jacob's is in *Jacob's Room*, or Rose's in *The Years*. They surround the tea table and inhabit the parlors, and the nurseries of the households of that privileged segment of English society to which Virginia Woolf's own family belonged. Sometimes they step into the library. But they also play on the streets of London's less fortunate neighborhoods and they run to fetch their parents from pubs. Taken together, Woolf's portraits constitute one of the most impressive and significant galaxies of children and their experiences as "prisoners of childhood"[31] in the world's literature.

In her novels, Woolf enacts the idea that personality is determined by one's personal history, and one's personal history can only be understood in terms of gender, class, social movements, and history. As she wrote in *Three Guineas*, "psychology would seem to hint that history is not without its effect upon mind and body."[32] In this, she anticipates the work of some of the most sophisticated explorers of the formation of human personality, like Alice Miller, whose work takes into account the interrelationship between child-rearing practices, national character, and historical events.[33] When Woolf described her memoirs, she disparaged them because, as she put it, they were "always private, and at their best only about . . . seductions by half-brothers."[34] But the fact that they were indeed private and about her trauma is of paramount importance. In her memoirs, one can see Woolf forcing a revision of the concept of history to include women's history, and personal history, and the fact that within the lives of so many girls and women, there was always something hidden—"hidden either by silence, or by flourishes and ornaments that amount to silence."[35] She persisted in this endeavor throughout her life.

She believed in the fundamental accuracy of memory and she understood that telling what you remembered, and writing down what had happened to you when you were young were radical acts of personal history that would force the rewriting of social history. She understood that the memoir was a radical form of history because it so often described pain, sorrow, suffering, humiliation, trauma, and sexual violence, sometimes meted out by those very people who were the heroes of history. Rewriting history from the point of view of the victim, of the outsider, was a project to which Woolf was personally committed.

Woolf understood that when men write history, women's history often gets lost or misrepresented. At the very end of her life, Woolf devoted a considerable amount of her writing energy to describing the common experience of sexual assault in women's lives. She was interested in recording her own exploitation, but at the same time she was also interested in recounting the fact that it had happened to the other young women in her household, to her sister Vanessa, and to her half-sister, Stella Duckworth.

Writing and speaking openly of the incest in her own life and the sexual violence endured by the characters she created in her novels and the historical figures whose lives she described were acts of supreme courage on Virginia Woolf's part. As we now know, the victim of incest runs a great risk in breaking the silence about her sexual abuse.[36]

But as she put it near the end of her life, "Only when we put two and two together—two pencil strokes, two written words, . . . do we overcome dissolution and set up some stake against oblivion."[37] Virginia Woolf was engaged in a lifelong effort to put together those words which helped her overcome her own feelings of dissolution, which set up her own stake against oblivion. And, fortunately, we too can read her words.

PART ONE

A Family Pattern

Chapter One

LAURA, "HER LADYSHIP OF THE LAKE"

It has been commonly accepted that the Stephen family was characterized by its liveliness, its affectionate concern for the well-being of
its children, its economic and emotional security—that it was, in
short, the archetypal serene and secure family of Victorian ideology,
with Julia Stephen in the role of the angel/mother in the house and
Leslie Stephen in the role of the Victorian patriarch, somewhat difficult to live with, but lovable nonetheless, the stalwart father, riding
herd on a lively household filled with energetic well-cared-for children.[1] The fact of Virginia Woolf's sexual abuse in childhood, by Gerald Duckworth—even when it is believed and taken seriously—is generally portrayed as a deviance within an otherwise well-functioning
and stable Victorian household.[2] And it has also been commonly held
that the paradisc that was Virginia Woolf's Victorian childhood was
shattered and utterly transformed by the death of her mother Julia
Stephen in 1895, when Virginia was thirteen years old, and then, of
her half-sister and mother-surrogate, Stella Duckworth in 1897, when
Woolf was fifteen years old.[3]

The Stephen family was, in fact, from before Virginia Woolf's birth,
through the death of her mother, and afterwards, a family in a nearly
perpetual state of crisis and instability that had a deeply disturbing
impact upon the well-being and emotional health of all of its children.
"Nothing," she wrote in her memoirs, "remained stable long."[4] The
children lived, she said, in a "state of anxious growth."[5] There were,
of course, moments of exquisite pleasure, and she remembers them,
chiefly in the summers that the family spent at St. Ives, and Woolf
herself describes them in loving detail,[6] although one must ask how

serene a paradise St. Ives could have been, considering that it was at St. Ives that Virginia Woolf was sexually molested for the first time.[7]

The image that Woolf used to describe her family was that of "some creaking old waggon, pitifully rusted, and yet filled with stirring young creatures" which "toiled painfully along the way."[8] In this and the next three chapters, I shall focus upon the lives of the girls, Laura, Stella, Vanessa, and Virginia, in that "pitifully rusted," "creaking old waggon," the Stephen family. And then I shall turn to Virginia Woolf's own fictionalized yet highly illuminating portrait of family life that she wrote when she was ten years old, before proceeding to an analysis of the children in the fiction of her maturity.

What happened to Virginia Woolf as a child cannot be separated from what happened to the other girls in the Stephen family. For what happened to Laura, Stella, and Vanessa was part of a family pattern as well as an historical pattern—the treatment of daughters within a middle-class Victorian family.[9] And what happened to her sister and half-sister profoundly affected the life that Virginia Woolf herself led as a child. Taken together, their lives vividly demonstrate that squelching of the spirit that was at the very heart of how the Victorians raised their daughters. In the case of Laura, Stella, and Vanessa, the attempt was successful, in varying degrees. Their names within the family embody the most salient aspect of how they were treated—Laura, "Her Ladyship of the Lake," isolated and confined as a prisoner within the household, banished, unseen; Stella, "the Cow," the archetypal nurturer, the mindless, unpaid household drudge; Vanessa, "the Saint," who supposedly transcended whatever suffering she endured, whose suffering was, thereby, effectively obliterated. (Virginia herself was called "the Goat.")[10]

After her marriage to Leslie Stephen, Julia gave birth to four babies within five years. In 1879, when she was pregnant with Vanessa she had five children to care for. Vanessa's birth was especially difficult, so that by the time Julia gave birth to Virginia, she was already feeling the effects of chronic fatigue and overwork that were to plague her until her death in 1895, when she was forty-eight years old.[11]

Even the most cursory examination of Julia Stephen's life exposes the extent to which Coventry Patmore's image of the Victorian woman as "angel in the house" seriously distorted reality. Maintaining that the woman in the house was an angel completely nullified the extraordinary hard work and effort that went into organizing and running a household, which, in the case of the Stephens, numbered eleven people, even given the fact that she had servants.[12]

Julia's treatment of any one child must be seen within the context of her family responsibilities. Living at a time when women were supposed to be angels, when women's capacities to carry on the business of family life were assumed to be boundless, when men did relatively little, if anything at all, regarding their children, she had no system within which she could set limits for herself.

One can well understand why Victorian mothers placed such a premium upon a child-rearing system that emphasized control,[13] and why they used their own daughters so early to help them with the work of the household, keeping them, even in a household like the Stephen's, from developing their own interests and capacities.[14] One can understand why any child who refused to be controlled was at extraordinary risk.[15] One such child was Laura Stephen.

When Virginia Woolf was born, there was a battle raging between Julia and Leslie, and Laura:[16] Laura wasn't reading well enough to satisfy Leslie and Julia and they were determined to make her read. On 4 February 1882, less than a fortnight after Virginia's birth, Leslie wrote to Julia that Laura's refusal was "intensely provoking," a direct challenge to his male authority as head of the household. According to Martine Stemerick, Leslie believed that it was his "most sacred duty, according to the Evangelical canon in which he had been raised, to secure . . . 'a wholesome moral atmosphere' in his home." If he perceived Laura's behavior as evil, it would be his moral imperative to correct her.[17]

Leslie was so preoccupied with his battle with Laura that he rarely mentions his daughter Virginia's birth. There is some evidence that Virginia's well-being was compromised as a result of this battle. Although Julia nursed her son Adrian (who was born after Virginia) for six months, she nursed Virginia for only ten weeks, at which point Virginia began to take milk from a bottle; the reason given was that Julia was overworked because of the claims that Laura was making on her time.[18]

Laura, as the daughter from a first marriage, was at great risk. When

Julia Stephen agreed to marry Leslie, she also agreed to care for his daughter, Laura, but it was not uncommon in the middle and upper classes in Victorian England to treat children from a first marriage more harshly than children from the new marriage; indeed, it was not uncommon to send them away to boarding schools, to have them cared for at a great distance from the household, by governesses or servants.[19]

In the period after Virginia's birth, Leslie was away from the household a great deal, and in letter after letter to Julia, there are complaints about Laura, queries about her, systems that they might try to control her, strategies for dominating her. Leslie conceived of his struggle with Laura as a battle: he believed, for a time, that he had "broken her in";[20] but he often wondered whether or not she would ever really acquiesce. One of Julia's punishments for Laura was to isolate her, to put her to bed.[21] But Leslie didn't believe that this was severe enough.

Julia and Leslie began to use increasingly stronger doses of medication to subdue Laura. The idea was Julia's. Leslie, at first uncomfortable with this, agreed nonetheless. Any means that would control Laura became acceptable.[22]

Leslie also probably used physical force with Laura; Leslie told Julia that his favorite forms of punishment were those which could be increased in severity or repeated.[23] When Julia described one of Laura's fits of obstinacy, Leslie replied that he wished he were there so that he could shake the little wretch.[24] At times, however, Leslie felt guilty, but he usually made Laura responsible; he wrote that he shuddered when he thought about how Laura forced him to treat her.[25]

Close to a year after Virginia's birth, the battle was still raging. Leslie described one victory, how Laura didn't hesitate over her words when reading; he thought, for a time, that he had been wrong to lose his temper. Yet this was short-lived, and in another letter, the war was on again, and he wanted to punish her.[26]

The battle, however, had taken on a new and horrifying wrinkle when Leslie began to insist that Laura should not whine or cry or work herself up into a fury in response to his punishments: he had now also begun to punish Laura for her response to his punishments. He expected her to submit to her punishments without responding because he couldn't endure hearing her cries.[27]

But the scheme to train Laura to submit did not work. In November 1882, Leslie wrote of Laura's "dreadful fits," of her "howls," of how her response to punishment was upsetting *him*.[28]

Julia and Leslie finally found a solution: they put Laura away in a different part of the house from the rest of the family, where she lived throughout Virginia Woolf's childhood; she was still living locked away within the family home when Virginia Woolf was seven or eight, and Laura was nineteen or twenty.[29] She ceased to exist, in any real sense, as far as the family was concerned. As long as she even lived within the household, however, she "acted as a source of irritation to Leslie Stephen."[30] In fact, rather than seeing his treatment of Laura as a form of torture, he wrote to Julia that she was torturing him.[31]

In the early 1880s, Julia Stephen wrote a group of stories for children. One of the more interesting and bizarre yet revealing stories, given Laura's history in the family, is "The Mysterious Voice," which describes how good children are supposed to regard punishment.[32] A boy named Jemmy Stone has decided that he is not going to be good any more, because he likes being naughty. Even though his mother always says that good children are always happy, every time he acts correctly and minds his manners, he feels miserable: but "when I just bang in and out and slam the doors so that the china plates on the wall shake and tumble, . . . then I feel quite happy, so I am sure it is much best to be naughty."[33] Jemmy Stone hears a mysterious voice asking him if he would like to be naughty always. He says that the only thing stopping him is that he is always punished. The voice asks if he would choose to be naughty if he were never punished, and it promises him that he can be as naughty as he likes, and he will never be punished again.

Jemmy makes his pact with the mysterious voice, and embarks upon a career of bad behavior. He burns holes in his boots; refuses to eat his breakfast in the nursery; amuses himself by throwing stones at the cat; trades a velveteen suit for a pet monkey, which wreaks havoc in the household. Then he uses the monkey to try to scare the nurse who has a horror of animals. He wraps it up and hides it in the nurse's quarters. The monkey suffocates, but Jem doesn't acknowledge his responsibility, saying that since the monkey was his, he was free to do anything with it.

After a time, however, Jem tires of this career of bad behavior, largely because he is being ignored, and his siblings are getting attention because they are good, and he cries out, "Oh! Oh! I wish I could be good. . . . Being naughty doesn't seem to be much fun" (102). The mysterious voice tells Jem that it will be difficult, if not impossible, to stop his bad behavior. But, the voice says, if "you try very hard you may get punished again" (103).

Jem begs for punishment from his aunt, and she replies, "I shall be delighted to punish you" (105). And Jem feels better "when it was done." Afterwards, "his father and mother both looked at him with [more] tenderness" than they had since that "evening which seemed so long ago when he had chosen to be naughty if he need not be punished" (106).

The message in Julia's story is clear. It goes far beyond the fact that good behavior is rewarded and bad behavior is punished. In the story, a child is defined as good only when that child *wants*, indeed *begs*, to be punished if the child has done something wrong. When Jemmy doesn't want punishment, the family behaves as if he isn't there. At one point, when he is bad, a relative doesn't recognize him, and says, "Who is this little boy?" (103).

When you don't want to be punished for misbehavior, you are not even recognized as yourself, as a human being: Jem's mother looks at him, "not as if she were angry, but as if she did not see him" (93). Like Mrs. Stone in "The Mysterious Voice," Julia, I suspect, could herself become stonelike in the presence of a child who displeased her.

Julia's story accurately reflects what happened to Laura: she was a child engaging in bad behavior; but she did not welcome punishment, she reacted against it as if it was unwarranted. Like Jemmy Stone, Laura was treated as a nonbeing, as a nonperson, within the Stephen household. One can only wonder what Julia and Leslie said to the other children, to explain the goings-on with Laura, if they said anything at all.

In 1887, when Laura was seventeen, she was sent to the country to live apart from the family (Woolf was five at the time); in 1891, when she was twenty-one, she was sent to an asylum in York.[34] After Julia's death, Leslie made Stella responsible for Laura; after Stella's death, he made his niece Kate Stephen Laura's guardian.[35] By then, he could not bear to be responsible for her care.

But while Laura still lived at Hyde Park Gate, the family home in London, Leslie "could hardly bear to see her, let alone show affection." A pathetic scene occurred at one time when Anny, Laura's aunt (Leslie's sister-in-law), who had shown her some kindness, came to visit her: "the child ran to her laughing and beaming to hug the only grownup she could remember [who] had shown her love."[36]

Leslie described a story that he allowed Florence Maitland, an intimate of the family, to tell the children when Virginia was five, at the time when Laura was being sent out of the Stephen home: he wrote that the children were well, and that it had been "very funny" seeing them respond to Florence's "ghastly story of how 2 wicked boys were slowly cut up."[37] A bad girl would be sent away from home; bad boys would be slowly cut up. The treatment of Laura was an example of how the children in the family would be treated if they misbehaved. The stories about what happened to bad children were no fairy tales: they predicted what could, and in fact, did happen to them.

The terms used in reference to Laura's behavior were quite different in the accounts that Leslie Stephen wrote during 1882 and the years following and in the memoir he wrote in 1895, after Julia Stephen's death. Current biographies of Virginia Woolf provide a third set of labels to describe Laura. In 1882 and the few years following, Leslie generally refers to Laura as "perverse." But in his memoirs, some thirteen years later, he describes her as having an inherent mental deficiency, a striking shift. In certain current biographies of Woolf, Laura is referred to as insane or psychotic,[38] although Leslie himself never uses those terms.

I believe that Leslie Stephen shifted his descriptions of Laura, not because it later occurred to him that Laura was, in fact, inherently deficient, but because to label her in this way provided him with a more acceptable reason for his harsh treatment of her. To lock a girl away in a house and then in an asylum because she is an "idiot" or because she is "psychotic" is unfortunate; to lock a girl away in a house and then in an asylum because she is bad, if classified as cruel and unusual punishment, might have been considered criminal. The British Parliament passed a law in 1889 protecting children from cruelty, a law that was not in effect during the time that Laura was being punished, but was in effect when Leslie penned his memoir. [39]

In his memoirs, Leslie explained the reason for Laura's treatment: although Laura appeared normal at birth, she was, in retrospect, obviously "a backward child," "mentally deficient," who "would require special treatment"; he also referred to her "strange waywardness and inarticulate ways of thinking and speaking." [40]

In Leslie Stephen's contemporary accounts, Laura is never described as an imbecile or even as mentally deficient: when she is described as not reading, the cause is her own refusal to use her mental abilities. In fact, on at least one occasion, in 1884, when Laura was fourteen, Leslie describes the harm that he believes would be done to Laura if they put her with "idiots"—quite obviously, Leslie himself did not at the time believe that she was one. [41] Biographers have explained this as Leslie's reluctance to admit to himself that there was anything congenitally wrong with Laura.

Nor do contemporary accounts support the later claim that she was mentally deficient. She was reading by seven; at eleven, she was reading *Aladdin*; at fourteen, *Robinson Crusoe*; at sixteen, *Alice in Wonderland*. Her sisters Vanessa and Virginia even wrote letters to her. There are accounts of recalcitrance, of troubling behavior, but not of mental incapacity: at seven, she spit the meat out of her mouth; at fourteen, she complained of choking throughout her meals; by the time she was a teenager, she was "suffering from nervous tics and speech impediments"; at times "she would become violent and would howl wildly." [42]

In contemporary accounts of Laura, Leslie describes her solely in terms of bad behavior: he describes her "sluggishness," her obstinancy, her "mulishness," and her "perversity." [43] All of the language used to describe Laura in later years point to her inherent deficiency or madness. The language used to describe Laura during her time in the Stephen household points to her moral failings, not to her stupidity.

Leslie said that she "lacked any moral sense"; that she was "'vain' but had a good character." Most significantly, he said that he was somewhat encouraged "when she became a little ashamed of herself and was 'dimly conscious' of 'something bad' in herself"; it was important that she understood that she had a " 'small mind,' " that she had " 'quenched' it by her 'perversity.' "[44]

It is impossible to know why Leslie believed Laura was "perverse"— but we know that he viewed her problems with reading as having been caused by her perversity and not by her stupidity. We know that Laura wouldn't accede to Leslie's wishes, and perhaps this is why he thought she was bad, but the term "perverse" was more often applied to Victorian children who were believed to be "depraved," and therefore, were "loathsome" and "repulsive."[45]

In the Victorian view, it was commonly held that all childhood problems stemmed from "an inherent failing in the child."[46] When "children failed to live up to their mythical purity, they risked harsh treatment."[47] Laura's father came to believe that the problems he was having in getting her to behave, in controlling her, in exacting acceptable behavior from her, were proof of her inherent depravity, of her evil nature.

The term "perverse" was also used to describe children who masturbated; masturbation was believed to be a deviant sexual practice which could lead to physical or mental collapse, even to death; any child found masturbating was assumed to be evil.[48] The letter in which Leslie Stephen describes how Laura had quenched her ability to learn by her perversity[49] suggests that Laura had been found masturbating. Children who masturbated, because they were believed to be bad, were often treated extremely harshly.[50]

In Victorian child-rearing practices, there was an overwhelming concern with developing self-control in children. This was perhaps due to the diminishing belief in certain quarters that childhood was a condition of depravity. Some began to believe that a child's character was "a product, not of sin or damnation, but of the influences of the domestic environment." The object of child rearing was to train children "how to regulate and control their behavior, to suppress their aggressive impulses." The tragedy of what happened to Laura was the consequence of a child-rearing system that equated a refusal to be controlled with pathology, that labeled as "perverse," and even "insane," any girl who refused to submit to her father's will, any child who acted outside the range of acceptable Victorian behavior. Laura's responses—her infantile forms of speech, her stammering, her tantrums, her hesitancy in reading—were logical responses to her treatment in infancy, to how she was raised as a child, and how she was mistreated within the Stephen household, rather than symptoms of imbecility or pathology.[51]

While her mother Minny was still alive, Laura had been raised by a German nurse whom Leslie described as "a silly woman enough."[52] Leslie seriously questioned her competence, but he was always looking for a bargain, and she probably came cheap. She seems to have spoken very little, if any, English to her young charge. (In one account, Laura, at seven, was being taught German,[53] probably so that she could communicate with her nurse.) As an only child, Laura would have spent almost her entire day, with the exception of the children's hour, in the company of this woman. (In Julia's story, "The Mysterious Voice," the children's hour is not even a full hour, but the half hour before late dinner.)

After her mother's death, she was essentially abandoned to the care of this nurse. Victorian ideology normally precluded a man from engaging in primary care responsibilities for children, the father's role being defined in terms of authority, not emotional involvement. To make matters worse, Leslie is known to have shut out the world when he grieved, so he must have been completely unavailable to his little girl. Laura, who had lost her mother, was left to grieve alone without the support of a father who would help her through this difficult time, who would grieve with her.[54]

After Minny's death, Leslie cast about for a woman to become responsible for overseeing his daughter's care. Minny's sister Anny treated Laura with great affection and was seriously concerned with her well-being. But Anny had a life of her own to lead, and she was not involved with Laura consistently, or for very long, although she visited Laura regularly while she was at Earlswood.

At one point, in desperation, Leslie turned to his sister, Caroline Emelia Stephen, and asked her to help out with Laura's education. Caroline only lasted for three weeks, until she "collapsed from the strain of having to deal with both Leslie and Laura."

Although Leslie was "very liberal in theory," in practice, he depended "upon the women in his life to supervise not only the day-to-day instruction of his children, but every other detail of domestic life." For all his lack of religious faith, Leslie was still "strongly influenced by an Evangelical vision of original sin and his forefathers' puritan distrust of women and children." Caroline's methods of dealing with Laura were "stern" and "authoritarian." She had decided views about "touching." She believed that children were to be taught that their outbursts would not be tolerated. Leslie shared her views.[55]

Leslie spent two years as a widower, until he married Julia, whom he had known before Minny's death. Even before he married Julia, he asked her advice about a governess for Laura,[56] and he knew that his new wife would assume primary responsibility for Laura's care.

Laura Stephen, unlike Virginia Woolf, has left no memoirs to describe how she felt, how she responded to her treatment as a child, or what her life was like for the two years that she was essentially abandoned to the care of her nurse. When her birth mother died, she had, in effect, lost both parents. This, combined with infant care that did not include sufficient contact for the development of the child's sense of well-being, was no doubt a crippling blow to Laura's psyche. When Julia Stephen came into the household that she had shared with her father, Laura probably already had problems that any child deprived of real contact and care for so long would have.[57] And she suddenly had three other children to contend with; a stepmother who had babies in rapid succession; a father who turned his attention to his new wife.

Victorian ideology did not permit children to have problems; children were supposed to be angels of delight, not demanding, insecure, unhappy, or angry. When Laura behaved in ways that today would be labeled as attention-getting, or as logical responses to emotional deprivation, or as an understandable regression attending her father's new marriage, she was treated instead as if she were inherently bad.[58] Victorian parents seemed unable to help children with problems. Experts on child care emphasized discipline, repression, and control. Experts warned of the consequences of spoiling children, but spoiling children was conceived of as tending to their needs. There were, to be sure, some who disagreed but articles on child care from the time manifest persecutory attitudes toward children. Emphasis on control was so great that "pot training" began at one month; failure to perform on schedule "usually led to some nasty laxative." If the problems continued, even more severe methods were called for.[59]

Laura received the most brutal and sadistic treatment of all the children in the Stephen household. Leslie's biographer, Noel Annan, describes how Leslie was "rather violent" and, throughout his life, had "a flaming temper." His sister-in-law told the story of "Leslie hurling a flower-pot at his mother," of how, as a child, no one was able "to control him."[60] But I believe that Leslie's treatment of Laura, his bullying of her, cannot be separated from the so-called tradition of bullying in English schools, which really itself amounts to an institutionalized form of child abuse. Parents who abuse and bully their children almost always were abused and bullied when they were children themselves. The behavior of abusing parents, according to E. Milling Kinard, is a "perverted version of the golden rule: 'Do unto others as ye have been done unto.'"[61] I believe that he hated in Laura the same kind of behavior that he had been taught to be ashamed of in himself, the displays of what he would see as weakness.

As a child, Leslie had displayed some behavior—a love of poetry—that suggested to a doctor that he was in danger of becoming effeminate. The doctor "advised a boarding school 'to have the sugar taken out of him.'"[62] Instead, he and his brother James Fitzjames Stephen were sent as day boys to Eton: Leslie was nine.

As day boys, they were despised, according to the elitist nature of the institution, for it was believed that day boys could not afford board, and the children of the upper class had already been taught to regard any boys below them as encroachers upon their natural privilege. From the day that he arrived, he was "bullied systematically."[63] What the bullying actually consisted of, in Leslie's case, we can only guess at; we know that he was beaten on a daily basis, but we know from other accounts that the cruelty could be so severe as to be life-threatening or physically damaging. One unfortunate boy was "literally scalped" "through being tossed in a blanket and remained disfigured for life";[64] we know that anal rape was a common occurrence; we know that the tradition of "fagging" meant that a younger boy could be taken as the sexual slave of an older boy, and that he was forced to endure a miserable form of servitude, which he would then, in turn, inflict upon younger boys. James Fitzjames Stephen, Leslie's brother, said of his experiences at Eton: "The process taught me for life the lesson that to be weak is to be wretched, that the state of nature is a state of war."[65]

All of this went on with the full knowledge and collusion, even the approval, of their elders; English boys cannot but have felt abandoned at a very young age to a brutality that was aided and abetted by their elders who failed to put a stop to this abuse. Indeed the abuse was described as necessary, even good. The system perpetuated itself inside the schools as the boys who were bullied turned into the bullies of younger and weaker boys. This institutionalized form of physical and sexual abuse was described as if it were a necessary part of the "toughening up" of boys. It is no wonder, given this history, that Leslie treated Laura as he did, that Gerald and George treated the girls as they did. For all of them as boys had been brutalized. One wonders how many other children with fathers with histories identical to that of Leslie Stephen became the object of their father's rage. As Elizabeth Stoneman has remarked, the very structure of schooling that the British patriarchy provided for its boys, in "trying to produce a race of men who are in control," turns out men who want *to control*: but in fact, it "turns out men who are weak, ignorant [of their motives and feelings] and pathetically vulnerable. . . . They react; they do not act." Their strength is a facade.[66]

What happened to Laura Stephen should also be understood as the tragic outcome of that institution of Victorian child rearing—the nursery—which had supplanted the institution of the wet nurse, where the labor of young, displaced, and poor girls, living in often disgusting surroundings, far removed from their own families, was used to rear the children of the Victorian middle and upper classes. According to Lloyd de Mause, the nursery allowed "institutionalized abandonments" of Victorian children.[67] Often no more than children themselves, nursemaids were the youngest and most poorly paid of Victorian household servants. These lonely, harassed, overworked, depressed servants became responsible for child rearing, and also for maintaining and enforcing the exacting standards of behavior expected from children. It would be too much to expect that they could do it well; yet that is precisely what the Victorians expected. That any children were well-treated is a miracle; that many servants mistreated or ignored their charges is completely understandable.[68] As Alice Miller has remarked, one must keep in mind "what satisfaction it must have given oppressed household servants to pass the humiliation meted out to them from 'above' on to the little children in their charge."[69]

The nursemaid had to make her charges conform to the outrageously strict standards of Victorian behavior in order to keep her position. Various strategies, such as the use of drugs and sexual stimulation, were known to have been used to keep the children in the household quiet. When no one was there to check, it was common practice to ignore the children completely. (There is just such a scene in Virginia Woolf's *The Years*.) And if, in fact, their children were being abused or ignored, it was entirely possible that Victorian parents would never find out. Lady Amberley, Bertrand Russell's mother, regarded as an exceptionally good and involved parent, nonetheless missed the fact that her first child "was being starved, neglected and lied about." She concluded that it was the institution of the nursery that made this possible.[70] The Victorian middle and upper classes created the ideal of the well-mannered child; they created the nursery to keep children out of sight; and they created the children's hour that sustained the illusion that they were involved in their child's well-being. But the interaction of children with their parents during the children's hour was so carefully regulated, so free from actual intercourse about real issues, real feelings, and real problems, that it is fair to say that it was nothing but a ritual: the reality of parenting was never encountered. Much that was unpleasant, uncomfortable, or difficult about child rearing became the responsibility of another class of women.

We know that there was a dramatic change for the worse in Laura's behavior when the Duckworth and Stephen households were combined. She relapsed into "baby-ways and apathy,"[71] sure signs of regression or depression.[72] Given the fact of Virginia's and Vanessa's own sexual abuse, it is appropriate to wonder if Gerald or George Duckworth also molested Laura.[73] Some of Laura's symptoms—choking, rages, doing poorly at reading although she knew how to read—are known to be symptoms of sexual abuse.

In 1921, Virginia wrote Vanessa about a visit that Kate, Laura's guardian, had made to see Laura in the institution. (Laura was fifty-two at the time.) She describes Kate's report, that Laura "is still the same as ever, and never stops talking." Much of what Laura said was described as gibberish, but the one intelligible phrase, which Laura seems to have repeated, was "I told him to go away."[74]

The psychoanalyst Alice Miller has stated that neurotic symptoms, such as repeated phrases, must be understood as attempts at communication. Could it be that Laura was telling her guardian, her only connection with the world outside the asylum, something about her personal history, something about what had happened to her?

In a letter to Vanessa, written when Laura was sixty-four, and still institutionalized, Virginia Woolf described George Duckworth's recent death. Woolf wrote that her husband Leonard says "Laura is the one we could have spared."[75] Given the context of Woolf's letter—the fact of George's death—and that we know the history of George's sexual abuse of both Virginia and Vanessa, Woolf's statement is curious and provocative. This letter suggests that Laura could have been spared, and suggests that what happened to Laura was not inevitable and that it had something to do with George.

There is an indication in a description of Anny's visits to Laura during Virginia Woolf's adolescence that Laura had not always had problems. At times, Anny would take Laura away for a quiet country holiday where she "might be rewarded by seeing a flash of her former self." This indicates that Laura was indeed at one time "normal," not backward from birth, as Leslie had stated.

But in her memoirs, read in public, Woolf holds to her father's description of Laura as "idiot."[76] In a private letter to her friend Violet Dickinson in 1904, however, she writes that the facts about Laura's history will have to be suppressed in her father's biography. She describes how she has read her father's letters and memoirs in conjunction with Frederic Maitland's biography of Leslie Stephen: the "history of Laura is really the most tragic thing in his life I think; and one that *one can hardly describe in the life*. The letters are full of her."[77] The letters Woolf refers to are the ones which label Laura as perverse. If Laura really had been an idiot, would there have been any reason to exclude her history from the life that Frederic Maitland was preparing of Leslie Stephen? Would it not have added to the portrait of Leslie that he contended with the difficulties of a retarded child? Rather, had not Woolf learned that Leslie's treatment of Laura, if described, would be an indictment that no "official" biography of his life could contain?

It is no wonder then that Stella became "the Old Cow," the family helper, and that Vanessa became "the Saint." They were purchasing their right to stay within the family by their exemplary behavior. One of the effects of scapegoating one child within a family is to exact seemingly impossible standards of behavior from the other children. Seen in the light of Laura's treatment, Virginia Woolf's childhood and adolescent habit of reading voraciously—"Gracious, child, how you gobble,"[78] her father would say—becomes terrifyingly comprehensible. Laura had been locked away, it must have seemed, for not having read well enough, for having stumbled over her words. Every time that Virginia knocked on the door of her father's study, and asked him to hand down yet another volume, she was proving that she was not Laura: she was keeping herself from being called perverse; she was buying the right to live a life within the family; she was keeping herself from being locked up, from being locked away, from being sent to an asylum.

As I have said, it is my belief that Leslie penned the account about Laura's idiotic nature to justify his treatment of her. But a careful reading of his explanation reveals inconsistencies. He reached back into his first wife Minny's family history to explain Laura's deficiencies. He records a "vague dread" that Minny "might not be without some hereditary taint." After Minny's birth "her mother had a fever; the fever affected her brain," and she had to be put under care. It is surely stretching the point to claim hereditary insanity for his daughter Laura by pointing to a disease his wife's mother contracted *after* his wife's birth. Moreover, he had recorded no suspicion of Minny's "taint" until after the death of his second wife Julia, until after Laura had been locked away in an institution. And he never explores the possibility that if Laura inherited her disability, it is entirely possible that he could have contributed. His father James Stephen had a "nervous breakdown" in 1824; another in 1832. His brother James Fitzjames Stephen resigned in 1891 from office because of a disease affecting his mental powers. Leslie himself was thought to have inherited this propensity for breakdown and he suffered from several throughout Virginia Woolf's childhood.[79] But with Minny dead, he placed the blame for Laura's inadequacy on her.

The view of Laura as idiot completely absolved Leslie and Julia from blame: it suggested that they were somewhat noble to have tried to put up with her, and to do something about her. There is no evidence that Leslie ever took any responsibility for what was done to Laura, or that he even regarded his treatment of her as abusive; he seemed to come to believe the story about Laura's congenital abnormality. In the words of one of his biographers, however, the "daughter who suffered most at Leslie's hands is usually forgotten. This is Laura."[80]

If my re-creation is correct, then, throughout the most formative years of her life, Virginia lived in a household where an adolescent girl was locked up and severely mistreated. The Stephen family had its very own madwoman in the attic.

Laura outlived Virginia Woolf and died in 1945, at seventy-five, still confined to the asylum.[81] That the treatment which Laura received was reserved for a girl within the family becomes clear when one examines the histories of the Duckworth and Stephen boys. Laura was not the only one who had trouble with her lessons. Time and again the boys did poorly, even abysmally, at school. In 1883, Leslie wrote Julia how George was making a mess of his exams;[82] in 1897, how Thoby's inability to do well in school was due to "some slackness due to rapid growth"; in 1901, Leslie records how Adrian was sent to board at Westminster because accounts of "his school progress were unsatisfactory"—the reason Leslie gives is that his "great growth—over 6 ft. 2 in.—has tried him." When the boys did not do well, or when they behaved bizarrely, their behavior was either overlooked, or excused, because they were growing.[83] Once Thoby "allowed a playful friend to stick a knife into his femoral artery";[84] he also "tried, screaming, to the terror of the other boys, to throw himself out of the window."[85] The behavior of girls, whatever it consisted of, was far more likely to be considered perverse than the behavior of boys, whatever *it* consisted of. Laura was not the only child in the family who manifested bizarre behavior, but she was the only child locked up for it.

Laura's treatment prefigured what Virginia herself could expect and how she was, to some degree, treated, especially during her adolescence, when she did not measure up to the standards of behavior that were expected of her, or when she exhibited unacceptable behavior.[86] I believe that Leslie always needed one scapegoat within the family, for it wasn't until Laura was moved outside the home that he turned his attention to Virginia, and began to interact with her in some of the same ways that he had with Laura.

The language that Leslie Stephen used to justify his treatment of Laura reflected one of the prevailing Victorian beliefs about child rearing, that any means employed by a parent to exact acceptable behavior from a child was legitimate. And this included the use of force, the use of violence, and the use of drugs. Laura's childhood was a time of extreme neglect, emotional deprivation, and abandonment; her life became one of abuse and torture. Her life dramatically reveals the perils inherent in the method chosen by the Victorian middle and upper class to raise their children; what happened to Laura was a consequence of the way that she had been raised.

There are very few references to Laura in Virginia Woolf's extant correspondence, or diaries, or memoirs, written during her adult life. There are a few letters: one, written to Violet Dickinson in 1904, after Woolf had read her father's correspondence, referring to the history of Laura as the most tragic episode in her father's life; three written during 1921 to her sister Vanessa regarding Laura's expenses, Kate's visit to Laura, and one describing George Duckworth's expectation that Adrian's knowledge of psychoanalysis might "be able to cure poor Laura"; the last, written in 1934, upon the occasion of George's death.[87] There are no references to Laura in the diary which Virginia Woolf kept after her marriage to Leonard Woolf. A visit to Laura is mentioned in the diary that Woolf kept when she was fifteen, when Woolf herself was going through a very difficult time;[88] the visit to

Laura cannot but have reinforced the possibility that Woolf herself might be dealt with in the same way.

I have already remarked upon the disparity between the portrait of Laura which Woolf draws in her letters to Vanessa, where she seems to describe Laura's fate as avoidable, and the one she draws in her memoirs meant to be read to friends, where she describes Laura as an idiot. The difference between Woolf's private and public descriptions about Laura suggests that Woolf was not willing to subvert the story her father told about her half-sister's treatment. Otherwise why would she have written differently about Laura to her sister? If Woolf *really* believed Laura was an idiot, would she not have disputed Leonard's view that Laura could have been spared? Although she was willing to break the silence about her own abuse, about Vanessa's, and about what had happened to Stella, she supported her father's explanation about Laura in public.

The fullest statement Virginia Woolf made regarding Laura's life was in the papers which she presented to the Memoir Club, in "A Sketch of the Past" and "Old Bloomsbury," and she wrote these in the last years of her life, for a public audience. It is the portrait of Laura that Woolf's biographers have most often used. In these memoirs, Laura appears as the vacant-eyed idiot. In "Old Bloomsbury," Woolf distances herself from Laura, describing her, not as Leslie and Minny Stephen's daughter, but as Thackeray's granddaughter,[89] as if Laura were not her half-sister.

When Virginia was young, about ten or so, she referred to Laura as "Her Ladyship of the Lake," after the Lady of the Lake of Arthurian legend, with which Virginia was no doubt familiar.[90] The name appears in the Stephen children's family paper, *The Hyde Park Gate News*, which was left around for the grownups to read. If Leslie Stephen had been more alert, he might have been able to see, in Virginia's naming of Laura "Her Ladyship of the Lake," his daughter's uncanny insight about Laura's treatment within the family, her feeling about Laura at the time, and there is something astonishingly precocious and terrifyingly apt about the name.

The nucleus of the story of the Lady of the Lake is the folktale "concerning the theft of a king's son by a water-fairy"[91] who brings up the child in a fairyland under the water. In one Arthurian tale, the Lady of the Lake steals Lancelot, as a baby, from the Lady Elaine. Using "Her Ladyship of the Lake" as a name for Laura indicates that Woolf felt that her own infancy was robbed by "Her Ladyship's" presence in the Stephen household. In the same Arthurian tale, the Lady of the Lake is responsible for the profound sorrow and mourning of the Lady Elaine. Woolf must have believed, or was told, that Laura was causing her mother's sorrow; indeed, in Leslie Stephen's letters to Julia, Laura's behavior is used to explain Julia's profound depression, even though Julia had been profoundly depressed at least since the death of her first husband, and, quite possibly, even before.

The deep-seated and perhaps unacknowledged rage that Woolf must have felt toward Laura's seemingly preeminent position is also evidenced by the name. The slaughter of the Lady of the Lake is connected to the loss of a mother and to the chaos of King Arthur's realm: Balin, with a sword, "cuts off in full court the head of the Lady of the Lake who had slain his mother." Balin's act signals the "deep disorder and moral confusion obtaining everywhere," the "anarchistic condition of the realm,"[92] the loss of self-control that has, in fact, led to chaos. The young Virginia might indeed have felt murderous toward "Her Ladyship of the Lake" who had brought grief and distress to her mother, who was probably blamed for the chaos and disorder in the Stephen household.

The Lady of the Lake takes Lancelot under the water to a fairyland, where he lives in utter bliss and contentment, free from the cares of the world that he would have had to endure as the child of Elaine and King Ban. There Lancelot is brought up lovingly by his foster mother; tutors train him; the "woods and wilds await his pleasure."[93] One wonders how Leslie and Julia explained Laura's departure to their other children; the name, "Her Ladyship of the Lake," suggests that they might have said that Laura was being sent to a special place of great privilege, where her special needs would be catered to, where she would be happy. But the name also suggests that Woolf experienced Laura's departure as if she herself was stolen from the family, and that her loss was felt at a deep emotional level.

From a child's point of view, it must have seemed that Laura was the cause of her parents' severe and violent behavior—like the Lady of the Lake, she was the giver of the sword. Yet Laura, like the Lady, was locked away, unseen, as if she were underwater, or in a private realm of her own. The fact that the young Virginia used a name that locked Laura in an underwater realm is immensely significant. For the image of being underwater, or of drowning, recurs again and again throughout Woolf's life, in connection with her own sorrow and suffering, in connection with wanting to escape from violence. The image of Laura as the Lady locked under the lake indicates that at some deep level Virginia believed that she and Laura were akin, that they were sisters under the skin, and that they would ultimately share the same fate.

Chapter Two

STELLA, "THE OLD COW"

Stella Duckworth was Virginia Woolf's other half sister, the daughter of her mother Julia's first marriage to Herbert Duckworth. Stella and Laura were born within a year of one another and there is a fearful symmetry in what happened to each of them. As Frances Spalding, Vanessa Bell's biographer, has observed of Stella: "An awful helplessness surrounds the story of her life."[1]

Stella was born in 1869; her father died in 1870. Her infancy and childhood were spent in the atmosphere of overwhelming grief and profound depression that was Julia's response to Herbert's death. After her first husband's death, Julia was never again fully able to turn her attention to Stella's needs, although she lavished a great deal of love on George and Gerald, her two sons from that marriage. The effect on Stella was deadening and continued for the rest of her life; she developed a "passive, suffering affection" toward Julia.[2] Because she was deprived of her mother's love, she became welded to her, continually seeking her favor, forever carrying out those tasks by which she no doubt hoped she could win her mother's affection. This never happened. Leslie Stephen tried to explain Stella's treatment by saying that during Julia's widowhood, "a cloud rested even upon her maternal affections."[3]

It was Stella who told Virginia Woolf how their mother used to lie prostrate upon the grave of Herbert Duckworth at Orchardleigh as a way of expressing her grief.[4] At the wedding of Anny Thackeray, which Julia attended with Stella, who was eight at the time, a bridesmaid described Julia, seven years after Herbert's death: she wore "a thick, black velvet dress and heavy black veil," giving "the gloomiest, most tragic aspect" to her side of the chancel. But Stella, too, "looked as tragic as her mother."[5]

Stella's infancy and childhood have been amply documented. Her half sister Virginia said that "Stella came to her first realization of selfhood and of life during Julia's saddest years."[6] We know that Julia Duckworth was "ruthless" to Stella; "indifferent" to the "personal suffering" that the girl endured. Although she protested that "she did not love the boys better than Stella," she said that she treated Stella so harshly because "Stella seemed to her more a part of herself" than a person in her own right.[7]

The merging of their identities is dramatically illustrated in a photograph taken of Julia Stephen and the Duckworth children, by the famous Victorian photographer, Julia Margaret Cameron, Virginia's great-aunt.[8] In the family photo, taken at Saxonbury, after her first husband's death, Stella is seated behind her mother, leaning into her, with her hand on her mother's arm, but Julia isn't touching her. The mother looks severe; the daughter looks sad. A lock of Stella's hair has been taken and draped over her mother's shoulder, so that it seems as if it, in fact, belongs to Julia.

Julia's upbringing had been far from ideal. From a very early age, she had cared for her mother, described as an invalid, but, according to Jane Lilienfeld, quite possibly a drug addict. Her mother's care became Julia's responsibility, and not that of her physician father. Julia's life is a classic case of nurturance deprivation and role reversal, the child assuming the care and nurturing in a household that has not rendered the child appropriate care. Julia's parents continued to expect her to take care of them well after she was married, with children of her own.[9]

Just as Julia's mother had reversed roles with her, at a very early age, so that Julia was forced to become her mother's mother, so too did Julia require Stella to become a little mother within her own household. The historian of childhood Lloyd de Mause has observed that this role reversal is cued in photographs which commonly show the child touching the mother: in this photograph, Stella touches Julia; Julia touches no one. This role reversal, in which a child, often the eldest daughter, assumes responsibility for practical and emotional tasks usually performed by an adult, is a common feature in incestuous families.[10] Julia, in fact, did not love Stella. Except for Laura, Stella was the least-loved of all of the children in the household; her mother felt differently toward her than she did to the four Stephen children, who "were to her a pure delight."[11]

Stella retained a lifelong sense of her own "inferiority which led her from the first to live in her mother's shade." Deprived of the kind of love which would have encouraged her to form a coherent sense of self, she became, as a result, not only Julia's "handmaiden," but an unpaid servant within the Stephen household when she was but ten years old. Her compliance with this role was no doubt assured as a result of the example which Laura provided to the household of the treatment that a recalcitrant child could receive. She was taught her subservience; Julia did not reward Stella's work with praise, but instead, treated Stella as "a slower and less efficient part" of herself.[12]

Stella was ten when Vanessa, the eldest Stephen child, was born; she was only thirteen when Virginia was born and there were then three young Stephens to care for. At the time, she lived a very different life from the Stephen children, because of the work that was required from her. As soon as Vanessa was born, Stella was given the responsibility of helping her mother and the servants. The amount of care that Stella rendered must not be underestimated: she fed the children, shopped with them and for them; taught them their letters, and superintended their play. She ran the entire household on the frequent occasions when her mother was away caring for her own mother, sometimes for weeks at a time, or "doing good" in the homes of the poor. It was Stella who "gave Vanessa her first music lesson and taught her the art of letter writing." It was Stella and not Julia who observed Vanessa's "love of drawing and gave her some chalks." It was Stella who provided comfort when, after their mother's death, Virginia thought that she saw a man "sitting bent on the edge of the bed." Stella said, "It's nice that she shouldn't be alone."[13] In fact, it seems as if Stella interacted with the children far more than Julia; she functioned as a primary caretaker, not just a half sister.

Stella was really a kind of household Cinderella. Vanessa remarked, many years later, that "it filled her with horror to contemplate Stella's life." The responsibilities crammed into the pages of Stella's diary after her mother Julia's death made Vanessa "wonder how Stella ever lived to be 28." Adrian Stephen had discovered the diary, and had read parts of it to Vanessa. Vanessa wrote Virginia, describing the "most gloomy and terrific account" of Stella's overworked days, with "never a moment's praise."[14] In fact, her chronic overwork probably hastened her death, just as Julia's had.

One reason for this was that Leslie, like so many other Victorian men, thought nothing of leaving his wife in the most desperate straits and going off on jaunts of his own with his male cohorts. One example of this occurred soon after Virginia's birth. At the time, the problems with Laura were at their peak. Leslie went off on his trip, leaving Julia or Stella to cope with the chaos. His common excuse for not canceling a trip during a time of crisis (and there were many crises) was that his plans had progressed too far for him to be able to cancel without embarrassment. But while he was away, he wrote many letters of comfort and support for Julia's plight, sometimes two or more a day, remarking upon what a dreadful time she must be having, stating that they must find a way to end her misery.[15] These letters have earned him the reputation for being a Victorian father more concerned with his children than most.

When Leslie was home, he would not have superintended the children's care in the nursery; the notion of separate spheres precluded the Victorian patriarch from issuing orders concerning the children to the servants. Julia desperately needed someone to help her and that someone was Stella. Leslie's freedom was purchased at the expense of Stella's.

Like so many other Victorian girls, Stella had no real childhood, no adolescence. She was in fact far less free than Julia for her entire life, because Julia could escape from the household alone to visit the sick and the poor. But as a Victorian girl, Stella had no such opportunity. Any time she left the household, she had to do so in the company of one of the younger children who would chaperone her; this meant that she was never without the responsibility of caring for one of the younger children; Stella constantly had a child in tow as she ran errands in London's business district.

43

The life that Stella led was far from the stereotype of the pampered daughter of the middle classes. Such a life of service is usually associated with the daughters of the working classes in Victorian England, many of whom were running entire households by the time that they were ten.[16] True, Stella had the servants to assist her, and her role was probably not unique, but her hard work and many responsibilities dispel the myth that the children of the middle classes always led a life of privilege and ease. Her position within the family probably devolved to her because, as the daughter from a first marriage, she was in a position of less importance within the family than her half sisters, even though her father was far richer than Leslie and her dowry was substantial.[17] The family name for her, "the Old Cow,"[18] portrays her as a mindless, slow-witted supplier of the family's needs for nurture.

A dramatic example of Stella's responsibility for the household occurred in 1887; at that time Virginia was five and Stella was seventeen. Julia had been called upon to attend her father upon his deathbed; after her father's death, her mother required (or insisted upon) Julia's remaining to care for her. Julia was away from her own household for a period of six weeks, during which time Stella was put in charge of running the household. Leslie, although he wrote that he did not want to leave the children alone, nonetheless went on a trip to Scotland that he had planned before the crisis. Florence Maitland was eventually brought in to help. During the crisis, Leslie wrote to Julia constantly, requiring responses and assurances from her that it was all right to leave Stella with the children. Leslie could never be counted upon to suspend his pleasures, even in times of acute crises. But it must also be said that Julia very often put the needs of her mother before the needs of her children.

Stella's efforts were not rewarded with praise. Not only did Julia chide her with her inferiority at performing tasks, Leslie also criticized her "for being less capable than Julia."[19] Once when Julia was away and Stella, at fifteen, was in charge of the household, Leslie wrote Julia that Stella "'was too lenient with the children,'" that she "'could-not converse with him,'" and that she "'hadn't provided him with writing paper.'" He complained that when Stella was put in charge of his needs he "'was very hard up.'" At sixteen, "he called her a firstrate housekeeper, concluded that she would make a good nurse but complained that she snubbed him when he was unusually silly."[20]

Stella was not only to act the part of surrogate mother when Julia was away; she was also expected to act the wife to Leslie, which included his expectation that she would fetch his writing paper and respond to his silliness. Stella never had even the semblance of a life of her own until the brief period of her marriage (and even then she was responsible for Virginia, as we shall see), and she married much later than she might have because she continued to take care of her half siblings after Julia's death. Stella's treatment, though not overtly brutal, as Laura's was, resulted in an almost complete extinction of Stella's own sense of self.

Stella was literate, but not educated, although she had the most musical talent in the family.[21] Julia Stephen adhered to the philosophy of "the sanctity of separate spheres and the futility of votes, careers, or a university education for women," and she wrote "impassioned essays" defending her views. Julia was also a "staunch supporter of the patriarchal system": she was a social conservative and believed in the right of women to rule the home, as the men of this class "ruled the realm; she adhered to a belief in a strict hierarchical order between the classes and the sexes within the home," which was treated as a "small domain." Julia believed that the family was "the smallest unit of the patriarchal state"; she had the right of "physical and moral rule" over the lives of the family members and servants. The duty of the mistress of the household was to maintain the moral atmosphere within the home by "a firm, just rule" which was believed to be beneficial to the whole family.[22]

During the 1870s and 1880s, there was agitation for the greater liberty for women and workers. Julia Stephen responded by writing an essay on the servant question which defended the "established patterns of deference and subordination between the classes in the home." Inherent in this scheme was the subordination of women and daughters within the household, and a belief in a form of family governance which insisted upon keeping "the laboring population in servitude through legal and economic sanctions."[23]

Julia's treatment of Stella cannot be separated from her acceptance and defense of a strict order within the home. Within this order, she had the right to command Stella; Stella had the obligation to obey. The justification for this doctrine was that it was the only way to ensure the "moral health" of the home, indeed, the moral health of the nation and of the empire: she believed that "loosening the bonds of control over a subject group" would result in sexual license; because the strength of a nation depended upon its morality, "social discord or even revolution by the lower orders would quickly follow" any relaxation of this rigid control.[24]

But it is precisely this family arrangement—a careful and uncompromising regulation of every aspect of the behavior of the daughters by the parents—that often leads to sexual abuse within the home.[25] The supreme irony of Julia Stephen's beliefs and practice was that although she believed that through her control she was maintaining a moral atmosphere within her home, the fact was that her treatment of Stella made her so submissive that she became the victim of the abusive and violent behavior of her cousin, J. K. Stephen.

J. K. Stephen was the son of Leslie Stephen's brother, Fitzjames. Fitzjames had displayed his belief in the inherent evil of women during the Maybrick case, with which he was involved. During his summation, he told the jury, without evidence, that Mrs. Maybrick, on trial for the murder of her husband, was an adulteress and that "an adulteress by nature was likely to commit murder."[26] After this, he was advised to resign his position as judge, but it is significant that this irrational behavior revealed how deeply seated Fitzjames's belief was in the depravity of women.[27] As Jane Marcus has described, the legacy of Stephen misogyny went as far back as James Stephen of the Colonial Office, Leslie and Fitzjames's father, who was a tyrant at home, and "the architect of an ideology of oppression which used the model of patriarchal domestic tyranny as a basis for colonial imperialism." This master-servant relationship was refined by James's son, James Fitzjames Stephen, "as the relation of a father to his wife and children."[28]

Woolf described her cousin "Jem," as he was called, as that "great figure with the deep voice and the wild eyes" who always brought to Woolf's mind the image of "some tormented bull."[29] Indeed, J. K. acted out that Victorian belief in male sexuality as pure aggression, as demonic possession.[30] The unfortunate object of J. K.'s passion from 1890 to 1892 was Stella Duckworth. During this two-year period, J. K. would often dash into the Stephen household in search of Stella, "with his madness on him."[31]

His behavior must have created quite a stir within the household because it was so flamboyantly aggressive and hostile; it must have deeply affected the children, especially the girls, for Woolf remembered how J. K. would "burst into the nursery and spear the bread on his swordstick." His explosive violence surely directly threatened the children because Woolf recalls how, on at least one occasion, "we were told to go out by the back door."[32] But Leslie Stephen and Julia persistently refused to admit J. K.'s violence: Leslie, in fact, referred to him as "pathetic," as "charming."[33]

The onset of J. K.'s madness was described by Leslie in his biography of his brother, J. K.'s father. He reports, without comment, the fact that his brother saw "comparatively little of his elder children in their infancy."[34] Leslie describes J. K.'s career as an Etonian, and as an "Apostle" at Cambridge, remarking that he was "most definitely marked out for distinction."[35] That early promise was never fulfilled, however. At the end of 1886, he had an accident. He received a "terrible blow on the head" by an "engine employed in pumping water."[36] By the summer of 1888, he began having periods of excitement and depression. Leslie attributes the change in J. K.'s behavior to this blow on the head. He insisted that "under all the distressing incidents, the old most lovable nature remained absolutely unaffected. No one could be a more charming companion."[37]

During the peak of this mania, J. K. was in chronic and violent pursuit of Stella. Part of the responsibility for controlling J. K.'s behavior, illogically and unfairly, fell to the Stephen children, who were instructed, although Vanessa and Virginia were just ten and eight when it started, to deny him access to Stella: if the children met him, they were not to discuss Stella's whereabouts.[38]

These spectacles must have worried and deeply troubled the children, impressing them with the view that an ardent male is a violent male, a "tormented bull," a view which Woolf herself had to accept on the basis of what she witnessed.

Neither Julia nor Leslie took strong measures to protect Stella, to stop J. K. from terrorizing their children, or to prevent him from having access to their home. Indeed, Julia seemed not to recognize the very real threat that J. K. posed to her children, or if she recognized it, she chose to ignore it and to continue to expose them to risk. More importantly, the raving J. K. held a greater place in her affections than the docile, obedient Stella, whom she did not love.[39]

Julia "took the warmest interest in him and his fate"; "she loved him very dearly";[40] and she did all that she could for him.[41] Although J. K. was so potentially violent that "the committee of his club were compelled to post a policeman at the door to restrain him forcibly from entering,"[42] yet Julia's constant saying was, "'I cannot shut my door upon Jem,'"[43] and he continued to have access to the Stephen home, except for one period, until the day the specialist Sir George Savage confined him to an asylum.[44]

By the time of J. K.'s assault on Stella, Virginia herself had been sexually abused. The effect of J. K.'s unbridled rage was a repetition of the violence that Woolf had already experienced. She and the other children must have felt unprotected and threatened. They saw their own mother refusing to shut her door on this threatening and violent man; in fact, he came "very constantly" to their home during this time. But Julia believed "allowances" should be made for him.[45] The children might have also learned to get her attention by behaving like him.

The family myth about Julia's relationship with J. K., described by Leslie Stephen, was that "in his most excited moods" Julia's "gentle grace and dignity commanded him absolutely." This is an example of the Victorian myth of the power of a good woman's love as an agent of salvation and transformation.[46] Myth it was, however; there is very little truth to it. Though Julia might have calmed J. K. from time to time, she did not transform him at all, nor did she rescue him. He was committed to an asylum where he starved himself to death. He died on 3 February 1892.[47] His death was one of the losses to which Julia "found it hardest to become reconciled." On the anniversary of his death, just before her own, she visited Jem's grave.[48] Leslie Stephen's account of J. K. Stephen's life portrays it as essentially a "sad story." But Jem's love for Julia, as far as Leslie Stephen was concerned, exhibited "all the strength of his fine generous nature."[49]

There is another side to the J. K. Stephen story that directly bears upon his pursuit of Stella Duckworth. J. K. became tutor to Eddy, the Duke of Clarence, while he was at Trinity College, Cambridge, in 1883–84; there were rumors that Eddy and his cohorts were leading a "dissipated and unstable" life,[50] so much so that the Prince of Wales visited his son's rooms to check on the story. During this time, there is evidence that J. K. became involved in some sexual difficulty, which became the subject of a song at Cambridge. The song suggests that he may have conceived an illegitimate child.

> There was a maid of the mountain glen,
> Seduced herself with a fountain pen;
> The pen it broke and the ink ran wild,
> And she gave birth to a blue-black child.
>
> . . . They called the bastard Stephen
>
> . . . Stephen was a bonny child
> Pride and joy of his mother mild,
> And all that worried her was this:
> His steady stream of blue-black piss.[51]

J. K. Stephen's hatred of women is in evidence in his poem called "A Thought," published in *The Cambridge Review,* in February 1891:

> If all the harm that women have done
> Were put in a bundle and rolled into one,
>> Earth would not hold it,
>> The sky could not enfold it,
> It could not be lighted nor warmed by the sun;
>> Such masses of evil
>> Would puzzle the devil
> And keep him in fuel while Time's whiles run.
> But if all the harm that's been done by men
> Were doubled and doubled and doubled again,
> And melted and fused into vapour and then
> Were squared and raised to the power of ten,
> There wouldn't be nearly enough, not near,
> To keep a small girl for the tenth of a year.[52]

These beliefs about the inherent depravity of women and the excellent moral nature and inherent superiority of men were being penned at a time when, ostensibly, men believed in the purity and power of a woman's goodness. But J. K.'s poetry was very popular and well-received at Cambridge. This misogyny was not only accepted at Cambridge: it was learned there "in the valorization of homosexual over heterosexual love, . . . in the study of Greek and reinforced by the philosophy debated in the meetings of the Apostles."[53]

J. K. Stephen's poetry not only articulated a belief in his sex's superiority. His hatred of women often was expressed in murderous and rapist fantasies. In one poem, "In the Backs," he describes how he was strolling by himself in the Backs at Cambridge. This traditionally all-male enclave is intruded upon by a woman who refuses to conform to the inhibiting traditions of behavior and dress of the proper lady. J. K. writes:

> As I was strolling lonely in the Backs,
> I met a woman whom I did not like.
> I did not like the way the woman walked:
> Loose-hipped, big-boned, disjointed, angular.
> If her anatomy comprised a waist,
> I did not notice it: she had a face
> With eyes and lips adjusted thereunto,
> But round her mouth no pleasing shadows stirred,
> Nor did her eyes invite a second glance.

J. K's response to finding this woman merits close attention:

> I did not like her: and I should not mind
> If she were done away with, killed, or ploughed.
> She did not seem to serve a useful end:
> And certainly she was not beautiful.[54]

There is nothing subtle in this. Women who do not behave as men want them to should be murdered or raped. Within this poem is the paradox that the appropriate standard of behavior for a woman is to both appear demure but not to ward off "a second glance" from a potential male admirer. But if the man does not get his way, then the woman should be punished by murder or rape.

These are the sentiments of the man who was allowed to pursue

Stella, and she did not respond to his advances. Leslie Stephen was familiar with his poetry, but he did not find it terrifying, he found J. K.'s verses "humorous"; he referred to them as "playful."[55] Indeed, the poems were the talk of London.[56]

Michael Harrison has put forth the startling thesis that J. K. Stephen himself was Jack the Ripper, the notorious Whitechapel mass-murderer of women,[57] and he uses, as part of the evidence for his case, quotations from J. K.'s profoundly misogynist poetry and correspondences between it and the notes sent to Scotland Yard by the person who claimed to have committed the murders. The association of the Stephen name with the Ripper murders has made its way into the public imagination.

In fact, J. K. Stephen was violently pursuing Stella during 1891, precisely the time of the Ripper murders. If the ten-year-old Virginia Woolf heard anything of those murders, and we must assume that she had, for they were the talk of London and commanded attention in the papers, the impression of J. K. Stephen running amok within her home must have been doubly terrifying. The impact upon Stella must have been tremendous. She was going through her own private hell, which no one was stopping, just as no one seemed capable of stopping the madman loose in Whitechapel. A man whose poetic fantasies include murder and rape was allowed easy access to Stella during precisely those years during which the Ripper murders occurred.

I do not support Harrison's view that J. K. Stephen was, in fact, Jack the Ripper. But I do believe it is significant that J. K. Stephen was penning his verses and publishing them in the periodicals of England's ruling class during the same time when the Ripper murders were occurring. It suggests that the Ripper murders were not an aberration from the norm of reverence of women as "angel in the house," believed to be the dominant ideology of the ruling classes. Rather, J. K.'s poetry demonstrates that Jack the Ripper was acting out the murderous sentiments publicly expressed by one of the highly esteemed and influential young men at Cambridge. And his expressions of violence in the treatment of women were not confined to women of the lower classes, but were also directed at women of his own class, as we shall see.

In his love letters to Stella, there is a supreme confusion surrounding the issue of whether Stella is good enough for him to love. He seems conflicted, even within the same letter, about whether he should venerate her or punish her. He calls her "my Star" and he uses his own inconsistent variant of the Victorian language of intimacy: "Do not expect to find a man worthy of your love. . . . No man can be really worthy of any good woman's love. Nor any woman worthy of a good man's. You are not worthy of mine. . . . And so good bye, my Star: good bye, perhaps for ever to your lover, but never till he died to you."[58]

Whether J. K. Stephen acted out his rage against women by raping Stella is impossible to determine. There are indications that he tried to. For one thing, J. K. was not prohibited from entering the Stephen house even after his violent rampages, because Julia could not shut out poor Jem even though he would often drive up to 22 Hyde Park Gate in a state of insane excitement.[59] At some point, however, J. K. was not permitted access to Stella, and it is safe to assume that there must have been a crisis that went beyond the usual violence. Rape is defined as "violent seizure"; J. K.'s behavior toward Stella has been termed a "violent pursuit."[60]

But there is further evidence. In J. K.'s collection of poetry, *Lapsus Calami*, a signed copy of which Virginia Woolf herself owned, which probably belonged either to her mother or to Stella,[61] there is a poem called "The Last Ride Together" which depicts, from the point of view of a woman, her treatment by a man whose attentions she has not responded to. The woman in the poem describes how she has rebuffed a man's advances and that she believes that her "no" will be enough to stop him: "When I had firmly answered 'No,' / And he allowed that that was so, / I really thought I should be free / For good." She believes that she has gotten this unwanted suitor to "soberly acquiesce."

She thanks the man for his "amorous zeal," promising him that she "would always feel / A kindly interest" in his well-being, and that she could promise to be a friend, a sister to him, even though she could not be his lover.

J. K. Stephen's poem reiterates the situation as it stood between himself and Stella: she, like the woman in his poem, had rebuffed his advances. But like J. K. Stephen, the man in the poem will not take no for an answer. Although he acts properly, he invites the woman on "'one more last ride'" with him. Although the woman is uncertain, she acquiesces, telling herself that "a ride, no doubt, would do me good"; and, besides, she believes that agreeing to the ride would be the "only way of ridding" her of her "pertinacious" suitor.[62]

The double entendre of the ride introduces one of the standard Victorian images for rape. In Victorian pornography, women assumed the images of horses which men rode; in rapist fantasies depicted in pornography, the stock figure is the woman, who, like a horse, must be "broken to the bit." In several pornographic novels of the time, women are "repeatedly subdued and tied down so they can be 'mounted' more easily, and they always end as grateful victims, trained to enjoy the whip and the straps, proud to provide pleasure for their masters."[63]

In J. K. Stephen's poem, the woman declaims: "I won't say much of what happened next," but she will "own I was extremely vexed." For, as she "leaned forward to stir the fire, / He advanced before I could well retire." And she finds herself in an "embrace in which I found no charm."[64]

J. K. Stephen uses the standard Victorian pornographic language which alludes to anal rape: the unwilling victim is approached from behind, "the hem of her dress" is swept up "over her hips," and she is sodomized.[65]

The rape, or "ride," in J. K.'s poem goes on for four interminable verses, during which the woman "at first . . . thought of little, save / The way to escape an early grave." Throughout the rape, she tries a number of ploys to get him to interact with her, hoping that she can force him to recognize her humanness, but he "rode with a fixed and gloomy stare"; this rape, of course, is not about pleasure—it is about power and inflicting pain and teaching a woman that she does not control access to her own body.[66]

Because these poems belong to the period during which J. K. Stephen was violently pursuing Stella, it is fair, I think, to assume that the revenge and rapist sentiments which he expresses in his poems were probably transcriptions of what he himself felt when Stella rebuffed him. The important issue is that he was permitted unlimited access to Stella even after expressing himself in print and in public. Could the family have been so charmed and disarmed by him that they could not read the very clear message of his work? Or, rather, did they so associate violence with male sexuality that J. K. was, quite simply, just another one of the men—no different, no worse than, say, Leslie Stephen himself, or Jack Waller Hills who, in time, married Stella? Was the misogyny in the·Stephen family so commonplace that there was nothing unusual about J. K.'s beliefs?

There is a curious postscript to a letter which J. K. Stephen wrote during this period in which he cautions Stella "Dont be sentimental: dont be excitable: dont be over sympathetic: dont above all be unreasonable, so as to think you did wrong when you did right."[67] What event this postscript refers to can never be determined; but J. K. is telling Stella how she should *not* behave in response to an event that has occurred between the two of them. He seems to be commanding her not to believe that she has done something wrong, and not to react to the fact that she knows that she has done something wrong.

These are precisely the sentiments in "The Last Ride Together": the woman *wants* the ride (rape) because it will be good for her; and she gets raped because she really wanted it. This is the thinking that prevails in Victorian pornography: the upper-class male fantasy that is endlessly repeated is that a woman really wants to be "taken" even when she says no: Victorian pornography encodes the belief that women have no choices to make about their sexuality because they are always ready for sex, even if they think they aren't: it signifies and enacts the "victim's loss of freedom." What is required of the woman at the end of the rape is that she tell her rapist that she really wanted it in the first place: "the young woman is to accept gratefully the domination of a man and learn to like it."[68] This is the covert content of "The Last Ride Together"; it is also the content of J. K. Stephen's confused postscript to Stella.

Stella Duckworth was supremely at risk at precisely the time when the middle and upper classes of London were focused on the morality tale of the Jack the Ripper murders, whose victims were prostitutes in London's East End, where do-gooder philanthropic activities had centered. As the historian Judith R. Walkowitz has observed, the Ripper

murders "contributed to women's sense of vulnerability in modern ur-
ban culture." One of the moral messages derived from those murders,
which became embedded in the consciousness of women, was that
"the city is a dangerous place" when women "dare to enter public
space."[69] The Ripper murders were "the latest of a series of sexual
scandals linking highlife and lowlife in London in the 1880s"; among
other things, the Ripper murders once again turned the spotlight on
the idea that upper-class men were leading double lives, that they were
therefore complicitous in a "system of vice that flourished in the undergrowth of respectable society." To middle- and upper-class readers,
the Ripper murders "constituted a morality tale of stark proportions.
These were economically desperate women, who violated their "womanhood" for the price of a night's lodging, and for whom the wages of
sin were death. The media used the events to write a sexually titillating
script "based on the association of sex and violence, male dominance
and female passivity, and the crossing of class boundaries in the male
pursuit of the female object of desire."[70]

Walkowitz has documented the extent to which the Ripper episodes
"covertly sanctioned male antagonism toward women and buttressed
male authority over them."[71] She has described how many men acted
out the Ripper role, intimidating their wives, and how, because of the
Ripper murders, many women were placed under virtual "'house ar-
rest' and made . . . dependent on male protection."[72]

Florence Fenwick Miller, however, had argued that "'attacks on
prostitutes were not different from other violent assaults on women by
men.'"[73] But if the Victorian middle and upper class could continue
to maintain that events like that happened *only* to the poor, that events
like that happened *only* to people well away from where they lived,
then what happened within the confines of the middle- and upper-
class Victorian home would not be subjected to public scrutiny. But
the sexual violence toward girls of the privileged classes like Virginia
and Stella continued unabated and undetected behind the screen of
those beliefs that associated depravity and sexual violence primarily
with the lower classes.

It is both ironic and tragic and chillingly fitting that while a Victorian do-gooder woman like Julia Stephen made her forays into the

homes of the poor in order to help them, she was leaving behind three girls—Stella, Vanessa, and Virginia—who were enduring the very sexual abuse and violence that she went abroad in order to expel. Her belief that her class was immune from depravity was grounded in an ideology of superiority that prevented her from seeing what was going on within her own home. That her own system of belief contributed to the mistreatment of her daughters never would have occurred to her. If her daughters were mistreated, she probably would have argued, it was because they invited it, or that they deserved it.

J. K. Stephen died in 1892, Julia Stephen in 1895. It was an all too brief respite for Stella, and it was, in all likelihood, one of the easier periods of her life. She received a serious proposal of marriage from Jack Waller Hills in 1894, when she was twenty-five, which she rejected; either she did not love him sufficiently or she was not yet ready to set out on her own. Vanessa Bell told her son Julian that Stella refused to marry while her mother was alive "because she could not live without her."[74]

Stella was hit very hard by Julia's death. Stella was the one who had watched Julia's health take a steady turn for the worse; she had tried "to warn Leslie"[75] that Julia's health was failing; she really believed that Julia's death could have been avoided if Julia could have stopped working so hard.

After Julia's death, Stella was required to take on all of the burdens of the household and all of her mother's philanthropic duties. Leslie was wrapped up in his own grief; he ignored the children; he "would do nothing for himself. Stella had to buy the underclothes, pay the bills and listen to complaints that she had ordered fish too often that week."[76]

The position into which Stella was plunged was very difficult, and also very dangerous. She was, in fact, living out a real-life version of a less common variant of the Cinderella legend, in which the daughter, because of her extraordinary resemblance to her mother, becomes the object of her father's desire. Indeed Virginia speaks of her father's "illicit need for sympathy," of Stella's "unqualified self-surrender" to Leslie's needs.[77]

In fact, Leslie indicated that he wanted Stella to slip into Julia's position. On 30 May 1895, shortly after Julia's death, on Stella's birthday, Leslie gave Stella a chain "which I gave to her mother upon her marriage." The message delivered together with the chain was, "We will cling to each other." Stella had to "assuage his grief and remorse"; she had to put her own grief second. When Stella was intruded upon after Julia's death, she was usually found in tears.[78] But when Leslie and Stella were intruded upon, after Julia's death, they were usually locked in an embrace.[79] Virginia Woolf said "resentfully that Stella had confused her father because she had behaved 'indiscriminately' when she was thrown into a position of intimacy with him."[80] Woolf clearly interpreted Stella's and Leslie's behavior as incestuous.

As Jean O. Love has so astutely observed, the trauma of Julia's death was made far worse because the children observed their father and Stella in compromising and confusing circumstances. Leslie's demands also removed Stella from the children; he was terrified of losing her as he had lost Julia and he would not allow her to leave him. As Virginia phrased it, "I do not think that Stella lost consciousness for a single moment during all those months of his immediate need." He would insist upon her constant attention and "whatever comfort she had to give."[81] Woolf implied that her father demanded, and that Stella might have given him, comfort of a sexual nature. The letters that Leslie wrote to Stella on the occasion of her marriage are the letters of an unrequited lover, not the letters of a loving father.

In one sense, Leslie had always seen Stella as a romantic figure. On the occasion of Vanessa's birth, which fell on the same day as Stella's, Leslie suggested that Julia and he name their firstborn daughter Vanessa. In the biography of Swift that Leslie was writing at the time of Vanessa's birth, the "two women who worshiped Swift"[82] are called "Stella" and "Vanessa"—not their real names, but the names that Swift gave them. Leslie, in choosing that name for his firstborn daughter, was clearly indicating that he perceived Julia's daughter Stella as the coequivalent of Swift's Stella, to whom Swift had written his famous journal.

Leslie's tremendous identification with Swift, "the famous Dean of St. Patrick's,"[83] is constantly alluded to in the pages of his biography. Leslie is fascinated with the attention which Swift seems to have commanded from Stella and Vanessa, the women in his life, whom Leslie describes as "his two slaves."[84] Leslie's treatment of Stella was, in part, a reenactment of Swift's relationship with Stella. Swift had known Stella from girlhood and acted out his power over her by confining her to a household over which he himself was master, which might have included a secret romantic and sexual relationship with her. In his biography of Swift, Leslie implies that Swift's relationship with Stella was sexual, for Leslie believed it to be impossible to be constantly in the presence of a beautiful woman without falling in love with her and wanting to consummate the relationship. Leslie writes that "it is singular that a man should be able to preserve" a mere friendship with a beautiful woman; an "ordinary man who was on such terms with a beautiful girl as are revealed in the *Journal to Stella* would have ended by falling in love with her";[85] a man in the same household with such a girl was powerless to overcome his inevitable attraction to her. But Stella Duckworth's situation is precisely the one that Leslie describes.

If Leslie really believed what he wrote, then clearly he would believe it to be the natural thing for an ordinary man in his position to fall in love with Stella. Stella, in order to accommodate the needs of her stepfather, did not marry until 1897, and she then lived on the same street as he did after her marriage; she continued to supervise his household. Like Swift's Stella, Stella Duckworth became Leslie's personal property after her mother's death. This situation only came to an end when Jack Hills again began to court Stella, and not without Leslie's trying to stop it.

On 22 August 1896, while the Stephen family was at Hindhead, Jack Hills asked Stella again to marry him, and this time he was accepted.[86] Leslie Stephen behaved badly, acting the part of the disappointed suitor rather than the part of the parental surrogate, interested in the well-being of his stepdaughter. He didn't want to lose her, and he treated her impending marriage as an act of utter selfishness on her part; he stated that his happiness was "a matter of rapidly diminishing importance"[87] to her. He "began to abuse Jack to his own children. Jack's name, he said, cut him like the smack of a whip."[88] He did everything that he could to complicate the wedding arrangements and to forestall the marriage.

Jack had been a special favorite of Julia's. Jack Hills had not gotten on well at all with his "worldly, snobbish mother" and he had become one of Julia's "special protégés."[89] A suitor like Jack would come to court Stella; Julia and Stella would discuss his particular merits; but because Julia held "exalted views of love and marriage," some seeming defect would be found. (It was probably Julia's unconscious way of keeping Stella for herself.) But then, once Stella rebuffed the young man, Julia became preeminent in the young man's affections: "she felt a pity for their disappointments which led her to show them a touching kindness and to do all she could to soothe the trouble."[90] She was, however, competing with her daughter for male attention. And she was winning. Stella was the bait; but Julia was the woman whom they all wound up loving. Julia was especially sympathetic to young men "who seemed to her to be not sufficiently appreciated."[91] But she herself set Stella up so that she did not sufficiently appreciate them. As Virginia herself baldly phrased it, Stella's emerging womanhood, her beauty, and her suitors "excited many instincts long dormant in her mother; she liked young men."[92]

It is impossible to tell whether Stella accepted Jack because she loved him, or because she needed to get out of the Stephen household and out of the impossible and compromising position that Leslie had placed her in and Jack was the first man to offer to marry her after Julia's death. Leslie, whose word cannot be relied upon in the matter of Stella's marriage, hinted that Stella had never loved Jack, and that Julia had known it and had therefore cautioned her daughter against marrying a man to whom Stella could not "give herself without hesitation."[93] But according to Virginia, Stella was at her happiest during her engagement to Jack; during the seven or eight months of the engagement, "her radiance unveiled her joy."[94]

When Stella was married in Kensington Church, on 10 April 1897, Leslie wrote that he would not commit to paper "the thoughts which have agitated me." He wrote only this: that the wedding caused him "many selfish pangs: but—well, I should be a brute if I really complained."[95]

What kind of a man was Jack Hills? And were the few months of Stella's marriage to Jack happy ones? Virginia Woolf has described him on several occasions as a thoroughly decent sort, who was, "affectionate, honest, domestic, and a perfect gentleman." He was fond of the country and its pleasures, such as riding and fishing, but he also was able to describe things poetically.[96] He brought much happiness, not only into Stella's life, but also into the lives of the Stephen children. He taught them how to sugar trees for moths; he gave them frank answers about sex; he explained Plato to Virginia, Vanessa, and their cousin Marny Vaughan;[97] he was a breath of fresh air in what Virginia described as that period of Oriental gloom. Most importantly, Virginia associated him with Stella's happiness: she believed that Stella once again exhibited "the exquisite tremor of life."[98] Woolf no doubt was also relieved when Jack's presence broke the deadlock of Leslie's and Stella's relationship.

But Jack Hills was also the son of a woman who despised women,[99] and it seems as if something of this was passed on to Jack, not only from his mother, but also from the prevailing misogyny inherent within his culture. Virginia described Jack's mother's attitude in her diary: "She said an odd thing to Nessa once—that she hated girls, especially motherless girls. . . . It was the terror of her life—that she was losing her charm. She would never have a girl in the house."[100]

Stella was the daughter of a woman who preferred her sons and her daughter's suitors to Stella; Stella was marrying a man whose mother shared Julia's beliefs. There was a side to Jack Hills which Violet Dickinson, a family friend, discussed with Vanessa. According to Violet, who had gotten it from a nurse's gossip, Jack was a "tiring lover" who had injured Stella on their honeymoon,[101] either because of the violence of his lovemaking, or the unceasing nature of his demands. The accuracy of this story is impossible to verify, but Violet claimed that Stella's illness, which the doctors diagnosed as peritonitis, was caused by Jack's sexual conduct.

Woolf herself recalled and recorded conversations with Jack Hills about sex that support the possibility that something like this could have happened. In a conversation about male sexual attitudes, Jack told Virginia that "young men talk incessantly of women; and 'had' them incessantly." Woolf records being shocked, and asking Jack if sexual relations had anything to do with honor. He replied that they didn't; they were "a mere trifle" to a man, and "made not a jot of difference to their honourableness";[102] "every young man had his whore."[103]

Woolf describes that Jack's shocking her with this information was good for her, but Woolf was unaware of what Violet Dickinson had told Nessa about Jack, and might have viewed Jack's statements about a man's "incessant" need for sexual gratification differently if she had known. Clearly Jack believed that men's sexual needs were boundless, incessant, uncontrolled, and uncontrollable. Although, given Jack's beliefs, he surely would have taken a lover when he returned from their honeymoon, I cannot help wondering whether he acted as Violet Dickinson claimed, on their honeymoon. If Stella's illness and death were directly caused by Jack's sexual aggression, then Stella's honeymoon must have been an even more brutal repetition of the way J. K. and Leslie had treated her.

Stella returned on Sunday 25 April 1897 from her wedding trip. She was taken ill on Tuesday; Leslie Stephen's contemporary account was that the attack "soon appeared to be peritonitis."[104] On Thursday, things looked very serious; that night she improved; by Sunday, the doctors believed she was out of danger. She had recurring bouts of pain and illness,[105] but there was a moment of hope when, on 30 May 1897 Stella announced that she was pregnant. She died, however, on 19 July 1897. According to Vanessa, Stella's death was "a time of horrible suspense, muddle, mismanagement, hopeless fighting against the stupidity of those in power."[106] No cause of death was noted by Leslie; but Woolf's contemporary record states that an operation was performed on 18 July, that it appeared to have been successful, but it does not describe what the operation was for. Virginia was told at 3:00 A.M. on the morning of 19 July that Stella was dead,[107] a mere three months after her marriage to Jack Hills.

It is significant that when Woolf remembered Jack's proposal to Stella, she always associated it with the appearance of a tramp: "I remember the moonlight night at Hindhead: the tramp: the shadow in the garden; Stella & he in the summer house; Thoby shouting at the tramp."[108] In another recollection, she wrote how "Thoby thought they were tramps."[109] It is clear that at some level she regarded Jack as a thief who stole Stella from the family; she saw Jack as a potential threat to her sister's well-being.

What did Virginia Woolf make of all this? How did she see Stella's life? How did she interpret it? How aware was she of the nature of Stella's relationship with Jack, with Leslie, with J. K., with her mother?

Virginia Woolf's letters, diaries, and memoirs contain descriptions of Stella's continuous concern for her, of Stella's attentions to her, and of Stella's generosity. Among her earliest memories was that of running errands with Stella, after which "she would take me to a shop and give me a glass of milk and biscuits sprinkled with sugar on a marble table."[110] When she was fifteen, she described how she was sitting in an armchair that Stella had given her; knowing how difficult Leslie was about finances, Stella arranged for Vanessa and Virginia to have an allowance upon her marriage.[111] She described walks that she took with Stella through the Park, how they hoped to see the Queen.[112] Even when Stella was sick, Woolf would "spend most of my day over there" at Stella's house.[113] And she described how generous Stella was with gifts, how, in contrast to her father, who sometimes gave his daughter gifts that had been given to him, when Stella came back from a trip, she was always heavily laden with presents.[114]

She speaks of her lovingly, although when she was fifteen and Stella was dying, there were difficulties in their relationship, which I shall later describe. But when Woolf was a grown woman, she discovered, through some old letters that Madge Vaughan sent her, the terrible reality of Stella's life: "Here are two dismal letters," she wrote to Vanessa in 1915. "I should rather like to keep Stella's—miserable though it is."[115]

Virginia Woolf explained that Stella's nickname, "the Old Cow" had been chosen because of Stella's association with "large white flowers— elderblossom, cow parsley" or "a white faint moon in a blue sky."[116] The nickname suggests that she associated Stella with some primal, natural, life-giving, maternal force; she was both beautiful and fragile. In fact, if it weren't for Stella, Virginia, Vanessa, and the other Stephen children would have suffered far more than they had. While still a child herself, she was the one who brought care and nurture to the nursery, but she did this at the cost of her own well-being. That Woolf also suffered profoundly from this is no doubt also true. Woolf's most constant mother figure was herself never nurtured, so how could she

possibly have given Woolf the security and support which she required. And Woolf was forced to witness for many long years Stella's
mistreatment by J. K. Stephen, and to watch Stella and Leslie. Nonetheless, in many ways, the woman that Virginia Woolf became was
due far more to Stella's daily care than to Julia's chilly and distant
supervision.

When Woolf spoke of Jack, in her letters and diaries, she described
him as "emphatic, sententious, & very trusty & kind"; he reminded
her of "an excellent highly polished well seasoned brown boot"; she
spoke of his "open air honor & sagacity." Though "nominally a conservative," he was turned by "his human sympathies" "in the direction
of women's suffrage."[117] At one time, the two of them planned to work
on a piece of writing together, the subject of which would be "oceans
of talk and emotions without end."[118]

On three important occasions, her rage at Jack surfaced. Once, after
the death of her father, when she was helping Maitland with his biography of Leslie by reading and sorting through his correspondence,
Virginia exploded at Jack's "thickskulled proprieties," how he "always
manages to put his great hoof down."[119] Jack apparently thought Woolf
would choose correspondence that would reveal her father in a damaging light. Woolf doesn't describe why Jack felt this way, but Stella
had been the recipient of some compromising letters from Leslie,
which Woolf had probably read; Jack might have been concerned
about the reputation of his dead wife had Woolf chosen to include
excerpts from those letters.

Another time was when she described Jack's behavior after Stella's
death. Woolf records how Jack vented his feelings on Virginia and
Vanessa. Woolf remembers Jack gripping her hand in his, she remembers him wringing her hand, his "hand gripping my wrist." Once
again, when a woman died, there were men demanding sympathy, and
young women were expected to provide it. Virginia Woolf referred to
it as "our immense task of piecing together all the torn fragments of
his life." In her memoir, Virginia associates the violence and insistence
of Jack's grip on her wrist with George Duckworth's grip on her arm.
Jack wanted to impress upon her, in the days after Stella died, not how
much he missed Stella, but the fact that "his sexual desires tore him

asunder."[120] This lesson Jack taught her as an adolescent about the effect of a wife's death was entirely in keeping with everything else that Woolf had learned about male sexuality. Stella had been reduced, in death, to the receptacle for Jack's lust. It is no wonder that throughout her life Woolf associated heterosexual love with violence and with death. After the death of her mother, she was sexually assaulted by George Duckworth; after Stella's death, Jack held her captive while he lectured her on how overwhelming were a man's sexual needs. On one occasion, Virginia lumped him together with the Duckworths, calling the lot of them "a plague of males."[121]

Woolf describes how Jack behaved in this way, week after week, in the summer after Stella's death, while the family stayed at Painswick. Every night Jack would take either Vanessa or Virginia for a walk, impressing upon them his terrible pain. As Virginia put it, the two of them "bore the brunt of his anguish,"[122] and she refers to "those appalling evenings at Painswick."[123] Woolf's two impressions from that summer were of a "leafless tree," and "Jack's hand gripping my wrist."[124] With Stella, the "Old Cow" gone, all fecundity was gone from the world; once again, without a woman to protect her, Virginia was subjected to the violent sexuality of the Stephen men.

Not long after Stella's death, Jack began to court Vanessa, and there were those who believed that she loved him.[125] Why Vanessa felt this way about Jack is a complicated issue which I shall take up later; but it is clear that Vanessa knew at some level that unless she married quickly, she would inherit Stella's position in the household. She could not, however, legally marry Jack in England: the law at the time precluded a man from marrying his widow's half sister, but she might have gone abroad to marry. Why Jack chose to court Vanessa, no one can say. But according to Noel Annan, Leslie's biographer, it was because after Stella's death, Jack Hills was "in a state of sexual frustration."[126] Jack's behavior after Stella's death does lend credence to Violet Dickinson's claim, however.

But perhaps the most virulent legacy of Jack Hills's marriage to Stella and his subsequent behavior to Nessa was the impression that one woman was interchangeable with another as an object of a man's desire; that a man's desire could cause him to forget very quickly indeed a woman whom he supposedly loved. The tragedy of Stella's death was that Woolf had to watch how Jack responded to it. When Woolf recorded Jack coming again to see Nessa, she wrote, tellingly, that "Nessa has her cisterns full again":[127] Nessa was nothing but a cavity into which Jack could ejaculate his grief. She also recalled how, later, Jack would write her letters from Italy, saying "Never think that I've forgotten Stella, tho' I've loved other women."[128] But his behavior said it all.

In 1940, as she was listening to the droning of the German airplanes in the skies above her, she recorded a saying of Jack's: "The weak are the wrong doers. . . . The drifters that foul the nets."[129] In 1940, Woolf saw Jack Hills as a fascist, who, like Hitler, believed in the inherent evil of the weak. In her diary entry, she refers to herself as "a drifter" who fouls the nets. She had come to see herself as someone who had been weak, and who, like Stella, had been the victim of Jack Hills and his errant masculinity.

Virginia Woolf analyzed the impact of her relationship with Stella twice in her life: when she was twenty-five, and when she was near sixty. Both times, she contemplated what the reality of Stella's life must have been, she carefully considered Stella's relationship with Julia Stephen, and she examined the nature of Stella's relationships with Leslie Stephen, with Jack Hills, and with J. K. Stephen.

Woolf stresses that Julia had trained Stella for submission and victimization. She described that as a child, Stella had been "suppressed"; that Stella lived in her mother's shade, that she imputed to herself "an inferiority" which her mother both instilled and encouraged. Virginia described the drastic consequences of the Victorian tradition of raising a daughter as if she were an appendage of the mother; she described how Julia had offered "her up . . . freely."[130] Woolf did not romanticize her mother; she described the process whereby a self-sacrificing mother, responding to the demands for care made upon women, turns to her daughter and, in turn, enslaves her.

In the meantime, Stella's dependence upon her mother was assured, Woolf understood, because Julia trained Stella to believe that she could not survive apart from her mother. Stella was a "part of herself." Julia was the sun, Stella, the moon. Stella regarded her mother as a divinity; she was "always the beautiful attendant hand-maid."[131] This arrangement reproduced Julia's own relationship with her mother, Julia Jackson.

Woolf used the example of Stella's life to explain to herself that the creation of a strong ego, one that would enable a woman to take care of herself, requires that what Woolf referred to as this "almost excessive"[132] bond between mother and daughter must be reformed. The mother could then care for herself and not require her daughter to meet her own desperate and unfulfilled need for care—by not over-taxing her own resources, by not putting the needs of men above her own needs, and by insisting that men care for themselves (Woolf did not go so far as to state the possibility that men could care for women). The mother could then also help fulfill her daughter's very real need for validation and for care.

This reforming of the mother/daughter dyad Woolf saw as an urgent and compelling necessity if women were to move beyond passing on their own enslavement to their daughters. By describing what happened to Stella and herself after her mother's death, Woolf also indicated that this restructuring of the mother/daughter relationship was necessary if incestuous abuse was to be forestalled.[133] If one continued to maintain that women were solely responsible for nurture within the family, then this cycle would never be broken, no matter how many political reforms were enacted. To reform the family, Woolf understood through the example of Stella, it was essential that women not train their daughters to serve, not teach their daughters that it was their duty to respond to any and all claims for attention made by men, to put the well-being of men and boys above the well-being of girls and women, to make the well-being of men and boys the responsibility of girls and women.

When Woolf commented upon what happened to Stella (and to herself) after her mother's death, she described how and why both she and Stella became the victims of incest, and Woolf linked Stella's relationship with Leslie to the submissiveness training that she received from Julia; and she linked her own abuse to the fact that Leslie had abandoned his children and Stella had put his needs before theirs. In turn, because Stella was "claimed" by Leslie, both Virginia and Vanessa became the targets of George Duckworth, who might have been responding to his own stepfather's behavior, by turning his own aggression and rage at Stella's position into an onslaught upon Leslie's own daughters.

Although Woolf chides Stella for failing "in proper discrimination" and though it is clear, and understandable, that Woolf's life at the time was, as she described it, "in a chronic state of confusion," Stella had been taught, by the affair with J. K. Stephen, and her treatment in general, that her integrity and her physical and sexual well-being were of no apparent concern to her mother or to her stepfather: a man's violent assault took precedence whatever the cost; not having been cared for, or protected, when she required it, Stella could not protect and care for herself. If Julia and Leslie had permitted, even encouraged, the two-year onslaught by J. K. Stephen, and, in all likelihood, his rapist behavior, to intrude into their home, how can Stella ever have learned that it was within her power to say no to a man? She clearly could not say no to Leslie.[134]

Stella became Leslie's sexual and emotional support. Virginia must have learned in consequence that any veneration that her father supposedly had felt for her mother Julia was suspect, for it seemed to be quickly abandoned as he sought comfort and relief in Stella's embraces. (This whole vicious cycle would repeat itself when Stella died, and Jack Hills turned his sexual attentions to Vanessa.) The view of Julia as the "angel in the house" whom Leslie venerated, the view of Stella, as the beautiful "star" whom Jack adored, was desperately, even hysterically maintained by the Stephen family, even though the men in the family hardly waited for their wives' bodies to be buried before they turned their attentions to their next "victim."[135]

Virginia Woolf (and her siblings) lost not one parent, but two, in addition to the attentions of Stella, who really had been their primary caretaker. They were left alone with their grief. Their father abandoned them just as he had abandoned Laura when her mother died.

In the meantime, Woolf's own sexual ordeal began afresh: George chose this time to begin his incestuous assaults on her and perhaps on Vanessa, too. Woolf describes how "the sultry and opaque life" after Julia's death "choked us and blinded us." But as she put it, a "finger was laid on our lips."[136] Because it was impossible for her to break the silence by speaking out, Woolf's "breakdown" was a desperate attempt that, no matter how costly, would ensure that the privacy of those hermetically, incestuously sealed "hot rooms," upon which the continuance of incest depends, would be broken into by the outside world, by those doctors who were summoned to care for her.

When Woolf remembered the effect of her mother's death, she associated it with having "protection removed," of being "tumbled out of the family shelter."[137] And it is no wonder. Julia provided Stella with a semblance of a defense against Leslie (but not against J. K.; nor had she provided a defense for Virginia against Gerald). But with Julia gone, Stella, Virginia, and Vanessa were left with no defense at all. These three suffered from the consequences of a belief that men cannot control their lust; that women, merely by their presence, are enough to drive men wild; that the moral well-being of a household requires the constant vigilance of the "angel in the house." Woolf understood that this ideology was at the core of incestuous abuse within families: it was the ideology that her mother and father subscribed to; it was the ideology that they lived by. Incest was not, therefore, an aberration within this family; it was, Woolf understood, the natural, logical, necessary outgrowth of the family's Evangelical code.

Chapter Three

VANESSA, "THE SAINT"

In 1907, Vanessa Bell began writing her own memoirs, in which she intended to describe her life until the age of fourteen, and she suggested that her sister Virginia should also begin writing her own biography.[1] It was one of the most difficult times in their relationship: Virginia was suffering terribly, feeling that her sister had deserted her finally by marrying Clive Bell. Virginia wrote to her friend Violet Dickinson that her sister's marriage "does seem strange and intolerable sometimes. When I . . . see that funny little creature twitching his pink skin and jerking out his little spasm of laughter I wonder what odd freak there is in Nessa's eyesight."[2]

Virginia took up Vanessa's challenge to write, but she chose instead to write Vanessa's life for her. She could not give up the chance to write a memoir that would best Vanessa's own, and, through the writing of her sister's life, she could try to reclaim Vanessa or, failing that, to regain the spirit of the childhood that they had once shared. She wrote Clive Bell that she was writing Nessa's biography: "I ask myself why write it at all? seeing I never shall recapture what you have, by your side this minute."[3]

The memoir which Virginia Woolf wrote served yet another purpose. As she penned her memories of her and her sister's past, she sent what she had written, a few chapters at a time, to Clive Bell, who really was her intended audience for the piece.[4] In the "Reminiscences" themselves, Virginia pretends to be writing for Vanessa and Clive's as-yet-unborn children, but that is only a pose, for the first message that Virginia delivered was to Clive and she delivered it loudly and clearly in chapter 1. It was that she and Vanessa had been lovers long before Clive came on the scene, that they formed "a close conspiracy," that they were a "private nucleus,"[5] as she described it later in her life. She wrote of meeting Vanessa in "the dark land under the nursery table, where a continuous romance seemed to go forward. . . . We drifted together like ships in an immense ocean."[6]

The work was written, ostensibly, to celebrate Vanessa's virtues. Virginia speaks somewhat romantically of how Julia Stephen would smile at Vanessa, as she took on the role of a little mother in the Stephen family, caring for the "little creatures who were younger," so concerned with the well-being of her siblings that she insisted the nurse properly fasten her brother Thoby into his highchair before eating. She describes how Vanessa was "outwardly sober and austere, the most trustworthy, and always the eldest"; how she would sometimes "lament her 'responsibilities'"; how she "took it upon her to be what people called 'practical'"; how she was so honest that the other children "persecuted her" with her nickname "Saint."[7] Indeed, Virginia's "Reminiscences" seems, at first glance, to be the portrait of Vanessa as "the Saint," sent on to her husband Clive so that he, together with Virginia, could celebrate his wife's superior qualities as a human being.

However, by the time she began the memoir, Virginia had written of her wish to redress the commonly held impression, which she believed Clive shared, of "Saint" Vanessa, which so irritated her because of its implicit criticism of her own far from saintly character. She wrote to Clive, soon after their marriage, of the "general opinion . . . that no one can be worthy of her"; she wrote that she wished Vanessa's portrait were "a little more various," and she added, with apparent sarcasm: "I do homage all day long prostrate and acquiescent, before her shrine. And I suppose incense rises in the fields of Wiltshire [where Clive's family lived, and where the couple was staying] also." But in a letter to Violet Dickinson, she called Vanessa the "old fraud."[8] In her "Reminiscences," she takes her revenge on Saint Vanessa by describing, in great detail, ostensibly as just another fact of Vanessa's life, precisely how Vanessa had behaved with Jack after Stella's death.

Virginia was sharing with her sister's husband news that he might not yet have known, information about a love affair that his new wife had once had. Regardless of how broadminded Clive may have been, it is important that Virginia took the offensive and flaunted, for Clive to read and for Vanessa to share, this portrait of her sister, all too eager to fall in love with her dead half sister's widower. She chose her words carefully, but they were pointed. She wrote how Vanessa had "of old an affection for him"; she wrote of how Jack took "a regular and unthinking satisfaction in being with her." And, most tellingly, she described how those old feelings were the "starting point of much quicker and more fervent feelings, and the incentive was now urgent."[9] Virginia's implication was clear: Saint Vanessa was not a saint at all.

Virginia also graphically described how George behaved to the two of them after their mother's death. She told Vanessa's husband that the two of them had been the target of their half brother's amorous attentions, something Vanessa herself might not have shared with Clive. She described George's "violent gusts of passion," how his "abundant animal vigour" was not held "in control" by "an efficient brain," that he "allowed himself to commit acts which a cleverer man would have called tyrannical," that he "behaved little better than a brute," even as he claimed to believe in the "purity of his love."[10]

That Virginia broke the silence about their mutual exploitation in 1907 is astonishing; that she did it to her sister's husband is important. It seems that she wanted more than anything for Vanessa to continue to share with her the burden of the lives that they had led together. She did not want Vanessa to retreat from her, to deny what had happened to them, to pretend that it didn't exist, to "impose our conventional heroic shape" on "the tumult" of George's character.[11] She wanted Clive to know the real history of the woman he married; she wanted to assert that the stereotype of the image of the good woman denied Vanessa her pain and her past, and, in the process, negated that the two of them, because they shared the same past, were more alike than they were different; together, after all, they comprised a nucleus.

Vanessa responded to her sister's description of their past in a letter. She wrote that she "felt plunged into the midst of all that awful underworld of emotional scenes." And she asked, "How did we ever get out of it? It seems to me almost too ghastly and unnatural now ever to have existed."[12]

Virginia Woolf again publicly revealed what had happened to the two of them when she read her "22 Hyde Park Gate" to the Memoir Club, which began meeting in 1920, to an audience which included her husband, Maynard Keynes, E. M. Forster, and others. Part of Woolf's intention was to differentiate between the lives of young men and of young women during Victorian times. She wanted to point out that while the men in the assembled audience had been at Cambridge, learning, as Cambridge Apostles, to reverence all things Greek,[13] their sisters were at home, living through what Virginia referred to in a private memoir, as the "'Greek slave'"[14] years, performing duties of service and servitude.

Virginia described how Vanessa "in her white satin dress" "wearing a single flawless amethyst" and "a blue enamel butterfly in her hair," gifts of George, went forth with him "lavishing embraces which were not entirely concealed from the eyes of strangers."[15] Woolf wanted to make the point that she and Vanessa were subjected to incestuous assaults that should have been, and probably were, quite obvious to anyone who saw them.

Vanessa was George Duckworth's preferred companion in society from her "coming out" in 1897 until at least 1904.[16] She was his victim after her mother's death, in 1895, until at least 1904, a period of nine years. She accompanied him everywhere—to a dinner party given by Lady Arthur Russell; to a weekend with the Chamberlains at Highbury;[17] even abroad to Paris.[18] The cards would come daily, addressed to "Mr Duckworth and Miss Stephen." Vanessa indeed tried to resist, but, according to her sister, the more she did, the more George persisted.[19] Although there may have been scenes which put a temporary halt to what she had to endure, like one in which George and Vanessa circled round and round the same square, unable to emerge from the carriage because of the evidence that they had been fighting, and although Vanessa would continuously complain to her sister, George was still carrying on his behavior, often in full view of spectators, in 1904.[20]

After George's death in 1934, Vanessa sent her sister a memoir of what George had done to her, describing, perhaps, certain events about which her sister had been unaware, although she surely knew much of what had happened. Virginia wrote Vanessa that her memoir "so flooded me with horror that I cant be pure minded on the subject."[21]

In her private memoir, Woolf believed that George's behavior stemmed from "sexual jealousy";[22] he was Vanessa's constant companion ostensibly so that he could secure her a good match; in fact, Virginia understood, it was so that he could regulate her conduct and gain access to her. In trying to keep Vanessa to himself, George Duckworth was aping his stepfather Leslie Stephen's treatment of Stella, then of Vanessa, and enacting as well one aspect of the submerged meaning of Vanessa's name. In the words of Vanessa's biographer, Frances Spalding, she was "cruelly named." Hester Vanhomrigh, the woman whom Swift called "Vanessa," had lived a life of sexual deprivation, "a long agony of unrequited passion"[23] as a result of her association with Swift.

What can Leslie Stephen have had in mind when he named his and Julia's first child Vanessa? The fact that the name he chose for her so accurately signified the circumstances of her life suggests that he had some unconscious sense as to what he wanted to create in her when he named her, of what he would foster in her—a lifelong attachment to him, perhaps, his "ownership" of her, as Swift had turned Vanessa into his devoted slave. Can he also have unconsciously wished for a life of sexual abstinence for his daughter, as many Victorian fathers did, to ensure themselves of a caretaker if or when their wives died? Swift writes in *Cadenus and Vanessa* of his feeling for her, of "That innocent delight he took / To see the virgin mind her book."[24] Swift understood that, if Vanessa remained a virgin, he would have no competition for her affection; he would remain the idealized lover because of his inaccessibility, and, through denying himself to her, he bound her to him more truly by subjecting her to a lifetime of sexual longing.

Vanessa was "thrust into the role of hostess and housekeeper"[25] when Stella died; for seven years, until Leslie's death, when she was twenty-five and able to establish a household for herself and her siblings in Bloomsbury, far away from Hyde Park Gate and all it represented,[26] she ran her father's household, and bore "the brunt of his demand that, as the daughter of an eminent man of letters, she should tailor her life to his needs":[27] "When he was sad," he explained, "she should be sad; when he was angry, . . . she should weep."[28] For these seven years she lived a life of servitude to him, and he was as cruel to her as Swift was to "his" Vanessa, so much so that, after his death, she dreamt more than once of murdering him.[29] As Virginia described in her memoirs, his treatment of her was "brutal";[30] he had taken Vanessa "for his next victim."[31]

Vanessa had to work continuously to ensure that she could carve out some small space of the day to cultivate her talent in art, for she had become, at eighteen, the female head of a Victorian household in which her father's needs and wishes were a priority. During this time Virginia described him as "the tyrant father—the exacting, the violent, the histrionic, the demonstrative, the self-centred, the self pitying, the deaf, the appealing, the alternately loved and hated father."[32] The difference between Virginia and Vanessa was the ambivalence Virginia felt: all Vanessa ever felt was pure rage.[33]

While Vanessa ran his household, she had to order dinner; she had to arrange for Virginia's care on the frequent occasions when she was ill; she had to pour tea for her father, who, according to the tradition of the time, could not pour tea for himself; and she had to carry on a steady stream of conversation with his callers, because he was becoming increasingly deaf and unable to do this for himself; she had to dress for and appear at dinner; she had to accompany her brother George on his daily round of social engagements. Every day, according to Virginia, they "did battle" for "that which was always being snatched from us."[34]

The name given Vanessa was prophetic in yet another sense. Like Swift's Vanessa, she lived out much of her life, from about 1914 until her death in 1961, in an essentially asexual relationship with the painter Duncan Grant, who was the father of her third child, Angelica.[35] She began to live with Duncan after the collapse of her marriage to Clive Bell and after her love affair with Roger Fry had ended. Like Swift's Vanessa, Vanessa, too, suffered within the relationship with Duncan Grant, who was a committed homosexual. Throughout her entire life with Duncan, until her death, Vanessa made accommodations so that Duncan's current male lover would choose to live in the household which Duncan and Vanessa had established, rather than setting up a separate household alone together away from her; about his affairs, she always remained, as Duncan phrased it, "'the perfect darling,'";[36] she had once again become the "Saint."

Vanessa had begun to fall in love with Duncan when he was still involved in a relationship with her brother Adrian, which had been ongoing for a few years; and she decided that she wanted to have a child with Duncan when Duncan was involved with David (Bunny) Garnett.[37] Vanessa could not predict that she was inviting trouble and pain for herself; but she was unconsciously reproducing a set of conditions that would involve her in an emotional life very much like the one that she witnessed and also lived with in her childhood home.[38]

In fact, the emotional contour of Vanessa's life greatly resembles how she was entrapped by the demands made upon her by Leslie, by the sexual jealousy of George which would not let her go free, and by the emotional maelstrom of an incestuous family in which virtually all of the members were involved. In addition, her life with Duncan repeated the pattern of perpetual mourning and profound depression of her mother Julia Stephen. Vanessa also manifested something of Julia's belief that the presence of a good woman could transform a man; it was said of Vanessa that her presence had, among other things, curbed Duncan's drinking and somewhat quieted his emotional outbursts.[39]

Duncan stopped sleeping regularly with Vanessa soon after she became pregnant, but on at least one occasion Duncan slept with her again specifically in order to get his current lover, Bunny Garnett, jealous. In 1918, Duncan wrote into his diary, hopeful that Bunny would later read it, that he had "copulated on Saturday with her [Vanessa] with great satisfaction to myself physically. It is a convenient way the females of letting off one's spunk and comfortable. . . . That's one for you Bunny!"[40]

Vanessa tolerated an extraordinary amount of outrageous behavior from Duncan, a common pattern in women who have been incestuously abused.[41] On one occasion, Duncan was supposed to come and help Vanessa pack up the household and move it, together with the children. Duncan came so drunk that he vomited all over the cab that carried them. Duncan would become "uncontrollably jealous" if his current lover showed someone else any attention. At one time, when Bunny was involved with other women (in fact, he had tried to get Vanessa to sleep with him, which she wouldn't do), Bunny found Duncan in the barn at Charleston, "banging his head against a beam and threatening suicide"; they fought with one another constantly, and violently and vociferously, to the point that "both were half dead with exhaustion."[42] After these scenes, Vanessa would provide comfort and consolation.

Vanessa also took upon herself the self-imposed task of assuaging Duncan's guilt for hurting her, for she feared that, if he felt guilt at how he behaved or that he didn't make love to her, he would leave her. Duncan was assured of the constant services of a woman who ran their household with apparent ease and efficiency at very little cost to himself, other than protestations of continuing affection and unceasing love and unaltered devotion and utter dependence. Vanessa listened to the language rather than to his behavior: and so with her running their household, he could keep on painting, and loving, without impedance. When his love affairs went well, and a lover moved in with him and Vanessa, the bonus was that Vanessa would care for them both; when his love affairs did not go the way he wanted them to, he had her there to comfort him. As he wrote to her when he was involved with Paul (Don) Roche, late in her life, in a letter which was characteristic of the many that he had written to her throughout their long relationship: "I absolutely rely on you for everything. You do everything for me, and I can never do anything for you which distresses me." And then he went on, "I do not think that Don is in love with me, though he does love me. . . . I have been lately through rather a bad time with him . . . but I think now we understand each other a good deal."[43]

It has been said that Duncan loved Vanessa, although it seems that he had never been "in love" with her. They shared a lifelong passion for art and their best times together were when they were painting, either side by side, or in their separate studios. The problem for Vanessa was that she was, in fact, "in love" with him. Duncan, for his part, seemed to fear that if he showed her that he loved her, he would unleash a passion in her that would devour him.

Leslie Stephen might have been describing her relationship with Duncan Grant, and not Swift's affair with Vanessa when, in his biography of Swift, he quoted Vanessa's words to Swift: "Put my passion under the utmost restraint; send me as distant from you as the earth will allow, yet you cannot banish those charming ideas which will stick by me, whilst I have the use of memory."[44] Vanessa never stopped wanting a sexual relationship with Swift, just as Vanessa never stopped wanting one with Duncan.

According to her daughter, Angelica Garnett (who married Duncan's former lover Bunny Garnett), because of this relationship, Vanessa lived in a state of "chronic unhappiness."[45] Vanessa lived out her life in a state akin to mourning for what she had had for a brief time with Duncan, which corresponded to the emotional quality of Julia Stephen's life. Vanessa continued to try to engage Duncan in a sexual relationship; she wrote him of how sorry she was for bothering him continually about it, especially at night.

Vanessa's life with Duncan Grant was not vastly different from the one that she had lived at Hyde Park Gate, although she was able to paint unimpeded. Nonetheless, she spent her adult life structuring her various households around the needs of men, none of whom took much responsibility for the children's daily care—first, her husband Clive Bell and then, Duncan Grant.

In 1907, when Vanessa began to write a memoir of her childhood, she pondered the characters of her parents, and wrote her sister Virginia, wondering whether they too, as parents, would repeat their "old abuses" of not knowing what their children were like or what they wanted to do.[46] She wrote, feelingly, of being terrified of the responsibility of having children, primarily because she felt sure that, given her own upbringing, she would not be a good parent, and that she would be "unreasonably fond" of them, overly dependent upon them for satisfying her own emotional needs which had not been satisfied in childhood,[47] in that "appalling" life that she had lived at Hyde Park Gate which was directly traceable to the childhood which her mother Julia had experienced.[48] Her words were a brave admission of the difficulty in breaking the chain of treating one's children as one was treated in childhood. The tragedy of Vanessa Bell's life was that, according to Angelica Garnett, she came perilously close to organizing her own household in the same ways as the one that she herself grew up in.

We can get a sense of what Vanessa Bell's childhood was like, and how she conceptualized that period, from two of her paintings. Vanessa Bell painted two works depicting the nursery in her maturity, in addition to decorating both her own children's nursery and others for the Omega workshop, to which she contributed designs. The first, *Nursery Tea*, was painted in 1912, after the birth of her two sons, Julian and Quentin.[49] It was her largest painting to date, and she wrote to Roger Fry: "I am trying to paint in an entirely new way (for me)."[50] The painting is dominated by the figures of two nursemaids, seated opposite each other, at the head and foot of an oblong table, facing one another. There is a pile of food in the center of the table, a pitcher, some glasses, some pieces of bread. Two children are seated diagonally across from each other: the younger one, a boy, in a highchair, close to the nurse with her back to the viewer; the other, an older girl, just next to the other nurse. What strikes the viewer immediately is the expression of the nurse facing the viewer: her features are sketched, not fully drawn, but she appears, nonetheless, clearly reproachful. In fact, it is precisely because her expression is suggested that the impact of her reproof is so powerful, for it is not the censure of a singular nurse, but rather that of a generalized caretaker. The nurse is condemning and stern. She looks severely at her young charge, but the girl looks away and down, as if to avoid her glance. But, in looking down, her gaze is met by the other nurse, monumental, with her back to the viewer. The two nurses castigate the girl. The little boy looks to his sister; he does not smile, but rather looks puzzled, interested, alert.

This is not a painting about the sustenance and happiness and lively glow of how children are treated in the nursery. Rather, it is a telling evocation of an institution which is the locus of much pain and sorrow, rather than of pleasure. It is immediately evident that although the figures are all involved with one another emotionally, they are all separated from one another physically and pictorially by Bell's brilliant use of the surface of the table. The figures of the nurses predominate; the children, isolated, dwarfed, diminished in importance, are pushed out to the edges of the composition; the girl, in fact, is cut off by the right edge of the canvas; the boy, lighter in tonality than the rest of the figures is ignored, as all attention turns to the girl.

When Vanessa Bell decorated the nursery at Gordon Square for her own children, she avoided traditional images of good cheer. Rather, the nursery was filled with images of beasts of prey: "with stalking lions, zebras and jaguars pouncing on deer."[51] She wrote her sister that she had decorated the nursery with realistic portraits of Indian and African animals.[52] In fact, Vanessa may have been depicting the nursery as she herself had experienced it. At least one of her children seems to have reacted to it traumatically. Angelica Garnett has described her house as "a kind of petrified zoo." She describes a recurring dream that she had, "a gruesome dream of white-skinned children whose arms and legs, like parsnips, were chopped off in a sea of blood."

Vanessa's design for a nursery, done for the Omega workshops, is equally forbidding. A photograph of one corner of a room which she designed shows bold, powerful shapes. One wall is dominated by an elephant in a jungle landscape; the tusks are prominent. Virginia once associated the quality of Vanessa's love for her with "a South American forest, with panthers sleeping beneath the trees,"[53] which suggests that, as loving as Vanessa was, Virginia unconsciously perceived something threatening or predatory about the nature of her love. Vanessa herself believed that maternal love was "one of the worst of the passions, animal and remorseless. But how can one avoid yielding to these instincts if one happens to have them."[54]

In a later painting, *The Nursery*, which was perhaps inspired by her sister's *To the Lighthouse*,[55] there are also four figures: a nurse, a mother, and two children.[56] This painting, like *Nursery Tea*, presents the nursery as a sad place.[57] Both children are in the process of turning away from the mother and the nurse. The nurse is not happy; rather, she tends to the child, who pulls away from her, with an expression of sadness on her face; her gesture is automatic, reflexive, uninvolved. Nor does the infant appear happy. The mother looks at her son, but her son looks away. Both children are naked; both women are clothed.

The nakedness of the children, within a room that is filled with toys and plush furniture, seems out of place, jarring, incongruent with the clothed figures of the adults. Rather than their nakedness signifying freedom and a lack of inhibition, here, because of their nakedness, the children seem exposed, vulnerable, set apart, alone. Although there are two women present, there are no gestures of warmth or easy familiarity: the nurse is preoccupied with her own sorrow, the "elegant mother watches with greater detachment her elder child."[58] In this work, two caretakers are little better than none at all.

Vanessa Bell described this sense of detachment from her own children in a letter to Duncan Grant: "I feel somewhat detached," she wrote, "and really don't much mind what happens—the whole thing is rather like what it used to be when one saw a nurse being foolish with one's child and had to wait till it stopped."[59] This statement reproduces precisely the emotional content of her painting of the nursery. Vanessa writes that she as a mother would remain detached when she witnessed a nurse mishandling her child. One would expect that a mother *would* intervene on behalf of her child. This, apparently, Vanessa did not do. This, apparently, was not done for her. If this painting depicts Vanessa Bell's recollection of childhood, as her sister's *To the Lighthouse* represents hers, and Vanessa Bell's own experiences as a mother, then it is a grim, bleak view. As in *Nursery Tea*, neither mother nor nurse is directly involved in an interaction with a child. It illustrates, tellingly, the paralysis of depression, which manifests itself as detachment, and shows how depression is passed on through the generations by everyday interactions.[60]

Although Vanessa might have been detached in her mothering, she was, according to her daughter's account, very dependent upon her children for her own fulfillment. In this way, she repeated the mother/daughter relationship that had existed in the Stephen household, primarily between Julia and Stella. Vanessa has been described as "voraciously maternal, unconsciously possessive, in a way that exposed her to suffering."[61] She and her son Julian had a relationship that Angelica and Virginia both described as being more like lovers than like that of a mother and son. She told Julian how happy it made her to be told of his sexual relationships;[62] he obliged and wrote her long, involved detailed letters describing his love affairs. On the one occasion when he seriously contemplated marriage, she intervened, and "persuasively steered him away" from marrying.[63]

Although Julian loved his mother, he believed that he needed to put some distance between them, and he took a position in China, to set himself "straight internally," to "produce a kind of peace of mind"[64] which he apparently did not have. Like his sister Angelica, he too felt the strain of his upbringing. He wrote Janie Bussy, not long before his untimely death, that he had worked himself into "a genuine enough resignation to an early death."[65] He then volunteered for the ambulance corps in Spain, because of his politics. But he was wounded at a time when he chose not to seek shelter in a nearby trench that was available, where he might have been safe; he was engaged in repairing a road which was, in fact, under direct fire when he was hit.

Contemporary accounts depict Vanessa Stephen as a depressed child when she was in the nursery. In 1894, when Virginia was twelve and Vanessa thirteen, Leslie reported that both of them were seriously depressed;[66] this was the year that Thoby Stephen threw himself out of a window, so *all* of the Stephen children suffered from a serious, ongoing depression. Rather than their sadness being a response to their mother Julia's death (as is commonly held), contemporary reports indicate that the children were seriously depressed well before her death. It was surely caused by a combination of things, but it probably resulted from the detachment of the care which they received in the nursery; the events that they witnessed, such as Laura's treatment and Stella's, which would inculcate feelings of hopelessness; that Julia Stephen was chronically depressed and often absent; that Leslie Stephen did not see himself as responsible for child care, that he was infantile, and that the abuse that he had received as a child had surely affected him; that the Victorian system of child rearing insisted upon ignoring infants, rather than interacting with them. The Stephen children, Vanessa included, were never given the engaged, considerate, warm kind of care that we now know is essential for a vigorous sense of well-being in adulthood. The Stephen household demonstrates how depression continues through the generations: both Vanessa Bell's daughter, Angelica Garnett, and Angelica's daughter, Henrietta Garnett, have written important documents about depression. Virginia Woolf's "A Sketch of the Past" is as important a document analyzing a lifelong depression as one will find.

Although there were times, such as when Virginia wrote her memoirs of Vanessa's life and her own, when she recognized the extent to which her sister had suffered, there was an overriding tendency, nonetheless, for the two of them not to share their feelings in adulthood, so that Virginia misrepresented how "in control" Vanessa was of her life throughout their maturity. Calling Vanessa "the Saint" fixed her image as Virginia so often needed to see her, as Virginia wished her to be: "How much I admire this handling of life," Virginia wrote into her diary of Vanessa, "as if it were a thing one could throw about; this handling of circumstance."[67]

In adulthood, each sister depended upon the other to be strong because each had been trained that to show emotions or to demonstrate real feelings was not permitted and was even dangerous. Rather than arriving at authentic strength from a recognition of their fears, they both believed that strength was, in fact, an absence of negative feelings. As Angelica Garnett has stated: "They were very, very self-controlled . . . we were all very good-mannered with each other; we didn't step beyond certain limits, and our feelings, I think, seethed underneath and didn't come out."[68]

This view of Vanessa's control is important, because it debunks the popular notion that the Bloomsbury group was openly expressive. In the last letter that Vanessa wrote to Virginia before her suicide, the theme, again, is the necessity for control. Rather than each sister permitting the other to have her own feelings, however troubling they might be, each typically told one another that it was necessary for the other to be strong: "What shall we do when we're invaded [by the Germans] if you are a helpless invalid—what should I have done all those last 3 years if you hadn't been able to keep me alive and cheerful. You don't know how much I depend on you."[69]

Vanessa was, essentially, making Virginia responsible for her own well-being, as she so often had been made responsible for her sister's. In the Stephen family, rather than the children learning that they could develop the emotional strength to care for themselves, they learned that their well-being was out of their control, in the hands of another family member who was responsible for making them happy. Their well-being did not come from within. Vanessa was so fragile because she was completely dependent upon others to make her happy, and when they didn't, or couldn't, or wouldn't, she could not create the conditions that would assure her own emotional well-being.

The view of Vanessa's life that prevails is that she took whatever life threw at her and triumphed because she remained largely unaffected by what had happened to her, particularly by what had happened with George Duckworth. Unlike her sister Virginia, who was thought to be the "crazy" one, Vanessa was "a bowl of golden water which brims but never overflows."[70] But Vanessa was profoundly and deeply affected by her upbringing and the fact that she was sexually molested. Her way of responding was through withdrawal and depression.

Leonard Woolf believed that Vanessa and Virginia were more alike than they were different. He thought that her "tranquility was to some extent superficial" and that she, too, manifested "a nervous tension which had some resemblance to the mental instability of Virginia."[71]

After her marriage, Vanessa suffered "bouts of mental instability. These terrified her as she feared she was losing control of her mind." Her doctor's advice was to "throw herself into life," but she worried that she was "'on the verge of some obscure abyss.'"[72] Her depression lasted for over two years, during which she was virtually incapacitated. Throughout her life, she was chronically depressed: "Self-denigration and timidity became a habit," according to her daughter.[73] After the death of her son Julian, she experienced yet another severe breakdown, and she was never able to shake off the impact of his death, never again able to transfer her affections and attentions fully to the world of the living. In this she was very much like her mother. In her old age, there is a "sense of isolation and poignant sadness" in the photographs and portraits made of her at this time. There is no picture of her in which she truly looks happy.

What had perhaps triggered her first severe period of depression was her husband Clive Bell's and her sister's response to her childbearing. Clive once described himself as a "loiterer in life's pleasant places," and he wrote a poem describing his psyche: "I was made for airy thinking / Nimble sallies, champagne-drinking, / . . . Friendship, anything but love."[74]

As soon as their first child was born, Clive Bell essentially abandoned Vanessa. He was "fearful of mess and alarmed by fragility." He would not hold his son, Julian, he was infuriated by the baby's loud screams, and he started sleeping apart from Vanessa.[75] Vanessa had, unwittingly, married a man very much like her father, who was also incapable of a direct and committed responsibility for his children.

Soon after the birth, Virginia Stephen and Clive began an affair. It had the effect of isolating Vanessa from her two sources of support. She did not lash out at them, insisting that they put a stop to behavior that was hurting her. Instead, she was polite, and she responded by withdrawing, and by directing her attention to her child.

The conditions under which the children in the Stephen family were raised precipitated a lifelong history of sexual rivalry that manifested itself in Virginia and Clive's flirtation. One can only speculate about why this was so, but it seems related to Virginia and Vanessa repeatedly witnessing their father and other men in their life, such as Jack Hills, turning their attentions so quickly from one woman to another, so that the children had no chance to internalize a sense of loyalty to one another, or a sense that any one particular person was "off limits," for no one in the family was "off limits." They had never been taught that to control one's sexual desires was sometimes desirable, that it was, in fact, possible.[76] What they experienced was not sexual freedom at all, but rather the use of sexuality as a means of expressing or of gaining power. Children who have been reared in incestuous households tend, in their adulthood, to try to sexualize every relationship, because in early life the relationships within the family have been sexualized. Being able to accomplish a seduction substitutes for having authentic power and it seems that Virginia was using her ability to lure Clive away from Vanessa for that reason, at least in part.

In an incestuous family, it is not an uncommon pattern for family members to be intensely jealous of one another: in fact, a covert aim is to link its members indissolubly together so that escape from the emotional dynamics within the family is impossible. Sometimes this is accomplished through attention, and then its withdrawal. In adulthood, family members repeated the pattern of their childhood: Virginia flirted with Clive, her sister's husband; Vanessa took up with Duncan, her brother Adrian's lover; Angelica, Vanessa and Duncan's daughter, married Bunny Garnett, Duncan's former lover; Virginia said that she would seduce Angelica—on one occasion she wrote Vanessa "I shall rape Angelica one of these days"; Bunny teased that he would seduce Quentin.[77]

In 1897, when Virginia Woolf was fifteen, Vanessa appears in Woolf's daily-entry diary both as a co-conspirator within the household but also as an object of profound jealousy, for Vanessa was permitted to leave the household in order to take art lessons, and Virginia, who was believed to be ill, had to stay at home and was prevented, for the better part of the year, from doing lessons. Virginia resented the fact that Vanessa took her friends home from school, that they closeted themselves, shutting her out. The sound of their laughter and conversation coming from behind the closed door upset her and made her angry.[78]

The fact that each had been the object of George Duckworth's sexual attentions solidified the bond between them but also, paradoxically, contributed to their rivalry. Virginia and Vanessa were set up as rivals for George's largesse, a common condition in households in which more than one child is involved in incest, and in which presents are lavished upon the preferred sexual partner, not only to foster her acquiescence and to set her condition apart as one that is to be envied, but also to masquerade what is actually happening.

George showered presents upon Vanessa after her "coming out" and during the many years when she was his preferred companion to balls and parties in London—opals, amethysts, dresses, a blue enamel butterfly, an Arabian mare, a trip to Paris.[79] When Vanessa started presenting George with problems, he made it clear to Virginia that if *she* were tractable, he would shower *her* with presents—he immediately gave her a jeweled jew's harp to wear when she became his companion.[80]

Virginia and Vanessa shared information about what had happened to them: in 1904, Vanessa wrote Virginia a letter describing how "George embraced me and fondled me in front of the company."[81] And it was Vanessa who put a stop to George's sexually molesting Virginia after their father's death. She told Virginia's doctor, who chastized George about his conduct.[82] George was still involved with Vanessa after this, so it might have been that Vanessa allowed herself to be subjected to George's molesting, to spare her sister, who had had a breakdown. Vanessa's behavior—to offer herself up in order to save a younger sister—has been frequently reported in case histories of incestuous families.[83]

Because Virginia and Vanessa had been physically involved with one another, Virginia viewed anyone else as a rival for her sister's affection. She had a childhood habit of "fingering her sister's amethyst beads and enumerating with each the name of a friend or relative" who had aroused her jealousy.[84] Her affair with Clive was her way of making her sister pay for having deserted her. But when Vanessa saw Virginia with Leonard Woolf, she also wrote about how confused she felt.[85]

The sisters were still physically involved with one another as late as 1905, when Virginia was twenty-three; Vanessa wrote, during an absence, how Virginia would probably be "pining for a real petting" when she arrived; "perhaps *if* you have been good . . . you may get it." But because each had been subjected to the association of sexuality with violence, their own relationship seems far from idyllic, and overt hostility is sometimes included in their expressions of physical desire. Just as Vanessa promised Virginia affection, she also wrote, using a pet name, that "Poor little monkeys are easily trampled on and squashed." Vanessa summarized how she had experienced Virginia as a partner: "As long as the ape [Virginia] gets all he wants, does not smell too much and has his claws well cut, he's a pleasant enough bed fellow for a short time."[86]

Frances Spalding, Vanessa Bell's biographer, has written: "Without any doubt Vanessa's marriage [to Clive Bell] was sexually a great success."[87] George's "malefactions," it is claimed, did Vanessa no harm. But Vanessa herself saw the matter differently. After Virginia's marriage, Vanessa wrote, asking her sister if she was "a promising pupil." And she added that she thought she was "very bad at it." Vanessa teasingly suggested that perhaps "Leonard would like to give me a few lessons."[88] Leonard wrote to Vanessa that he was dissatisfied with Virginia's sexual performance on their honeymoon, describing "his night with the Ape," to which Vanessa responded, "I pity him sincerely," adding that *she* would never stand for such a poor performance, suggesting, "He ought to try a whip."[89]

Sharing these intimate sexual details of mutual heterosexual failure no doubt solidified their own relationship. But they also provided the opportunity for rivalry rather than mutual support. Although the image persists of Vanessa's sexuality as a kind of voluptuous abandon, nonetheless both she and Virginia lived the greater part of their lives in a condition of celibacy which, I believe, is best understood as an accommodation to the fact that each had received unwanted sexual attention for so long. Vanessa believed that her sister's primary sexual identification was lesbian; she wrote to her in 1910, wondering when she would "come out"[90] as a Sapphist. Vanessa, in choosing Duncan Grant, whom she knew to be a practicing homosexual—her brother Adrian had described for her the intimate details of their " 'inverted' " passion[91]—was committing herself to life without heterosexuality, perhaps unconsciously. Vanessa, unlike Virginia, never became involved in a serious lesbian affair in her adulthood.

Angelica Garnett, Vanessa's daughter, has written a memoir in which she directly addresses the issue of her own and her mother's depression. Garnett's memoir, *Deceived with Kindness*, traces the effect of her childhood on her character. She wrote that the attitude of her parents was a "threat"[92] to her well-being; she wrote that, as she thought about her childhood and adolescence, she "began to realise that the past may be either fruitful or a burden; that the present, if not lived to the full, may turn the past into a threatening serpent; and that relationships that were not fully explored at the time can become dark shapes, in the shadow of which we do not care to linger" (11).

The prevailing version of Bloomsbury which Garnett's memories challenged had depicted it as a place where that pillar of patriarchal domination, the nuclear family, had been supplanted by a life lived in harmony with one's husband, one's wife, one's husband's lover, one's wife's lover, one's lover and one's lover's lover, and a melange of adored and pampered children unencumbered by the heterosexism and petty sexual jealousy that afflicted the less liberated.

Garnett's memoir makes clear that although this myth may, indeed, hold true for the male inhabitants of Bloomsbury, it was far from true for her mother and for herself. This is effectively demonstrated by contrasting Garnett's description of the occasion of her birth with that of Leon Edel in *Bloomsbury: A House of Lions*. First Edel:

> Vanessa Bell found herself pregnant a few months before the [first world] war's end. It seemed to her a part of the fitness of things that a baby, a daughter, was born at 2:00 A.M. on Christmas Day, the first Christmas of the peace. In the Charleston of that Yuletide it was as if some Sussex Nativity Play were being enacted. . . . In the frosty dawn, when her travail was over Vanessa might have felt that hovering angels had attended, for she named her daughter Angelica. . . . The child of the love of two artists became the daughter of the Bell family and grew up with two fathers, Duncan, close at hand, and the visiting Clive, who continued to arrive bearing gifts. [93]

Garnett's version quotes her mother's account of the same time, written in a letter:

> It was very romantic then—the first Christmas of peace and a most lovely moonlit, frosty night. I remember waking up in the early morning . . . hearing the farm-men come up to work singing carols . . . — perhaps I seem very sentimental, do I? but the horrors afterwards, when she nearly died through the doctor's idiocy and every possible domestic disaster seemed to happen altogether, were so great that I rather forgot the happy part of it. I don't think I've ever had such an awful time. (40)

In fact, Vanessa "lay in bed in a house without running water, electricity or telephone" (40). Although the men may have prostrated themselves before the supine Virgin Mother Vanessa after she gave birth to the angel-child Angelica, they were nowhere to be found when Vanessa needed help with the children. Angelica's half brothers, Quentin and Julian, were sent to their aunt Virginia, not their father Clive, who was otherwise engaged. (Clive was always otherwise engaged.) When Virginia took to her bed, at Leonard's insistence, after a tooth extraction, the children were peremptorily sent back to their mother, who had all she could do to cope with an apparently dying infant. Virginia then callously expected her sister to entertain her with hilarious accounts of her trials and tribulations which denied the reality that Vanessa was living through. And Vanessa complied: Leonard wrote, "your letter was a great entertainment to her [Virginia], and she would like another with news of yourself and the servant problems."[94]

After Angelica's birth, Vanessa retreated into an increasingly severe depression, which no one took the time to understand, and which was interpreted by the men in her life as a natural reserve, not as an indication of profound stress and dissatisfaction.

Angelica records in her memoir that the occasion of her birth was not the first time that Vanessa was abandoned. Although her marriage to Clive Bell began by her being "transfigured; she was bowled over not only by sex itself but by the intimacy it conferred on their relationship," (25) Angelica records how the honeymoon lasted a very short time, until the birth of their first child, Julian, after which Clive turned his attentions to Virginia. Later, when her brother "Quentin's refusal to put on weight was causing Vanessa considerable anxiety, Clive offered her little support" (31). And it was just after the birth of Angelica that Duncan had told Vanessa that he felt incapable of having further sexual relations with her. During this year, Vanessa began to age dramatically. The accumulated suppressed rage, and living within the lie of Bloomsbury, had begun to take its toll.

Vanessa Bell was deserted again and again, and the men in her life reverted to being children whenever she gave birth to a child. Garnett tries to understand why her mother persisted in relationships that were so obviously self-defeating and masochistic. She traces the source to Vanessa's early history of emotional deprivation, excessive responsibility, and to her repeating the pattern of her own mother's marriage to an infantile, self-indulgent man. She understands that Vanessa, like her mother Julia, organized her household "in favour of men: in Julia's mind women were, if not slaves, doomed to serve their better halves" (20). But Vanessa manifested more loyalty to the men who abandoned her than she did to her daughter, who needed her but who had less of her than they did.

The Bloomsbury of Garnett's childhood, although it may have been a source of nurturing for its male denizens, was, for her, a "precarious paradise" (176). As a girl-child, she was adored, lavished with presents, pampered, petted, photographed, and painted. Angelica's concern with her appearance was encouraged; "her beauty was constantly admired"; it was implied that her beauty was enough to bring her complete happiness, an attitude not vastly different from that of her Victorian forebears to her mother Vanessa's beauty. Her love of dressing up was encouraged to the point that Vanessa stood in a boat on Charleston pond in order to photograph Angelica's "floating in the water in a white dress in imitation of Ophelia."[95]

Angelica was so infantilized that, at seventeen, she was totally ignorant of sexual matters. Joan Malleson, the doctor to whom Vanessa sent her for sexual instruction, on the eve of her entrance into drama school, "was so flabbergasted at how little this seventeen-year-old girl knew that she was able to say very little and Angelica emerged from her room almost as ignorant as when she went in."[96] In 1940, when Angelica was twenty-two and living with David Garnett (her father's former lover) whom she later married, Virginia Woolf still wrote her letters in "baby-talk": "Its a tearing gale, and the Witcherinas [Virginia and Angelica] are floating past in a roaring rhapsody of circumgyration."[97]

Garnett records that she felt as if she were treated as an object and a plaything and as an extension of Vanessa, and not as a person with needs and feelings and with a future that she should prepare for. Although she painted, took music lessons, went to boarding school, and attended acting classes, she was never encouraged to develop her talents into a life-sustaining or life-supporting profession. If a task became too challenging, rather than supporting her through it, her mother encouraged her to drop it. Garnett describes how her teachers were so enamored of Bloomsbury that many of the rules which applied to other girls were ignored for her—sometimes upon the intervention of her mother. Perhaps her mother wanted to create an idyll of childhood for Angelica so that she would always have one child who would not abandon her, as her lovers did; perhaps her mother wanted to create a happy place for Angelica to supplant the painful, difficult world, filled with responsibilities, which she herself had inhabited as a child. But for Garnett, the results were almost deadly. As she phrases it, "one's maturity should be a better time than one's childhood" (176).

Throughout her life, Garnett was denied important information, which was an outgrowth of being denied her personhood. Like so many girls, she was defined out of existence by being defined as an angel, a wraith, a sprite, a pixie. When her beloved brother Julian, who had functioned as a father-surrogate, left for Spain to join the ambulance corps during the Spanish Civil War, no one told her, and she never had a chance to say good-bye to him before he was killed. When her mother was dying at Charleston, no one summoned her, even though Garnett's own daughter was summoned to the bedside: Duncan Grant, immune to the effect of Vanessa's death upon Angelica, suggested that Angelica "should do a drawing of her" (171).

An important reason for her "tangled web of repressed emotion" (5) was that until she was seventeen, after the death of Julian, she was not told that Duncan Grant and not Clive Bell was her father. Her mother's timing of the disclosure was doubly damaging. Suffering the immense loss of her adored son, it seems as if Vanessa wanted to inflict a great loss upon her daughter so that they could be locked together in mutual bereavement. Thus, Angelica had to endure the death of Julian, the loss of Clive as father, and the loss of her mother to crippling grief, all within a very short space of time. These losses were experienced against the backdrop of a world gone mad with war: as Garnett puts it, "I was horrified by the glimpses of a world where individuals counted for nothing and were simply the pawns of powers who themselves were struggling to supersede each other" (124).

One can imagine how enraged Garnett must have been at the news; she describes her inability to understand this dishonesty about her parentage in light of Bloomsbury's ostensibly liberated attitudes about sexuality: "given the freedom that Bloomsbury supposed it had won for itself, it is, on the contrary, the conventionality of the deception that is surprising" (37). Rather than having two fathers, as her mother claimed, Angelica quite accurately perceived that she had no father at all. She describes the "murderous rivalry" (5) she felt for Paul Roche, Duncan Grant's companion, for Duncan openly gave him a fatherly kind of affection which she longed for. Duncan was, quite obviously, capable of fatherly behavior; but he was not capable of fathering a daughter. Through the years, Garnett hoped for some recognition, some sign, from Grant that he regarded her as his daughter. It was not forthcoming; the subject of his paternity was never even broached as a topic of conversation between them.

The crisis with which Angelica begins her memoir was the logical outgrowth of Bloomsbury's virulent if unconscious misogyny, masquerading beneath the veneer of a sexually liberated, enlightened humanism, and the logical outgrowth of a pattern of parenting that goes all the way back from Vanessa Bell and Duncan Grant, through Julia and Leslie Stephen, to Julia and Dr. Jackson.

Garnett's prologue describes how, at the age of fifty-six, fourteen years after her mother's death, she found herself living alone in London, profoundly disoriented. While shopping for vegetables, she looked into a mirror, and "saw a vagueness, almost a hole, where I myself should have been" (1–2). She begins with the boundless rage of the child against the mother's incapacity to love in a life-enhancing, life-sustaining way; she ends with "a dialogue with the dead" (12), a recognition of the reality of the circumstances of her mother's life, which prevented her, through no fault of her own, from loving her daughter well. Before she understood the causes of her own and her mother's depression, her mother had been a monolith; after, Vanessa "shrank into a mere individual in a chain of women who, willingly or not, had learnt certain traits, certain attitudes from one another through the years" (12).

It is not that Garnett's life was unremittingly horrible; far from it: "I was not completely solitary, lonely and withdrawn. On the contrary, I was often full of high spirits. . . . I was given pleasure and returned it" (176). She describes moments of her childhood which were filled with exquisite pleasure: being in a room with her mother and Duncan painting; being in front of the house at Charleston, watching "tiny creatures [which] threaded their way among the boulders: spiders, beetles, ants, busy, intent and unaware of me, a female Gulliver in their midst" (44).

Garnett shatters the icons of madonna, saint, earth-mother, lady bountiful, sex-goddess, enchantress, superwoman, that her mother was locked within. As Garnett sees it, Vanessa Bell was trapped inside a Bloomsbury version of the Victorian icon of the angel in the house that had guided her own mother's life; she was frozen into the ideal of woman as unwavering center of a household organized to serve the needs of men. Like so many single mothers, she had no one to nurture her; she was overtaxed, extremely depressed, isolated, and frozen with an incapacitating rage. Vanessa Bell emerges, for us, as a real woman, and, in consequence, Angelica Garnett replaces the hole with a self that she has discovered as a result of writing this memoir. One of the most important aspects of her book is her honest, difficult, liberating attempt to come to terms with the rage that she felt against her mother for her emotional inaccessibility.

Garnett describes her mother as a "limpet" (33), in terms of her need for affection; she describes how she was "suffocated with caresses" (43), with unwanted displays of affection: it was "at the age of five, that I at first became aware of my own identity, and with it of an exaggerated sweetness in Vanessa which troubled me." "In photographs of the time I am grave, round-eyed and healthy, held by a smiling Nellie [a family servant] or a Madonna-like Vanessa, whose long straight fingers are too apt to find their way into every crevice of my body" (42). Garnett's recognition of her own identity is conjoined with the unpleasant memory of this violation of her body. She describes how Virginia Woolf, too, when she visited, would force a display of affection; she "would demand her rights, a kiss in the nape of the neck or on the eyelid, or a whole flutter of kisses from the inner wrist to the elbow" (107).

The child learned that she had little control over what was done to her body. During her childhood, her doll Judy's "stockinette limbs [were] splashed with red ink," which she "carefully explained, resulted from numerous operations" (48). Her marriage to David Garnett, more his choice than hers, was an attempt on his part to recover his old lover Duncan Grant, to retaliate against Vanessa, and, once again, to make Duncan jealous. When Angelica was born, he had predicted that he would marry her. Just after her birth, Bunny said, "I think of marrying it—will it be scandalous?"[98] Her marriage, rather than removing her from the family circle, swept her into the very center of the vortex of familial emotions; as Angelica phrased it, it was "incestuous" (156).

Angelica's violation repeats Vanessa's and Virginia's violation by their half brothers Gerald and George Duckworth. The horrifying familial symmetry of Virginia's memory of Gerald's abuse and Angelica's memory of Vanessa suggests that Virginia and Vanessa, victimized by the Duckworths, themselves in turn victimized Angelica. Her object status within the family is evident in family photographs, published in *Vanessa Bell's Family Album*.[99] There is something deeply disturbing about the pictures Vanessa Bell took of her daughter. Angelica's frail, fragile, and timorous nudity contrasts sharply with the unselfconscious fully developed male bodies of her half brothers. In one photograph Angelica is seated on a stone seat, naked except for her shoes, folding herself inward, so that her private parts do not show; she is seated between her fully clothed father, Duncan Grant, who looks down at her, and a three-piece-suited, smiling, smoking Roger Fry, who looks confidently at the camera. These photos of Angelica, far from being innocent demonstrations of a mother's affections are, to this viewer, a stunning demonstration of Angelica's powerlessness and vulnerability.

Garnett's book ends with an epilogue which, in fact, at fifty-seven years of age, she saw as a new beginning for her, an entrance into maturity, although a much belated one. She describes how the writing of this memoir marked her "emergence from the dark into the light" (175). One understands why Leonard Woolf's gift to her, of a "splendid Victorian copy of *Pilgrim's Progress*, filled with pictures of Christian marching onwards" (108–9) was so important to her: she had been through her own private pilgrim's progress.

Rather than ending her memoir on a falsified note of triumph, of having achieved insight once and for all, Angelica offers something much more essential and inspiriting: a recognition that insight is a continuous process, and the insights that she has achieved are only imperfect. Garnett refuses to become for us the icon that her mother was for her, the icon of the wise woman. Rather than deny her feelings, she acknowledges that although it "is generally believed that to understand all is to forgive all, . . . to talk of forgiveness smacks too much of superiority" (175).

In writing her memoir, she has given us an important document which records how one woman has tried to understand the patterns of her past, and, through therapy and self-analysis, how she has tried to change them. Angelica Garnett acknowledges that understanding, by its very nature, is fleeting, temporary, and tenuous. Her memoir joins her to many other women in the process of trying to understand their own and their maternal history.

PART TWO

Virginia Woolf
and Childhood

Chapter Four

A DAUGHTER REMEMBERS

In April 1939, Virginia Woolf began to write her autobiography, "A Sketch of the Past."[1] It was the bravest writing task that she had ever set out to accomplish, because she knew that for her introspection was a dangerous and difficult enterprise, and that if she probed too deeply into the past, she could pay dearly for it by becoming agitated, depressed, and even suicidal; she was, moreover, "afraid of autobiography in public";[2] and she feared that if she wrote about her youth, she would stop writing altogether.[3]

Nonetheless, she began, prompted perhaps by writing Roger Fry's life, to rethink the relationship between childhood experiences and personality. She was spurred on, perhaps, by meeting Sigmund Freud, and by reading his work. A few months before she began writing her life, she went to see him, and he gave her a narcissus. She was challenged by the openness of her friend Ethel Smyth, the composer, to examine her feelings more carefully than she had ever examined them before.[4] So, late in her life, she began a project that she came to describe as autoanalysis.[5]

She had written other accounts of her life, other memoirs of the past. But in writing this one, she had a different aim. She would not only tell what had happened to her, she would try to recall her feelings. Most importantly, she would try to understand her depression, and the reasons for it: "I'm interested in depression," she wrote on 15 April 1939, "& make myself play a game of assembling the fractured pieces."[6]

She began to take very careful notes in her diary about the pattern of her feelings. She wrote when she was depressed, when the mood came over her, in order to understand it, so that she would not feel so hopeless when it happened. She began to examine the history of her depression, and to look for its causes in her own personal history; she began to assemble the fractured pieces of her emotional life.

In doing this, she was giving up the way that her family (and she) had explained her behavior ever since she was a little girl. The "poor goat," her half brother George Duckworth would say, "which I suppose means that I'm permanently mad."[7] For the first time, she was fully exploring the possibility that her life might have been otherwise, that the bouts of depression and despair, the suicide attempts, were not an inevitable part of her makeup, but that they were, instead, caused by her reaction to what she had lived through.

In writing "A Sketch of the Past," she examined a number of extremely significant issues—her father's character, his good points as well as his violence, rages, and despotism; her mother's character, her goodness, but also her unavailability to her children, her overwork, her early death and its effect on the family; the treatment of her sister Vanessa after their mother's death and her all-too-intimate relationship with George Duckworth; her memory of being abducted by J. K. Stephen, along with her mother, and his pursuit of Stella Duckworth, her half sister; of Stella's life, her courtship, and untimely death.

But even more significant were Woolf's attempts to recapture the memories of her feelings from infancy and early childhood, those elusive moments that explain so much, if we can remember them. In the process, she uncovered one memory that I believe she had repressed— the fact that her half brother Gerald Duckworth had abused her when she was very young. Although she had written and spoken of George Duckworth's "malefactions," as she phrased it, and although she spoke of both of the Duckworths in conjunction with her abuse, this is the first recorded instance in which she directly implicates Gerald. And this is the first time I believe that she remembered how far back the history of her abuse went.

I believe that this memory triggered feelings that frightened her. But she was able to explore the relationship between these feelings and the fact that she was sexually abused as a child, and to link them to her depression.

Uncovering that memory confronted her with some extremely disquieting realities: that the pattern of abuse lasted for many, many years, from roughly 1888, when she was six or seven, through 1904; that she was abused by more than one family member; that it was a central formative experience for her; and that a pattern of abuse existed within the Stephen family. She began to understand that sexual abuse was probably the central and most formative feature of her early life.

She had taken on this frightening task under the worst of all possible circumstances. Dealing with the feelings of rage and powerlessness which these memories inevitably elicit would have been troublesome enough if confronted with someone's help or with the knowledge that a cause-and-effect relationship exists between abuse and emotional trauma.

But Virginia Woolf was quite alone. She was a pioneer in exploring the effects of her abuse at a time well before incest survivors reported their experiences in works like *I Never Told Anyone*.[8] Vanessa had suggested that she begin writing her life,[9] and although she shared some of her insights with Ethel Smyth about how hard writing autobiography was for a woman, because the truth about a woman's sexual life had to be suppressed, writing "A Sketch of the Past" was a solitary journey, a journey back in time to her childhood, and a journey deep within to explore her psyche, that she shared with no one. This had not always been the case. Throughout her life, Virginia Woolf had told a number of her friends and acquaintances about what had happened to her, and had even read memoirs describing George's sexual abuse of her and Vanessa in public. But this was different.

As she worked on "Sketch of the Past," the threat that England would be invaded by Hitler became ever greater, so that this task was undertaken at a time when she felt powerless in the face of the Nazi threat. This feeling perhaps allowed her early memories to surface, but it was surely exacerbated by what she was remembering.

The threat of the invasion gave her work great urgency, for she and her husband Leonard Woolf had decided to kill themselves if the Nazis invaded. As she neared the end of her life, she became committed to putting down the significant facts of the life that she had led. Of all the possible ways she could have chosen to write this final document, one that might shape the way biographers would write her life, she wrote of her experiences as a daughter in an upper-middle-class Victorian family. Because she saw her family as representative, she was describing what could and probably did happen in other "typical" upper-middle-class Victorian households.

Her first memory was of sitting on her mother's lap, and of seeing "red and purple flowers on a black ground—my mother's dress,"[10] which opened up "the most important of all my memories" (64), so important it explained the base upon which she had built her life: "It is of lying half asleep, half awake, in bed in the nursery at St Ives. It is of hearing the waves breaking, one, two, one, two, and sending a splash of water over the beach." And she continues, "It is of hearing the blind draw its little acorn across the floor as the wind blew the blind out. It is of . . . feeling, it is almost impossible that I should be here; of feeling the purest ecstasy I can conceive" (64–65).

This memory might suggest an idyllic childhood. But Woolf says that she remembers it so well because it was so *unusual*; this feeling was so unusual for her, that she hung onto it as a reference point, to show herself that once it had been possible to feel ecstasy. What makes this early memory poignant is that Virginia is calling into question her very right to exist—"it is almost impossible that I should be here" is another way of saying "my existence is threatened; that I should cease to exist is a very real possibility." From as early as she could remember, from her first significant memory, she did not take her right to exist for granted; she considered it almost a miracle that she continued to survive. The fact of her own simple survival is what she remembers as having given her the purest ecstasy that she has known as a child. Her existence had been threatened from the very first days of her life.[11]

That moment of rapture was such an intense feeling for her, precisely because the more usual feeling for her, the "normal" way that she experienced life as a child was "the feeling . . . of lying in a grape and seeing through a film of semi-transparent yellow" (65). As she tried to turn up other early memories, she continued to turn up a variation on the metaphor of experiencing life as if she were living it inside of a grape. She wrote that if she were to describe what things looked like to her as a child, "I should make a picture that was globular; semi-transparent. . . . Everything would be large and dim" (66).

She also recalls sounds as muddled and unclear; the air at St. Ives seemed "to suspend sound, to let it sink down slowly, as if it were caught in a blue gummy veil" (66).

Woolf explains that these sensations from childhood are still with her. Although the day that she began writing "A Sketch of the Past" had been good, it was nevertheless "embedded in a kind of nondescript cotton wool. This is always so" (70). She realizes that a "great part of every day is not lived consciously" for her, that "non-being" alternates with "separate moments of being" (70). Her periods of connection with the world alternate with fuguelike states. She once associated this "disembodied trance-like intense rapture that used to seize me as a girl" with an erect penis, and she said that the memory of that state still comes back "with a violence that lays me low."[12] The rapture is not always pleasurable; it can be incapacitating.

She recognized the discontinuous nature of her perceptions as "separate," not connected, "moments of being." This is not an expression of Woolf's philosophy about the nature of existence; rather it is an attempt to describe her own emotional makeup, an attempt to analyze how depression interfered with her sense of connection to experience; it is a description of a continuing fragmentation, disconnection, and detachment. She wanted, however, to find the "pattern hid behind the cotton wool" (73), the reason the cotton wool existed, and she did.

The similarity between Woolf's feelings as an adult, of being encased in cotton wool, and her description of her childhood memory of living life inside a grape is significant, for it suggests that Virginia was depressed even as a child. She was able to determine that she had a history of feeling that way, and that her feelings went way back.

Children who have spent their lives in a state of chronic depression report precisely what Woolf describes in "A Sketch of the Past"—a sense of not being connected to the experiences of childhood, a feeling that life has been lived behind a screen, within an envelope which protects the child from trauma or from neglect.[13] This deadening, a state of suspended animation, is what Woolf describes as her nearly constant state as a child. When she describes memories of intense feeling—the recollection of her mother's dress, of waves breaking, of ecstasy—she reminds herself that these memories are so intense precisely because they are moments that pierced her usual sleepwalker state, moments in a childhood that was otherwise experienced through "a film of semi-transparent yellow" (65). No more accurate, articulate, or convincing portrait of the state of childhood depression has perhaps been drawn.

After describing this feeling in childhood, she interjects a long analysis of what she calls her "looking-glass shame" (68), shame about her body, in a passage in which she describes, for the first time, perhaps because she is remembering it for the first time, the fact that, at age six or seven she was sexually abused by Gerald Duckworth. Because the memories of feeling deadened are connected to her memory of sexual abuse, one can read a cause-and-effect relationship between the two, although Woolf herself did not explicitly make the connection.

She wonders why she feels shame about her body, so in contrast to a positive sense of self, a pride in one's body, that she has seen and admired in other people. She wonders where it came from, and she toys with the idea that it was inherited, that this Puritanical streak came from her Clapham ancestors.

But while exploring that she was "ashamed or afraid of my own body" (68), she writes of "the shame" at "being caught looking at myself in the glass" at St. Ives which leads to another memory of the looking glass in the hall, the memory of how, at six or seven, she was sexually assaulted by Gerald Duckworth on a ledge *in the same hall in which that mirror hung,* outside the dining room door. The ledge was usually used for stacking dishes. But Gerald lifted her onto it and "as I sat there he began to explore my body. I can remember the feel of his hand going under my clothes; going firmly and steadily lower and lower. I remember how I hoped that he would stop; how I stiffened and wriggled as his hand approached my private parts. But it did not stop. His hand explored my private parts too" (69).

No more significant a place could exist for sexual assault than this— being fingered by someone on a ledge where plates of food were placed on their way to and from the dining room. Can there be any mystery in why Virginia Woolf had trouble eating later in life? That ledge with its dishes was the very same place where "he began to explore my body," the very same place where she "stiffened and wriggled as his hand approached my private parts." The very sight of a plate of food must have made her sick, recalling her feelings of disgust and shame, although perhaps not the incident which prompted them.

I strongly suspect that what intensified the horror of the experience was the fact that Virginia was able to see herself in the mirror: she was watching herself being assaulted. No wonder that she developed a dread of looking at herself in that mirror, in any mirror. No wonder, in an early draft of her first novel, she writes the disturbing image of a disembodied hand, some "malicious arm with knobs at the elbow and coarsely haired."[14]

In "A Sketch of the Past" she writes, described a dream which she thought might be related: "I dreamt that I was looking in a glass when a horrible face—the face of an animal—suddenly showed over my shoulder. I cannot be sure if this was a dream, or if it happened" (69).

That face was surely a mental image of the bestial nature of what the person who had abused her looked like to her. He/it frightened her; he/it could pop into the picture at any time; there was no peace, no rest from the possibility of his appearing at any time. And there is this, too. The experience had forced her into proximity with bestiality; the figure of an animal appears over her shoulder; it seemed to emerge from behind her. Was the animal separate from her, or did it come out from her? This memory of the horrible face in the glass is, I believe, the origin of what she referred to, in a letter to Ethel Smyth, as her "suicide dream," a recurring dream that overwhelmed her with terror: it was a dream of being alone, on the inside of a drainpipe, and, at the end of that drainpipe is madness: "suddenly . . . I approach madness and that end of a drainpipe with a gibbering old man."[15]

Two other important moments of being which Woolf describes: the one, when "everything suddenly became unreal; I was suspended; I could not step across the puddle" (78) in a path. She cannot explain why she couldn't step across the puddle, but the act of opening her legs wide enough to stretch across a puddle of water was horrifying to her possibly because she would be able to see in the puddle a reflection of her legs, open wide, which she might have associated with her abuse. Another moment that also aroused a feeling of horror was seeing the face of an idiot boy, who appeared "mewing, slit-eyed, red-rimmed" (78). It must have reminded her of those distorted faces of male lust, of what Gerald's and George's faces must have looked like. It was the face that inhabited her nightmares, the face at the end of the drainpipe in her suicide dream.

When Woolf summarized the emotional contours of her life in "A Sketch of the Past," she said, simply, that as a child and in the present, her life "contained a large proportion of this cotton wool, this non-being. . . . Then, for no reason that I know about, there was a sudden violent shock; something happened so violently that I have remembered it all my life" (71). She gives, as instance, a terrible physical fight she had with her brother Thoby on the lawn. They were pommeling each other. "I felt: why hurt another person? I dropped my hand instantly, and stood there, and let him beat me" (71). She had already internalized the fact that she should not fight back, that she should, simply, take it.

Cotton wool. Non-being. Incest. Physical violence. The outgrowth of this pattern of experience was to make her have "a feeling of hopeless sadness. . . . I became aware of something terrible; and of my own powerlessness. I slunk off alone, feeling horribly depressed." Another experience with violence, of hearing of someone's suicide prompted a feeling that she was "dragged down, hopelessly, into some pit of absolute despair from which I could not escape. My body seemed paralysed" (71). Sexual violence. Hopeless sadness. Powerlessness. Horrible depression. The face in the mirror. Being dragged down into a pit of absolute despair, from which there was no escape. Paralysis. This was the shape of Virginia Woolf's early childhood as she saw it.

It is worth dwelling for a moment on the image of cotton wool which Woolf used to describe her depression, for this image points directly to the Duckworths. In "22 Hyde Park Gate," which she read in 1920 or 1921 to the Memoir Club, Virginia described how the Duckworths were cotton merchants, that "old Duckworth had sold cotton by the yard."[16] Being covered in cotton wool was being covered in stuff that was associated with the Duckworths. But the cotton wool also points to another family member, to Laura Stephen. Laura Stephen's health was so fragile that for the first months of her life she was wrapped in cotton wool.[17] In one sense, Woolf is using a metaphor which suggests that she herself needed a covering. But if Virginia knew the story about Laura and cotton wool, then her metaphor reveals an unconscious fear that she and Laura were similar, that she would be seen as bad, and would be treated like Laura.

The word pictures which Virginia Woolf has painted here of her images from childhood are identical to those found in the drawings of children who have been sexually or incestuously abused. Their drawings reflect the sense of powerlessness they feel, their attenuated sense of self, their perception of themselves as entrapped and ensnared. Indeed, the most common and repeated feature of these drawings is that swirling, swooping lines of color cover the children and nearly obliterate them, a pictorial equivalent of Virginia's "cotton wool" image.

The children also depict themselves as tiny beings, often within enclosed spaces, just like Virginia's grape image. They often put themselves at the edges of the picture, or entrapped by webs of lines. In one picture, a girl abused by her father drew a tiny figure of herself on a gigantic bed, from which there appears to be no escape; his face is tremendous, animal-like, and leers at her from around a corner. When the abusers are shown, they are angular, hostile, frightening figures, who are enormous on the page. They bellow; they stare; they are revolting; their nostrils flare. They are just like the animal-man of Virginia's memory.

In adulthood, like Virginia, survivors of incestuous abuse speak most frequently of the emotional isolation that they felt as children. "I feel so alone, so alone, so all alone," an entry in the diary of an incest victim reads. A woman described how even an operation she had for appendicitis did not stop her father from abusing her; she felt totally alone; absolutely powerless, that if he could not stop himself even when she was in terrible pain, recuperating from surgery, then nothing would ever stop him. [18]

If the time frame of Virginia's memory—that she was six or so when the abuse began—is accurate, then she was sexually assaulted during a period when she was recuperating from a bout with whooping cough, which was so severe that it was life-threatening. In April 1888, when Virginia was six, all of the young Stephens developed whooping cough at the same time. Julia did not leave the nursery for five or six weeks. Virginia was the sickest of them all; she would tremble and moan for an hour before the whooping spasm would come, and then when it came, she suffered severely. At her worst, she had about twenty-four of these spasms a day, and with each spasm there were twenty or so whooping attacks.[19]

She emerged from the sickroom a different child; she had become thin and frail; she seemed "more thoughtful and more speculative."[20] The sadism of Gerald Duckworth's act—accomplished in the summer after this attack, while she was still recuperating at St. Ives—cannot be overstressed. The full significance of that first memory, of her lying in a bed hearing the waves, being grateful that she continued to exist, can only be fully comprehended given her near death and the abuse which came so soon after. Virginia depicts herself as being caught in a tank with Gerald, who is described as an alligator. This image of rapacity becomes understandable when the frailness of her condition and her vulnerability are taken into account.

But embedded in Virginia's retelling of her memory is the idea that *she herself* was responsible for causing what happened to her: she says she remembered "resenting, disliking it"; but she also says that she believed "it is wrong to allow" parts of the body "to be touched."[21] What she no doubt carried around with her throughout her life was a deep-seated feeling of guilt, a feeling that somehow she should have been able to prevent what happened to her, that she was responsible, that she was bad, that there was something about her that invited this abuse. In the Stephen family, by the age of six or seven, she had already been taught that if something bad happens to you if you are a girl, it is your own fault; indeed, Victorian ideology held girls responsible for the morality of their brothers.[22]

Yet this is not at all uncommon for contemporary victims of sexual abuse. The victim often takes over feelings of guilt that the abuser *"should have had,* but being psychotic, *did not."*[23] One reason is that victims of sexual abuse are often told that they're bad. A survivor described how her abuser called her names during the abuse, telling her she was bad, filthy, and evil.[24] It is no wonder that victims of incest often feel that they are responsible: they have been told by trusted family members that they are responsible. An unfortunate and often tragic consequence is the victim's unconscious need for punishment which often manifests itself by self-mutilation, alcoholism, drug abuse, or suicide attempts.

There is abundant evidence that Woolf's suicide attempts were directly related to her incestuous experiences. She herself had come to understand this as early as 1921 or 1922, when, in a contribution she made to the Memoir Club, she described her family life at 22 Hyde Park Gate. She wrote how that house was crowded with "violent emotions," "with rages" at George and Gerald: "I feel suffocated by the recollection. The place seemed tangled and matted with emotion." She described that, after her mother's death, George abused her. She wrote that her subsequent breakdown was an "illness which was not unnaturally the result of all these emotions and complications,"[25] so that she clearly understood the causal connection between it and her sexual abuse. Her feeling suffocated is significant, I believe, in that she ultimately chose a death by drowning. Her breakdown might have been a desperate (if uncontrollable) attempt to stop the abuse, for it brought doctors into the household.[26]

In 1936, Virginia Woolf was suicidal. She wrote that she had "never been so near the precipice to my own feeling since 1913," another time when she had entered a period of prolonged breakdown.[27] The fact that she explained her suicidal feelings as being "near the precipice" is important. This illness is often explained as the result of her revising her novel, *The Years*. But I believe the cause lies elsewhere.

On 1 April 1936, near the time of the onset of her illness, she wrote in a letter that she had seen Gerald Duckworth for the first time in twenty years. (In fact, she had seen him in 1924, but she apparently repressed that meeting.)[28] She wrote that visiting him was "like visiting an alligator in a tank, an obese & obsolete alligator, lying . . . half in & half out of the water."[29] After she came out of the most dangerous phase of this breakdown, she wrote in her diary, "Always . . . a feeling of having to repress; control."[30]

The early memory of Gerald Duckworth molesting her had not yet fully surfaced, so far as I can tell. Yet there was something about seeing Gerald that troubled her deeply. Her image of him as the alligator in a tank containing her indicates that she clearly saw him as dangerous. And the words that she used to describe her suicidal feelings, that she was nearer to "the precipice" than she had been for many years, directly point to Gerald.

Precipices, ledges, strips of pavement over an abyss; the threat of these giving way, and of her slipping over them into disaster—Woolf frequently describes her suicidal feelings and her feelings of utter despair in this way. It is no wonder. These metaphors retold what had happened to her with Gerald. They pointed to the scene where she experienced the first, and a deeply repressed episode of abuse. On 1 March 1937, when she began to take notes on her "ups & downs,"[31] she wrote:

> I wish I could write out my sensations at this moment. . . . A physical feeling as if I were drumming slightly in the veins: very cold: impotent: & terrified. As if I were exposed on a high ledge in full light. Very lonely. . . . Very useless. No atmosphere round me. No words. Very apprehensive. As if something cold & horrible—a roar of laughter at my expense were about to happen. And I am powerless to ward it off: I have no protection. And this anxiety & nothingness surround me with a vacuum. It affects the thighs chiefly. And I want to burst into tears, but have nothing to cry for. Then a great restlessness seizes me. . . [;] the exposed moments are terrifying. I looked at my eyes in the glass once & saw them positively terrified.[32]

She had not yet written out the memory of Gerald molesting her on the ledge in "A Sketch of the Past," and it had not yet surfaced, so far as I can tell. But we can see the memory trying to tear its way through—"exposed on a high ledge in full light"; "No words. Very apprehensive"; "something cold & horrible"; "I am powerless to ward it off: I have no protection"; "it affects the thighs chiefly." And then, entwined within these fragments of memory, other statements which suggest that the incident might have been accompanied by a roar of laughter at her expense, that it included him humiliating her, or telling her that she was worthless, that it terrified her, and that she cried, but that he told her she had "nothing to cry for." She lived with these sensations, but they pointed to this episode, the fractured pieces that she could not yet assemble into a coherent, meaningful story to help her understand her depression, although she would ultimately remember it. She was able to connect her depression with these feelings, but she was not able to understand their origin.

Woolf saw Gerald as an alligator in a pool; her suicidal fantasies often included images of water; and she remembers feeling suffocated by the presence of her brothers. Once, in 1926, when she was suicidal, she wrote into her diary: "(The wave rises)." She wrote that she could almost feel "the wave spreading out over me."[33] It is significant, too, that any illness scared her. She had been molested in the aftermath of an illness, but she probably lived for her entire life without realizing this. Any illness must have reawakened her panic, her sense of vulnerability, and her feelings of disintegration. I believe that this is why Woolf's physical illnesses—her bouts of flu, for example—were so often accompanied by panic, depression, and a deeply felt anxiety and why her suicidal feelings were sometimes the sequelae to her physical illnesses.

Drowning metaphors are frequently used by incest victims. Woolf wrote of being left an orphan "in a sea of halfbrothers";[34] of being "drowned in kisses"; of feeling, around George, like "an unfortunate minnow shut up in the same tank with an unwieldy and turbulent whale."[35] In one of the most important extant works that we have from her adolescence, which I discuss in a subsequent chapter, she describes nearly drowning in a pond covered with duckweed and she signed her work, "One of the Drowned."

In 1931 she had lunch with George, and she had decided to "refer delicately to our past." After, she wrote a letter describing that she felt herself drowning as a result of this meeting, that she would write again when she could get "my head above these vast whirlpools."[36] This was when she was preoccupied with suicide, when she wanted to hear, and share with her friends, arguments for and against it,[37] so that talking to George about her past, her image of drowning in a whirlpool, and her thoughts about suicide were all connected.

The fact that Woolf used drowning images when she spoke of her sexual abusers is important for it signals how life-threatening that abuse was. Virginia Woolf clearly felt herself unprotected and exposed. Yet, although she expresses rage at her father for his violence, she never seems to have directly confronted the fact that her parents had left her unprotected enough to be molested. In all the retellings of her abuse, she does not express anger at her parents; rather, she exhibits a loyalty that is a common feature of victims of incest.[38] She comes near admitting the powerlessness of her mother in the face of rapacious male sexual violence in a cryptic story in "A Sketch of the Past" about how J. K. Stephen abducted her and her mother, taking them to his room, where "he painted me on a small bit of wood" (99). Given J. K. Stephen's rapist mentality, and the threat which he posed to Stella Duckworth, and the fact that he was violent within the Stephen household, this experience must have contributed to Woolf's sense that her mother was unable to protect her. We do not know whether J. K. shared the Victorian preference for painting his young girls naked,[39] but we do know that his feelings about women were murderously misogynist.

When Woolf describes the life that she was plunged into after her father's death and the scenes with her half brothers, she states that "over the turbulent whirlpool the ghosts of mother and Stella presided. How could we do battle with all of them" (156). Having her mother and Stella actively "presiding" over Virginia's drowning in a whirlpool of unwanted incestuous activity is the closest that Woolf comes to connecting the maternal figures in her life with her abuse. And she wrote this near the end of her life.

When she describes her father, she uses language that is similar to that describing her sexual abuse. She writes how, after Stella's death, she was "fully exposed without protection to the full blast of that strange character" (107). Rather than offering any protection, Leslie Stephen was himself a problem for her. When she wrote of her rage at him, she used a rape image: how "deep they drove themselves into me, the things it was impossible to say aloud" (108). She describes herself as "shut up in the same cage with a wild beast" (116), as "a nervous, gibbering, little monkey . . . leaping into dark corners"; she saw her father as a "pacing, dangerous morose lion," "sulky and angry and injured; and suddenly ferocious" (116). Although there is no indication that Leslie Stephen himself abused Virginia, the menacing figure, associated with incestuous feelings, in both *The Voyage Out* and *Night and Day* is a father,[40] and Woolf in "A Sketch of the Past" described how, in adolescence, she "lay awake" at night "horrified hearing, as I imagined, an obscene old man gasping and croaking and muttering senile indecencies" (123). She is told by a family member that what she heard was a cat, but the figure is very much like the one in her suicide dream, and it is the figure of an old man.

Yet she probably had wished for parental protection, although it is clear that she did not receive much. An indication of Julia's severity with children is indicated in the essay that she wrote about nursing, "Notes from Sickrooms," in 1883. She describes how hysteria should be treated. She writes that the caregiver "should never speak to the person in hysterics, nor look at her"; if she "feels that there is any danger of becoming upset herself, she should at once leave the room."[41] Because a frequent symptom of sexual abuse in children is acting out, it is clear that Julia would have dealt with this behavior by ignoring it until it went away.

Indeed, Julia was no doubt far too busy to see what was going on with Virginia. In 1888, she had nursed all her children through whooping cough and her own mother was ill. When the children were recuperating, she bundled them all up and packed them off to her mother's house. She had five invalids on her hands. In 1888, the year of Virginia's abuse, her father had one of his several breakdowns.[42] He too was unavailable. This first episode of her abuse coincided with serious family emergencies.

The Duckworth brothers' sexual molestation of Vanessa and Virginia is surely reprehensible. But they lived as outsiders within the Stephen family. Leslie admitted in his memoirs that he had never acted as a father to Julia's children, so that when she married they lost her to Leslie and to the Stephen children.[43] Gerald and George probably took out their rage against their mother and stepfather on the bodies of their stepsisters, who might have seemed to have been given preferred status in the Stephen home. Acting out their rage more directly against Leslie was dangerous: they had seen what had happened to Laura. There were other, younger, and weaker targets. From the evidence which remains, it seems as if their abuse coincided with the loss of their mother. They attacked their half sisters when their mother had been preoccupied with the care of the younger ones, or after her death, or after the death of their sister Stella. The Stephen sisters were attacked when they were most vulnerable—after an illness or a death in the family. Whatever the pathology of George and Gerald, it was part of a family pattern that involved emotional deprivation. They were not monsters. They were victims who victimized in reprehensible ways. Both George and Gerald had learned, from watching Leslie, that self-control was not a watchword for male behavior.

In family memoirs, Julia's life of overwork is often described using a drowning metaphor. Virginia herself used it in reference to her mother, and so did her father. When Virginia described her mother's overwork, her chronic fatigue and exhaustion, she wrote "she sank, like an exhausted swimmer, deeper and deeper in the water."[44] Leslie described Julia, after the death of her first husband, "like a person reviving from drowning and that the process must be painful." After he shared his perception with her, she replied that she sometimes felt "that she must let herself sink."[45] Her death was described as a metaphoric drowning; she was "sinking quietly into the arms of death."[46] But Woolf's drowning fantasies were also associated with her father. She often describes him as voyaging "alone in ice-bound seas" (37). When he spoke of the family's imminent financial doom, which he did regularly, he said they were "shooting Niagara" (144). In 1926, when she was contemplating suicide, she wrote in her diary that her new "vision of death" was "as the river shoots to Niagara . . . ; active, positive."[47]

Her depression had a family history. Her mother's photographs depict a seriously depressed woman;[48] as Woolf wrote, she had no idea "what my mother was like when she was as happy as anyone can be" (89). Julia's depression, I believe, was a response to her own lack of parenting. From when Julia was no more than a child, she was required to "parent" her mother. Even then, "she was used to nursing; to waiting on a sick bed" (86).

Leslie was seriously suicidal during Virginia's childhood. During 1891, he had "fits of the horrors"[49]; he was so ill that Julia persuaded him to stop work temporarily. On Virginia's ninth birthday, Leslie wrote that Virginia "is certainly very like me I feel."[50] Neither he nor anyone else in the family provided a model for treating the self with care.

Because suicide might very well be a learned response, and because feelings of helplessness or worthlessness can be learned from one's family, it seems clear that Virginia's suicidal tendencies in part were learned and in part were an outgrowth of her sexual abuse.[51] Her father was seriously suicidal; her mother spoke of not wanting to go on. Her cousin J. K. Stephen in all likelihood committed suicide; J. K.'s father, James Fitzjames Stephen, was suicidal after his son's death.[52] Her brother Thoby tried "to throw himself out of the window" in 1894; there was another episode within a month.[53]

When Virginia chose to kill herself by drowning, by walking into the River Ouse in 1941, she was responding to feelings of helplessness, and she was using a way of dying that had an important family and personal history. She would drown as her mother had drowned: it was the metaphor that connected them. She would actively pursue death by "shooting Niagara"; she would sink "like an exhausted swimmer": she would drown in a "sea of halfbrothers."

When Woolf described her general condition as a child, she wrote of herself as a plant which grew without cultivation or care. She was "the little creature . . . driven as a plant is driven up out of the earth, up until the stalk grows, the leaf grows, buds swell" (79). It is a curious and singularly illuminating metaphor, for it describes a sense of growth unguided, unmediated, and unchecked. It squares with the facts of Woolf's infancy and childhood.

On 25 January 1882, when Virginia Stephen was born, her household was as chaotic and crisis-ridden as one can imagine. She was unplanned-for,[54] and she was born when the problems with Laura Stephen had reached such a crisis that in letters from Leslie to Julia there is virtually no mention of Virginia. Both parents were obsessed with trying to correct and control Laura's behavior. Vanessa and Thoby were two and three at the time and the household also included three adolescents, Stella, Gerald, and George, who were fourteen, fifteen, and sixteen. Julia Jackson, Julia's mother, was sick, and Julia was responsible for her care, despite the fact that she had seven children to care for.

Given these circumstances, it is impossible to imagine Virginia getting consistent, loving attention. Indeed, Julia decided to stop nursing Virginia in April. She wrote, asking Leslie's permission. Leslie responded that he would not object if the effort became really trying,[55] which, apparently, it did. Virginia was weaned in her third month, exceptionally early for a nineteenth-century baby. Being fed by bottle was a risky matter because milk supplies were unreliable. It also meant that Virginia lost the contact with Julia that she would have had. She was passed to the care of nursemaids, who commonly propped a baby's bottle for feeding, so that she was held less frequently than if Julia had continued to nurse her, if she was held at all. Victorian infants, in upper-middle-class homes, were left very much to themselves. Self-regulation was a principle of child care in upper-middle-class families; if infants cried, they were ignored so that a firm moral character would be ingrained from the beginning.[56]

Because we now know how essential it is to hold infants, and to comfort and care for them when they are in distress, it is fair to say that many Victorian upper-middle-class children would be classified as emotionally deprived by contemporary standards. No one believed more completely in children developing self-control than Julia and Leslie Stephen. We have ample evidence in the stories Julia Stephen wrote for children, and in the beliefs expressed by Leslie in his letters about Laura. It is safe to assume that Virginia was not cuddled and played with very much during her infancy.

She often depicted herself as a helpless and uncared-for child: "I feel at the moment a helpless babe on the shore of life, turning over pebbles. . . . So the ocean tosses its pebbles, and I turn them over, naked, a child, and no one helps me."[57] It is precisely this view of the condition of childhood that she dramatically presented in "The Experiences of a Pater-Familias," written when she was ten, and it is the informing principle behind *The Waves*, her novel about childhood.

There is evidence that she was left very much alone in the nursery. It took her a "very long time to talk properly; she did not do so until she was three years old." She was described as "incalculable, eccentric and prone to accidents."[58] She was probably saved from Laura's fate because of Vanessa and Thoby, and, most importantly, Stella. Being accident-prone is usually an indication that a child is not being properly supervised. In fact, she exhibited the common behaviors of neglected children—a delay in the onset of language; being accident-prone; exhibiting seemingly eccentric behavior.[59]

I believe that in the first years of her life, Woolf's care was seriously compromised. The family's pressing needs diverted attention from Virginia but the Victorian child-care system was probably also responsible. It is no wonder that she considered the fact of her being alive a reason for celebration and that she described herself as a plant left to grow as it might. Adrian, too, born a year after her, suffered. He always seemed infantile.[60] As an adult, he entered psychotherapy because of the deprivation he believed he had endured as a child.

Julia had help in managing her household—there were seven maidservants[61]—and she relied on help from Stella and Vanessa. But it would be incorrect and unfair to underestimate the amount of stress and sheer physical labor that was required of Julia. She provided nursing care every time that Leslie became ill. He could not even go to sleep unless she eased him into it. He would not cut his own meat. She was the primary caregiver during her mother's numerous illnesses, and she often had the Stephen children ill at the same time.

Julia could not provide close, continuous care, and there is plenty of evidence in what Woolf herself says. She wrote that, given her mother's responsibilities, she "must have been a general presence rather than a particular person to a child of seven or eight. Can I remember ever being alone with her for more than a few minutes?" (83). After writing *To the Lighthouse*, Virginia Woolf wrote her sister, "But what do you think I did know about mother? It can't have been much."[62] Julia died when Virginia was thirteen; a child in even fairly frequent contact with her mother for thirteen years surely would have known something more than Woolf's "It can't have been much." Under ideal conditions, Virginia's contact with her mother would have been limited to the "children's hour," a time when parents and children engaged in formalized behavior, rather than an interaction in which problems were faced and crises were resolved. In Victorian England, children were supposed to be a comfort to their parents, not vice versa. To whom could Victorian children take their problems? And what happened to Victorian children because they could not air their problems? As the case of Laura Stephen illustrates, when Victorian children had problems, their parents tried to control their behavior. If that didn't work, they were punished, drugged, and labeled as deviant.

At times Woolf understood how little she knew about Julia, how hard it was for her to paint an accurate portrait of her mother's character. When she described how she arrived at her mother's character, she wrote: "I dream; I make up pictures of a summer's afternoon" (87). This accounts for the idealized portrait of Julia Stephen as "angel in the house" that Virginia drew of her so often. She had also read her father's attempt to explain his wife's character to the children in his *Mausoleum Book;* many features of her portrait of Julia are borrowed from her father's descriptions.[63]

But when Julia died Virginia had to suppress laughter and when she kissed her mother after her death, she says "it was like kissing cold iron" (92). Her lack of response has been interpreted as a "quarrel with grieving,"[64] but Virginia had spent so little time with her mother that her lack of grief is understandable. Julia had been, in fact very like "cold iron" to her daughter. She had been unavailable and severe far more frequently than joyful. She was never approachable. Her last words to Virginia were, "Hold yourself straight, my little Goat" (84).

When Woolf read Freud in April 1940, she explored the possibility that her mother was not the unqualified "angel in the house" that Leslie Stephen had painted in his memoirs; she wrote into her diary, "My mother, I was thinking had 2 characters."[65] In June 1940, when she began to think of her ambivalence toward her parents (108), she thought of her father. Yet I believe at some level there existed in Woolf a tremendous rage toward Julia, although it seems to have remained unconscious.

We can see Woolf looking at the possibility that a mother is not necessarily committed to the well-being of her children (particularly of her daughters) in the stunning sequence in "Professions for Women" where she describes murdering the image of the Angel in the House, which is, so clearly, an image of Julia Stephen. She writes that the Angel was "intensely sympathetic. She was immensely charming. She was utterly unselfish. . . . She sacrificed herself daily. . . . she was pure." The Angel, however, is not life-enhancing; she stunts her symbolic daughter's growth. In an exceedingly violent sequence, she describes the murder. It is the only place where she allowed her rage to surface, although through the controlled vehicle of art: "I turned upon her and caught her by the throat. I did my best to kill her. My excuse, if I were to be had up in a court of law, would be that I acted in self-defence. Had I not killed her she would have killed me."[66]

In January 1941, shortly before her death, when she was writing her autobiography, she wrote Ethel Smyth a letter of extraordinary importance. She continued their ongoing discourse about her reticence about certain features of her life; Virginia had thought that Ethel could be forthcoming about her sexuality, but, on hearing that she might not be, she speculated that it was impossible for any woman to write an honest autobiography. She wrote: "I'm interested that you cant write about masturbation. That I understand. What puzzles me is how this reticence co-habits with your ability to talk openly magnificently, freely." Virginia wrote how limiting this attitude was: "But as so much of life is sexual—or so they say—it rather limits autobiography if this is blacked out."

In an apparent association with the idea of self-censorship, Virginia then told Ethel that she believed that telling the truth about sexuality is "like breaking the hymen—if thats the membrane's name—a painful operation. . . . I still shiver with shame at the memory of my half brother, standing me on a ledge, aged about 6, and so exploring my private parts. Why should I have felt shame then?"[67]

The association between her abuse, "breaking the hymen," and self-censorship is significant. It is a detail that she does not include in her autobiography, which was written earlier. It is quite possible that she had not yet unlocked the fact that Gerald had broken her hymen. In this letter she seems to have been able to uncover the memory of the *pain* of Gerald's sexual abuse, which she had probably repressed. It was surely an extremely traumatic possibility. Gerald had injured her; he had broken her membrane, an event over which she should have had control; he had robbed her of her virginity. Her lifelong response to her prolonged abuse was a dislike, perhaps even a terror, of heterosexual sexuality. She wrote to Ethel, "I was always sexually cowardly. . . . My terror of real life has always kept me in a nunnery."[68] But she chose lesbian love, with Violet Dickinson and with Vita Sackville-West, as a positive, adaptive response to her abuse,[69] as other women have as well. But at the age of six or seven, Virginia Woolf was no longer a virgin. Ironically, she had been called Virginia, a name linked with the ideal of virginity.[70]

In a documentary on the impact of incest on children, a narrator advises the audience that in order to really understand what it feels like to be incestuously abused, you must think back to what the world was like for you as a child, how small you were, how needful of care, how trusting.[71] In a Victorian household, children were expected to be pure. It must have been extremely traumatic to have been violated in a Victorian household, one in which Leslie Stephen liked his men "manly," but his women "pure" (151). If children masturbated, or showed too much interest in their genitals, they were punished, sometimes severely, sometimes even brutally. What can it have been like for Virginia, who had seen what had happened to Laura, who was labeled "bad"? As an adult, Virginia read in her father's memoirs that Leslie was "thankful" that Julia never had to "bear the pain—the worst pain a parent could suffer and the only one which could be some excuse for regretting even love—the pain of seeing a child go wrong morally or proving by conduct that her faith had been an illusion."[72]

There is evidence that Woolf tried to tell her parents that something was wrong. She tried in the oblique way that children do, because telling is dangerous, and it must have been even more dangerous during Victorian times, a time when involvement in incest, no matter how blameless, would probably have been seen as an indication of a girl's inherent evil.

Self-destructive behavior, paintings, stories, play—these are the child's vehicles of communication. Virginia tells us of one important story, "a Talland House garden story," which was about "spirits of evil who lived on the rubbish heap; and disappeared through a hole in the escallonia hedge" (76–77). She told it to her mother and her godfather, James Russell Lowell. And we have an extraordinary document that I discuss in the next chapter, which Virginia wrote at ten, which describes, as graphically as one could, what it feels like to be abused and unprotected. But her parents seemed not to hear the messages signaling that Virginia was being molested.

Or had they heard? Woolf writes how, after the death of her mother, when George was molesting both her and Vanessa, "A finger was laid on our lips" (93).[73]

But a finger was not laid upon Virginia's lips for very long. She did not keep the story to herself; she told a number of people about it, often in graphic detail. Nor did Vanessa keep it a secret. She told Dr. Savage about what George had done to Virginia.[74] In 1908, when Virginia was twenty-six, she wrote the first account of their sexual abuse in "Reminiscences" for Clive Bell, Vanessa's husband. She wrote of their "sultry and opaque life which . . . swam about us, and choked us and blinded us." She wrote of George's "violent gusts of passion"; how he behaved "little better than a brute." She became interested in the issue of incest, and, in 1918 wanted to join the British Sex Society, whose chief object was "Incest between parent & child."[75]

In her extraordinary contribution to the Memoir Club, "22 Hyde Park Gate," written in 1920 or 1921, she describes George Duckworth graphically as "lover" to the Stephen sisters. She wanted to shatter the image of George Duckworth as a pillar of society and to correct his public image as the generous half brother who took such good care of the Stephen sisters. And she did it in public. She tells how, in a "confused whirlpool of sensation," she undressed in her room in her adolescence, how she stretched out on her bed to fall asleep, and how George invaded her room: "creaking stealthily, the door opened; treading gingerly, someone entered. 'Who?' I cried. 'Don't be frightened,' George whispered. 'And don't turn on the light, oh beloved. Beloved—' and he flung himself on my bed, and took me in his arms."[76] She wanted to inform the men who were present that her adolescence was very different from theirs. She wanted to explain that her "madness" after her mother's death was the direct outcome of her abuse. She "came out" as an incest survivor.

In 1922, she told Elena Richmond, the wife of Bruce Richmond, editor of *The Times Literary Supplement*, and family friend. She wrote Vanessa how "I told her the story of George. It is only fair to say that she began it." She told Vanessa that Elena Richmond said that she had never liked George: "She was shocked at first; but very soon reflected that much more goes on than one realises. . . . Now she'll tell Bruce [Richmond], who being a perfect gentleman will probably have to spit in Georges face in the Club." She told Vanessa that "a noble work for our old age" would be "to let the light in upon the Duckworths—and I daresay George will be driven to shoot himself one day when he's shooting rabbits."[77]

What surely infuriated her was George's patronizing attitude toward her so-called madness. He believed that Virginia's emotional problems were due to her madness. This absolved him of any blame. Indeed, his promulgating the view of her as insane was immensely (if unconsciously) self-serving: if Virginia ever told anyone about what he had done, they might automatically dismiss it—after all, he could say, "the poor goat" was mad and could not be trusted. Yet she understood that he also brought her pleasure and that much of her childhood was associated with him: "the laughter, the treats, the presents, taking us for bus rides to see famous churches, giving us tea at City Inns."[78] She confronted him directly on at least one occasion, and, when, before he died, she learned that he had wanted her to contact him, she hoped that perhaps he had had "some regret."[79]

She wrote other memoirs, which she read in public, in which George's abuse figures predominantly. She continued to tell the people who mattered to her about what she had lived through, but her aim was not purely personal, for she wanted to know how widespread this phenomenon was. In the last years of her life, she came to the conclusion that it was widespread indeed.[80] She surely derived some release by sharing her story with others, and she encouraged others to tell her about what had happened to them. Leonard Woolf's mother once shared with Virginia the extraordinary fact that she had "slept with a governess as a child who had given her a terrible disease, & been expelled from Holland on that account. I fancy she had never told anyone this . . . I was moved by her; could hardly speak."[81]

Throughout the years, Woolf described her abuse to numerous people in letters, conversations, and memoirs: to Vanessa Bell, Clive Bell, the members of the Memoir Club, Elena Richmond, Vita Sackville-West, Janet Case, Ethel Smyth, Violet Dickinson, Adrian Stephen. The fact of the Stephen sisters' abuse was not a secret; it was not hidden; it was common knowledge. It was discussed and debated, even in a public forum. Nowhere in any correspondence is it implied that Virginia lied, exaggerated, or misrepresented the truth. This fact is completely overlooked by those biographers who impugn her account or even question that she was sexually abused.

Some of her letters suggest the extent of the abuse that Virginia had endured. In 1911, she wrote Vanessa about a conversation that she had had with Janet Case, her Latin teacher. Virginia's revelations about George were precipitated by Case telling Virginia that she had discussed her sister Emphie's "symptoms with a male doctor." Something was wrong with Emphie, and Janet's description "led to the revelation of all Georges malefactions." This surely suggests that whatever George did resulted in either Virginia or Vanessa coming to some harm. Janet told Virginia that "she has always had an intense dislike of him" and used to say " 'whew—you nasty creature' when he came in and began fondling me over my Greek." But Virginia wanted Janet Case to know that what George did to her did not stop with these public embraces: "When I got to the bedroom scenes, she dropped her lace, and gasped like a benevolent gudgeon." Virginia's story was not a short one, for she told Vanessa that "By bedtime she said she was feeling quite sick, and did go to the W.C."[82] Although Virginia does not report the content of what she told Janet (for of course Vanessa already knew), her story was prompted by an illness, it included bedroom scenes, and it took a very long time to tell. It was upsetting enough to make Case sick enough to have to excuse herself to go to the W.C.

In 1923, Virginia wanted to discuss George with Violet Dickinson. In June she wrote: "one of these days I hope to see you again; and then we can discuss George, better than on paper."[83] In August, Virginia collapsed, and she suffered, for many months, from headaches and exhaustion.[84] There were other times that dredging up her past seemed to make her ill. It could sometimes cause her acute pain although sometimes telling her story was helpful.

In 1928, Virginia took a trip to France with Vita Sackville-West. Virginia discussed with Vita the fact that she had been molested by her half brother. There is an entry in Vita's diary from their trip to France which reads, "After dinner V. read me her memoir of 'Old Bloomsbury,' and talked alot about her brother."[85] On the trip, Virginia bought herself an antique mirror, an extremely significant act, given her "looking-glass complex," which suggests that telling Vita provided temporary comfort. At some point either Vita or Ethel Smyth suggested that Virginia confront George about their past, for Virginia wrote Vita in 1930: "Off to lunch with Sir George and shall refer delicately to our past."[86] Although Woolf did not record exactly what she said, she wrote Ethel that she had lunched with George and "have been given Pattles picture as reward."[87] At about the same time, she began a serious discussion with Ethel about suicide, and promised her that "one of these days" she would tell her about "the suicide dream,"[88] the one about being locked into the end of a drainpipe with the "gibbering old man."[89] She was seriously suicidal and told Leonard that if he weren't there, she would kill herself.[90] Over the years, she continued to share the story of her past with Ethel, referring to George Duckworth as "her seducing half-brother" or her "incestuous brother,"[91] revealing to her that, as a result, she rarely felt sexual passion.

And, finally, at the end of her life, she wrote of her abuse and the causes of her lifelong depression in "A Sketch of the Past." In doing so, she was anticipating, by thirty years or so, inquiry into the relationship between childhood abuse and the formation of personality, between family structure and childhood abuse. What she seems not to have understood, for she was in uncharted territory, was that her depression was also an outgrowth of Victorian child-rearing practices which minimized the contact between child and caregiver, which emphasized control of one's bodily functions and of one's feelings, at all costs, although she clearly described the results of such an upbringing.[92]

The very way that the Victorian family was structured contributed to the possibility that she, and others like her, would be victims of sexual abuse. If suicide attempts by children are an index of abuse, as they are believed to be, it is significant that, in the 1890s, "child suicide appeared . . . to be rising sharply."[93] Florence Rush has remarked that the Victorian cult of the little girl and the deification of the immature female, in addition to male privilege, quite possibly contributed to incestuous abuse. She has observed that child molesters from respectable families were well-protected, and points to the case of Ruskin, who, at thirty-nine, fell madly in love with his nine-year-old pupil, Rose la Touche: "He never stopped pursuing (and tormenting) her until this sickly, deeply disturbed child died in her mid-twenties."[94]

Virginia Woolf wrote an analysis of how life in the upper-middle-class Victorian family contributed to the exploitation of her and her sisters in "A Sketch of the Past." She described its household arrangements, its organization, the role of the father, and of the mother. Her analysis is visionary. She describes her family as a lonely "caravan, absolutely private silent, unknown."[95] When she described childhood, she saw it as always "surrounded by a vast space." She describes how the family members were "wedged together," the "shrouded and curtained rooms" at 22 Hyde Park Gate, how it was "impossible to break through" the "dark cloud" over the family. She described the house as a cage, herself as an animal trapped within it, a prey to any "wild beast" who chose to harm her.[96] This description of the family as insulated, surrounded by a space that is impossible to penetrate, is precisely the description of the structure of incestuous households provided by contemporary researchers like Judith Herman, in *Father-Daughter Incest*.

Woolf also understood that the very *structure* of the patriarchal family invites child abuse. She wrote that her father occupied an "extraordinarily privileged position," that he had a "godlike, yet childlike" position; she described how her mother conveyed to her the idea that her father "was licensed," that he was "not bound by the laws of ordinary people."[97] She understood that his rages and his lack of control were the product of male privilege. This is precisely the portrait of fathers within incestuous households; they are childish, lacking in control; a different set of rules obtains for them (and often for their sons); most importantly, they are permitted to do anything that they choose, and, because the family is insulated from public scrutiny, the abuse can go on unimpeded for they are not held accountable for what they do and other family members have no power to stop them or to escape from the abuse. Toward the end of her life, she began to see that not only was her father a tyrant, he, too, was implicated in some way: she told her physician Octavia Wilberforce that "he had made too great emotional demands upon her, and because of him she could never remember any enjoyment of her body."[98] She described her mother's chronic overwork; her preference for boys; her use of Stella's labor; her acquiescence to Leslie's lack of control; the fact that she was a generalized presence to her children, traits that were the result of her father's privileged position, and of her mother's support of it. Her portrait is very like that of the mothers of abused children painted by researchers like Herman.

Woolf had set herself the task of figuring out why she had been plagued by a lifelong battle with depression by looking into the past, by analyzing her family, in 1939, when the world seemed to have gone mad with war. It was extraordinarily brave for her to try to reject the notion that human beings were the sum of internal drives, of forces beyond their control, during a time when it surely appeared that England would one day be invaded by the Nazis. She noted in her diary that a Nazi raider had been shot down near their home in Rodmell, and that "the country people 'stomped' the heads of the 4 dead Germans into the earth"; her home in London had been hit in an air raid—"all our windows broken, ceilings down, & most of our china smashed"—fortunately, for her autobiography's sake, and for our own, she was able to salvage twenty-four volumes of her diary, "a great mass for my memoirs."[99]

She was writing her life under the threat of imminent death. She believed that she did not have long to live. She knew that if the invasion of England by the Nazis ever materialized, or if England capitulated to the Nazis, as was rumored, she and Leonard, a Jew, would be seized and carted off to the death camps; indeed, their names were on a list of people to be taken immediately following the invasion.[100] She knew that no woman was safe from rape by an invading army, and, given what she had lived through, her fears of being violated again must have been overwhelming.

She and Leonard made plans to commit suicide. But she was ambivalent. Leonard had gasoline in the garage so that they could asphyxiate themselves when the time came; she carried a lethal dose of morphia around in her pocket.[101] The closer the date of the predicted invasion, the more agitated, suicidal, and depressed Woolf became. She herself chose as the occasion of her own suicide the very week that had been predicted for the Nazi invasion of England.[102]

During these troubled times, she was writing her autobiography. She was also reading Freud and how he had come to describe human behavior, not as the logical outgrowth of childhood experiences, as he had believed early in his career, but as the result of drives, complexes, fantasies, wish-fulfillment and other subterranean and seemingly uncontrollable forces.

Toward the end of her life, as she was writing "A Sketch of the Past," Woolf looked to Freud to establish an essential vantage point that might help her make sense of what she had experienced. She "tried to center by reading Freud."[103] At some point, she must have realized that she and Freud would describe the etiology of depression in completely different ways. She was ascribing her depression and her "madness" to her abuse. He was describing reports of incest as fantasies which were wish-fulfillment. She wondered whose view was correct and there is evidence that, after a lifetime of struggle to establish the view that I have described here, she wavered, reconsidered, and accepted Freud. This meant that she would have to see herself as mad. I believe that it contributed to her suicide and there is evidence to support my view. On 9 December 1939 she wrote: "Freud is upsetting: reducing one to whirlpool; & I daresay truly. If we're all instinct, the unconscious, whats all this about civilisation, the whole man, freedom."

Just as the Duckworth abuse made her feel that she was drowning, reading Freud upset her, reducing her to "whirlpool." The language that she uses to describe both experiences is the same. What am I to make of my past if we're all instinct, if the unconscious predominates, she seems to be saying.

I have come to believe that the cause-and-effect view that she was striving to maintain was seriously eroded by her reading Freud, that reading Freud, in fact, urged her to abandon her own insights into the reasons for her depression and madness.

From her vantage point, she was trying to establish that her madness had been caused by her childhood experiences with incest; but if she followed Freud, she would have to factor in several possibilities: that her memories were distorted, perhaps even completely untrue; that her memory was a projection of what she desired rather than what she had experienced; that the incident was perhaps even a fantasy that she had invented. Throughout her life, she continually described how repulsive and physically offensive the Duckworths were to her: she described them as pigs and as alligators; George was "fat as a louse, . . . beady eyed like a rat," he was an "overfed pug dog," he was "swollen," with transparent flesh "that one longs to slice." To contemplate the possibility that the erotic impulses for these "pigs," who she believed came from "a very incestuous race,"[104] originated in her own psyche would surely have been cause for despair.

I believe that reading Freud precipitated a crisis, plunged her into the "whirlpool," by irrevocably damaging her belief in the logic of what she had established. I believe that it eroded her sense of self. If she was right and Freud was wrong, she was not a madwoman, but a woman whose response to her childhood was appropriate, though painful. But if Freud was right and she was wrong, she was, indeed, a madwoman, a prey to uncontrollable urges and forces, whose memories might have been wishes, for contrary to Woolf's belief in the fundamental accuracy of memory, for Freud, much was distortion. Before she took her life, she tried to verify that her memories were accurate. But in the closing days of her life, we know that Virginia Woolf had come round, again, to believing that she was in fact, a madwoman, that she had been mad, and that she would go mad again. She responded to reading Freud in the same way that she had responded to seeing her brothers earlier in her life.

It is illuminating to isolate the statements that Virginia Woolf made about Freud in the last few years of her life, and to juxtapose them with her work on her autobiography.

On 29 January 1939, she went to see Freud, who gave her a narcissus. On 15 April, she recorded her interest in her own depression. On 16 April she started "A Sketch of the Past," writing the part dealing with her feelings in childhood, the "grape" section, the "cotton wool" section, the incident of her being abused by Gerald on the ledge, and her "looking-glass shame."

On 2 May, she continued her autobiography, beginning the section describing her feelings about her mother, Julia's severity, the fact that she was only a generalized presence to her children, and a description of her death. On 20 June 1939, she wrote about Stella; on 19 July 1939, about J. K. Stephen's violent pursuit of Stella. Then she put the memoir aside for nearly a full year. So far she had written the history of the violence within her family, explored her childhood depression and her sexual abuse, and the violence directed toward Stella.

Then she began reading Freud. For the first time, she began thinking about "Censors. How visionary figures admonish us" (7 August). On 6 September, she wrote that war had been declared, and that the world felt empty and meaningless. On 1 December she was reading Freud, "to enlarge the circumference," "to give my brain a wider scope: to make it objective; to get outside." A day later, for the first time in writing her life, she felt the need to censor herself. She wrote, "my memoir will have to be compacted." On 8 December, she was "gulping" Freud and she had discovered, through him, the idea of ambivalence.

And then on 9 December, that most significant of entries about how reading Freud on instinct and the unconscious was profoundly upsetting, reducing "one to whirlpool," for it denied the principle of freedom. As if she were reaching for an antidote to Freud, she began "Mill on Liberty." By 17 December, she was again reading Freud, now "on Groups."

She now began talking to people about her past, as if to reaffirm that her memories were accurate. On 19 January 1940, she talked with Sybil Colefax about "our family life"; Sybil said "She never liked George." On 25 April, she was thinking about her mother's two characters for her memoir; and that she could see her father from two angles—as a child, condemning, as a woman, "tolerating." She wondered if both views were true.

In May 1940, she and Leonard were seriously discussing suicide; but on 15 May, she protested that she didn't want to die, and wrote "I've a wish for 10 years more, & to write my book." She said that thinking was her fighting. By 29 May she realized that she couldn't "plan, any more, a long book." The threat of capitulation or of invasion was imminent. She and Leonard would be "in concentration camps, or taking sleeping draughts" (2 June).

With the likelihood that she would never have an audience for her work, and poised on the brink of disaster, she continued nonetheless. On 8 June, she began again. The Germans were flying over England. She wrote of Stella's husband, Jack, and Jack's needing to relieve his sexual urges after Stella's death.

On 19 June 1940, against the background of reports that the French had stopped fighting, that "the dictators dictate their terms to France," she wrote of her father's behavior after Stella's death, how she and her sister were now without protection and fully exposed to his brutality. The day after, she began to carry morphia in her pocket, to be ready in case the Germans invaded.

On 27 June, she turned once again to Freud. Because the war had "taken away the outer wall of security," she was looking for support: "I tried to center by reading Freud." On 18 August, "five German raiders passed so close over Monks House that they brushed the tree at the gate."[105] On the same day, she began writing about her brother Thoby.

5 September 1940. She has a real failure of nerve, and suggests that she has misapprehended her past; she writes that all "writers are unhappy. The picture of the world in books is thus too dark."[106] On 18 September, her house in Mecklenburgh Square is hit by a bomb; all of the windows are smashed. The bombing of London was "preparatory to invasion."[107]

22 September 1940. She turns again to her memoir, and she describes St. Ives again. But now the tone of her memoir changes dramatically. She begins to write what can only be called an idyll of family life at St. Ives. Why now?

She discovered that she had been an unplanned-for child, perhaps by reading her father's letters to her mother. She wrote it into her memoir: "they wished to limit their family," she wrote, "and did what they could to prevent me."[108]

I believe that the shock waves caused by learning this fact, at this critical and anxious time, contributed to her disintegration and to her suicide. In reading Freud, she had been forced to question the accuracy of her vision of the past; in reading her father, she learned something new that, in the best of times, would be difficult to integrate. She believed that England would soon be invaded; she had relived or uncovered one traumatic insight after another in writing these memoirs, from her first defilement at St. Ives, through those horrible memories that she had dredged up about George's behavior after her mother's death, and her father's behavior after Stella's. And now this. She had been unwanted.

By 1 November, she again found fault. She believed that her autobiography was "too circuitous and unrelated: too many splutters: as it stands." But even more fundamentally, she began to question the view of her life as a series of violent shocks punctuated by nonbeing, for she wrote, in criticism of what she had written, "A real life has no crisis: hence nothing to tighten. It must lack centre. It must amble on. All the same." She had begun to deny the fundamental accuracy of her memory of the past.

On 15 November, she began to write about her father again and she began the sequence describing George's abuse. But by 22 December, she began a process that can only be called denial, a reversal into the opposite view of her family that she had established, so painstakingly, since 1939. After having written of her father's violence and her half brother's abuse, she read her father's letters and memoirs. She now wrote the image of her childhood as idyll in complete contrast to what had come before. She wrote into her diary:

> How beautiful they were those old people—I mean father & mother— how simple, how clear, how untroubled. I have been dipping into old letters & fathers memoirs. He loved her—oh & was so candid & reasonable & transparent. . . . How serene & gay even their life reads to me: no mud; no whirlpools. And so human—with the children & the little hum & song of the nursery.

This is extraordinary because it is a distortion of her father's letters and memoirs and also because it denies the insights that she had fought to arrive at. It misrepresents what her father's letters and memoirs contain. Both are filled with descriptions of family troubles, of his illnesses, and Laura's behavior, of their sons' school problems, and Julia's mother's needs, of the children's diseases, of Julia's fatigue. What could Woolf have been doing? And why was she doing it at this time?

I believe that one possible reason was her reading of Freud. Faced with Freud's view, she might have felt a need to deny the reality of her experience rather than reinterpret it in light of Freud. It is clear that she was not strong enough to continue in her pursuit of the past and that she needed to deny what she had uncovered. She let what she had written in her autobiography stand essentially as she had penned it. She did not destroy it. But she began to think about it differently. She now needed to erect a vision of her family in these stress-filled, traumatic, closing months of her life. In her diary entry about the idyll of childhood, she was writing about the parents she wished she had had, the child she wished she had been, the childhood she would have wanted—"the little hum & song of the nursery." She wanted "no mud; no whirlpools." She wanted to stop thinking about her abuse and the violence that she had lived with, or she wanted to deny it. As she was reading her father's letters, however, she must have encountered the reality of her parents' lives, because she wrote "if I read as a contemporary I shall lose my childs vision & so must stop. Nothing turbulent; nothing involved; no introspection" (22 December).

She wanted to see her parents as if she were a child again. She clearly wanted to regress. But that was dangerous. For rather than escaping the turbulence and avoiding the whirlpool of her emotions, she would be plunged right back into her state of being as a child. The stress had become too great. She chose to return to her view of the world from inside the grape, to her vision of her childhood from behind the cotton wool. Although it was her timeworn means of self-protection, it was a regression that this time would be deadly.

Yet she seems to have uncovered one final memory. On 12 January 1941, she wrote Ethel Smyth the letter about how Gerald had molested her which also described the pain that accompanies the breaking of the hymen. Soon after, she wrote that she had become ashamed of her own words (15 January). By late January she was fighting "depression." She was trying to fend off overwhelming feelings of "rejection" which had no doubt surfaced from having learned that she had been unwanted. She felt as if she were being engulfed by a "trough of despair." She tried two more days of memoir writing, but it didn't work. She had come to "dislike introspection."

8 March 1941. She had dispensed with writing autobiography. Her life was almost over. She would live twenty more days. "I intend," she wrote, "no introspection."

What she wanted now was peace. Many years before, she described her feelings of powerlessness, of everyone "jerking wires and making me jump like a jack-in-the-box, when I wanted to be ten miles deep under the sea."[109] Waiting for the invasion was a terrible strain. During the second week of March, she had seen incendiaries lighting up the downs. She now wanted the invasion to come: "Its this standing about in a dentist's waiting room that I hate."[110]

She knew that Hitler's invasion was expected during the third week of March.[111] The site of the invasion would be Newhaven, just three miles from her home in Rodmell.[112] And it was during the third week of March that Virginia Woolf became certain that she was going mad again. In her suicide letter to Vanessa, written during the third week of March, she wrote that she knew she was going mad again; it was just like the first time; she was hearing voices: "I know I shan't get over it now."[113] She had no fight left. She had taken too many blows.

Virginia Woolf killed herself during the fourth week of March. During that week, she spent some time arranging her father's old books,[114] those relics from moments in the past that she remembered most fondly, how she would go up into his study at Hyde Park Gate, and he would interrupt his work to hand her down a book. But many of his books hadn't fared very well during the bombing of her London home. They had arrived in Rodmell waterlogged and dirty and she really didn't know what to do with them.

She ended her suicide note to Leonard with the words, "Would you destroy all my papers."[115] But fortunately Leonard Woolf did not comply. Then, she took up her stick, and walked through the water-meadows to the River Ouse. "I will go down with my colors flying," she wrote.[116] She put a large stone into the pocket of her coat, and walked into the water. This was the place that she now "wanted to be, . . . deep under the sea."[117]

Chapter Five

IN THE HOUSE OF THE PATERFAMILIAS

In the summer of 1892, Virginia Stephen wrote a juvenile novel, *A Cockney's Farming Experiences*, and a sequel, *The Experiences of a Pater-familias*[1] for the family newspaper, the *Hyde Park Gate News*, that the Stephen children had begun in February 1891, when Virginia was nine.[2] The first installment of Virginia's juvenile novel appears in the issue dated 22 August 1892. It is an extremely important document that has been virtually ignored or misread,[3] for it explores in graphic detail the experience of child abuse and child neglect, written three years before the death of Virginia Woolf's mother, at a time when biographers of Woolf generally maintain that she was well protected and cared for, living in what has been called "almost a period of pre-lapsarian bliss."[4]

In a photograph of Virginia Woolf taken in that same summer of 1892, at Talland House, St. Ives, when she was ten years old, she sits behind her parents, her chin in her hand. They are absorbed in their reading—Julia in her book, Leslie in some papers. They might be Mr. and Mrs. Ramsay in *To the Lighthouse*, sitting together, reading. In the photograph Virginia looks at them intently but they are unaware of it; she studies them, as if to capture the moment as completely as the photograph has captured her in the act of regarding them.[5]

This tenth year was a memorable one for Virginia Stephen; it marked a turning point in her consciousness, in the way that she regarded herself. In 1921, when she was visiting St. Ives, she wrote a letter to Saxon Sydney-Turner, "of how I was a nice little girl here, and ran along the top of the stone walls, and told Mr Gibbs after tea that I was full to the chin." She mentions, in particular, the summer of 1892. She asked him "Do you like yourself as a child?": "I like myself," she wrote, "before the age of 10, that is—before consciousness sets in. Still I expect I muddle it all up with Cornwall."[6] Her letter also describes the countryside that she so loved, the "sea spread out," "blue, with purple stains on it, and here a sailing ship, there a red steamer," and her memories of summers.

Pater-familias is the longest and most complete work that we have from Virginia's pen during this year which she regarded as a watershed in her development. *Pater-familias* helps us understand why Woolf links the beginning of consciousness with the beginning of her disliking herself.

1892 and the years preceding had been filled with tragedy for the Stephen family, which informed this juvenile work.[7] Like the Brontë children's juvenile tales of Angria and Gondal, *Pater-familias* explores, in vivid detail, a family in chaos and disorder, the experience of child abuse, neglect, and abandonment, an environment in which grownups repeatedly forget that there is a child who needs care, yet who have the power of life, death—"even resurrection"—over their "diminutive" subject.[8]

The Stephen family had lived through a number of significant—and, for a child, extremely traumatic—events by the year 1892. There was Virginia's sexual abuse (about which no one but Virginia and Gerald might have known); and Laura's experiences. In 1888 and 1889, Leslie Stephen had suffered two serious work-related "breakdowns."[9] He may have been suicidal—he praised the Duke of Bedford for having the courage to shoot himself,[10] and a few days later endangered his life by crossing an avalanche which had come down ten minutes before[11] while he was in Switzerland for his health.

During these years, he was out of touch—as he put it, "paying very little attention to what is passing around me." He had taken on the gargantuan task of editing the *Dictionary of National Biography*, which became overwhelming, and it is no wonder; it contained 29,120 biographies in 63 volumes, 378 of which Leslie wrote himself.[12] He became anxious and stressed; his daughter Virginia believed that her growth and well-being had been impeded by the weight of those volumes which had "crushed and cramped"[13] her in the womb, before she had even been born. Once Leslie's well-being became precarious, Julia, who had once found him "in a state of unconsciousness,"[14] had even less time to concern herself with her children.

Leslie began to have serious sleep disorders; his dreams were punctuated by images of the dictionary devouring him "like a diabolical piece of machinery, always gaping for more copy, and I fancy at times that I shall be dragged into it, and crushed out in slips."[15] During the worst times, over a period of four years, he was given various narcotics, and was only able to fall asleep if Julia eased him out of his restlessness: "She used to put me off to sleep like a baby," he wrote in his memoir.[16] Leslie collapsed again, in 1890 and 1891,[17] the same two years during which Virginia's cousin J. K. Stephen was pursuing Stella Duckworth. Leslie was taking holidays for his nerves as late as 1893.[18]

On 2 February 1892 J. K. Stephen died, having starved himself to death in the asylum to which he had been confined after his violence became unmanageable. Virginia's uncle, J. K.'s father, James Fitzjames Stephen, began a period of rapid decline. He died in 1894; his death profoundly affected Leslie, especially because it was believed to be related to his emotional state, and Leslie had so recently had a serious breakdown.

As if this were not enough for Julia and the family to bear, in 1891 Julia's mother had "a serious access of weakness"[19] and, in the spring, came to stay with the Stephen family to be cared for by Julia. (She had, in effect, two invalids on her hands, in addition to her intermittent care of J. K. Stephen.) Julia's mother died on 2 April 1892 at the Stephen family home, 22 Hyde Park Gate. Julia had nursed her through her terminal illness. And to add to the trauma, 1892 was the year in which Laura Stephen, Virginia's half sister had been settled out of the house; and they would soon stop taking her to St. Ives for the summer.[20]

During these years, although Julia Stephen clearly had her hands full with caring for all of the illness that descended upon the family, she could usually be counted upon to be a good audience for the *Hyde Park Gate News*. After picking up the paper and reading one excerpt, Julia responded, "Rather clever, I think," which "was enough to thrill her daughter."[21]

Vanessa Bell has described how her sister was "very sensitive to criticism and the good opinion of the grownups." She remembered how they would put the paper on the table by her mother's sofa when the grownups were eating their dinner, and then, looking through the window with her sister, "she trembling with excitement," "we could see my mother's lamplit figure quietly sitting near the fire, my father on the other side with his lamp, both reading. Then she noticed the paper, picked it up, began to read."[22]

The children's paper contained news items, articles on proper behavior, and stories. On 18 January 1892, an article, echoing Julia Stephen's own stories for children, described how "Young children should be nipped in the bud of cheekiness otherwise impertinance which when the child increases in years it grows into audacity. It is then a great hinderance [sic] to mankind."[23] On 12 September 1892, there is a description of a trip to Godrevy lighthouse, that event which is so important in *To the Lighthouse*: "On Saturday morning Master Hilary Hunt and Master Basil Smith came up to Talland House and asked Master Thoby and Miss Virginia Stephen to accompany them to the light-house."[24] In 1895, when the paper was resumed after a hiatus, there is an article describing a dream that Virginia had that she was God; and there is a news item that reported the onset of the illness (influenza) that would eventually end in Julia Stephen's death.[25]

Virginia has described how important it was that her mother took pleasure in her work, how excited she was when her mother read something she had written in the *Hyde Park Gate News*: "Never shall I forget my extremity of pleasure—it was like being a violin and being played upon—."[26]

Vanessa Bell described the earliest story that Virginia composed as a child. It was of "the discovery under their nursery floor of immense stores of gold" and of the wonderful things that the children could buy, "especially the food, which was unlimited, though mostly consisting of not then very ruinous eggs and bacon,"[27] their favorite dish. The earliest extant story in the *Hyde Park Gate News* was called "The Midnight Ride." It appeared on 1 February 1892 and described how "a boy will have to ride at midnight through a dangerous North American bog to see his brother, who lies ill at school."[28] These two early stories share one central idea: children bring food, fortune, and hope for the ill; they are helpful fantasies of courageous and resourceful children who take risks or who are clever and who are able to care for themselves or their siblings; but they are also fantasies which illustrate the extent to which care and food are not forthcoming from adults.[29] In these two early stories, there are no grownups; "The Midnight Ride" is a rescue fantasy, a story in which a child becomes completely responsible for the welfare of his brother.

On 6 June 1892, Virginia published in the *Hyde Park Gate News* a story mocking adult heterosexual love and its conventions; it may have been inspired by Stella and Jack Hill's courtship. She used a series of love letters to tell her story: "you have jilted me most shamefully," writes Mr. John Harley to Miss Clara Dimsdale; who replies: "As I never kept your love-letters you can't have them back. I therefore return the stamps which you sent."[30] Here, Virginia used her sense of humor, which, according to her sister, brought her "the greatest success with the grownups" who "laughed at her jokes but so did we all."[31]

Vanessa Bell has written, "I cannot remember a time when Virginia did not mean to be a writer."[32] By 1893, her father Leslie was convinced that Virginia indeed *would* be a writer:[33] he wrote to Julia that writing was a fitting profession for a woman, "& Ginia will do well in that line,"[34] but he did not want his son Thoby to write: he had grander plans for him and thought that some day he might be Lord Chancellor.

By encouraging her writing, Leslie was not challenging the conservative norms of proper conduct for women which prevailed within his society, to which he adhered, and by deciding to become a writer, and by practicing her craft as a child, Virginia Stephen was not violating her parents' expectations of the gender-determined proper roles for girls and boys. She would, however, use her art in ways that challenged traditional beliefs about men and women and she did it as early as 1892 in her juvenile novel.

By the time that she wrote it, Virginia seems to have learned how she could use the *Hyde Park Gate News* to tell her parents what she wanted them to hear. She seems to have also learned that fiction can present a truth and yet at the same time protect the writer because it can act as a screen behind which the writer can hide, should she need to. *Pater-familias* is a very subversive story, and it is different from anything else that Virginia wrote as a child.

A *Cockney's Farming Experiences* relates the misadventures of a young Cockney couple who try to change their lives by becoming farmers in Buckinghamshire. It is a brilliant fictional analysis of salient features of Cockney life; it is remarkable that a ten-year-old has recorded what far older and more mature observers have also perceived. It mimics the voyeuristic and do-gooder interest that Virginia's elders took in the lives of the poor. But it also uses the fictional screen of a Cockney's life to explore the economic realities and marital and filial relationships in her own family, to describe the Stephen household and to sketch details of her own family history.

She had apparently learned a great deal about Cockney life. We know that Virginia accompanied her mother as she made her rounds in the working-class districts of London as a Victorian "do-gooder." Her half brother George Duckworth was working with Charles Booth on his analysis of Cockney poverty for many years, and Virginia once visited Booth's offices with Stella Duckworth. She records how George was at work there, correcting proof.[35] By the time Virginia wrote her story, Booth had written his analysis of the effects of poverty on Cockney family life, the frequency of husband-wife violence, and that Cockney wives were, nonetheless, "ready to stand their ground" and fight back against their husbands. Although husbands were "supposed to 'keep' their families," "everyone knew that in reality they would regularly fail."[36]

Virginia describes the newlywed couple as "energetic and hopeful." But that youthful hope soon turns into misery, despair, and hopelessness. They had taken an "imprudent step" in buying a farm, because they "knew nothing of farming" (1). The story is told from the husband's point of view, and it chronicles how impossible it is for the poor to change their economic status. But inherent in Virginia's story is the assumption that Cockneys are their own worst enemies; they bring disaster upon themselves because they act rashly, without forethought and planning.

And yet, embedded in Virginia's story there are hints of the deeper understanding of class which Woolf would develop as a grown woman. The story describes how it feels to never have quite enough food to feel satisfied. It suggests that in a marriage like this one, most of the arguments between the wife and husband are about money, and it suggests how difficult it is for the poor to keep their spirits up and to refrain from fighting with one another because of the hopelessness of their situation. As the Cockney puts it, "Next morning I determined to be as agreeable as I could to Harriet as I did not think it proper for two young people to be always falling out as we had done." His inability to provide for them results in Harriet's berating him constantly, and he is driven out of the house by her continual "nag nag nag"; a remarkable day is one when Harriet "did not say one nasty word to me" (2).

Soon after they set up housekeeping, the Cockney goes out to milk the cow and after "an hour's hard work managed to get about half an inch of milk at the bottom of the milk jug" (1). There is a tremendous disparity between the physical effort that the Cockney must make and the amount of sustenance which his efforts bring; yet Virginia seems to be ambivalent about whether this is because milking a cow is, in fact, hard work, or because the Cockney is, by nature, stupid and inept.

The Cockney and Harriet repeatedly try to feed themselves; but they never manage to succeed. First there is not enough milk; then Harriet tries to boil the only two eggs which they have, but they turn out to be "as hard as bricks"; then the Cockney tries to toast the bread, but he "burnt the toast to a cinder." The Cockney is so hungry that he winds up eating his "nestegg but I had to eat it as there was nothing else to eat" (1) but he immediately regrets having done so, because he realizes, although it is too late, that his thoughtless action will assure their future hardship.

Neither can the Cockney feed his cows; he has no training in husbandry, no real skills which could provide him with a way out of his life lived on the edge of survival, but Virginia suggests that it is a personality defect rather than a lack of skill: he remarks, "I went out to inspect the cows and found that I had forgotten to give them any food or water" (1).

When Harriet abuses him, she says things like, "What are you squinting like a sick rabbit for?" (3). Their squabbling and marital strife prevent them from banding together; it also prevents their arriving at a mutual understanding that he is unsuccessful because for a man of his class, success is nearly impossible, or highly unlikely. Traders bilk him, so that his meager resources are exhausted more quickly than they might be. In pointing out how inept the Cockney is, Virginia suggests that a lack of training or formal education ensured his failure. Harriet, however, continues to see it as the Cockney's personal failure.

The couple has quickly moved from hope to despair; by the end of *A Cockney's Farming Experiences,* he overhears his wife planning a new marriage with a man called Buskin; she tells him that she would be happy to have the Cockney dead. Her hope seems to have become transmuted into a murderous rage.

Like many novels read by women, *A Cockney's Farming Experiences* describes a woman who is, in every way, "superior, though often miserable,"[37] and a man who is pathetic and needs help. Because his wife continually abuses him, to stop the abuse the Cockney pretends to be seriously ill: "I went and chalked my face white and staggered into the room where she was and pretended to faint" (3); but she doesn't respond, so he pretends to be dying.

Relief comes, however, just in the nick of time, when a "telegram boy" arrives on the scene with a message that "Aunt Maria is dead and she has left me a jolly lot of money." Harriet abandons her plan, and settles for sharing the benefits of his newfound wealth. At the end of the story, she is fixing up the house, buying armchairs which she covers with "very expensive stuff" (4). The Cockney hires an expert farmer by the name of Marston; Harriet employs a domestic maidservant. He observes that "a little money seemed to have entirely reformed Harriet and made her quite agreeable to me" (4). Now that his days are not so "fatiguing," (3) he can take "Harriet to the theaters" (4). Because of their wealth, they are now happy, peaceful, and comfortable. Their ability to become economically secure is made possible not by their efforts, but because of an inheritance. But their newfound wealth will not buy them acceptance; rather, as they take on the trappings of respectability, they will be berated for their pretension. Class is not an easy prison to escape.

But what was Virginia using her invention, the Cockney, to say about her own situation? The story contains an almost nightmare-like series of descriptions of the inadequacy of food. There is the "half an inch of milk at the bottom of the milk jug" (1); the milk that the Cockney wastes by milking "with the pail upside down so that all the milk rolled down onto the grass" (4); the eggs, as hard as bricks; the toast that is burnt to a cinder; the starving cows; the cow who refuses to eat; the cow that dies of starvation; the rustic boy who says he doesn't know "what his mother eats" (1).

I do not believe that this preoccupation with food is an accident. Priscilla Robertson has described of the Victorians that, when "it came to punishments other than beating, favorite methods were often connected with food." She describes how "English children's food was at best extremely simple and monotonous," and that "it was held that fancy food was bad for children's digestions and morals." Most important, I think, an "almost universal tenet was that children should never be allowed to ask for anything, or to express a preference, but simply to eat what was set before them."[38] If these methods were used in the Stephen nursery—and Virginia's novel suggests that they might well have been—then Virginia must have felt a kinship with the plight of the Cockney and Harriet, who, like children in the nursery, were deprived of being able to control their own need for food.

Moreover, in emphasizing the insufficiency of milk, it is possible that Virginia is reaching back to an infantile memory of deprivation at having been weaned so young; the dead cow might signify the mother who no longer provides her child with milk. Nonetheless, the lack of milk surely signifies a lack of nurturance, of warmth and care.

The Cockney's inability to achieve success, in any way other than through luck, duplicates, I believe, Leslie Stephen's sense of hopeless failure in regard to his own achievements, which he dwelled on repeatedly in his letters to his wife, and which, I believe, the young Virginia perceived. The portrait of the Cockney as a bumbling idiot is how Leslie depicted himself. In just one of dozens of examples, in a letter to Julia, he writes: "I do wish that I had been more self confident & then I should have stuck to one thing & done something." He apologized for being a chronic complainer, and for venting his sense of dissatisfaction with himself to her, but he knew that he complained in large part in order to get "a little comfort from her.[39]

Virginia writes that the Cockney feigns illness in order to get his wife's sympathy and attention. Virginia might have been dealing with her terror at her father's extremely serious illness by exploring the possibility, in fiction, that his illness was feigned. There is no evidence that Leslie was a malingerer. In fact, he repeatedly assured his wife that he was well.[40] Julia had to insist upon his recognizing the seriousness of his illness, and she once had to force him to go away to recuperate, and to stay away for as long as he was supposed to.[41] Writing Leslie's illness as pretense could have protected the ten-year-old child from what was probably one of her worst fears, that her father would die. From the time that she was four years old until she was eleven, she lived with the reality of her father's serious illness, and the possibility of his death.

Virginia describes Harriet as absolutely unconcerned about the Cockney's illness. Leslie believed that his wife wore herself out with caring for the sick,[42] although he demanded constant attention when he himself was ill. Leslie hinted that Julia's mother was a professional invalid—which is another way of saying that her prolonged illness was feigned.[43]

When Virginia writes that Harriet was unaffected by the Cockney's disease, she may have been writing things as she wished they were. Virginia might have used Harriet to explore a response to illness different than her mother's—Harriet treats illness as if it were not serious. Harriet exercises far more control over the deployment of her energy than Julia did. Virginia writes another possible script for a woman's role by inventing one who does not automatically respond to the needs of others, but rather makes her own independent assessment of whether her caretaking is required. Harriet is immensely irreverent about the one thing about which Julia was in dead earnest: the role of woman as caregiver. She also explores the possibility that her concern will in fact do no real good. Harriet says, in effect, if he is going to die, let him die; there is nothing that I can do or am willing to do to stop it. And yet Harriet's lack of concern about his illness might also be Virginia writing of how she perceived her mother responding to her own childhood illnesses or to her own abuse.

The quarrels within the Cockney household, which are invariably about money, accurately reflect the quarrels in the Stephen household. The Cockney is forever squandering money on affectations which he believes will make him more highly regarded—a walking stick, "an ebony one with a silver handle" (3), or the right kind of dog. In the Stephen household, Leslie was the one who constantly accused the rest of them of spending foolishly, of ruining him; as Virginia later wrote, when the accounts were presented to him on Wednesdays, he would "roar" and "beat his breast" and claim that he was "dying."[44] Leslie's biographer has written that his "preoccupation with money . . . arose partly from his determination to make it clear that those dependent on him were really dependent and partly from his desire for gratitude and appreciation."[45] By rewriting the man of the house as the one who squandered the money and the woman of the house as the one who berates him, Virginia revises what went on in her own family.

In *A Cockney's Farming Experiences*, Virginia writes about a man who cannot be depended upon; she rewrites the traditional image of the Victorian paterfamilias. According to the letters which remain and memoirs which describe Leslie's behavior, Leslie had enough money to support his family, but acted as if he didn't, and he created the less-than-secure image of his family on the verge of ruin, which is how Virginia depicts the economic reality of life within her Cockney house-hold. She was also relating how frightening it was for a young child to think that her family was perpetually on the verge of bankruptcy.

There are seemingly incongruous details in the story which call such attention to themselves that the possibility that they are highly significant episodes must be explored. In the first, the Cockney describes how he has been driven out of the house by his wife's nagging:

> I pursued my path to the stream when I saw a bull (as I thought) with ereck [*sic*] tail, dilated nostrils, fiery eyes come tearing towards me. I rushed forward but tumbled into the stream. I then being somewhat awakened from my fears saw that it was only a calf running to the stream to drink who was much more frightened than I was. I scrambled home and went up to my room by the back door and changed my dress. I remained there till supper time for I did not wish to be seen by Harriet who would only laugh at me for being frightened by a cow. (2)

The image of a male animal with an erect tail, dilated nostrils, and fiery eyes tearing towards its prey, the soiled dress, cowering within a room after the incident, not wanting to be seen, the fear of not being taken seriously, of not being believed, of being laughed at if the incident was reported—each and every detail of this apparently incongruent incident becomes meaningful if sexual assault is read as a subtext. I believe that it transcribes sexual violence or incest as Virginia herself had experienced it. She wrote A *Cockney's Farming Experiences* about four years after Gerald Duckworth's sexual assault, and in the year after J. K. Stephen pursued Stella Duckworth. Near the end of her life, Virginia referred to J. K. Stephen as a "tormented bull."[46] But Julia Stephen did not believe that J. K. was a tormented bull; she believed he was a pathetic man in need of care. In the story, Virginia transforms the menacing bull into a calf. I believe we are witnessing the process of denial, one that she might have been taught by her mother—one can almost hear Julia saying to the children, after one of J. K.'s rampages through their household, "Poor Jem. Pay him no mind; he may seem scary but he's really helpless. You musn't be afraid." In her story, however, Virginia preserves the integrity of her own impression, and I believe that she records how she was trained not to trust that her own fears were significant and real.

I believe that the incident also records that Virginia anticipated the response of her family if she told what had happened to her. There is no indication that anyone knew about Gerald's conduct; there is no indication that anyone inquired about how the children were affected by J. K.'s conduct. Leslie, in a letter to Julia, speaks of Gerald's upright moral character.[47]

By the time that she wrote this story, Virginia had been abducted at least once by J. K. Stephen,[48] and she had experienced at least one incident of sexual violation that we know of. In her text, the narrator transmutes the bull with the erect tail first into a frightened calf running to the stream to drink, and then into a cow. The traumatic experience of incest, or of sexual assault, is being detoxified, as it were, so that it will not become a pernicious memory. I believe that we are seeing Virginia using that process which psychoanalysts refer to as "reversal into the opposite"—taking something terrifying and denying its potentially lethal nature by turning it into something innocuous. Parents sometimes teach children to do this; rather than recognizing a child's fear as valid or rooted in reality, parents tell a child that there is nothing to fear.

I also believe that we are watching her beginning to deny the reality of what had happened. Judith Lewis Herman has discovered, in a study of fifty-three women who had been childhood victims of incest, that the "earlier, longer and more violent the incest, the more it had been forgotten."[49] I believe that A *Cockney's Farming Experiences* shows us Virginia in the process of creating a story which will enable her to forget. Yet in another sense, the story stands as a record of what might very well be a plea for help.

The second incident which calls attention to itself occurs when the Cockney pretends to be sick, because he is afraid of how his wife will respond to his having broken his expensive walking stick. He believes that his wife is either going to allow him to die or that she is plotting his death, and that she is already planning on marrying Buskin. He overhears them talking, and then he says: "I wondered if she could be as base as she seemed so I jumped out of bed and ran down stairs to find her talking and grimacing to the empty air" (4). A plan to get rid of him thus instantly evaporates into a plot that Harriet has concocted; she changes from being fearsome to being clever.

Harriet is not as base as she had seemed; she is not capable of getting rid of the Cockney. She instantly becomes just a clever woman. He admires her, and admits that "it is just like a man to blunder," and they resume their proper roles: she "scuttled away to attend to her domestic duties and I went away to attend to my agricultural duties" (4).

The year that Virginia wrote her little novel was the year that Laura was put out of the house. Given how her mother and father had acted to Laura—and one must assume that Virginia had witnessed some of that behavior over a ten-year period—Virginia must have wondered about the true nature of her parents. Were they dangerous? Did they intend harm? Were they, to paraphrase her, as base as they seemed? Or were they, instead, as they probably told their other children, only trying to arrange the best situation for Laura?[50]

At the end of the story, the Cockney and Harriet resume their proper roles within the household, much in the manner of the ending of a Shakespearean comedy. It is, I believe, Virginia's attempt to make some sense out of the chaos that she had observed, to make some sense out of her parents' behavior, to use her narrative to effect an order in the chaos of her household which was repeatedly threatened with illness, violence, and loss. But in her sequel, *The Experiences of a Paterfamilias*, she shatters almost immediately the temporary artistic order that she had created at the end of her first tale.

In the sequel, set some three years later, the birth of a child causes the couple even more problems than they had before. For one thing, the husband is tremendously jealous of the attention which his wife pays the child, so much so that he wishes that "he had never been born" (5). The Cockney perceives his son as a rival, one who demands attention, who leaves Harriet less time for him. Their marriage is clearly not a partnership, especially when it comes to the child, because this man does absolutely nothing for his child that he is not cajoled or harassed into doing.

The attitude of the father toward his son is consistently "cross"; the Cockney and Harriet enact a continuous battle in front of the infant; she tries to force her husband to pay attention to the baby, to play with it, to care for it, which he eventually does, unwillingly, after much bickering, and many threats. Virginia, at ten years, was able to embed in this fiction her observation about the unwillingness of most fathers to participate in child care.[51]

But rather than admitting that the child is primarily his wife's responsibility, and that she is, in one sense, trapped by the condition of motherhood, he remarks that because his wife forces him to pay attention to their son, *he* has come to regard "the nursery as a cage where I am made to perform compulsory tricks and therefore I avoid it as much as possible" (5). Virginia has apparently observed and here records that fathers perceive having children as a trap, and that they view any marriage which has produced a child as a cage which contains them. This reverses the reality of the conditions within the household: in fact, it is Harriet who is trapped within the nursery, who cannot escape it very easily if at all; yet it is the Cockney who portrays himself as caged. She also implies that the act of becoming a father has turned the father into another child who will demand that his wife become a mother to him at the very time that she must nurture their child; and she also suggests that the father's behavior toward his child is beastly.

Harriet is portrayed, through the point of view of the husband, as having a very bad nature, as being constantly angry. He never connects her unhappiness and her rage to his behavior as a father. When she comes "down stairs looking quite good-natured," he calls it "a wonder" (5). He assumes that, whatever his behavior, no matter how many problems he causes, it is her obligation to be kind to him. He renders himself blameless by lapsing into a litany of abusive language about how ill-tempered she is by nature, not by virtue of her circumstances. Virginia identifies precisely the rhetoric by which unhelpful and irresponsible men excuse themselves and exculpate themselves from responsibility either for their children or for their wives' unhappiness.

When the Cockney remarks that he has come into some money, and has "the satisfaction of feeling my money steadily increasing per annum," Harriet says, "Then I shall buy the dear little Alphonso a nice little carriage, shan't I then Baby?" He has kept the extent of his good fortune from her and she has, apparently, refrained from buying a carriage until she is sure they can afford it. Although a baby carriage cannot possibly be considered a self-indulgence, the Cockney cannot bear hearing Harriet say this, and he " 'shuddered and bolted' out of the room as I always do when Harriet begins her baby talk." Her desire to care for her child results in her husband's running out of the house. He tries "to think how I could escape from the baby for the rest of the day" (5).

Virginia at ten captured arguments about how difficult it is to get men to give women the money that they need to care for their children. She understood that, within the house of the paterfamilias, "his" money is "his"; any increase in his own fortune is not, as a rule, passed on to his wife and children. In many instances, he will continue to give his wife the same amount of money to run their household as he pockets his salary increase or his inheritance for his own pleasure.[52]

When he finally agrees to buy the baby a pram, it is not because he believes that it is necessary, nor because that would be the "fatherly" thing to do, "not because I had succumbed to his baby charms (if he had any)," but because he will temporarily be in Harriet's "good books" (6), and he will be able to escape her wrath. The young Virginia has precisely described that quality of working-class women, that relentlessness in pursuit of what they believe is necessary for their children's survival, that has been described as a distinguishing feature of women of this class.[53] This toughness and resilience and essential optimism are very different qualities from the eternal pessimism and resignation that seem to have marked how Julia Stephen responded to life. I believe that Virginia here was writing a woman as she could be (as indeed many women in fact were), rather than a description of how her mother saw herself. I also believe that she was responding to the tough qualities that her mother had, in fact, demonstrated, for Julia had been thrown virtually every trouble that one could conceive of, and yet she endured and went on.

Virginia describes the following cycle: the mother believes the child needs something; the father refuses to buy it; a fight ensues; the father uses the fight as the excuse for escaping his household (the cage); he gives in, he says, to placate his wife, but what he has done, in reality, is to remind her that it is he who controls how the money will be spent in this family.

Once the baby is born, the Cockney escapes from his household as often as he can. He uses various pretenses, one of which is that he needs to go to his farm "on the excuse of seeing how things were getting on there but my real intention was to get away from the baby." He apparently causes so much chaos in the household that Harriet is just as glad to have him go, for "she agreed readily" (6), provided that he will only be gone for two weeks.

But the day after he gets there, Harriet comes, because the baby "wanted to go to the country." She describes how the baby hated the train, which she refers to in baby talk as the "nasty Puff puff." He is so disgusted by her that he remarks: "I will not repeat all that passed between Harriet and Alphonso" (7). Harriet seems incapable of interacting with her husband as a grown woman when she is in the presence of her husband and the baby; her husband is incapable of being anything but disgusted by his wife's attentions to his son. She has become an object of revulsion to her husband. He is no doubt jealous; perhaps as a response to his behavior, she has begun to align herself with her son.

The next few chapters describe the horrors that befall the baby who has been unfortunate enough to be born into a household which is headed by a "pater-familias" like the Cockney. On the day after the baby and his mother come to the farm, the baby, like any baby, begins to assert his need for care, and begins to cry because he is hungry. The Cockney says, "I was not prepared for this," as if the baby's crying is an unanticipated or even an unnatural act. At first he engages in a contest of wills with the baby, expecting him to stop crying without being fed; when Harriet wants to feed him after he has been crying for five minutes, he suggests that the baby should be made to cry far longer than that. He is appalled that Harriet asks him to participate even indirectly in the act of feeding the baby, by going upstairs to "fetch down the bottle" (7). Virginia understands that child care is perceived to be women's work, yet she also understands that child care is organized to satisfy the *father's* needs, rather than the baby's or the mother's. It is the Cockney who wants the baby to cry longer, and it is he who dictates that Harriet will not "give in" to the baby: he insists upon the form of care the child will receive.

Virginia uncovers the virulence that underpins this withholding of food from the infant. She writes that the Cockney is conscious of his desire not to have this baby fed, to starve his own child, for he reports how he has "trouble" with bottles, having already "smashed" one of them, and how "all the milk [had] run out in the cab." Seeing the milk spill thrilled him, "for I had fondly hoped that that would be the last I should see of bottles." Yet he does Harriet's bidding, "without a murmur," and he fetches the baby's bottle which he describes as "the odious thing" (7). His rage at the baby goes underground; outwardly he acquiesces to Harriet; inwardly he wants the baby dead.

If the reader begins to identify with the plight of the baby, Virginia's narrative becomes an extremely painful evocation of the experience of child abuse and neglect. The father treats the baby in ways that must be called sadistic and murderous, although the language which the father uses to describe what he is doing beclouds and masquerades what is going on.

His father takes him to "the stables" and puts him "on to a pig's back"; the baby "soon tumbled off into the pigwash." He falls down; he is covered with excrement. Later in the day, she again gives the child to him. He repeats what he has done earlier; this time he puts the baby on the back of a donkey "but the donkey began to kick and the little beast [who is his son] hadn't the sense to stick on but tumbled off into a puddle." The child takes another fall; this time the baby is covered with mud. But the father is clever enough to pretend that he is doing these things for the baby's amusement, so as to evade responsibility for what has happened. Using a language that is common with neglectful and abusive parents, the father blames the child himself for what has happened—he says that it isn't his fault that the baby "hadn't the sense to stick on" (7).

When he comes back with the baby wet and soiled, Harriet berates him, but she continues to give the baby over to his care even though she knows that he will harm him. We know that she yells at him; we know that she is "disgusted" with him; but we also know that she doesn't intervene actively to protect her child either by prohibiting the Cockney from having access to the baby or by walking out and leaving him. This is because he controls the money in the household. At ten Virginia understood that it is difficult for a woman without economic resources of her own to act in the best interests of her child, even when she knows that child is being mistreated.

When the baby shows even greater evidence of neglect or mistreatment, the Cockney does not hand the baby over to Harriet, but rather to "the nurse"; he knows that the nurse, because of his control over her, will hide the evidence of his abuse, whereas "Harriet . . . would probably make it hot for me after my little escapade" (8). At ten, Virginia understood that nurses were forced to hide the evidence that children were being mistreated because of their dependence on the paterfamilias for their sustenance and for future employment.

He knows that if Harriet sees the baby wet, she will know that he has again acted in a way to cause his son harm, so he decides that he will try to hide the evidence of his abuse by wiping the baby off. Instead, however, he fastens "his sash to a branch of a tree and left him dangling there" (8); in effect, he is really abandoning the baby or, perhaps, even trying to hang the baby. He walks away as innocently and as unconcernedly as if he were leaving an article of clothing behind.

His intention is clearly, if unconsciously, to have the baby die or to have someone else pick up the baby: "I was away rather longer than I meant to be," he says, "and when I came back I found the baby gone!" (8) His response to the missing baby is inappropriate—"I had almost forgotten the missing baby"—unless he really wants it gone. Harriet, in the meantime, has found the baby's wet sock, and when he returns home, she responds to his having "lost" the baby with a look that "was meant to be cold haughty and dignified" (8). This is telling, for, as the narrative progresses, the mother begins to respond to the loss of the baby inappropriately as well, and this suggests that Harriet might also want the baby gone; the narrator seems uncomfortable with an overt declaration of the mother's malice toward her child, but has no difficulty expressing the father's. After the Cockney "loses" the baby, he states that "I thought that Harriet wasn't very much disturbed by the Baby's loss" (9); yet she scolds him until she is hoarse. She does not, however, go looking for the baby at first, although she eventually sends the police out to look for him.

The words which are used to describe the Cockney's treatment of the baby are telling: he uses words like "escapade" and "prank" to describe what he has done; his wife, however, calls it "unparental conduct" (9), which also understates the case. The Cockney repeatedly uses the term "to nurse the baby" to describe what he has done. He says Harriet looked grave when "I take it into my head to nurse the baby" (8). To nurse the baby means to remove the child from its proper home, so he is clearly aware of his intention to get rid of his own child. When the baby is missing, he expects to carry on with his life as if nothing has in fact happened: he tells Harriet that they will be going to a party, but she responds that he is "barbarous to think of worldly gaieties when my only child was lost" (9). Harriet uses the word "barbarous" to describe his wanting her to go to the party. She does not use it to describe his attitude toward the baby, even though she knows that her husband wants her baby dead.

Throughout *Pater-familias*, the Cockney hides his abusive behavior behind a veneer of boyishness and helplessness not only to diminish the impact of his cruelty toward his son but also so that he can continue to act out his sadism. Virginia describes with astonishing accuracy the personality traits that researchers have discovered in abusive parents. He simpers toward his wife; he cowers; he pretends to be inept; he acts the part of the bumbling incompetent fool. No one would believe for an instant that he could be capable of such cruelty. His behavior seems to throw Harriet off the scent, for she vacillates between being absolutely sure that he has abandoned the child to questioning her own perceptions, by asking herself how could someone who seems so weak be so cruel.

The middle section of *Pater-familias* deals with Harriet's discovery of the baby; she has then sequestered him in another part of the house. She seems to be waiting for some admission from her husband that he has abandoned his son. But because the story is told from the Cockney's point of view, there is a real dramatic tension—is the baby in the house or isn't he? Has he been lost forever, or is he safe and sound? What are those cries that seem to be coming from some part of the house? Are they the baby's? And why has Harriet hidden the baby?

When Harriet admits that the baby has been found, that he is safely in the house, he asks her why she has hidden him. He learns that her "motive in hiding the baby from me was to find out if I was really as brutal as I seemed" (10), which echoes his plot in the first part of the narrative to discover whether she was as brutal as she seemed.

The stories of children who have been abused or who have witnessed abuse are "full of aggression and brutality." In their play and enactments, dolls and fictitious persons are "constantly being beaten, tormented, and killed." The repetition indicates the extent to which brutality is enacted repeatedly, and how consistently threatened these children feel by violence. The drawings of children who have been sexually or incestuously abused reflect the sense of powerlessness that they feel. They reflect the children's attenuated sense of self, their feeling entrapped or ensnared, their hurt and their pain, and sometimes, if therapy is effective, their anger and their rage. They show themselves as tiny creatures, stick figures, whose faces show their pain; once therapy begins, they often show themselves crying, their eyes dropping big tears, their mouths, an anguished, open space, screaming or pleading with their abusers to stop. [54]

On two facing pages of *Pater-familias* there are no less than four overt acts of brutality that directly threaten the baby's well-being, in addition to the desire of the father to starve his child; but the incidents which Virginia describes may seem bizarre, even absurd—hanging a baby from a tree; putting a baby on top of various animals that will surely fling him to the ground. Alice Miller has cautioned that it is especially important not to dismiss the stories of children which seem to contain "absurd fantasies" for these are often, in fact, "a retelling."[55] Moreover, brutality toward children in families is often enacted in ways that are bizarre and incomprehensible to an outsider; within the household, however, these acts take on a grotesque kind of internal logic. Because this is the only reality that the child has seen and learned, these bizarre acts appear to be rendered without affect; in fact, they are rendered as if they were a normal part of daily life, because in many cases the child has been taught that this punishment is the logical outgrowth of a bad nature, or of bad behavior—that it is, in fact, nature, or of bad behavior—that it is, in fact, deserved.

The behavior of the paterfamilias can only be called disturbed. And I believe that Virginia's narrative is an attempt to understand behavior that she had witnessed, such as the treatment of Laura, in order to explore for herself whether it was, indeed, as brutal as it seemed.

For in her work the young Virginia is writing a brave and a provocative narrative: she is shattering the myth of the Victorian child as savior and she is exploding the definition of the Victorian father as just and as wise. In her story, a child does not bring salvation; nor is the child treated with reverence. Rather, every day of its life, the child's life is endangered. Although by the end of the narrative Harriet is satisfied that her husband is not as lethal as he seems, there is no indication that he has reformed; although he states that he is now "getting more reconciled" (10) to the baby's presence, in the last chapter, he is in the process of buying a gun, ostensibly to go and hunt rabbits.

I believe that *Pater-familias* is Virginia's attempt to come to terms with what had happened within her own household, both to Laura and to herself. In one significant scene that explodes with meaning, largely because it is one of those incongruous moments in the narrative, the Cockney records that Harriet says that "a lie is sometimes better than the truth. I said that even if it was better to tell a lie (which it never was) her morals ought not to let her tell a lie whatever her natural self said" (9–10). I believe that Virginia is communicating something of great significance here, that she is testing the possibility that she has been lied to about something, perhaps about Laura and the reasons that were given for how she was treated.

The emotional contour of the narrative, a repetition of the baby being "lost" and "found," duplicates the conditions under which the children lived with Laura locked away in another part of the house. She would appear for a bit, then disappear, then reappear again. At around the time when Virginia was writing *Pater-familias*, Leslie was discussing whether they would permit Laura to come to St. Ives. It seems as if Virginia was using her narrative to deal with the cloud that surrounded the treatment of Laura; I believe that she was writing both the possibility that Laura was as badly treated as it seemed—that she was being "nursed" out—and the possibility that she was really being well-cared-for. But because the narrative ends on an ominous note and because the Cockney never really proves he is less brutal than he seems, I believe that at some level Virginia understood what had happened, although to recognize that one's parents can be brutal is perhaps the most terrifying insight that a young child can have, and surely one that a young child must obscure if she is to live in anything but perpetual fear.

I also believe that Virginia was rewriting the myth that the Victorian family was a refuge and a haven for its children. Because she locates her narrative within another class, I believe that she is obscuring the fact that she is writing, in fact, about fathers within her own class. In the second part of her narrative, when the family moves to the country, they take on all of the trappings of upper-middle-class life—they have servants and they go to a party with a table laden with food—but the story slips into the upper middle class without the reader even being aware of what the narrative is accomplishing.

When Virginia calls her central character a "pater-familias," she is using a term in reference to the father as the legitimate head of household government which goes back at least as far as the reign of the Stuarts.[56] The term points to a belief in masculine authority (and, by extension, a belief in feminine dependence), but it also assumes that the father will care for his children and his wife and his servants, as if they were his children.

At significant points in the narrative, when the Cockney is threatening his child with bodily harm, Virginia capitalizes the word baby, which becomes "Baby" at those moments. Virginia used her story to debunk the notion that the head of the household is, by nature, just and good. The term "pater-familias" indicates an inherent belief in the fact that "differences in status and authority," as between men and women, husbands and their wives, fathers and their children, "are not just normal, but good and desirable."[57] Virginia shatters every one of these assumptions. The "pater-familias" (who has no other name) is both less intelligent than his servants and less able than his wife; as Harriet puts it, on the subject of which sex is superior: "I don't know what you men do think of. You leave all the thinking to your wives"; and, on the subject of the natural superiority of the higher classes, of their servants, she remarks: "though they are low bred they have more common sense than some people I know" (9); on the issue of the inherent goodness of the paterfamilias, Harriet wonders whether her husband is as brutal as he seems.

In her novel, Virginia shattered the assumption that it was the father's right to rule because he was naturally superior, naturally intelligent, naturally just, naturally kind. In *Pater-familias*, she asks, for the first time in print, the question that she would return to in the major works of her maturity: What happens when the paterfamilias who is the absolute ruler of the household is neither wise nor just nor kind? Here she suggests that absolute power always entails abuse. If the father is neither wise nor good, and the rule within the house is not just, then the conditions for life within that household will be neither good nor desirable for his dependents, although to outsiders the family may seem to be representative of all that is admirable. In her story, no one outside the family (except for the servants, whom the "pater-familias" controls completely) has any inclination about what is going on within the household. Harriet and the paterfamilias get invited to dinners; he behaves well to everyone but his family.

There are several overt descriptions of acts of sexuality in *Pater-familias*. Virginia Woolf is often accused of not being able to describe sex overtly in her mature novels, yet she had no apparent reticence in describing sex at ten.

The sex that she describes is between the servants. The paterfamilias describes being awakened at half-past six "by the sound of 'lovering' outside my door." He finds the housekeeper and her lover at their love-making, and scolds her "severely," telling her that he will have "no nonsense" in his house. But after breakfast he catches them again, and "found to my horror my housekeeper and her lover snivelling by the pigsty" (7).

Virginia describes lovemaking which she herself had apparently witnessed; she describes it as disgusting, associating it with a pigsty. But she also understands that the sex life of servants is regulated and controlled by the master of the house.

The nursery, then, was not the place where children were carefully screened from knowledge of sexuality; rather, Virginia knew and could recognize the sounds of "lovering." At the same time, her father believed it was his duty to protect his daughter's virtue. He believed it was his fatherly duty to control the reading of the girls in the house; he would not permit Stella to read *Cousine Bette*: in a letter to Julia he reports: "I dont think that pretty reading for young ladies."[58]

There is a nightmare sequence in *Pater-familias*, that I believe, is a symbolic retelling of the abuse she suffered at age six by Gerald Duckworth, when he molested her on the ledge by the dining room. The scene takes place in a dining room; it has nothing to do with the rest of the story; it proceeds according to an emotional logic, rather than a rational one. The story is a profoundly disturbing one of near death and violation and terrible shame; it seems out of proportion to the events being narrated, unless the real event being narrated is elided.

Husband and wife are invited to a dinner party; as the paterfamilias drinks a toast to his hostess's health and makes a "pretty speech," the "table gave a tremendous crack and tumbled to the ground." Throughout the meal, Harriet has been repeating over and over, though no one listens to her, "Oh I know this table will break down soon" (10).

Afterward, Harriet tells her husband how she has saved herself as the table broke, crashing to the ground, threatening to pin her underneath at best, or to crush her beneath its weight. She told him

that luckily for her she had lifted one of her legs from the ground to scratch it and when the legs gave way she had drawn it up on to her chair and made it's fellow follow it so that she was left standing on her chair looking on the wreck before her. Soon she remembered that there were gentlemen present and that she was not in a very dignified position but she could not move for as the table tumbled she had not remembered to pull her skirt up after her and so the table tumbled onto her train and she was left sticking onto the chair not wanting to stay there and not knowing how to get down.

She cannot get down by herself, she is frozen with fear and unable to move. A servant comes by and finds her, standing on the chair, with her torn train, and her dress soiled and in shreds, and she says, "Lor mum 'owever did you manage to get that torn? It'll take a deal of time to sow [sic] it up" (11). The paterfamilias is not happy that his wife has been spared the fate of Mrs. Robinson, his hostess, who was the only one "who had got really stuck" under the table; instead, he is ashamed at his wife's appearance.

What the young Virginia is describing, I believe, is a disaster, and it is important that the scene is a dining room, ostensibly the locus of those social rituals which serve to demonstrate how civilized we are, which was near where Virginia was violated for the first time. The table is "almost cracking with cake, wine, fruit and candles," and Harriet is terrified that the table will break, but more and more evidence of wealth and position are piled upon the table—"all the swell silver on [sic] which is of no use and we have got enough stuff" (10).

The incident concerns the smashing of respectability; it concerns an event in which she has had to lift one of her legs; in which she speaks of her legs as if they are not parts of her own body; in which parts of her body are exposed to gentlemen which leaves her ashamed; in which she is "left standing on her chair looking on the wreck before her." It is an event which leaves her so paralyzed that she cannot come down off that chair; a servant finds her, finds her with her dress soiled and torn, and scolds her, rather than inquiring about what has happened to her. The narrative resumes as if this event had never occurred; it is enfolded within the narrative, just as episodes of incest are enfolded within the trappings of conventional life. The servants are left to clean up all the evidence of this disaster which, as the young Virginia tells it, has really been caused by an excess of appetite. Life goes on as if nothing had happened.

When Virginia, in adulthood, described her feelings of hopelessness, she often referred to feeling as if she were standing on a ledge over an abyss. In her adulthood, the word that Virginia used in reference to the two men who had assaulted her in her childhood—Gerald and George—is the word "pig"—ironically, George Duckworth raised pigs, and once wrote a story on pigs which was published, and which he encouraged Virginia to read. [59] In *Pater-familias*, the disaster occurs because the people are pigs. In her adulthood, Virginia explained that she had been abused because her brothers' appetites were not checked, had gone out of control, had run amok. This scene in *Pater-familias* suggests that she used this same paradigm to explain what had happened to her when she was a child. She saw it as a ravenous appetite that masqueraded behind the veneer of society which could be unleashed at any time. No wonder the world was frightening, for society is not what held the passions in place; it was the cover behind which the passions ran wild.

When, later in her life, Virginia referred to the effect of being sexually molested, she described her shame, her sense of being disconnected from her body, her feeling exposed, her fright, her dread, her feeling of being pursued by something animal, of being locked in a cage from which she cannot escape the bestial attention of her animal pursuers, of being left on a ledge, of immobility, of not being able to use her legs to cross a puddle: these are precisely the feelings described in this phantasmagoric interlude and in the other unusual incidents in *Pater-familias*.

"I now look upon the nursery as a cage where I am made to perform compulsory tricks." Can this be the voice of Virginia, speaking through the mouth of the paterfamilias? Can she have been trying to tell her parents something as she penned these words?

It is highly likely that Gerald Duckworth's sexual molestation of Virginia Woolf had not been confined to that one episode which she describes in her memoirs, which had occurred at St. Ives some four years before she wrote her juvenile novel. These words suggest that Virginia had come to regard the nursery as a cage where she was made to perform compulsory sexual tricks. They tell us why Virginia stopped liking herself at ten, when consciousness set in. For, if *Pater-familias* is any indication, what Virginia become conscious of at ten was that as a child she had not been cared for, she had been abused. Such a realization has a shattering impact on a child's sense of worth and self-esteem. If someone molests you, it is because they believe you are worth molesting, that you are worthless. It takes a great deal of effort, and time, and escape from the conditions which allowed these events to occur in the first place, to learn that having been victimized does not mean that one has deserved it. For many survivors of sexual abuse, that time never comes because it demands a break from the perverted logic which prevails within the incestuous family, and the incestuous family makes breaking away extremely difficult. When George Duckworth died, Virginia Woolf wrote, in her diary, how sad she was, because he represented an important link with her past, even though she recognized the extent to which he had harmed her.[60] In fact, I do not believe that Virginia was ever able to separate herself from her family to the extent that she could perceive her abuse as having nothing to do with her, but rather as being *their* problem.

A *Cockney's Farming Experiences* and *The Experiences of a Paterfamilias* are important documents, not only for our understanding of how much the young Virginia understood about the conditions under which she was raised, but also for our realizing the extent to which children who have been brought up in situations like hers realize what is happening to them and to their siblings. At ten, I believe that Woolf was fully able to comprehend what was happening in her own home, but she was unable to convey its effect upon her directly, quite possibly because of a fear of reprisal. So she embedded her story within a story which is, in and of itself, an extremely important analysis of married strife and paternal abuse, of childhood neglect and abandonment. She is telling both her story and Laura's story. She seems to be split off from feelings, such as terror and rage and sorrow, that are appropriate responses to such a childhood, for much of the tale is told without affect; but then there are those moments when the terror, rage, and shame at her situation explode on the page, hidden, it is true, within an incident that will not call attention to itself.

This juvenile novel retells a story of barbarity toward a child on the part of a severely disturbed father, who hides behind the persona of an infantile innocuous fool, and of a mother whose attitude toward her child is ambiguous and inconsistent, but whose actions do not serve to deter a male history of abuse from repeating itself.

Although biographers of Virginia Woolf might claim that she was bathed in a protective love, *Pater-familias* counteracts those claims, if anyone chooses to read the evidence in its pages. It documents that Woolf's terror of abandonment preceded her mother's death. Moreover, the portrait of the father in this juvenile work associates him with abandonment and the portrait of the mother suggests that, even at ten, the young Virginia understood that her mother would not or could not protect her or others within the household from the violence of men. What is especially important about the *Pater-familias* is that it confronts more directly than any other Woolf document which has survived the possibility that parents can in fact be the destroyers of their children. It is the only place where the possibility of maternal complicity is sketched. It is possible that much of her life was spent denying the possibility that parents could behave in the deadly ways that she seems to have been able to recognize when she was ten years old.

Chapter Six

"IN THE BEGINNING
THERE WAS THE NURSERY"

In the beginning there was the nursery. These are the words of Bernard, the writer in Virginia Woolf's novel *The Waves*,[1] a novel which traces the life cycle from childhood of its six characters. Here and in other works, Woolf articulated the idea that in order to understand how and why human beings behave the way they do, one must begin with how they were treated in the nursery. For Woolf, the essential beginning of life, the most important act of creation, occurs in the nursery.

As we have already seen in *Pater-familias*, she began to interpret the nature of families and the condition of childhood almost as early as she was able to record her insights. Close readings of major works of her maturity indicate that she repeatedly drew upon the facts, shape, and substance of her childhood in her work, but that she used her own experiences, and those of the other members of her family, to examine the conditions under which children live out their lives in that middle-class British institution, the nursery. Virtually every one of her major novels begins with, or flashes back to, the childhood experiences of its protagonists.

This chapter will provide close readings of childhood experiences in eight major works of her maturity. Although they all share the idea that childhood is a terrible time, each adds another dimension to her analysis. Taken together, her portraits of the children in her fictional families—the Vinraces and the Ambroses in *The Voyage Out* (1915), the Flanders in *Jacob's Room* (1922), the Ramsays in *To the Lighthouse* (1927), the children in *The Waves* (1931), the Pargiters in *The Years* (1937), the Olivers in *Between the Acts* (1941)—demonstrate that Virginia Woolf might well be called one of the greatest interpreters of the condition of childhood, of the betrayal of the child, and the history of the family who has ever written. In nonfictional works as well, such as in her biography *Roger Fry* (1940) which I discuss in this chapter, she describes in great detail the growing experiences and the family interactions of her subject's life, well before many biographers took an interest in childhood as a formative and important period in the lives of the great. In *A Room of One's Own* (1929), *Three Guineas* (1938), and "Thoughts on Peace in an Air-Raid" (1940), Virginia Woolf also grappled with ideas about human development and child rearing and their relationship to education, the organization of households, and society, the relations between the genders, between the generations, between the rulers and the ruled, the economy, and international relations. Her insights about the fundamental nature of the family as a patriarchal institution which functioned to maintain the superiority of men can be found scattered throughout the major nonfictional works of her lifetime.

Virginia Woolf's first published novel, *The Voyage Out* (1915),[2] begins with the portrait of a mother crying for the children she has left behind. Her name is Helen Ambrose, and she and her husband Ridley, a scholar, are wending their way through London to the *Euphrosyne*, a ship that will take them for a long journey to an island off the coast of South America, where Ridley will spend many months leading the secluded scholar's life, working on an edition of Pindar. Her mouth trembles; the tears roll down her face. Ridley tries to console her, but it is clear that he doesn't understand her grief and does not share it; he is not attached to his children at all. Some local boys who see her crying think that he must have been bestial toward her, that he might even be murderous. They call him "Bluebeard."

She is leaving behind two children, a boy and a girl, aged six and ten, in the company of a nurse whom she doesn't trust. She is sure that during their very long absence (which will be for the better part of a year—the voyage out alone will take three or four weeks), their nurse will teach them how to pray. The choice hasn't been Helen's; she already misses her children tremendously. She brightens only when talk turns round to them, only when people ask her how they are. She tells anecdotes which illustrate her liberal views on child rearing. She tells her brother-in-law, the ship's owner, Vinrace, how they are "quick brats," how her son once ran across the room with a pat of butter to put it on the fire, for the fun of it but also because he was curious and wanted to find out what would happen. Vinrace, an old-fashioned father, assumes that Helen has punished her son to show him that "these tricks wouldn't do" (21). When the mail comes, Helen pounces upon the letters which inform her about her children.

That the Ambroses' treatment of their children is not idiosyncratic, but, instead, part of a cultural pattern, is indicated when Woolf explores the heroine Rachel Vinrace's childhood. Rachel, whose mother died when she was eleven, had also been left behind by her father in the care of two aunts, as her father has made his seafaring voyages in order to build a mercantile empire.

Woolf here challenges unquestioned assumptions about raising children. What is childhood like for these children who are left behind? Why do Helen and Ridley really leave them? Why does Helen accompany her husband, who will be spending hours of his life alone in his study surrounded by books, shut off from the world and from her, to make his edition of Pindar? And why is it necessary for Ridley to leave England and his children to make his edition of Pindar in the first place? Woolf reveals the fact that the most significant feature of child rearing among the privileged classes in England is that contact between parents and children is minimized, while the father's control of child-rearing practices is retained.

Helen is separated from her children so that Ridley can exact a kind of maternal care from her that might not be forthcoming if the children were with them on the journey. With the children in London, Ridley can act like a child, which he does for the better part of the novel, and he demands a kind of mothering which he expects his wife to provide. He complains that he is uncomfortable, and so Helen must see to it that he is not chilled; he rants that he will never be able to work on board the ship, and so Helen must convert a space in the ship into a suitable work area for him; he is unsure about his intellectual powers, so Helen must feed his ego to ensure that he continues his work.

Woolf suggests two reasons why the very presence of children is an enormous threat to male privilege: fathers might have to act like grownups, and fathers might have to share the attention of their wives.

Without children present, male behavior can continue to be infantile, self-absorbed, and narcissistic; and men can be the center of female attention. Woolf indicates that men are more than willing to compromise the well-being of their children so long as their own needs are met. The safeguarding of the rights of men to act in infantile ways will always mean that the needs of infants will not be met.

Indeed, Helen wonders why nursemaids are the most poorly paid of household servants.[3] Woolf suggests that their low pay reflects the fact that their work is not considered valuable, nor are the children whom they care for important enough to warrant highly paid, professional care. Rachel's caregivers, her aunts, are, in fact, expected to provide for her care without recompense. That they are singularly incapable of providing a warm, loving environment for Rachel doesn't concern Vinrace at all. But to provide well-paid, professional care for children, to have fathers provide care for children, and/or to allow mothers to provide care for children would be to challenge the fundamental tenet of the primacy of adult males in a patriarchal society.

Helen is also being separated from her children so that her impact upon their development will be minimized, so that the bonds between her and her children—particularly her son—will be loosened, if not severed completely. Part of this dynamic will result from the children's rage at having been left behind, rage that they will not be permitted to express. It is clear from the glimpse that we get of Helen as a mother that her views are liberal; it is also clear that she and her son are close—indeed, she prefers boys to girls—that she invites him to be intellectually curious, and that she treats him with kindness. Because the men of her class must be made into conformists, and must be educated for the sake of England, her influence upon her son must be squelched before it can bear fruit. The powerful, developing bond between a mother and her son must be severed to minimize the impact that she might have upon his upbringing, were she to remain close to him. Meanwhile, it seems essential that there be no bond at all between Helen and her daughter. Perhaps it is because a lack of affection or trust between women prevents a solidarity, which would give them power. Helen does not like her own sex, and she passes on her society's devaluation of the female to her daughter.

In this novel, Woolf demonstrates that the greatest threat to an imperialist state is a warm, loving, intact family, in which parents share equally in child rearing, in which contact between parents and their children are maximized, an idea which she developed fully in *Three Guineas*. *The Voyage Out* suggests how this operates. Richard Dalloway, a former M.P., who travels on the ship, is a great believer, together with his wife, in an imperialist policy, which he describes as "a lasso that opened and gradually opened and caught things, enormous chunks of the habitable globe" (50). His wife Clarissa understands that all of this depends upon "sending out boys from little country villages" and she hopes that they will have a son, not for themselves but for the Empire, who can avail himself of the numerous opportunities to rule.

But in order to be able to send boys away from England, it is imperative, in the view which this novel provides, that you not be too attached to them, that you not value them so highly that you want to have them around. Richard Dalloway briefly describes his upbringing, which is clearly related to the politics that he has chosen, which is the paradigm for the rearing of children in an imperialist country: he was one of two boys in a family of six children, and, in public, Clarissa describes him as having been spoilt, or, as he puts it, "appreciated." In private, however, he admits his extreme and constant unhappiness as a child, his loneliness, and his sense of deprivation. He tells Rachel, "It's a fallacy to think that children are happy. They're not; they're unhappy. I've never suffered so much as I did when I was a child" (68). When Rachel asks him why, he says that it was because his father was "hard" (68),[4] and he remarks that "children never forget injustice" (68). What he can't understand, but what Woolf explores, is the relationship between his father's severity, his unhappy childhood, his desire to control the world, which will make him feel powerful, and his desire to make conquests among women, which is illustrated in the scene when he kisses Rachel Vinrace, which causes her so much pain. Although children don't forget injustice, when they become adult members of the ruling class they inflict precisely the same kind of injustice—the abuse of power and authority—upon others, upon subjugated peoples, and upon women.

When the novel opens, Rachel is in her twenties. But throughout, a clear picture emerges of her life as a child. Rachel was left to her own devices as a child. She was provided with no real care, no real comfort, no real information about the world, no real companionship. She has spent most of her life alone. She has had only one friend, a religious zealot. Her aunts never explained a thing to her, either about the world or about their feelings, nor did her teachers. Her father was consistently absent, away on his voyages. Rachel was provided with no information about why people behave as they do, why "did they do the things they did, and what did they feel, and what was it all about" (36). And so the whole world appears to Rachel as if it is "something quite unfamiliar and inexplicable" (36).

Even more devastating is the fact that Rachel's attempts to find out about the world are viewed as a pathology by her aunts: when she asks as simple a question as whether or not her aunts are fond of one another, they refuse to answer, and intimate that her question is bizarre: "Her efforts to come to an understanding had only hurt her aunt's feelings, and the conclusion must be that it is better not to try" (36). The impact of this upbringing is pernicious, yet Woolf suggests that it is the norm: "To feel anything strongly was to create an abyss between oneself and others" (36). Feelings separate people, rather than bind them together: choking off feelings is necessary if one is to be acceptable in a society in which "nobody ever said a thing they meant, or ever talked of a feeling they felt" (37).

The most terrifying insight that Woolf conveys is that Rachel has been rendered unfit for life: "The shape of the earth, the history of the world, how trains worked, or money was invested, what laws were in force, which people wanted what and why they wanted it, the most elementary idea of a system in modern life—none of this had been imparted to her" (34). She has, in fact, been infantalized and brought up in a way that would not result in her having a healthy self-confidence: as a girl, she was "brought up with excessive care, which as a child was for her health; as a girl and a young woman for what it seems almost crude to call her morals" (34). Woolf describes how circumscribed and hemmed in is the life of a girl whose father is suspected of abusing her. But Rachel's past is not available to her, because she has blocked off her memories; she uses the metaphor of "sealed packets" to describe the image of her past.

Helen Ambrose suspects Rachel's father of "nameless atrocities with regard to his daughter" (24); she also suspects that he bullied his wife, her sister. But she never asks Rachel directly if her father has abused her, she does not confront Vinrace about her suspicions, nor, apparently, did she ever ask her sister. If Rachel has suffered and Helen has suspected it, it seems clear that she would have been powerless to stop it, which is, perhaps, why she really doesn't want to know. Helen believes that Rachel's behavior is infantile, as indeed it is. As far as Helen is concerned, Rachel, although she is twenty-four, "really might be six years old" (25). Helen sees, but does not understand, the fact that Rachel is stuck in childhood both because of her upbringing but also because of those "nameless atrocities."

The Voyage Out describes the effect of childhood experiences which are sealed away and unavailable to Rachel. Her experience is juxtaposed against that of the Ambrose children in London. The novel is extremely realistic in its portrait of the deadly effect of sexual abuse upon a young woman, who is not even fully aware of what has happened to her, who only becomes aware in the images that crowd her dreams. In the novel, Rachel dies inexplicably, after a delirium which suggests sexual abuse. Woolf is suggesting that sexual abuse and inexplicable death are connected. One can only imagine what the future of the Ambrose children will be.

An earlier version of the published text is extremely explicit in suggesting that Rachel dies because she has been abused:

> She began to be tormented by the sights, which now were always chasing her, and to try by swimming or jumping off high towers to escape from them. . . . [She] found herself by a great dark pool into which she plunged. But it was not full of water but of a thick sticky substance which closed over her head. . . . While all her tormenters thought that she was dead she knew that she was not dead, . . . though right under the sea. (6)

The images of drowning used here echo those that Woolf used in relationship to her own personal experience. But she described, as well, abandonment and neglect through the Ambrose children and in her portrait of Rachel's childhood.

In *Jacob's Room* (1922),[5] Virginia Woolf provides a critical reading of how male children are raised, as well as detailing the problems faced by single mothers. By the time that Virginia Woolf began *Jacob's Room*, she had had ample opportunity to observe the life of her sister Vanessa Bell, who was, for all intents and purposes, a single parent. As Kathleen Walsh D'Arcy has put it, in *Jacob's Room* Virginia Woolf portrays the plight of single parenthood as insightfully as any contemporary sociologist.[6]

The novel begins with Betty Flanders, whose husband has died in an accident some two years before, writing to Captain Barfoot, the man who presumably provides money for her to care for her three small children. The time is before World War I—her infant son Jacob will die in that war. Betty's fate will be repeated by the many young war widows, forced to raise their children without a man in a society that does not enable mothers to do so with dignity.

Jacob, who is very young when the novel begins, has wandered off while Betty has been writing her letter, which she needs to write so that she and her sons can simply survive. As a single mother, Betty does not have the emotional resources to give Jacob the kind of attention such a young child requires because she is consistently worried about how she will find the money for their needs.

When Betty realizes that Jacob is nowhere in sight, she does not go off to find him herself; instead, she makes her son Archer responsible: "Run and find him. Tell him to come at once" (7), and she calls Jacob a "tiresome little boy" (7), presumably because he has wandered off.

Nearby, Steele, a painter, is upset because his subject, Betty Flanders, has moved. He hears Archer calling for Jacob, and he is "exasperated by the noise," yet he thinks he loves children. He tells Archer that Jacob has wandered over to the rocks. Steele has felt absolutely no obligation to collect Jacob and return him to his mother, even though he is getting near to danger; the painter has more important things to do than to concern himself with the well-being of a little boy. He is trying to find the right tint, the tint that will bring his picture together. It is no wonder, then, that Woolf describes Archer's voice, the voice of childhood, as "going out into the world, solitary, unanswered" (9). No one is really paying him any attention.

And where is Jacob? He is perched at the very top of a tremendous black rock, looking at a crab in a tidepool. To get there, he has had to climb up and up, to stretch his legs wide, and to summon up his courage, which has made him feel "heroic" (9).

He takes the crab, plops it into his bucket, and climbs down. He is in even greater danger now, for as he climbs down from the cliff, the "waves came creaming up to him" (10); the force of the water battering the rocks presents a great danger to children. That danger is underscored when Jacob finds a whole skull lying under the cliffs.

He suddenly realizes that he is lost, and he becomes frightened. The first person he calls for is his nanny, Rebecca, who is elsewhere taking care of the baby. He is "about to roar" (10) but picks up the skull instead. Sobbing, with his bucket and the crab and the skull, he runs along. Betty, who by this time has started looking for him, sees him. She tells him to drop the skull; asks him why he didn't stay by her, and calls him a "naughty little boy" (10). She sees Jacob as "a handful," as "obstinate already" (11). Thus she makes him responsible by suggesting that it is his nature. She herself has endangered her son's life, but she just labels him naughty. Her young son becomes the locus for many of her uncomfortable feelings, her feelings of betrayal and abandonment and helplessness, which have resulted from her husband's untimely death, and the fact that she has "no man to help" (11).

She angrily grabs the hands of both children and pulls them along, and responds to what has occurred by telling Archer the story of a gunpowder explosion in which a man has lost an eye. Rather than training her children to understand their limits, by creating a safe space in which they can explore the world under her watchful eye, she tries to get them to behave by scaring them, by telling them that the world is a dreadfully dangerous place, which indeed it is, especially for children who are left to their own devices. Archer responds by not being able to sleep at night, a problem which lasts for years. His mother tries to comfort him by telling him to think "of the fairies"; to think of the "lovely, lovely birds settling down on their nests"; to think of "the old mother bird with a worm in her beak" (12). During the day, she tells him about explosions, and insists that he repeat the story back to her; at night, she tries to comfort him with the myth that she is a mother bird and all is well.

Meantime, the crab that Jacob has taken from the tidepool, and left in the bucket, is about to die. As it has tried, with its "weakly legs," to "climb the steep side, trying again and falling back, and trying again and again," (14) Jacob is asleep, "profoundly unconscious" (14).[7] The crab is so insignificant that he and his mother aren't even conscious of its struggle to survive. In the novel, the crab's plight is a metaphor for what will happen to an entire generation of young men.[8]

As a widow, Betty is regarded by the community as a potentially disruptive force, as indeed she is, because it is imperative for her to attach herself to a man if she and her children are to survive. Mrs. Jarvis, the rector's wife, looks at Betty at church, and thinks "that marriage is a fortress, and widows stray solitary in the open fields, . . . lonely, unprotected, poor creatures" (8). But it never occurs to Mrs. Jarvis that marriage is a weak fortress if every married woman may become a widow.

And so Betty, without a way of supporting herself and her children, writes Captain Barfoot, who is married, long, tear-stained letters. She tells him what their lives are like; she hints that they need more help ("packed though we are like herrings in a barrel"); but she can't overtly ask for money, for that would be to break the rules of their unspoken agreement: he gives what he chooses, rather than what she needs. She lives in "poverty," (15) he is well-to-do; their relationship must be one of inequality. She is forced into depending upon the largesse of a man who has no legal responsibility for her; she has been clever enough to find one whose care is consistent and ongoing. Part of Captain Barfoot's attentions are due to the fact that he has no son of his own. His wife is an invalid; Betty makes him feel young and desirable. For twenty years, Betty has entertained Captain Barfoot on Wednesdays; she has been the sounding board for his plans and his political ambitions. Because of their relationship, Captain Barfoot provides the connections and the money that enable Jacob to go to Cambridge. Betty has been clever enough also to be slightly flirtatious with Mr. Floyd, who will give her sons free Latin lessons, but she refuses his offer of marriage, probably because he is less well-connected than Captain Barfoot, and ultimately, of less use to her.

The most important paradox in *Jacob's Room* is that a child whose growth we watch, whose mother must continually plot for his survival, will become nothing more than cannon fodder once the war has begun.[9] All of the love, time, and care that has gone into his rearing will count for nothing as he becomes one of the million like him who are killed in World War I. In this sense, *Jacob's Room* is Virginia Woolf's great pacifist novel. Because she begins with Jacob's childhood, because she details the attention that must be paid to small children by their caregivers, who are women, who engage in "the eternal conspiracy of hush and clean bottles," (13) she suggests that women have a great stake in preventing war.[10] She describes, with great accuracy, the fact that women like the servant Rebecca are made responsible for rearing the children of the Empire, while they themselves will not be permitted to have children of their own.[11] She points out the irony of making the rearing of children women's greatest and most important task, if those selfsame children are sent off to be killed as soon as their upbringing is over. In *Jacob's Room*, war becomes the ultimate devaluation of how women are required to spend their time as well as the ultimate expression of society's hatred of its own children.

When Virginia Woolf wrote of her plans for *To the Lighthouse* in her diary, she stressed that it would be about childhood and she attested to its autobiographical nature: "This is going to be fairly short: to have father's character done complete in it; & mothers; & St Ives; & childhood."[12] It was an ambitious undertaking, for instead of confining her attention to the lives of one or two children, she provides glimpses into the lives of the eight Ramsay children.

To the Lighthouse (1927) begins with what is one of the most famous family squabbles in literature.[13] Mrs. Ramsay, sitting with her young son, James, tells him that if the weather is fine tomorrow, the family excursion to the lighthouse that he has looked forward to will indeed take place. Mr. Ramsay, the ultimate realist, predicts, however, that "it won't be fine" (10). This unleashes a murderous fantasy in James; he imagines that if there had been "any weapon" nearby "that would have gashed a hole in his father's breast and killed him, there and then, James would have seized it" (10). James hates his father for many reasons: for continually interrupting the time that he has with his mother, for his aloofness, for his egotism, but most of all for "the twang and twitter of his father's emotion" which continually disturbs the peace. James also hates his father because his father confuses him; because he is inconsistent and unpredictable: Mr. Ramsay is indeed an egomaniac, but he is also tremendously seductive, and even tender. James hates him as well because he acts like a tragic hero, making sublime and grand gestures, holding his head in studied postures, forcing people to pay attention to his histrionics. But even as James feels himself to be Mr. Ramsay's victim, he believes that his mother has suffered more. In an earlier version of the novel, he describes her as "flaring up to be gashed and drunk and devoured by the beak of brass, the arid scimitar of the male which smote her, again, again, again, demanding sympathy."[14]

James's father holds a set of severe and unrelenting principles about how children should be dealt with. In an earlier version of the novel, Mr. Ramsay explains the reason for his statement about the trip to the lighthouse in this way: "children, of the male sex in particular, . . . should be from childhood made aware that life is hard, truth uncompromising," and they need, above all, "fortitude, truth, and the power to endure" (5h).

Although Mrs. Ramsay is able, for the moment, to pacify James, for she describes the trip as a possibility, she too inhabits a bleak cosmos. Indeed, the times when she believes in her ability to both support and guard her children and in her husband's ability to support and guard her are far rarer than the times when she sees life as a racing river which crashes "into the abyss" (25h).

Although we are not told the source of Mrs. Ramsay's world view, we are told that Mr. Ramsay's behavior is extremely unpredictable, and that he is given to moments in which his instability is exposed to public view, although his behavior is never described as anything more pathological than "eccentric." We also know that Mr. Ramsay, from time to time, is extremely cruel to his wife. At one point, Mrs. Ramsay is described as bending her head as he hurls abuse her way, "as if to let the pelt of jagged hail storm [and] the shower of dirty water bespatter her bowed shoulders" (62h). And yet, paradoxically, "there was no body whom she reverenced as she reverenced him" (63h).

From time to time, he retreats into a fantasy land in which he is "charging at the head of an army, and receiving wounds of which he died gloriously on the heights of Balaclava" (28h). His family and friends only know he is in that private place of his own when he bellows forth snatches of poetry which refer to his private nightmare. Mrs. Ramsay understands that "he needed privacy in which to regain his equilibrium" (6oh).

We can assume, from his recurrent fantasy of receiving wounds and dying, that at some time in his past, which is never described, he has in fact been severely emotionally wounded. He cannot control his outbursts just as he cannot control his rages: he is both "formidable" and "childish." He can both "frighten one to death" and then "behave worse than a baby" (31h). Lily Briscoe, a guest of the family, is so cowed by his rages that, when she looks at him, she is glad that she has never chosen to marry.

Both of the Ramsays are victims, even as they victimize their children. "Ramsay is the mutilated victim, cast out into the world, handicapped,"[15] but because he cannot understand his feelings, he reacts rather than acts. British society is the oppressor, the mutilator.

The Ramsays have eight children. A family friend, Mr. Bankes, refers to them as "vigorous, angular, ruthless youngsters" (49h). The point about their being ruthless is an important observation, for several of them already have developed a kind of barbarity in response to the code of ethics thrust upon them. We soon see one of them running off to engage in his favorite sport, shooting birds, which his mother thinks is a stage he'll grow out of. But she is myopic; her sons are being prepared for a war in which they will shoot the enemy rather than birds, so this is a stage that will not in fact pass at all.

The girls, we learn, are forced by their mother into a system of behavior which will render them handmaidens of the male sex. She permits no deviation from the life of service that she herself has chosen; nor will she even permit her daughters to speak of other ways of behaving: "it was only in silence that her daughters . . . could sport with those infidel ideas which certainly they had brewed for themselves, of a life far lovelier than hers, and less strict" (8h). One of them imagines a life on an "island among sea birds"; another, a life in Paris among painters; a third simply wishes for "a new life" (8h). She herself prefers the company of young men to that of her daughters. All of these men "had claims on her. It might be said indeed that she had taken the whole of the opposite sex under her protection" (7h). One of her daughters, Prue, "was a little afraid of her, and was her slave, and would never grow up or leave home, with her there" (192h). While Mrs. Ramsay is alive, Prue will have no life of her own.

In the beginning of the novel, although Mrs. Ramsay sits with James and thinks about him from time to time, there are only a few fleeting moments that she interacts with her youngest daughter, Cam, who is very close in age to James. When she makes a mental list of the members of the family, she forgets to include Cam, although she does include the family dog.[16]

We soon understand why she prefers to forget Cam. Although James contains his rage within his own thoughts, Cam acts her anger out. She is, in the words of Mr. Bankes, "wild and fierce."[17] In this family, the father is permitted to act like a baby, but "all emotion is bad to children" (69h)—the children are expected to act with reserve, but how are they to learn reserve if they live with outbursts? Nor will Cam perform those gestures of attention to men, so important to her mother, such as giving a flower to Mr. Bankes, as her nursemaid instructs her to. Cam is the child who deviates from what her mother wishes her to be, and she is already in the process of being frozen out of her mother's attentions, while James preoccupies his mother's time.

Mrs. Ramsay has her suspicions that all is not well with Cam, but she does not act on them. When she sees Cam, she uses language that suggests that her daughter has been harmed ("who had shot her") and she thinks of Cam as a projectile that "dropped dead to the earth in mid career" (94h). We do not know whether these images are the product of Mrs. Ramsay's own rage at Cam or whether indeed Cam has been harmed. Her mother's metaphor may indicate a subconscious knowledge that Cam has been harmed by her bird-shooting son. But there is something extremely worrisome about how Cam responds (or rather, doesn't respond) to her mother, and her mother thinks of her as "a sleep walker" (95h).

When her mother asks Cam to relay a message to the kitchen, Mrs. Ramsay wonders whether the message will be delivered accurately, for Cam always appears to be distracted. Her mind, according to her mother, is not clear; it is like a well whose waters are "extraordinarily distorting" (94h). When Cam talks, she uses "a parrot like instinct" to repeat her mother's words, which empties them of all content; she talks in "an absent minded singsong" (94h). Mrs. Ramsay does not, however, try to discern the reason for her daughter's vagueness. She turns, instead, to more pleasant matters: whether or not two of her guests, Minta and Paul, will marry. For Mrs. Ramsay, all hardship vanishes if she can engage in a fantasy about the possibility of romance.

Although it might be argued that she has so many responsibilities that she cannot be expected to pay close attention to any of her children, she can, however, find the time to be kind to the young men whom she refers to as "boobies," and she always has time for Minta and Paul. Nancy, one of her daughters, describes what it feels like to be one of so many children in this family: it was "being anonymous and amorphous as a jelly which floats hither and thither secretly absorbing nourishment" (97h).

Mrs. Ramsay wants and needs peace, and she is angry at Cam and James for fighting, but the fault, she believes in typical Victorian style, rests with Cam. She thinks "it was Cam's fault, mostly, because she was older and a little girl, and sisters ought to control their brothers" (99h).[18]

Completely oblivious to the sadness which permeates the lives of her children, Mrs. Ramsay continues to cling to the romance that a "child's power of happiness was something indescribable" (100h). She is able to maintain this illusion partly because of her own powers of denial—the "hidden pockets of emotion" in her relations with her children which "she never examined" (130h). But she has so little contact with her children that she can imagine that they're happy, and because her children cannot say what is on their minds. And so she listens to them from afar, in the nursery, and imagines them "absolutely happy," as happy as "birds among cherries" (100h). But she does not stop to examine the unconscious knowledge contained in that very metaphor, for throughout the opening pages of the novel, the birds around the Ramsay house are not safe at all: Jasper is continually trying to shoot them.

Mrs. Ramsay is relieved (as indeed any parent is) when her children go to bed, for, she thinks, "children never forget" (105h). She seems to wish that her children would develop amnesia; what they remember will be a source of trouble to her. She hopes for the free time, when they're grown, to be able to think about issues and problems which puzzle her, the main one of which is "how could any Lord have made this world . . . with its vice, its torture" (107h). But the lines are elliptical and the world's vice and its torture are never named.

Cam Ramsay has trouble sleeping; she is afraid of shadows. She is particularly afraid of the shadow that a boar's skull, which James likes, makes upon the wall. It hangs in the nursery, a present from a relative. One night when Mrs. Ramsay is called to put Cam back to sleep, she deals with the situation not by talking to Cam about her fear, but by taking her shawl and covering over the boar's skull; she croons to her daughter that the skull is nothing to be afraid of, that it looks lovely, that "the fairies would love it," that she would transform it into a "great bird's nest" (188h). James get his way; the boar's skull is not removed. Mrs. Ramsay tries to transform the skull into a less virulent image for Cam, but she does not find out why Cam is afraid and she is unwilling to take the boar's head down. She covers it up, just as she tries to get Cam not only to cover up her own fears, but to convert them into opposite feelings. By telling Cam that the fairies would love the skull she is training Cam to deny her fears rather than to express them.

But the most terrifying image in the early version of the "Time Passes" section of the novel, which records the events of ten years, the image which shatters the possibility for "harmony and completeness," is related to the boar's head that scares Cam. It is a reflection of "a pig's snout" in a mirror which "broke the mirror" (222h). This disgusting image is unlike those that Woolf would ultimately use in the "Time Passes" section. It must have been significant, for it is reworked many, many times in her various draft versions. In one version, the snout in the mirror "thrusting itself up meant death, and starvation, pain, it was difficult to abolish its significance, and to continue" (222h). In another, Woolf writes, "how could one forget" "that ugly snout" (222h).

In the longest and most fully worked version, the appearance of the snout in the mirror is the event which unleashes a storm of chaos and inappropriate matings:

> that black snout—that purple foaming stain—had so gravely damaged the composition of the picture that they had fled. They had gone in despair. They had dashed the mirror, to the ground. They saw nothing more. They stumbled and strove now, blindly, pulling their feet out of the mud and stamping them further in. Let the wind blow, let the poppy seed itself, and the carnation mate with the cabbage. Let the swallow build in the drawing room, and the thistle thrust up the tiles. . . . Let all civilisation be like broken china to be tangled over with blackberries and grass. (179h)

The tremendous autobiographic significance of the boar's head is apparent in the early version of the novel, for Virginia Woolf habitually called the Duckworth brothers "pigs" and the thing which scares Cam is a boar's head. The event that shatters the possibility of order, initiating, among other things, a period of unnatural cohabitations (the carnation mating with the cabbage) is the appearance of the pig's snout in a mirror, just as the event which so shattered Woolf's life was the experience of sexual molestation, which she probably saw in the mirror in the dining room passage.[19] Whether Woolf had access to the memory of Gerald Duckworth's molestation when she wrote *To the Lighthouse* or whether she was using an image the significance of which was not yet accessible to her, I cannot say. She had, by this time, described George Duckworth's sexual abuse and she referred to him as a pig.

I do believe it is significant that Mrs. Ramsay engages in the act of covering over the boar's skull with her shawl. In the early version of the story, as time passes Mrs. Ramsay's cover-up becomes undone. The shawl becomes unwrapped, and the boar's head is again revealed. Time undoes what Mrs. Ramsay had tried to conceal. This is the only instance that I know, in any of Woolf's writings, where it is even suggested, if only through metaphor, that her mother knew what had happened to her and had covered it up. But the image of the boar and pig's snout in the mirror unquestionably point to that trauma in Woolf's life, and to Woolf's knowledge that the dream of a harmonious life was shattered, just as "the snout broke the mirror" (222h).

In 1929, Virginia Woolf wrote of the new novel that she was planning, which became *The Waves* (1931),[20] that it might be called "Autobiography."[21] Musing about how it might begin, she wrote, "this shall be Childhood; but it must not be *my* childhood."[22] It was extremely important that the childhood that she depicted would represent, not her life, but, as she phrased it in her plans in an early draft, "the life of anybody."[23] *The Waves* is a powerful and sorrowful evocation of the condition of childhood. After her friend Ethel Smyth read it, she wrote that the book was "profoundly disquieting, sadder than any book I ever read."[24]

In the earliest version of the novel (which I will rely upon in the ensuing discussion), Woolf's portrait of childhood is even sadder than in the published text, and she addressed even more directly and uncompromisingly the idea that childhood is a universally horrible time. It is extremely disquieting that the "many millions"[25] of the world's children are presented as if they have no parents; they exist, but no one seems to care for them. In an image which she revised numerous times, the act of birth takes on an aspect of extreme violence, as the mothers of the world, who are depicted as waves, cast their newborn children upon the shore and abandon them to fate: the waves "were many mothers and many mothers; and each as it sank forced onto the beach a child";[26] the only difference was that some, "with rather higher velocity than the others threw their burden further."[27]

In this world without caring, an early truth that the children must learn is that "life . . . is . . . to be endured," and an early insight into the human condition must be that "life is vile." Nor can the impact of the "harshness" of these facts be blunted for these children (all children), for "there is nothing to temper it."[28] All that can be done to ease the bleakness, to "feel that all is not blank," is to share the sorrow: it is necessary to know that "when I weep, I am not the only weeper."[29] What unites children is the sorrow they share.

By the time they are ten years old, their hearts are not happy, innocent, gay, and free. They are "ravaged" by difficult emotions, by "jealousy and hatred."[30] By this time, they have already experienced sexual jealousy: the most disquieting moment of the character Susan's life is that she has seen two of the other children kissing. Rather than their hearts being filled with innocence, the hearts of these children are filled with something different, which can only be suggested by a trio of repulsive metaphors: "it was snail slime, the sticky fluid in the hollow stalk and the rat heaving with maggots" that was "in the hearts of those unfortunate children."[31]

In a carefully rewritten metaphor, Woolf compared the so-called innocence of childhood to the protection which is afforded by the white enamel in bathrooms. In an upstairs bedroom, she wrote, a child sleeps, seemingly innocent and pure. But life invades that "innocency" through "crevices" and "cracks in the armour of innocence." The crevice, the crack in the armour of innocence is the vaginal opening. And in a stunning and explicit metaphor, Woolf describes how the child is penetrated, deflowered, and how she loses her innocence: "Exposed to the battery, the enamel, so white and smooth as the child stood up in its bath, gave way; through the hard shell something penetrated."[32]

This would be bad enough if there were someone to whom the pain, the sorrow, the suffering could be communicated. But this is far from the case. Parents have "forgotten their own childhood."[33] When a child runs away from an encounter like the one described, people look, but they feel nothing but "some vague unbalance"; "the fact remained that there was only one receptive mind in the whole neighborhood."[34] The mind receptive to the suffering of children is the mind of the woman writing the story of these children. She becomes the children's ally, for she is telling their story, a story that must be told, a story that is a dirge for the idyll of childhood.

It is no wonder, then, that Rhoda (speaking for millions of children) sees herself outside the loop of time. She looks into the mirror of the self and finds either that there is nothing there or that someone else is there: when Rhoda looks into the glass, she thinks "that she had no face."[35] Thrown up onto the beach of life, left there to scramble as best as they could, these children are profoundly dispirited and disoriented. They do not know who they are; they do not know how to find out: they are "eyeless" but they are also "I-less." They are utterly alone. They say to themselves: "Here am I entirely alone in the world. I am on a rocky island like Robinson Crusoe; How shall I make myself a raft?"[36] Childhood is a desolate island which is inimical to survival; to escape it, children themselves must make a way to safety; but their being able to do that seems slim, given how young they are.

Each child feels that there was a world, somewhere, that was "complete, circular; . . . everything in order,"[37] but that they were not of that world, but "outside of it," where the experience is that of incompleteness, chaos, fragmentation, and a necessary profound and utter isolation, given that each encounter with another human being is pernicious. The character who feels this deeply is Rhoda.

When she is in school, she tries to close the "loop of the figure six." She hears "time beating," the world outside "continuing its enormous existence with complete indifference to her own shrunken body." She is stuck within the loop of the figure six, and she can't get out. She felt "all power of movement had gone from her; being outside the world, . . . her movements were indifferent, she had no existence."[38]

Rhoda's being stuck in the loop of the figure six surely points to Woolf's being stuck in the emotional trauma that occurred when she was six, although it is unclear whether the memory of her abuse had surfaced by the time she wrote *The Waves*. Like Woolf's memory of being unable to cross the puddle in the path, Rhoda too cannot cross a puddle which she meets in her path because "nothingness possessed her" and "the power to lift her feet was gone."[39] In this early version, Rhoda begins to write of her experience. (In the published text it is Bernard who is the writer, the maker of phrases.) She writes of her experience "bitterly in prose"; she writes of "the brutality of the rest" because she envies what she perceives as their pleasure; she thought that "nothing in the world could be so exciting as to go among them spontaneously laughing."[40] Their world, the world which the "sun shines on" is not her world; in her story, "the world was different."[41]

The other children share similar feelings to Rhoda's, although Rhoda's feelings are by far the most profoundly nihilistic.

As Kathleen Walsh D'Arcy has written of the published text, "School, for all children, is a war zone" where children are "caned or birched into submission."[42] D'Arcy has described how images of war and violence pervade Woolf's description of schooling: the children are like "convoys marching through a desert"; the children form pairs "and walk in order" (24). The extinction of the self, begun in the nursery, is completed in the classroom where, as Rhoda puts it, we are "unfriended . . . I will not cry" (33). As Susan says, "I would bury the classroom."[43]

What makes it worse is that "many of the million children were tortured by the revelations . . . made to them, almost daily, of unmentionable vices."[44] An important part of their education is to learn that they are, by nature, corrupt and vile. The effect is alarming, for without a loving person to reach out to, their vices become the only certainty for them, the only thing they really can be sure of—their vices, their evils become comfortable companions, almost their friends. As the children go about, each "named and hugged its vice, and went off to brood over the swollen vein; the startling vision; the burnt or bruised fibre in flesh only that morning white and sweet."[45]

In one enigmatic encounter, Woolf describes Susan's pain and how a boy, called Roger in this draft, responded to it. He feels her unhappiness and responds to it as if it is a real wound: he "had to stop the blood,"[46] in the one genuine moment of empathy that is expressed here. What happens as he follows her is uncertain, but it is phrased in this way: "He pulled at Susan's skirt lagging leaving her green and soft, parched no longer, no longer dry and sore; but astonished, amazed at what happens or can happen if somebody comes up from behind like Roger; . . . and then one goes exploring."[47] This might be an elliptical expression of an erotic encounter. If it is, it echoes other moments in which the children try to make contact with one another, but through quasi-sexual encounters, which echo those of Virginia and her sister Vanessa, which confuse them rather than enrich their parched souls. In one, the character Jinny sees a man looking at her on a train and she feels energized, but when he looks away, "the whole apparatus of her body collapsed like a shut parasol."[48] In another, Jinny kisses Louis against his will; it doesn't make him happy. Rather, "it was as if a spring, jagged and red hot, from a steel bolt had struck him on the nape of the neck."[49] Yet his body seems to respond to the unwanted kiss even against his will, which confuses him: a partially canceled passage uses nature imagery—Louis's hand "holding a stalk"[50]—to suggest how his body responds against his will; Louis becomes aware of "the thick sticky liquid inside the tube"; another passage suggests an erection: "the tube formed a thick bubble on the end of the stalk. Yet he had not wished it."[51]

In this early version of the novel, Woolf also attempted to describe the class differences between children and how that affected their lives. There is even a moment in which a socialist vision for the future is imagined: the waves toss up babies, and there is a hope that "all distinctions" among them based upon class would be "obliterated forever."[52] Woolf canceled this passage even in this version, and the issue was discarded almost entirely in the published text. Here, however, there are constant reminders of the lives of working-class children, and how they began to work for the rich while they were still very young: she writes that while some children were at their desks, "more children, not sitting at desks" were "washing up plates";[53] she describes how certain of the children "would be going to schools in Switzerland about the same time that Florrie went out for the first time as a kitchenmaid";[54] and she described that children were "doing odd jobs in their spare time like minding babies or carrying parcels."[55] It is a splendid description, for Woolf suggests, in her juxtaposition of caring for babies and carrying parcels, that the privileged classes are really not providing very much care for their offspring if they use the labor of girls who are mere children themselves. Yet it is these servants who provide the only real care that these children will ever have.

Perhaps aware that the condition of childhood that she was exploring was vastly different from other views, Woolf wrote, "I am not laying too great a stress upon all this. I am not exaggerating the intensity of children's feelings." And in an extremely direct and unequivocal statement, she wrote: "Nothing . . . exaggerates the torture of childhood. People say that children are happy. They forget the terrible revelations;

the faces that look out from behind leaves; the surprises; the intimations; the sudden shadows on the ceilings."[56] Woolf's vision of childhood phrased here is one of terror, and one of violence. What makes it worse is that the child can never rest from the likelihood that something horrible will happen.

In the novel, children are not a source of comfort to one another; "when . . . children [are] brought together, naturally they inflict terrible pain upon each other."[57] As Rhoda phrases it, closeness will inevitably bring, not pleasure, not even pain, but rather the extinction of the self: "if you insist upon drawing me into your life," she says, "you will destroy me."[58]

In childhood, Rhoda could not step over the puddle because her "own identity" was "nothing." She saves herself in childhood by touching something that is hard, something that is solid. What she touches so that she can come back to the world, so that she can reclaim her sense of identity is "the wall of the house."[59] The metaphor is obvious: Rhoda needs the solidity of what the house represents if she is to survive.

The other characters find some solace as adults, in love, in work, in children, in sex, in power, and in position, but beneath the veneer each of them continues to feel isolated, tortured, bereft, and alone. But Rhoda remains outside the loop of time. Just before her death, she tries to explain what she feels to the others: she remembers the puddle from childhood and not being able to cross it; she tells them that she has no body, that she cannot save herself, and that she hears the "roar of annihilation," the grinding of millstones, "one whirling round within an inch of the other and I am pinned between. All the palpable forms of life have failed me. Unless I can touch something I shall fall down and die."[60]

In adulthood, Rhoda can no longer fend off the reality that all that the house represents, upon which her identity is based, is a chimera, an illusion. The wall of the house ultimately dissolves for Rhoda because its solidity was an illusion. She reaches out to touch it, to steady her, to help her come back to herself. It is not there. And so Rhoda kills herself. Woolf explored the connection between childhood experience and suicidal impulses again, in the character of Rose Pargiter, in her next novel, *The Years*.[61]

In 1931, Virginia Woolf conceptualized a new book which would be about "the sexual life of women."[62] In 1932, she wrote "the child scene" of *The Years* (1937),[63] a scene that represented the nature of girlhood. The novel recounted the lives of generations of a single family, the Pargiters, from 1880 to the present day. The childhood scene was about a "man exposing himself" to Rose Pargiter, aged ten, as she left the Pargiter household alone one evening to buy a toy for herself at Lamleys, a neighborhood store. The scene reverberates throughout the novel. Rose recalls it throughout her life as the moment that has shaped her very being. It has caused her to become a committed political activist, a suffragist, who goes on hunger strike, who gets force-fed, sitting on a "three-legged stool having meat crammed down her throat" (232), and who, at one point, goes to jail for throwing a brick.

Rose has grown up in a typical middle-class Victorian household. In an earlier version of the novel, her father, Abel Pargiter, is described as believing that "a girl's place was the home."[64] When the novel opens, Rose's mother is dying; her father can't bring himself to enter the room of his dying wife. Instead, he distracts himself by going to the lodgings of his mistress, a working-class woman, who is pregnant, probably with his child. This leaves Rose, the youngest, overlooked, as the elder daughters brood about their entrapment within the household, to render their mother the care she requires.

It is within the context of her mother dying (very much like that of Virginia Woolf's own life) that Rose becomes traumatized by seeing the man exposing himself. In an earlier version of the novel, *The Pargiters* (which was published posthumously), Woolf described that nothing affected the lives of the Pargiter girls more directly than "the principle of that love which . . . may be called street love, common love."[65] It was because of this kind of love that the elder girls—Eleanor and Milly and Delia—"could not go for a walk alone." Their confinement to the house was explained by the principle that the lust of men was predatory, and that they would become its victims if they walked outside alone. Abercorn Terrace, where they lived, was "besieged on all sides by . . . street love"; the streets of London were not streets, but a "swamp alive with crocodiles."[66]

But Rose has already been experiencing difficulty with her brother Bobby at home. Now that her brother has become a "proper schoolboy," he has begun mistreating her—he "snear[s] at her and treat[s] her as if she were a baby." Most importantly, he has laid claim to the school room, which he tries to prevent her from entering, and she is confined to the day nursery when he is at his lessons. She is both dispossessed from a place that they had shared and confined to a place that represents her continued infantilization. This territorial battle signals the split between these siblings, who used to be close, and Rose refuses to "give up her claim" to the space that they had shared in common, "without a fight."[67]

Because a girl of ten is not permitted outside of the Pargiter household alone, and because Rose gets shunted around when she asks for help (all are preoccupied with her ailing mother), Rose tries to get Bobby to come with her to Lamleys. She realizes, however, that he has become the enemy, and she decides, in a burst of anger at having been displaced, both in his affections and from the school room, to do the forbidden thing, to go to Lamleys alone.

To quell her fear, she makes it into a game, a game that she and Bobby used to play in the nursery, "about Red Indians."[68] It is a game fit for imperialist children to play, about colonizing and dispossessing a race of people. Within the Pargiter household, Rose's plight—being displaced from the nursery—becomes aligned with that of the Red Indians, as Bobby takes on the colonizer's role of their old game, only now he is playing it (and winning) with Rose as the enemy. Imperialism, Woolf suggests, is learned at home in the way that boys are encouraged, after infancy, to treat their sisters.

Rose, uncomfortable with the image of herself as victim, goes out to Lamleys playing the role of the imperialist: she becomes, in her fancy, "Colonel Pargiter of Pargiters Horse," "riding by night on a deadly mission through hostile territory." Her responsibility is to bring a secret message to the English, who are besieged: "Her head was full of her father's old stories of the Indian Mutiny."[69]

Still in the persona of the game, Rose sees "the figure of a man"—the "enemy," under the gas lamp. She clenches her imaginary revolver, looks him full in the face, and pretends to shoot him: "Bang! she said to herself. What a horrible face." In her imagination, she has triumphed, and she trots past him, thinking to herself that she had "cut off the head of the chief rebel," which she "carried under her arm as a trophy"[70] and she makes her way, triumphant, into Lamleys.

On her way back, however, their roles are reversed. He is still there, under the gas lamp. The reader does not know whether Rose's posture as the assailant, looking at the man with such obvious revulsion, prompts him to expose himself as she runs past him. But he gibbers at her, sucks his lips, "and began to undo his clothes." More frightening, however, is that she thinks he starts to chase her. And that night she wakes up and sees a "grey leering face" above her; she believes that the man has gotten into the house: "She cried Nurse! Nurse! But no one answered her."[71]

Rose tries to get help, both from the nurse and from her sister Eleanor. But no one will listen to her tale to help her sort out her feelings, to help her understand the link between her rage at her brother, her behavior, her guilt at having transgressed a rule. Woolf suggests that this is because it is the aim of the Pargiter family to control Rose's behavior by having her become afraid of the outside world, so that she will not venture into it; no one intends to help Rose with her fear, because it is necessary for her to learn to be afraid.

When Rose tells the nurse that she has had a bad dream, the nurse tells her it's because of what she ate and tells her not to be silly. The nurse does not want to aid her young charge; she wants to be free of her to enjoy the one pleasure that she has, a "gossip with Mrs. C." Rose tries to tell Eleanor about her fear. Eleanor immediately thinks that it must have been Bobby who frightened her, so it is clear that Bobby has been mistreating Rose: "Eleanor thought it would be a good thing when Bobby went to his boarding school, and left Rose to settle down."[72]

In *The Pargiters*, Woolf used the device of an interchapter to explain the significance of her story.[73] Here she comments on Rose's experience: "The actual fact," she writes, "that children of Rose's age are frequently assaulted, and sometimes far more brutally than she was— is familiar to any one who reads the Police Court news."[74]

Woolf was using Rose's experience to make an important point, that children commonly experience sexual assault. It is important that Woolf interprets the man's exposing himself as sexual assault. Rose is so ashamed about what has happened, because she has been indoctrinated into the belief that it is a girl's responsibility to stay at home so that she won't invite assault (male lust being uncontrollable, even if the only female in sight is a ten-year-old girl), that she concludes that "she could not tell any one."[75] And she is quite right; she knows, already, that if she tells, she will be worse off than if she does not.

But Woolf remarks that it is very difficult to give "a faithful account" of the effect of the experience "upon her mind." Her first response, she says, was "to turn away and hide herself." Rose is ashamed because, within the context of Victorian culture, she has invited the attack. Woolf states that this common experience of childhood assault is ignored by novelists, because "biographers and autobiographers also ignore it." The ellipsis that the novelist is forced to insert after the sentence, "He unbuttoned his clothes . . . ," Woolf indicates, is a literary convention, "supported by law," which forbids any candid discussion of Rose's experience, an experience that she has "in common with many other little girls."[76] It is therefore impossible to write honestly and forthrightly about sexual abuse. The law prevents it.

The sexual assault of little girls, Woolf interpreted, was part of the way that girls were socialized into their own inferiority. What happens to Rose outside the house occurs at the same time that Bobby becomes "rougher" with her at home; and he is even rougher with her when his friends are there. Woolf indicates that he treats Rose like this because he himself is being mistreated by a boy at school. But Bobby is being initiated into an all-male fellowship. He is proud that his friend uses the word "prostitute" in front of him, for using that word "initiate[d] Bobby" into a great fellowship, "the fellowship of men together," and "it was essential that Rose should be kept out."[77]

In *The Pargiters*, Rose is very much in love with her father, who has played intricate games with his children. In the published version, *The Years*, the only reaction that Rose gets from her father, however, is that he notices a stain on her dress, he pinches her ear, and calls her "grubby little ruffian" (16). All of his playfulness is reserved for the daughters of his sister-in-law Eugenie, Sara and Maggie, with whom it is suggested that he is having an affair. Indeed, later in the novel, Maggie wonders if she is Abel Pargiter's daughter.

He brings Maggie a present for her birthday; he is irritated that Maggie's own father has forgotten her birthday, even though he himself has been less than intimate with his own children. While Eugenie and Abel lose themselves in one another's company, Eugenie permits her daughters to engage in the "game" of playing near a blazing bonfire.

In *The Years*, Woolf suggests that adultery serves to distance parents from their children: Abel Pargiter stays home only as long as appearances require; as his wife is dying, he is engaged in amorous play with Mira, his current mistress. And Sara, Eugenie's child, fares as poorly as Rose: "She had been dropped when she was a baby." Her deformity—one shoulder is slightly higher than another—makes Abel Pargiter "squeamish; he could not bear the least deformity in a child" (122). He is also deformed; his hand is clawlike as a result of a war injury, but he cannot connect his feeling about Sara with himself. Both Rose and Sara are the childhood victims of the kind of neglect that runs rampant in the nurseries of *The Years*. As the years pass, Sara comes to believe in the inherent depravity of human beings; she says that in time, people will say of them all, "Pah! They stink," a feeling which Maggie echoes; she sees human beings as "driven by uncontrollable lusts" (189). Sara believes that children should be brought up "on a desert island," isolated from grownups, where supply ships and possible contaminating influences only come once a month.

In *The Years*, Rose later tells Eleanor and Martin (who was called Bobby in *The Pargiters*) that she has tried to kill herself as a result of the Lamleys incident and Martin's turning away from her: " 'I dashed into the bathroom and cut this gash'—she held out her wrist" (157). Eleanor, who has lived in the same house with Rose, has never known that her sister tried to kill herself. Their isolation from one another occurs within a household that is itself isolated from the world: Sara calls the Pargiter household, "the caravan crossing the desert" (170). Martin's response to Rose's confession is bizarre: "Oh," he says in response to seeing the scar on his sister's wrist, "Rose always was a firebrand," and he attributes her suicide attempt to the fact that she "had the devil's own temper." He believes that Rose's suicide attempt is the result of her own nature, but he does concede that children lead "awful lives" (157), and later, comes to realize that "it was an abominable system; . . . family life" (222).

At the end of the novel, in the present day, Eleanor sees a picture of Mussolini, "a fat man gesticulating"; she suddenly shouts out, "bully!" but she soon connects the picture of the fat Fascist with what happened to Rose. Although Eleanor believes that things have gotten better with time, she does recall that a friend has described war as "children playing with fireworks in the back yard" (329). The connection between male privilege, the education of boys, the treatment of girls, and fascism was to become a major theme of Woolf's analysis of childhood in the closing years of her life.

In *Three Guineas* (1938), Virginia Woolf reexamined the position of girls and women in light of the turmoil in Europe, and argued that the position of "the educated man's sister" "in the house of freedom" has been vastly different from that of her brothers;[78] the condition of girls and women in the homes of England she saw as akin to being shut up "like slaves in a harem" (74).[79] Her comparison built upon the one made by John Stuart Mill between the condition of women and that of slaves,[80] but Woolf extended the simile by suggesting that the slavery includes the sexual use of girls and women by their brothers and fathers.[81] She believed that there was a link between patriarchy as an institution and the sexual servitude of women; she saw incest as an almost necessary outcome of the utter dominance over the lives of girls and their mothers by the men in a household.

As Judith Lewis Herman has phrased it, the incestuous family is "an exaggeration of patriarchal family norms, but not a departure from them,"[82] and Woolf was observing precisely this point. The condition of girls within middle-class Victorian households duplicated, in every respect, those that have been found to be a precondition for the sexual victimization of girls—"a male prerogative to supervise and restrict the activities of the females" with the father exercising "minute control over the lives of their wives and daughters, often virtually confining them to the house."[83]

But perhaps Woolf's boldest and most controversial comparison in *Three Guineas* was between the condition of girls and women and that of the Jews in Europe, who had become subjected to the psychotic purposes of Hitler. Woolf compared the patriarchal father in his household with the strutting, posturing, and demonic brutality of the Fascist dictator. There, in the private house, she said, "we have in embryo the creature, Dictator as we call him when he is Italian or German, who believes that he has the right, whether given by God, Nature, sex or race is immaterial, to dictate to other human beings how they shall live; what they shall do" (53).

Woolf suggests that it is perplexing that all are in agreement that "the dictator when we meet him abroad is a very dangerous as well as a very ugly animal," yet a father in a patriarchal household has always been able to behave like a dictator, and those same patriots who condemn dictatorship abroad do not condemn it when it is practiced upon girls and women within the confines of English families. Woolf's point was, quite simply, that there are dictators "here among us . . . in the heart of England," and that the men of England should help its women "to crush him in our own country before we ask her to help us to crush him abroad" (53). For Woolf, there was something utterly bizarre about asking women to join with men in resisting tyranny abroad, while requiring that women submit to the tyranny of their fathers and brothers at home.

Woolf stated that there was a vehement denunciation against "the tyranny of the Fascist state" because it subjected men to the same tyranny that women had been required to submit to: now men were feeling "in your own persons" what women have always felt "when they were shut out, when they were shut up, because they were women. Now you are being shut out, you are being shut up, because you are Jews, because you are democrats, because of race, because of religion" (102).

As she phrased it in "Thoughts on Peace in an Air Raid,"[84] "Who is Hitler? What is he? Aggressiveness, tyranny, the insane love of power made manifest." If that is, in fact, what Hitler is, then, Woolf says, one must agree with Lady Astor when she says that women have for long been victimized because of a "subconscious Hitlerism in the hearts of men."[85] Tyranny cannot be eliminated by combating it abroad without first confronting it at home. We must, Woolf argues, "drag it up into consciousness," this "desire to dominate and enslave."[86]

To suggest that the Englishman in his home behaved like a Hitler was a radical argument, for it attacked those who saw the Fascists as barbarians and the resisters to Fascism as civilizers. To argue that an Englishman was a tyrant like Hitler was to undercut the very essence of how the Englishman perceived himself. In *Three Guineas*, Woolf argued that Hitler was not an aberration and, moreover, that he was not a new phenomenon. Hitler's voice, she commented, "is an old voice, it is the voice of Creon in *Antigone*" who, in shutting up Antigone in the tomb because of her refusal to obey him, brought catastrophe to his land, littering his land with the bodies of the dead, as the bodies of the dead piled up all over Europe. Tyranny has a long history. The reason for the "ruined houses," the mutilated bodies of children, the corpses all over Europe was the direct outgrowth of a tyranny that begins at home in the dominion that men permitted themselves to exercise over their daughters and their wives: "the public and the private worlds are inseparably connected," she wrote, "the tyrannies and servilities of the one are the tyrannies and servilities of the other" (142): Hitler and his Germany were not different in kind from the rule of the father in England, simply different in degree.

Soon after Roger Fry's death on 9 September 1934, Virginia Woolf was asked if she would write the official biography of this man who was a distinguished art critic, her old friend, and her sister Vanessa's former lover. She began Roger Fry's life with an account of his childhood. Rather than try to describe it all, she struck upon the device of choosing moments that were significant—"specimen days."[87] Woolf chose four such moments—a memory of his family's garden in Highgate, London; one of his father skating; a "lesson" with his mother; and an episode at Sunninghill House, his boarding school. All demonstrated that Roger's childhood was far from idyllic.

Roger Fry's "first great disillusion" (15) came in connection with his first great passion, a clump of intensely red oriental poppies that he had coaxed into existence. Once, "the plant was full of fat green flower buds with little pieces of crumpled scarlet silk showing through the cracks between the sepals" (15–16). Roger remembered thinking that "nothing in the world could be more exciting than to see the flower suddenly burst its green case and unfold its immense cup of red" (16).

He sat down on a stool to wait patiently, throughout an entire day if necessary, to witness that moment.

But Roger was "duly laughed at" for his behavior by his elder sister. If that were not bad enough, she told the grownups, and he was laughed at by them as well. What he remembered as an adult—a specimen moment—stood for a pattern in his family: "all passions even for red poppies leave one open to ridicule" (16).

In an ideal world, or a different family, his diligence, excitement, commitment, perseverance, curiosity, and love for beauty might have earned applause. Yet he was ridiculed. An important moment for him was treated with scorn; he was left with feelings of isolation, humiliation, and self-doubt. The fact that he preserved his passion for beauty was a personal triumph, but it also caused him great pain and alienation.

This incident was rendered even more puzzling because of another specimen moment, a vivid memory of his father ice skating and his memory that his father was "passionately fond of skating." Fry also remembered that his father made an incongruous spectacle "as he scuttered along" (20) in severe long black coattails and top hat. On the days that he skated, Roger's father was *himself* enjoying something but no one dared censure him. How different Roger's father was then from the father whose "voice was of such an awful gravity" when reprimanding a child, "that one shrunk at once to helpless self-condemnation and overpowering shame" (21).

Roger was brought up in an austere Quaker household; his mother "drilled [him] to implicit obedience."[88] Another specimen moment occurred when Roger's mother was teaching him botany. She told him to go and pick a poppy so that she could illustrate the flower's structure. His training had taught him that this was prohibited, for it would be tampering with nature, "an almost sacrilegious act" (16). But his mother had told him to do it, and he was trained to obey. He ran to pick the poppy, overriding his internal sense that it was wrong.

But his mother had sprung a trap to test him.[89] She had set up a situation to demonstrate how easily one falls into wrongful behavior if one is not forever watchful. She was testing to see if he would violate one of their deeply held principles, regardless of what she told him.

He failed the test, and she "gravely reproved" when he returned with the flower.

It was the most painful moment he remembered. He felt betrayed, confused, and disillusioned. He came upon "the horrible discovery" that "justice is not supreme, that innocence is no protection." This experience was devastating because Roger's mother was not responding to something that he himself had done. She had initiated the act of wrongdoing; he saw it as a profound betrayal, for she had used his absolute obedience to her will, a product of her own training, to trap him. It was a shock that he would leave him "still tingling" (16) some fifty years later.

But he did not record that he was enraged at her, even though rage would have been appropriate. (He probably had already learned to suppress that emotion.) Woolf records the fact that Roger, even after this incident, "respected her" (18). Woolf does not blame Lady Fry: she briefly describes Lady Fry's *own* childhood, one in which "there were more denials than delights, more austerities than luxuries in the life of the little Quaker girl" and she quotes from Lady Fry's list of "things that were not . . . when I was a little child: night-lights; Christmas trees; . . . spring mattresses." She tells that, as a girl, her father had ordered the tight, fashionable sleeves to be cut out of her dress and replaced with large, out-of-fashion ones, which provoked ridicule; she always remembered how the boys jeered at her, shouting "Quack! Quack!" (17). Woolf wrote that "the effect of such an upbringing was permanent" (18) and was the reason why "her eyes remained firmly yet uneasily shut" to the sights which, to her son, were objects of great beauty.

The fourth specimen moment is horrifying. It was an extremely important moment for Woolf to describe, for it broke the silence surrounding the treatment of boys in public schools.[90] Roger was sent to Sunninghill House, chosen in part because his parents were assured by the headmaster, Sneyd-Kynnersley, that corporal punishment, which would be an infringement of Quaker principles, was not permitted. But Roger soon began sending Lady Fry letters which told a terrifying tale; she kept these letters "neatly tied in little bundles" (30), but they didn't seem to provoke any response from her or her husband.

Roger was routinely and repeatedly subjected to violence and abuse by two boys who teamed up to "bully me as much as they can." They hit him routinely, but their two favorite forms of torture were "to try and keep me under water" and "to upset me when we bathe" (30). These were obvious violations of the principles by which he had been raised and real threats to his well-being, yet his parents did nothing to intervene.

Roger's letters reported other disturbing events, beatings inflicted upon the boys by the headmaster who supposedly forbade corporal punishment.[91] Roger wrote about the severe floggings that were taking place routinely, and for very little cause. One letter told how a boy wouldn't submit to a beating for being in his friend's room. Roger, as head boy, was forced to perform a despicable duty, which went against his Quaker upbringing: "I . . . had to hold him down" (31).

Sneyd-Kynnersley explained to the boys, "with solemn gusto," that he "reserved to himself the right to a good sound flogging with the birch rod." Fry was forced to witness and to participate in these acts which "poisoned my whole life there" (32). Again, Roger wrote his mother letter after letter; again, neither of his parents intervened, even though the headmaster had lied to them.

The boys were beaten until they bled profusely; they were also beaten until they lost control of their bowels.

> In the middle of the room was a large box draped in black cloth and in austere tones the culprit was told to take down his trousers and kneel before the block over which I and the other head boy held him down. The swishing was given with the master's full strength and it took only two or three strokes for drops of blood to form everywhere and it continued for 15 or 20 strokes when the wretched boy's bottom was a mass of blood. . . . Nor did the horrors even stop there. There was a wild red-haired Irish boy, himself rather a cruel brute, who whether deliberately or as a result of the pain or whether he had diarrhoea, let fly. The irate clergyman instead of stopping at once simply went on with increased fury until the whole ceiling and walls of his study were spattered with filth. (33)

Fry was forced to conclude that the headmaster was a sadist, because he became excited "by the wretched victim's performance" (33).

Sneyd-Kynnersley was a man of the cloth, a graduate of Cambridge, who, as Roger phrased it, "was as high church as was consistent with being very much the gentleman, almost a man of the world" (32) and this was extremely unsettling. Yet he was not entirely despicable; what caused even greater conflict was that he so obviously enjoyed the boys' company, read Dickens to them each evening, took them on expeditions, treated them to lavish high teas. It would have been far easier for Roger if the headmaster had been completely reprehensible; then his behavior would have been comprehensible. But Roger had to deal with sadistic behavior in a person who, in other respects, was virtuous, kindly, and highly regarded.

Because Sunninghill was a school that prohibited corporal punishment, one wonders how boys must have been treated in schools which permitted it. Even this most "humane" school was being run by a sadist. By indicating that the Frys did nothing to interfere, Woolf implies that the brutality was not considered extraordinary. Mr. Sneyd-Kynnersley was representative of the kind of man who instructed boys like Roger; his parents apparently did not perceive him as a perverted psychopath, for they did nothing to intervene; this irony was not lost on Roger.

When Woolf first undertook the project, she had discussed her wish to say something about the family with Margery Fry (his sister); Margery replied, "Now there of course I'm afraid I should have to ask you to be careful."[92] Woolf, however, hit upon the solution of allowing Fry to speak of his family and his schoolboy experiences himself; she used fragments from his unpublished autobiography and his letters.[93] She would not omit recording what had happened to him; nor would she undercut the pain and brutality of his experiences. Rather, her solution was brave, provocative, and radical, and one that she would use herself in exploring her own past in her autobiography, "A Sketch of the Past." It was also a stroke of genius, because one can well imagine the furor if she herself had written of the Sunninghill incident. In using Roger's words, she was doing her duty by him; her critics might scoff at her method, but they could not accuse her of misrepresenting his life. Attention would have to be paid to the incident.

Her method is an early example of allowing the victim of violence to "speak out," to break the silence, without censure, without questioning the veracity of the memory. She acted as if the integrity of the child's memory must be respected and presented. She worked under the assumption that memories of childhood are essentially accurate representations of what happened. Although these moments may require a great deal of scrutiny to yield their full meaning, and although the full meaning and shape of what happened might not become understandable until adulthood, Woolf believed that their significance would ultimately become apparent. In recording Roger's childhood in this way, Woolf demonstrates a profound respect for the ability of the child to attach significance to events and for the adult to later comprehend what happened in childhood.

In *Roger Fry*, Woolf does not impose meaning upon the events that she records. Rather, she was trying to record the sense that Roger made of his own life. She cites Roger Fry's belief in the "hypocrisy of the Victorian age" (184), and she records that, from childhood, because of the kinds of specimen moments that she has recorded, he had developed a hatred of "families and patriarchalism of all kinds" (281). Family life, for Roger, was a lonely time, a time of pain and brutality, cruelty and betrayal. In writing Roger's childhood, unlike so many biographers,[94] Woolf refused to lie, to cover up, to mythologize, or to romanticize. For what Woolf had unearthed in her researches into the piles of documents that she read was a system of child rearing in the Fry household that undermined the integrity of Roger Fry's ego, sensibility, and vision, even though it instilled some fine qualities, such as intellectual honesty, hard work, and rigor, into his character. This system, she understood, was not due to any villainy on the part of Fry's parents, but rather reflected their own Quaker upbringing and the times in which they were raising their children—a climate of Victorian hypocrisy and a family system that was patriarchal.

Woolf recorded Roger's response to his school experiences as well: "my horror of these executions," he wrote, "has given me all my life a morbid horror of all violence between men" (34), one possible response to his childhood trauma. But she also records, through the example of the brutes who beat Roger and held him under water, that a likely response to this violence was to become violent oneself.[95]

The question that Woolf raises is the effect of this brutality inflicted upon boys in boarding schools. The boys who were flogged were expected to *endure* the beatings with stoic resignation. Fry recounts that he himself found it almost harder to hear the boys crying out from pain than to watch the beatings themselves: "sometimes there were scenes of screaming, howling and struggling which made me almost sick with disgust" (33). Rather than considering these reactions appropriate, Fry had already internalized a code which labeled the screaming, howling, and struggling as disgusting. If one bellowed, one was beaten even more, and so it was quickly learned that the only way to control the length of the beating was to control oneself.

Woolf undertook the writing of Roger Fry's life throughout the years when England was watching Hitler, wondering whether there would be another war: as she wrote into her diary, Hitler "adds so much friction to my work on Roger."[96] In 1937, by the time that Woolf was well into her biography, her nephew Julian Bell was killed in the Spanish Civil War. As England drew closer and closer to war, she witnessed the fact that "the man in uniform is exalted."[97]

In her biography, Woolf quotes Roger Fry's statement that "of all the religions that have afflicted man . . . Nationalism seems to me the most monstrous and the most cruel" (231), a view that matched her own. At a time when England was becoming increasingly nationalistic and militaristic, underscoring Fry's antinationalist sentiment was extremely brave. Equally brave, given the tenor of the time, was to criticize the English school system which, according to Fry and Woolf, was responsible for instilling nationalist sentiment. For both Woolf and Fry had come to understand, in their adulthood, that the brutality and the beatings in these schools were not there by accident; they were there by design.[98]

The aim of this system was to toughen boys up, to raise a nation of warriors. For the schools promoted a fervent nationalism, a sense of elitism and cultural mission served by the enlightened use of armed force, that amounted to jingoism. Toughening up boys was not an aberration, but a piece of the whole design, which Woolf criticized most eloquently in *Three Guineas*.

In April 1938, as she was grappling with the issue of how to present

Roger Fry's childhood, of what—if anything—she should delete from the "School fragment," Virginia Woolf suddenly conceived her last novel, *Pointz Hall*. She was still working on it at the time of her death in 1941, but she had changed its name by then to *Between the Acts*.[99]

At the very beginning of the novel, there is an act of unmitigated sadism directed at a very small child, which becomes the moment that signifies how children are treated within the world of *Between the Acts*. George (the central character, Isa's, child) is "grubbing" in the grass. He picks a flower; he is not content to let it be, but destroys it: "Membrane after membrane was torn." He takes it apart, as much to learn about it as to dismember it. He suddenly hears "a roar and a hot breath and a stream of coarse grey hair rushed between him and the flower" (11). George is terrified: he sees, coming toward him, "a terrible peaked eyeless monster moving on legs, brandishing arms" (12).

It is his grandfather, Mr. Oliver, who has come up upon his grandson. He has fashioned the beak out of the day's newspaper. Although he persuades himself that he is really just trying to play a harmless game, he really has wanted to test the child, to see whether or not he would be scared. Woolf's metaphor is profound: the novel takes place during World War II, as England confronts the possibility of invasion by Hitler. The beak which so terrifies the child has been fashioned out of a newspaper which holds terrifying news.

Mabel, George's nurse, is in no position to protect her young charge from his grandfather's behavior; rather, she urges George, despite his terror, to mind his manners, to say "Good morning, Grandpa." The niceties of civilization must be carried on even after an adult has terrified a child. George either can't comply or won't. At that very moment, bounding up to Mr. Oliver, and scaring George even more, is an enormous dog, called "Sohrab," whom Mr. Oliver bawls at as if "he were commanding a regiment" (12). The leaping, panting dog is the very last straw: George bursts into tears and his grandfather has won the day. His veins swell, his cheeks flush, he is angry. He calls his grandson "A cry-baby—a cry-baby" (13).

While this goes on, Isa, George's mother, is in her bedroom at her mirror, languorously combing her hair. She is removed from the welfare of her son, whom she entrusts to her servants. As she combs her hair, she is enmeshed in a romantic reverie about adultery. She looks out the window and sees George plodding across the lawn, lagging behind the two nurses, and the perambulator, which carries the baby Caro. In the only maternal gesture that she is capable of, she taps on the window "with her embossed hairbrush." Protected from the reality of child care, she looks at her children from a distance, and conceptualizes childhood in this stunning yet inappropriate metaphor: "Isolated on a green island, hedged about with snowdrops, laid with a counterpane of puckered silk, the innocent island floated under her window" (14). Later in the novel, William Dodge, whose wife has borne a child which is not his own, sees the nursery more accurately, as "a ship deserted by its crew" (71).

Dreams of romantic love isolate Isa from interacting with her children; using the labor of nurses permits her to maintain the romantic vision of the innocence of childhood. As her son lags behind, dealing with his fear, alone, with no one to comfort him, his mother is at her mirror, murmuring poems about the illusion of escape which adulterous love provides her: "Flying, rushing through the ambient, incandescent summer silent . . . air . . . there to lose what binds us here" (15).

Isa loathes, above all else, the image of herself as a wife and mother; she loathes "the domestic, the possessive; the maternal" (19). All of these bind her; all of these prevent her from being a romantic heroine. She wants to escape, in part because of her rage at her husband, who neglects her, so that when her father-in-law comes and tells her about what he has done to her son and that her son is a coward, she simply frowns and looks away. She does not confront her father-in-law, nor does she seek out her son to find out how he is feeling. She returns, instead, to reading the newspaper; she focuses on a story of a girl who has been gang-raped by soldiers; she reads the description of the girl, screaming and hitting her attacker in the face. That, she thinks, "was real" (20).

Woolf suggests that something has happened to Isa which is so painful that it renders her unfit for a connected, concerned parenting. Isa sees herself as having suffered since childhood. She sees herself as an overburdened donkey, making its way, alone, across the desert. The cause of this recurrent self-image, though it is connected with her childhood, is never explicitly described, although a confusing experience with an uncle, with whom she stayed as a child, is hinted at.

Isa tells William Dodge something about her life. She tells him that, when she had "the whooping cough" (50) as a child, she stayed with an uncle, a clergyman. (This sequence becomes especially significant in the context of Woolf's life, given the fact that she was sexually molested soon after she herself had whooping cough. Woolf was writing "A Sketch of the Past" at about the same time that she was composing *Between the Acts*.)[100] As she tells the story, a poem comes out of her, spontaneously. It is about going to the "dark antre of the unvisited earth," going to a "wind-brushed forest" (51). The "antre" of the earth is a cave, but it is also a sexual image. Dodge asks whether these are songs her uncle taught her, but Isa does not reply. An image instantly flashes into Isa's consciousness. It is of "an empty room and someone had stepped out from behind a curtain" (51). She immediately looks at Dodge's hands, "the white, the fine, the shapely," but it is clear that she is also thinking about her uncle's hands. William Dodge himself has been traumatized; he has told Mrs. Swithin about how boys at school have held him "under a bucket of dirty water," and he relates that experience, and others that he does not describe, as the reason for his becoming a "half-man" (73).

When Isa thinks of the burden that she carries, she connects it with "furtive findings and feelings, where hand seeks hand and eye seeks shelter from the eye" (154). She is burdened with "memories; possessions. This is the burden that the past laid on me, last little donkey in the long caravanserai crossing the desert." Isa is forced to carry it until her "heels blister" and "hoofs crack." The burden, "laid on me in the cradle," is "what we must remember: what we would forget" (155).

In an earlier version of the novel, Isa's burden forces her into thinking about suicide. She looks "into the water"[101] as she thinks about the past. If she kills herself, she will cast away the burden, she will enter into oblivion, a territory where there is no dominance, no victimization. In death, "all's equal"; in death, "change is not; nor the mutable and lovable; nor greetings; nor partings; nor furtive findings and feelings."[102]

In her poetry, Isa wishes for another and more innocent history, even as she describes a problematic past that might be her own, in which sex is associated with violence. She writes a story of rape; a story of how a man came up from the country, stripped a woman, and then killed her: "For there's always a worm," she says; and then, "Why can't we be simple? Why can't we be brother and sister?"[103] Isa wishes for an idyllic childhood which she describes as the simplicity and purity of what the brother/sister bond should be. But because she can't recreate her past, she now wishes "That the waters should cover me, / Of the wishing well."[104] She thinks of a death by drowning as the solution to a past that can't be recast.

There is a dazzling array of literary allusions to incest embedded in *Between the Acts.*[105] Mr. Oliver's mother has given him a copy of *Don Juan,* that Byronic epic alluding to his incestuous relationship with his half sister;[106] the lines "Swallow, my sister, O sister swallow," which Mr. Oliver repeats to his sister, Lucy, are from Swinburne's "Itylus" and they suggest forced oral sex;[107] Lucy is identified with Cleopatra, who married her brother, Ptolemy XII;[108] Isa is identified with Isis, whose life was one "long uninterrupted search for Osiris in the ideal form of a brother-husband";[109] Giles Oliver (Isa's husband) is identified with Oedipus, who marries his mother (60). These references point to the very long history which incest has had, and she suggests that this hidden fact must be included history. In the novel, there is a pageant, written and directed by Miss LaTrobe which, among other things, rewrites and revises English history.

In the pageant, Budge, a character who represents the imperialist vision, tries to persuade the viewers that home is the place where children play with toys, to which the breadwinner returns, where Mama pours out a cup of tea, where Father reads the children a story—Sinbad the Sailor, or something from the Scriptures: "*Be it ever so humble,*" he incants, "*there's no place like 'Ome.*" But Mrs. Lynn Jones, a member of the audience, disagrees with Budge. "Was there . . . something—not impure, that wasn't the word—but perhaps 'unhygienic' about the home? Like a bit of meat gone sour" (173–74).

But the children, who have played important parts, come out from behind the bushes to confront the audience with another definition of home, which challenges the view that Budge has tried to impose. They carry mirrors, shiny objects, fragments of "anything that's bright enough to reflect, presumably, ourselves" (183). What is reflected back to the audience is terrifying.

As they hold up these reflectors, the children declaim phrases from the pageant which redefine home: *"Home is the hunter, . . . Home? Where the miner sweats, and the maiden faith is rudely strumpeted"* (185). As the children chant these truths, the adults in the audience "evaded or shaded themselves" (186).

The children continue, unrelenting, as Woolf writes a moment that many victims of sexual abuse fantasize: a moment of confrontation, of accusation. Let us speak, they say, *"without larding, stuffing or cant,"* and *"calmly consider ourselves"* (187). Lest we *"presume there's innocency in childhood. Consider the sheet"* (187). Each child holds a mirror up to the adults and accuses them of sexual assault, pointing to the stained sheets of sexual experience, suggesting by the words, *"O we're all the same,"* that the experience is universal. As the children present these accusatory incantations, a little girl, who has taken the part of England during the pageant, stands before the audience, sucking "a peppermint drop out of a bag" (195), all seeming innocence, while a member of the audience waits for her to speak "something hidden. . . . But why always drag in sex." Faced with the chanting children, it is concluded, by at least one member of the audience, that "there's a sense in which we all, I admit, are savages still" (199).

What Budge says about the home and about childhood, during the pageant, suggests that the mistreatment of children, their exploitation, has been universal and, somehow, connected with the imperialist plan. Budge tells the audience of the necessity of protecting and correcting the natives of foreign lands. *"But mark you,"* he says, *"our rule don't end there"* (162). Budge says that he wields his "truncheon," too, over childhood: *"The ruler of an Empire must keep his eye on the cot. . . . Purity our watchword"* (163). The hypocrisy inherent in Budge's position, which the children uncover, is that although purity may be the watchword, it is the cover behind which the truncheon is wielded in the nursery. Another member of the audience, Etty Springett, remarks to herself that it is children who provide much of the cheap labor which the Empire extorts from its subject peoples: it is children who "did draw trucks in mines; there was the basement," where working-class girls and boys who were no more than children provided labor at very little cost to the ruling classes; and yet, while all of this was going on, "Papa read Walter Scott aloud after dinner" (164).

The supreme irony of the treatment of children in *Between the Acts* is cued in the lines in the pageant which state that "*time whose children small we be, / Hath in his keeping, you shall see*" (95), for time mistreats its children, and the passage of time is a threat to young innocence, not its safeguarding. The story of Sohrab and Rustum, to which Woolf alludes in the name of the dog Sohrab who so terrified George, is a story of intergenerational conflict.[110] It is not a pretty story, but the image of this relationship between grandparents, parents, and children permeates the novel: at its center is an act of infanticide. Rustum kills his son Sohrab in an unnecessary battle, and Sohrab redefines the parental role as one of cruelty: "No warmth paternal seems to fill thy heart" (34).

At the center of Woolf's last novel is a taboo topic: the hostility that often accompanies the interaction between the generations, which enacts itself in the lack of concern which Isa displays to her son's suffering, in her own elusive history, and in the acts described by the children in the pageant. Woolf takes on the history of the family and rewrites it by describing the "built-in antagonism" that parents often exhibit "toward their progeny, that their attitude toward them may range from ignorance and indifference, through denial and contempt, to open attack and ultimate destruction" (37). This is the parenting that George and Caro experience; it is the parenting that Isa and Giles have both experienced and inflicted upon their children; it is what Giles and Lucy have lived with but have also imposed. Giles sees himself as an Oedipal figure: "manacled to a rock," left to die.[111] Giles feels that something like this has happened to him; he sees himself as the victim of extreme, though unrecognized, cruelty in childhood. He understands this only to the extent that he sees himself as Oedipus manacled to a rock. Part of the pageant, part of the "indescribable horror" which Giles is "forced passively to behold," (60) is a story about how a father wants his son dead, and how that boy has been saved by an old woman, who has put him into a basket.

In *Between the Acts*, Virginia Woolf allowed herself to explore the hostility that parents have toward their children. The image of birth presented in the novel is revolting. Giles Oliver is on his way to a private meeting with Mrs. Manresa during a break in the pageant; it might be the start of an adulterous dalliance. He sees a snake in the grass:

> Dead? No, choked with a toad in the mouth. The snake was unable to swallow; the toad was unable to die. A spasm made the ribs contract; blood oozed. It was birth the wrong way round—a monstrous inversion. So, raising his foot, he stamped on them. The mass crushed and slithered. The white canvas on his tennis shoes was bloodstained and sticky. (98)

Birth and parenting become a "monstrous inversion" (98). The only sign of love between parent and child within the novel is the sound that a cow makes for her lost calf: "she lifted her great moon-eyed head and bellowed. . . . The whole world was filled with dumb yearning" (140).

When the pageant has ended, each of the characters thinks again of the children and of childhood. Perhaps Miss LaTrobe, who has conceived and written the pageant, has forced some self-knowledge. Mr. Oliver notices that he is jealous of whatever has happened between his son and Mrs. Manresa; he recognizes that, early in the morning, he had "destroyed the little boy's world" (199). Mrs. Swithin realizes that it was always "my brother . . . my brother" (206) who rose to the surface of her thoughts. Isa gives up her romantic illusion about adultery, for the briefest moment, but resumes it, wishing that her son were not her husband's child, but instead the child of an adulterous liaison. When the pageant is over, Woolf tells us, Isa and Giles will fight, but after they fight, they will embrace, and from that embrace another life might come.

As all this goes on, we are told that the babies are "sound asleep, under the paper roses" (217). The question that Woolf leaves unanswered is whether the babies will be treated any differently now that the pageant is over.[112]

Virginia Woolf established in her own thinking the primacy of infancy and childhood as an explanatory principle in the behavior of human beings and she expressed this idea in her life's work. In describing the childhood of the Ambrose children and of Rachel Vinrace in *The Voyage Out*, of Jacob Flanders in *Jacob's Room*, of Cam Ramsay in *To the Lighthouse*, of Rhoda in *The Waves*, of Rose Pargiter in *The Years*, of Roger Fry, and of George and Caro Oliver, the children in the pageant, and Isa in *Between the Acts*, she radically revised the commonly held Victorian myth of childhood as an idyllic time and replaced it with a view which stressed the pain that children experienced. Throughout her career, she raised the following issues: What are the choices human beings have made in the raising of children and why have they made them? Why have girls been raised differently from boys? Can human behavior be explained by innate drives? Why is child rearing such a hidden phenomenon? What is the relationship between the treatment of women and how women behave as mothers? Why are women from the lower classes used to raise the children of the well-to-do? Why do boarding schools exist? What is the function of corporal punishment in the rearing of children? How prevalent is sexual abuse? What is the function of control and repression in the rearing of children? What is the relationship between imperialism and child-rearing practices? What is the role of class in child rearing? Why are children's lives so unhappy? What is the relationship between war and experiences in childhood?

In a lifetime filled with many significant achievements, Virginia Woolf must also be credited with asking many essential questions about child rearing during a time when very few of these questions were being asked. In fact, her insights about childhood resemble the work that is being done today by psychoanalysts, educators, feminists, sociologists, and historians. Her descriptions of childhood as a terrifying time, although they grew out of her own experiences, nonetheless described what she believed was the shared experience of the world's children. In describing childhood, as in so much else, Virginia Woolf was a visionary.

PART THREE

Virginia Woolf
and Adolescence

Chapter Seven

1897: VIRGINIA WOOLF AT FIFTEEN

Julia Stephen died in 1895, when Virginia was thirteen. In the period after her mother's death, George Duckworth, and perhaps Gerald as well, began to sexually abuse both his half sisters.[1] In her "Reminiscences," Woolf referred to the fact that "George, on the full tide of emotion, insisted upon a closer and more mature friendship with us; Gerald even became for the time serious and sentimental."[2] Leslie Stephen insisted upon "comfort"[3] from Stella Duckworth in the wake of his wife's death. Woolf referred to her experiences after her mother's death as living a "sultry and opaque life which was not felt, and had nothing real in it, and yet swam about us, and choked us and blinded us," an "atmosphere all choked with too luxuriant feelings, so that one had at times a physical need of ruthless barbarism and fresh air."[4] It was during this time that Virginia Woolf experienced what has been referred to as her first nervous breakdown; it is the time that she described in her autobiography, "A Sketch of the Past," as a period of enforced silence.[5]

Between the time of her mother's death and the beginning of 1896, when she began a diary that she did not keep for long (which has not survived), Virginia Woolf stopped writing. She abandoned the family newspaper, the *Hyde Park Gate News*.[6] There is but one letter from 1896, from her to her brother Thoby. It contains a story of embarrassment and exposure, and her fear of going outside. She has begun to use the name "Miss Jan" rather than "Virginia" to describe what happened to her; it is a name that she continued to use throughout 1897. She writes: "It is so windy to day, that Miss Jan is quite afraid of venturing out. The other day her skirt was blown over her head, and she

209

trotted along in a pair of red flannel drawers to the great amusement of the Curate who happened to be coming out of Church."[7] The re-telling of this event is significant for it explicitly conveys the reason why Virginia Woolf became agoraphobic: she was terrified because her bottom had indeed been exposed. And she was afraid that everyone would see it.

Virginia Woolf's silence did not last for long. In 1897, she began to keep a diary. She kept it for almost an entire year. On Saturday, 1 January 1898, she bade the diary and that year farewell:

> Here then comes the "Finis" what a volume might not be written round that word—& it is very hard to resist the few sentences that naturally cling to it. . . . Here is a volume of fairly acute life (the first really *lived* year of my life) ended locked & put away. And another & another yet to come. Oh diary they are very long. . . .
>
> *The End of 1897*[8]

Eighteen ninety-seven was the year Woolf wore stays for the first time. The year her half sister Stella Duckworth married and died. The year Woolf experienced a recurrence of symptoms of the "breakdown" that followed her mother's death, which would plague her throughout her life. The year she acquired a writing desk—too high to write at, but one in which she could store her writing supplies. The year she read no fewer than fifty weighty volumes. It was the year she attended King's College, London. The year she discovered how the moment was enriched and preserved by the process of writing it down. The year she watched the procession for Queen Victoria's diamond jubilee. The year she attended performances of *Mariana*, with Elizabeth Robins; of Shakespeare's *Hamlet* and *As You Like It*; of Gounod's *Faust*. A year with numerous visits to the zoo; walks through Kensington Gardens, to Battersea Park, to the Round Pond, along the Serpentine; visits to the National Gallery, the National Portrait Gallery, Carlyle's House. A year in which she discovered the pleasures, and the perils, of ice skating and bicycle riding. A year in which one could catch a glimpse of the woman that the girl would become.[9]

At the end of her life, she described the emotional quality of this year as feeling as if she were caged in with her father, "a wild beast."[10]

She referred to the seven years 1897 through 1904 as "unhappy,"[11] the years during which George Duckworth continued to abuse her.[12] Like his brother Gerald, who abused her after an illness, George's sadism in violating Virginia in the years following her mother's and Stella's deaths, when she was vulnerable, cannot be underestimated. It poisoned her adolescence. What seems almost a miracle, however, is watching Virginia Stephen, at fifteen, in the process of creating herself as a significant, purposeful, dignified human being. Given what she lived through, it is a story of the triumph of the human spirit, and Woolf's courage and tenacity is nowhere displayed more directly than in her fifteenth year.

What is striking is the energy with which the fifteen-year-old Virginia Stephen tried, often against all odds, and with amazing success considering those odds, to effect the changes in the self essential for a productive and profitable adulthood. The 1897 diary provides an invaluable record of Woolf in the process of trying to make changes that would prepare her for adulthood.

During 1897, Virginia Woolf tried to loosen the ties that bound her to her family, a difficult task considering the fact that her family believed her to be mentally ill. On 13 October 1896, Stella Duckworth took Virginia to see Dr. Seton, the family physician, because Woolf had had an anxiety attack—her pulse was 160 and she was in an excited state. This time the recommendations were firm: Woolf would have to give up her lessons entirely until January at the very least, and she would have to spend at least four hours a day outside the house.[13] Although she began to do some Latin with her sister Vanessa by the beginning of March, and even some Greek,[14] much of 1897 passed without her having a normal schedule.

Seton's cure itself might have become the cause of Woolf's continuing anxiety and frequent bursts of temper throughout much of the early part of 1897. In an autobiographical fragment written near the end of her life, she describes the row of medications in her room,[15] some of which might have been responsible for Woolf's symptoms—a racing pulse, excitability, severe mood swings.[16] Deprived of the routine and the rigor of work, she was also forced to be out of the house for four hours a day, usually with Stella. Stella assumed almost complete responsibility for Woolf's care during this year. It is no wonder Woolf grew increasingly ambivalent and even hostile toward Stella as the year progressed. As a relative remarked, "it's bad for Stella to have Ginia always with her!"[17] It was also, no doubt, bad for Virginia to be always with Stella.

Woolf's 1897 diary describes a daily round of activities, often to the nearby zoo and to Kensington Gardens, to the galleries and museums, often to the workhouses that Stella visited, as she followed in her mother's footsteps as an "angel of mercy."[18] This daily round of activities seems harrying and exhausting—anxiety-producing rather than anxiety-relieving. On a typical Monday, 25 January 1897, Woolf's fifteenth birthday, she records a walk around the Round Pond after breakfast with her father; a trip with Stella to see about a book for Jack Hills, Stella's fiancé; a trip to Regent Street for flowers and fruit; a trip to see Miss Hull in Marylebone Road; a trip to buy an armchair, which was to be the children's wedding present to Stella; and, finally, the birthday celebration itself. All of this was usually accomplished using public transport. If Seton intended to calm Woolf down by this regimen, this daily round of activities hardly seems appropriate. In fact, Stella Duckworth herself had to go to the doctor for what was described as a case of the "fidgets." And Violet Dickinson once referred to the generally held opinion that Stella's death was in part linked to her exhaustion, just as Julia Stephen's had been.[19]

Denied an identifiable purpose in her fifteenth year, it must have been extremely difficult for Woolf to develop the notion of herself as an evolving, purposeful human being. Virginia was almost never alone before Stella's illness, except for the time she spent reading. And when she was alone, she was afraid that George would come and fondle her. She rarely records being with young women her own age. She watched Vanessa and her brothers Adrian and Thoby establishing friendships outside the household, largely as a result of their going to school, and she was irritated and lonely when they closeted themselves with their peers. But Woolf was kept very close to the family and, until Stella's illness and death, was supervised virtually every moment of her day.

Seton's regimen, although meant to cure her, removed from Woolf's life any semblance of structure, any meaningful work, any serious preparation for adulthood. In reading the 1897 diary, one is struck again and again with how Woolf was forced to become an observer— a voyeur of her family's activities, of *their* meaningful work.[20] She watched her sister Vanessa go to her art lessons, heard her talk about becoming a painter, and, later in the year, watched her "come out"; she saw Adrian going to Westminster, getting a microscope, a present that indicated the family's approval of his wish to be a scientist; she saw Thoby going to Clifton, where he was becoming somewhat adept at Latin; she saw her father, doing the work that would lead to *Studies of a Biographer*, talking to Henry James and his other illustrious friends; she saw Stella preparing for her wedding to Jack Hills; she saw George and Gerald Duckworth going on their endless social rounds.[21]

This "watching" was no doubt important to Woolf's development as a novelist. Yet there was something fundamentally unwholesome and potentially damaging in her being denied her lessons and a life that would define her as a person in her own right, with an emerging though fluid identity—as Vanessa had the identity of a painter in embryo and Adrian that of a scientist. Woolf's later comments about the significance of work in *A Room of One's Own* and elsewhere become even more significant when viewed against the imposed vacuity of much of this year, a vacuity that Woolf herself was aware of and railed against from time to time. She could barely conceal her resentment of Vanessa as she wrote, for example, that once again "Nessa went to her _____ drawing."[22] In her 17 March entry, after describing yet another walk through Kensington Gardens, her second of the day, she wrote sardonically: "I went in to the gardens and looked at the flowers—the almond trees out, the crocusses going over, . . . the other trees just beginning to seed. . . . I shall turn into a country clergyman, and make notes of phenomena in Kensington Gardens."

Seton's advice regarding Virginia Woolf echoed the cure prescribed for Leslie Stephen in 1840 when, as a boy, he was made to give up poetry after manifesting symptoms that his mother thought were associated with precocious genius.[23] But those symptoms were defined in another way in Woolf's childhood, as the symptoms of breakdown when Leslie became seriously suicidal. Leslie thought that his daughter Virginia was very much like him, that she had inherited his nervous system. (She had no doubt learned many of her responses from him.)[24] It is likely that Woolf identified herself and her ailment with her father and his earlier breakdowns, and perhaps even with what the family described as a history of madness, as evidenced in the history of J. K. Stephen and his father, James Fitzjames Stephen. It is also likely that Woolf identified her behavior, especially her displays of anger, with those of Laura Stephen, and that must have terrified her. In 1897 Laura was twenty-seven years old, unable (or unwilling) even to recognize Leslie Stephen when he visited her at Brook House, Southgate, where she lived, a constant source of anguish and despair to him.[25] Virginia Woolf accompanied Stella on a visit to Laura during 1897. How can this visit have impressed Virginia, given the fact that she was behaving as Laura had behaved and now Laura was locked up and given up for incurably insane or mentally defective? Given this family history, Woolf would have had good reason to fear that she too might become irrevocably insane. But what seems fairly certain from the 1897 diary is that Seton's cure itself exacerbated Woolf's illness, making her and her family react to anxiety as a symptom of even more serious illness.

Deprived of school and of the companionship of peers, Woolf had nothing against which to judge herself other than the measure of her family, no way to determine where she stood in relation to other young women her own age in terms of social, intellectual, and emotional growth, no mirror outside the family that could reflect a less distorted image of herself and her feelings, no companion who could share that she too experienced rages, disappointments, griefs, and fears. She was exceedingly and excessively dependent upon the goodwill and good wishes of Stella, Vanessa, and Leslie. Without them, she had no one. If they were angry with her and withdrew their affection or attention, she had no one her own age to console her. But for them, in this year she was almost totally alone. And when deprived of their company, when they went about their own business, she was frequently incapacitated because she had been denied the chance to become self-sufficient or to use friendships outside the family as a bulwark against the hard times she might encounter within it. On 30 June, with Stella ill, Vanessa occupied with her drawing, her father employed at his work, an entry reads: "Nessa went to her drawing—but the rest of the morning is rather vague—I went in to Stella for the first time, & found her very well—then afterward I may have brought strawberries, or I may have taken a solitary walk in the park, both of them the usual employments of mine nowadays." Woolf's lassitude, her depression, her feeling of living life as if within a grape—the way she described her affect in her autobiography[26]—are evident on the page, as is her tendency to describe her days in terms of what other people did and her activities in relation to theirs. In Woolf's diary there is none of that egocentric tendency one often finds in the diaries of adolescents.

The conditions imposed upon Woolf by Dr. Seton and complied with by the family certainly were not conducive to her loosening family ties, to experimenting with a way of being that was separate from their definition of her. And perhaps that was the point. In an incestuous household young women are rarely allowed to go free. But Vanessa was given a good deal more freedom than Virginia. Nonetheless, the diary records how Woolf kept fighting to cut free throughout this year and how the family often defined these attempts as symptoms of Woolf's illness rather than as healthy though sometimes desperate efforts at separation and self-definition. In February, for example, plans were being made for Stella Duckworth and Jack Hills to go on a holiday together. Woolf was to accompany them. As soon as the plan was conceived, Woolf voiced her opposition to going, opposition that soon took the form of outbursts of temper when the family would not heed her refusal.

The family—primarily Leslie—wanted Woolf to act as a kind of chaperone for the twenty-eight-year-old Stella and Jack—just weeks before their wedding. One can imagine how confused and enraged Woolf must have become, given that since November she had been treated as ill and very carefully supervised and now she was seen as mature and capable. Surely she realized she was being entrusted with seeing to it that Stella maintained her chastity until her wedding, a terrifying responsibility for an adolescent so recently defined as incapable of even being alone. Given the fact that Stella had lived through the nightmare of J. K. Stephen's advances, and possibly even an attempted rape, in 1890 and 1891,[27] Woolf's response is even more understandable. For during that horrible time, the Stephen children's help was enlisted in protecting Stella from J. K. Stephen. And here was Virginia, again being pressed into the same kind of service.

The family, however, refused to allow Woolf's pleas to be spared this charge. It was clear that nothing could now stop what she called the "whole thing most horrible" (5 Feb.). As the time approached, she became enraged. She lost the battle and she and Vanessa (a concession to Woolf's vehemence) accompanied Stella and Jack on the trip, which was a disaster. (I shall describe it more fully later.)

When Stella returned from her honeymoon in April, she was seriously ill. With Stella bedridden, Leslie Stephen made Woolf take on some of her household responsibilities. She records visits to the workhouse, a trip to High Street to buy a chair for George Duckworth, a visit to the bank to retrieve Stella's and Jack's silver, visits to sit with Stella, and, often, rides in the park with her.[28] All of this was demanded of a young woman who, until Stella's wedding, was not allowed to be by herself. Stella's illness might have permitted Woolf to redefine herself as a potentially capable human being, for now Leslie expected from her the kinds of services he had expected from Stella.[29] But he was requiring her to be of service to the family, rather than allowing her to do what she herself wanted.

It was probably too much too soon, however, because Woolf also began to record accidents that she noticed on her trips about town—a runaway horse (13 April), a hansom overturned (8 May), a collision between a runaway horse and a carriage—the "carriage was smashed up, & a waggon turned over" (13 May). Although these have been described as figments of her imagination, I believe that she was simply sensitive to the dangers which in fact existed on the streets of London because this was the first time in her life that she was allowed to venture out alone. It is important that she began to record them at the same time that she was required to take on running many errands for the household. Woolf's psyche seemed to have been telling her she was not yet ready to turn from invalid to "angel in the house." The family's expectations following the onset of Stella's illness put Woolf in a double bind: she was now expected to act responsibly, whereas formerly she was treated as ill. The new responsibilities made her feel both capable and anxious. Yet if she showed her anxiety, the family would again curtail her activities and inhibit her new freedom. It is also significant that Stella had to be sick before Woolf was redefined as capable. This too must have confused her. Stella, who had been Woolf's protectress, was now the reason she had to accept responsibilities before she was emotionally ready. Woolf also feared that Stella might die; her illness was serious. Given what had happened to her after her mother's death, it is no wonder that Stella's illness caused Woolf concern. It is also no wonder that Woolf was ambivalent about Stella—that she worried constantly about her health but also began to record irritation and then outright hostility toward Stella and her illness. Now the burden of the family was falling upon her own shoulders. Virginia was becoming Leslie's next "victim."[30]

On 6 May, with Stella bedridden, Woolf records that she brought home "something else which I cannot remember—a catalogue of the classes at King's College . . . which I may go to. After lunch I talked to father about it, and decided to begin next autumn if I begin at all. In the afternoon we went to the workhouse."[31] Bringing the King's College catalog home was Woolf's most serious attempt to separate from her family in a healthy and non-self-destructive way. But Leslie Stephen demurred, probably because he did not believe in the education of women. He permitted Vanessa her painting, for that was not a deviation from his belief in women's appropriate roles, but going to King's was different. How she was capable of going to the workhouse and running household errands yet incapable of attending King's College must have been difficult to understand. Woolf must have believed that she was capable, or she would not have brought the catalog home. At this very time Woolf was devouring Macaulay at the rate of a volume every few days. Woolf must have suspected that her hopes for a real education were not going to be fulfilled, and she must have been angry. Instead of having her capabilities verified, she was forced to see herself as incapable once again—but only incapable of going to school, not of working for the family. And she responded with those same symptoms that she had manifested in November.

On 9 May, Seton examined Woolf again. The regimen of no lessons was reinstated. On 11 May, Woolf wrote: "Father has taken up Dr Setons notion that I should be healthfully employed out of doors—as a lover of nature—& the back garden is to be reclaimed—That will be a truly gigantic work of genius—nevertheless we will try. Accordingly, a fork, a spade, a hoe & a rake were ordered . . . & tomorrow I begin operations." Woolf was reading, according to her diary entry, the very difficult fifth volume of Macaulay's history of England. The spectacle of the fifteen-year-old reader of Macaulay deprived of her lessons, not allowed to go to King's College, and forced to become a gardener to cure her nervous symptoms is so ludicrous and so pathetic that the humor and the pathos did not escape Woolf herself.

Whether Woolf's mental state was precarious is difficult to ascertain. She was surely anxious and enraged, and because no one had stopped her abuse, or allowed her to do what she wanted, it is likely that she became agitated, or "hysterical." But they seem to have had less difficulty dealing with Woolf's "illness" than with her emotions— her moments of anger and anxiety, her rages, her "tantrumical" self. Defining an adolescent as mad, after all, absolves a family of guilt and responsibility. Instead of seeking a cause for Woolf's behavior in the complex constellation of family interactions, it was far easier to see the anxiety as inherited. Then it could be seen as inescapable, incurable, the family curse. Julia Stephen had written in her pamphlet *Notes from Sick Rooms* that "in illness we can afford to ignore the details which in health make familiar intercourse difficult" and, even more significantly, that the "ordinary relations between the sick and the well are far easier and pleasanter than between the well and the well."[32]

Instead of allowing emotions to surface appropriately and then dealing with them, instead of taking on the difficult emotional work, the difficult family intercourse necessary to help her understand her anger, sadness, and rage, and see the potentially powerful emerging woman, the Stephen family, like so many others, required that unpleasant emotions be held in check. This is evident in many of Woolf's diary entries. At the time of Stella's wedding, for example, Vanessa and Virginia vowed that they would show no grief, despite their sadness at losing Stella. They would be "calm and most proper behaved, as if Stellas marriage were nothing at all touching us" (5 April). When emotions surfaced, sometimes inappropriately, they were defined as symptoms of insanity. Then a meaningless, dependent, carefully circumscribed existence was imposed that itself caused Woolf to regard herself as incapable. In fact, Virginia Woolf's life during her fifteenth year very much resembled the life of the animals she observed on her frequent visits to the zoo; it is no wonder that she described herself as living in a cage. She began to describe herself and her emotions in animal-like terms, probably because she had been taught that to have feelings was to become like a beast—her stubbornness was the "stubbornness of a mule"; her ardor the "ardour of a marmoset (my new title)" (29 March). And when Woolf tried to break away, even harsher restraints were imposed. As an adult, she saw herself as a caged animal and she saw her father as a beast.[33] Woolf carefully refrained from describing this aspect of her father in her diary; it is no wonder. What would the wild ferocious beast have done to her if he had read descriptions of his own behavior?

Nonetheless, Woolf did the best she could. She carved out an identity for herself as a historian in the making, despite the odds against her, and she did it largely as a result of her own efforts, though Leslie Stephen helped her. By the end of the year she had persuaded her father that she was able to attend classes. But even before Woolf went to King's College, one can see her educating herself to become a historian, or perhaps even a biographer. Not only was she reading, she also tried writing various works throughout the year, which I describe in a subsequent chapter.

In an 1893 letter to Julia Stephen, written when Woolf was eleven, Leslie Stephen stated: "Yesterday I discussed George II with 'Ginia.' . . . She takes in a great deal and will really be an author in time, though I cannot make up my mind in what line. History will be a good thing for her to take up as I can give her some hints."[34] In 1897 Leslie Stephen continued to encourage her to become a historian or a biographer—to follow in his footsteps. For her birthday, he presented her with Lockhart's ten-volume life of Sir Walter Scott—the "nicest present I have had yet" (26 Jan.).

Leslie Stephen had been working on his biography of Scott for the *Dictionary of National Biography* in 1896; Julia Stephen had especially liked the works of Scott.[35] The Scott was a gift that allowed Woolf to forge a link with both her father and her mother. Reading about the life of a successful literary figure who had his share of difficulties no doubt provided Woolf with a role model.

The extent to which reading history and biography gave Woolf a sense of purpose and structure otherwise denied her during this very difficult year is evident from her 18 May entry, written when Stella was seriously ill.

> I went for my now usual much to be dreaded drive in the Park with Stella. I have now got Carlyle's French Revolution—the 5th volume of Macaulay being restored to its place. In this way I shall become surfeited with history. Already I am an expert upon William (Hear Hear!) & when I have mastered Cs. 2 vols. I shall be eligible for the first B.A. degree.

The formal education denied Woolf she provided for herself by reading. Reading history and biography, even daring to mention the possibility that one day she might be eligible for the B.A., must have done a great deal for her during this year. And the extent to which she read history—in contrast to other types of works—is evident from a list of works she was reading. In January, for example, of the eight or so volumes she records, six are works of history—*Three Generations of English Women* (vols. 1 and 2); Creighton's *Queen Elizabeth*; J. A. Froude's *Thomas Carlyle* (vols. 1 and 2); the first volume of Lockhart's *Life of Sir Walter Scott*. In February she continued the Scott and the Creighton and read *Essays in Ecclesiastical Biography*, by Sir James Stephen. In March she read Campbell's *Life of Coleridge*, Carlyle's *Life of John Sterling* and Pepys; in April, Caesar, Macaulay's *History of England*, Carlyle's *French Revolution*, and Miss Mitford's *Notes of a Literary Life*; in June, Carlyle's *Oliver Cromwell's Letters and Speeches*, Cowper's *Letters*, a *History of Rome*; in August, her father's *Life of Henry Fawcett*; in September she continued Carlyle's *French Revolution* and read his letters.

In addition there were works of fiction and poetry that she either read or heard her father read aloud to the family. In January Leslie Stephen was reading *Esmond* and *The Antiquary* aloud, and Woolf was reading *The Newcomes* and *The Old Curiosity Shop*. In February she continued *The Newcomes* and read *A Deplorable Affair*; in March she read *Felix Holt*, among others; in April her father recited "The Rime of the Ancient Mariner," and she was reading *Barchester Towers*; in May her father read "Love in the Valley," by Meredith, and she was reading something by Henry James, *Caleb Williams*, and *The Scarlet Letter*; in July she read both *Shirley* and *Vilette*; in August *Vanity Fair* and *Adam Bede*; in September *Jane Eyre* and *Nicolas Nickelby*.

Although Woolf was diligent in recording the works she was reading, she rarely if ever entered extended comments about them, other than referring to them, for example, as "my cherished Macaulay" (1 May), "my beautiful Lockhart" (30 Jan.). She does note that reading relieved her anxiety. When Stella was seriously ill and Woolf was reading Macaulay, she wrote: "After all books are the greatest help and comfort" (1 May). Perhaps reading history and biography, in addition to providing her with information, did for her what it did for her father: demonstrated that there were people who not only had more difficult lives than she but overcame immense personal unhappiness and afflictions to succeed, not despite them, but because they generated idiosyncratic lenses through which to view the world. Reading history and biography also extended the range of her perceptions beyond the confines of her family, allowing her, while being raised as a young woman in a Victorian household, to measure herself and the way she was treated against other kinds of experiences, particularly the experiences of men. In this year the range and depth of Woolf's historical reading are an indication of how she developed the probing mastery of historical processes that is evident in everything she wrote, but especially in *Orlando*, *Three Guineas*, and *The Years*, and of how she developed an understanding of the way societal and historical forces impinge upon people's lives. Reading fiction no doubt also extended Woolf's view, but in a different way. Through fiction she probably learned about the ways people interacted and was thereby able to see her own life from the perspective of other alternatives.[36]

Reading in effect became her refuge, her solace in grief, her substitute for the friendships she did not have. It was the way she carved out an identity for herself as a human being, the way she secured her privacy, the way she began to determine the life she would choose for herself as a woman. We can see the extent to which Woolf was influenced by the works she read in this year: she wrote about virtually every one in her maturity; she used many of the literary allusions in her novels; and they provided part of the historical background for her numerous essays, biographies, and novels.[37]

To describe fully the influence these works had upon the mind and the manner of Virginia Woolf the novelist, the biographer, and the essayist would require many pages. As one example, however, let us observe how she referred later in life to her experience with Scott's *The Antiquary.*

In 1924, Virginia Woolf published an essay called *"The Antiquary"* in the *New Republic.* She began the essay around 16 October 1924.[38] On 17 October Woolf wrote the diary entry recording her inspiration for *To the Lighthouse*—"I see already the Old Man."[39] Beginning her review of *The Antiquary* probably brought up memories and unresolved issues from 1897—the year Leslie Stephen read the work aloud to his children—most particularly, from 27 January, when Woolf records, "Father began the Antiquary to us" through 31 March, when she records that either he or she completed the novel. This is the period when Woolf's freedom was curtailed, when she accompanied Stella and Jack to Bognor against her will. So much of *To the Lighthouse* explores the emotional confluence of the events of 1897—the life-giving yet stifling and inhibiting presence of a mother figure, then her sudden death and absence; the lovable yet irritatingly infantile, dependent father figure; the need to come to terms with these two as parents and with the absence of the mother and continuing presence of the father while simultaneously trying to construct an identity derived from each and yet separate from both. All these reflect Woolf's situation in 1897. And it is fascinating to note that one of the prototypes of the characters of the Antiquary, according to Lockhart's life of Scott, which Woolf read during this year, was John *Ramsay* of Ochtertyre.[40]

Woolf referred to *The Antiquary* in "The Window" section of *To the Lighthouse.* Mrs. Ramsay comes into a room where Mr. Ramsay is "reading something that moved him very much. He was half smiling and then she knew he was controlling his emotion. He was tossing the pages over. He was acting it—perhaps he was thinking himself the person in the book. She wondered what book it was. Oh, it was one of old Sir Walter's she saw."[41]

Later Mr. Ramsay is described as reading about "poor Steenie's drowning and Mucklebackit's sorrow." Thoughts of his wife, his family, and himself become intermingled with his response to the Scott novel:

> This man's strength and sanity, his feeling for straightforward simple things, these fishermen, the poor old crazed creature in Mucklebackit's cottage made him feel so vigorous, so relieved of something that he felt roused and triumphant and could not choke back his tears. Raising the book a little to hide his face, he let them fall and shook his head from side to side and forgot himself completely . . . forgot his own bothers and failures completely in poor Steenie's drowning and Mucklebackit's sorrow (that was Scott at his best) and the astonishing delight and feeling of vigour that it gave him.[42]

This portrait of Mr. Ramsay, a fictional surrogate for Leslie Stephen, was no doubt based upon Woolf's memory of her father's reading *The Antiquary* to the family in 1897. In the Scott novel the scene Mr. Ramsay reads is as follows:

> The body was laid in its coffin within the wooden bedstead which the young fisher had occupied while alive. At a little distance stood the father, whose rugged, weatherbeaten countenance, shaded by his grizzled hair, had faced many a stormy night and night-like day. He was apparently revolving his loss in his mind with that strong feeling of painful grief peculiar to harsh and rough characters, which almost breaks forth into hatred against the world and all that remain in it after the beloved object is withdrawn. The old man had made the most desperate efforts to save his son, and had only been withheld by main force from renewing them at a moment when, without the possibility of assisting the sufferer, he himself must have perished.[43]

In 1897 Leslie Stephen's continuing, unresolved grief over the loss of Julia was still upon him. For Woolf, hearing her father read of Steenie's drowning and Mucklebackit's sorrow, or reading of it herself, probably supplied a fictional analogue with which to comprehend the depth of her father's continuing grief, an analogue she would return to many years later when writing a fictional portrait of him in *To the*

Lighthouse. It is significant that *The Antiquary* itself contains the image of the lighthouse that is central in Woolf's novel. In a scene in which Sir Arthur, Isabella Wardour, and Ochiltree are stranded on the crag in a storm, a lighthouse beam that is temporarily hidden from view is essential to their survival:

> Deprived of this view of the beacon on which they had relied, they now experienced the double agony of terror and suspense. . . . The signal of safety was lost among a thousand white breakers. . . . "My father! my dear father!" his daughter exclaimed, clinging to him.[44]

Woolf singled this out as one of three scenes she commented upon in her 1924 essay. In *The Antiquary*—as in *To the Lighthouse*—the lighthouse beam is associated with a need for parental protection. In *Lighthouse*, as Cam joins her father in their journey to the lighthouse, she, like Isabella Wardour, thinks about her father's ability to protect her from harm:

> Now I can go on thinking whatever I like, and I shan't fall over a precipice or be drowned, for there he is, keeping his eye on me . . . and yet he was leading them on a great expedition where, for all she knew, they would be drowned.[45]

Earlier Cam had thought of Mr. Ramsay's character traits that had poisoned her childhood, and they are the very traits with which Woolf had to live in 1897:

> But what remained intolerable . . . was that crass blindness and tyranny of his which had poisoned her childhood and raised bitter storms, so that even now she woke in the night trembling with rage and remembered some command of his; some insolence: "Do this," "Do that," his dominance: his "Submit to me."[46]

In the final section of *Lighthouse* Cam recalls her father's reading in her youth, and she associates his reading with her ambivalent feelings about his ability to protect her:

> on he went, tossing over page after page. And she went on telling herself a story about escaping from a sinking ship, for she was safe, while he sat there; safe as she felt herself when she crept in from the garden,

and took a book down. . . . About here, she thought, dabbling her fingers in the water, a ship had sunk, and she murmured, dreamily half asleep, how we perished, each alone.[47]

Cam's ambivalence about her father—that she regards him somehow as both protector and prophet of her own solitary death by drowning—probably echoes Woolf's ambivalence about her own father in 1897 as he sat reading *The Antiquary*, while she listened to Isabella Wardour's ambivalence about *her* father in that novel. For in 1897 Leslie Stephen seemed to be doing all he knew to take care of his daughter, to prevent her from falling victim to yet another anxiety attack. In ensuring that Seton's orders were carried out, he was her protector and saw to it that she was safe. But the very nature of those orders, the very gloomy submission to Seton's view of her illness, must have led Woolf to view her father as believing in her fate, which was to perish, alone, by drowning in the sea.

Moreover, Woolf probably shared Cam's ambivalence about fatherly protectiveness because he surely had not protected her from sexual abuse. And in referring to him as a lion in the cage that contained her, she suggested in her autobiography that he himself was one of her tormentors. Her task of establishing a healthy sexual identity as an adolescent was confounded by all this. One of the truths that Woolf lived with was the archetype of the male as polluter, as despoiler of a woman's life.[48] Stella's death in 1897 surely reinforced Woolf's fears about the dangers of sexuality.

In *To the Lighthouse*, after the dinner party Mr. Ramsay feels he must read the Scott chapter in *The Antiquary* again. The chapter, chapter 32, opens with the following poem, purportedly written by "Mysterious Mother":

> What is this secret sin, this untold tale,
> That art cannot extract, nor penance cleanse?

The "untold tale" describing "this secret sin" is unfolded at the end of the Scott chapter, immediately after Steenie's sorrow is described. Evelina Neville, crazed and filled with grief and guilt, led to believe she is tainted because she has committed incest with her half brother, destroys herself by plunging off a cliff. Cam's fantasies of death by drowning, in the context of *The Antiquary,* are also associated with Evelina's suicide. But one wonders how Woolf must have felt in 1897 upon hearing or reading of Evelina's decision to commit suicide because of her guilt over what she thought was an incestuous relationship with a half brother, an experience Woolf shared. By this time, Woolf had already experienced incestuous relationships with both of her half brothers, either or both of whom might have been in the room while Leslie or Virginia herself read of Evelina's suicide.

What is equally fascinating about Virginia Woolf's use of *The Antiquary* in *To the Lighthouse* is an indication, in her published essay on the novel, that she misread or misremembered the Evelina Neville episode, the one Mr. Ramsay feels he must reread. There is an important inconsistency between the published version of the essay and its holograph draft. In the holograph Woolf writes of the Glenallan episode:

> For who breaks in upon that memorable scene? The cadaverous Earl of Glenallan, ~~who~~ the unhappy nobleman ~~who had the~~ who had married his sister, or—but we wrong the ~~lady, who~~ lady who expiated her crime by leaping from a crag. She was his cousin only—& it is we who are most to be pitied, for she ~~pitches~~ us necessitates romance.

The published version, however, is quite different:

> For who taps at the door and destroys that memorable scene? The cadaverous Earl of Glenallan; the unhappy nobleman who had married his sister in the belief that she was his cousin; and had stalked the world in sables ever after.[49]

In the short space of less than two months between the holograph and the published text, Woolf's memory has played a trick on her, and it is a very significant one, given her own background. One suspects that Woolf's misremembering *was* in some way connected with her incestuous childhood experiences and perhaps obliquely connected with her dredging up memories from the past as she began to think of 1897, when her father read *The Antiquary*. For in the published essay an episode of suspected incest is rendered as actual incest. When one recalls that Evelina drowned herself because of her guilt at an episode that was not in fact incest, the slip becomes even more significant.

Woolf carried her sense of shame and guilt, of anger and grief and impotence in regard to *her* incestuous experiences, throughout her life. Cam's association of her father's reading with a lack of parental protection and Woolf's alluding to that chapter in *To the Lighthouse* may reflect Leslie Stephen's failure to protect Woolf when she was subjected to the incestuous advances of her half brothers. It is horrifying to speculate that Evelina Neville in *The Antiquary* was the model Woolf would emulate many years later when she committed suicide by plunging into the River Ouse. But the similarities between *The Antiquary* and Woolf's life, and her later use of the novel, suggest that *The Antiquary* was immensely important to Woolf—that she used it to understand her father, to explain her own ambivalence about parental figures—but that somehow she projected her own experiences onto Evelina Neville.

It seems clear that by Woolf's fifteenth year she was still longing for her mother and had not yet worked through the ambivalence (the love and the rage) precipitated by her mother's death, compounded by Leslie Stephen's inability to deal with his children's grief. The 1897 diary makes it very clear that Stella Duckworth acted as mother surrogate to Virginia Woolf during her adolescence. And Stella was very much like Julia Stephen—"sweet and noble and affectionate."[50] But Woolf's diary also makes clear how difficult it must have been for an adolescent who was not sweet and noble, who was not perfect, to be in the company of someone as good as Stella. Woolf even occasionally alluded negatively to Stella's sweetness and nobility, referring to her mockingly as "Bella."

Woolf's resentment of Seton's regimen, therefore, would have been directed at Stella, and one can also imagine her wishing her half-sister would disappear, perhaps even die and leave her free—the common wish of the adolescent who seeks relief from parental overprotection.

In the months preceding Stella's wedding there is hardly a trace of resentment toward her in the diary, except what boiled over in response to the family's desire that Woolf accompany Stella and Jack on their trip to Bognor. One can imagine that Woolf was so imbued with the family notion that one should be grateful to Stella for carrying out Julia's functions that her healthy resentment was never allowed to surface in a wholesome way. Instead, one confronts her resentment of Stella in response to the proposed trip to Bognor with Jack Hills—the trip she described as "the whole thing most horrible." The trip to Bognor was a disaster. And there are indications that the trip had real traumatizing effects. The lodgings Stella and the girls took were unfinished. It was windy, "dismal and cold," raining or drizzling the entire time. It was muddy. The sea was black. Jack took lodgings nearby but came over for meals. On Wednesday, 10 February, Woolf describes how Stella and Jack pretended to be walking along with her and Vanessa but "soon turned and went back alone." The couple seems to have been trying to elude them, which exasperated Virginia. On 11 February, she records a day that would surely tax the nerves and health of the most even-tempered. A cold and rainy morning, but Jack declared that Virginia and Vanessa must go out, apparently so he could be alone with Stella. Virginia and Vanessa were sent out for a bicycle ride in the country, without a map, carrying biscuits and chocolate as emergency rations. They found the "roads muddier and worse than we have ever ridden on." They were soon covered with mud and soaked to the skin—cold, miserable, and angry. They were jeered at by a group of schoolboys marching along. When they returned for lunch, having been gone most of the morning, Jack asked them to go through the whole torture *again* in the afternoon, but they refused.

Woolf must have been very confused in her feelings toward Stella and Jack. Although memoirs of this year written later in her life describe how happy she was at seeing Stella so happy in a love relationship such as she had never seen before, the diary from that year records mostly resentment, and how difficult, if not impossible, it was for Woolf to be alone with "those two." On 4 April she refers to the wedding as "the beginning of the end." On 10 April, the day of the wedding, she records: "Goodness knows how we got through it all—Certainly it was half a dream, or a nightmare. Stella was almost dreaming I think: but probably hers was a happy one."

Shortly thereafter, when the family went to Brighton, Woolf began to record her outbursts of temper—probably at being left once again without a mother. On 13 April she describes being "tantrumical." On 19 April she records, with fascination, the execution of a woman, almost as if she were exorcising her anger at Stella. On 21 April she describes how she broke her umbrella in half. One can imagine that with time Woolf might have worked through her anger at Stella's marriage and in so doing might have resolved her separation from her mother by reliving it in a more wholesome way. Instead, Stella returned from her wedding trip seriously ill. It was extremely difficult for Woolf, ambivalent and resentful at Stella's leaving the family, to confront Stella's illness. If Woolf had harmful or murderous wishes toward Stella, as would have been normal given the circumstances, she might have blamed herself for Stella's illness.

Stella's illness, according to Woolf's diary, made her "miserable" (28 April). She wondered "how is one to live in such a world" (28 April). In the months that followed Woolf turned to books as her only solace. Her feelings toward Stella probably became even more confused when she was required to spend a large part of her time with her. In the months that follow, Woolf's well-being seems tied to Stella's. She writes, for example, on 3 May: "Stella had a very good night & no pain—so everyone went happily to their work as usual." But she seems to increasingly resent Stella. On 20 May she states that she wishes the drives in the park with her "would cease to exist!" By 23 June the constant stream of queries about Stella's illness had so exasperated Woolf that she wrote: I "answered the invariable 'How is Stella?' till I hated poor Bella & her diseases."

On 19 July Stella Duckworth died after an operation performed in an attempt to save her. Curiously, the family did not attend the burial ceremony. In a 1907 memoir Woolf describes the effect of Stella's death as a "shapeless catastrophe."[51] That Woolf felt unprotected and unmothered after Stella's death is highly likely. On 27 July—the date Woolf misremembered in her memoir as the time of Stella's death—she records in her diary that Seton thought she was flourishing and also the following entry: "I went for a walk (I insisted on the *walk*) with Gerald." It is entirely possible that Gerald Duckworth started up or continued his amorous advances toward Woolf once Stella was dead, just as George Duckworth had begun his after the death of Julia.[52] It is no wonder Woolf associated the loss of a mother figure with the terror of a certain kind of sexuality.

At the end of Woolf's life she seems to have misremembered the cause of Stella's death—to have forgotten the diagnosis of peritonitis and substituted appendicitis and to have associated the pregnancy with the death. According to a letter Violet Dickinson wrote to Vanessa Bell, this confusion was understandable, because there was a version of Stella's death besides the "official" one, a version Woolf might have heard as she herself convalesced in Stella's house. This other version of Stella's death is recorded in Jean Love's *Virginia Woolf*:

> In 1942, as a very old lady, Violet Dickinson passed on the nurse's interpretation (and gossip) to Vanessa Bell, telling her that Stella had been injured by Jack on the honeymoon. Evidently Vanessa demurred, for Violet went over the matter again, in more detail. The nurse had been quite definite, she insisted; Stella had had some inner malformation that made sexual intercourse difficult. Something—Violet supposed the uterus—that should have been convex was actually concave, or maybe it was vice versa. At a minimum, Violet insisted, Jack had been a "tiring lover." She said also that the difficulty was due in part to Stella's exhaustion at the time of the wedding and honeymoon.[53]

How much of this story Woolf heard or overheard as a girl of fifteen— from the servants or nurses or even from Violet Dickinson herself—is sheer speculation.

If Stella's death was described as resulting from exhaustion, caused in part by her responsibility for Woolf before her illness, then it seems reasonable to assume that Woolf might have felt partially responsible. Woolf might also have considered Stella's pregnancy her responsibility. Her careful records of the times she and Vanessa were induced to leave the engaged couple on their own in Bognor might mean that Woolf fantasized about their activities.[54] In *To the Lighthouse* we have the curious example of Prue Ramsay. In the "Time Passes" part of the novel the sixth section begins:

> The spring without a leaf to toss, bare and bright like a virgin fierce in her chastity, scornful in her purity, was laid out on fields wide-eyed and watchful and entirely careless of what was done or thought by the

beholders. [Prue Ramsay, leaning on her father's arm, was given in marriage. What, people said, could have been more fitting? And, they added, how beautiful she looked.]

The spring, as virgin laid out, careless of what was done or thought by the beholders, and the following passage, seems to synopsize much of what happened in 1897—Stella at Bognor, Stella's wedding, Stella's submitting to Jack. Two paragraphs later, again in square brackets:

[Prue Ramsay died that summer in some illness connected with child-birth, which was indeed a tragedy, people said, everything, they said, had promised so well.][55]

If one is very literal minded one can read the second set of square brackets as evidence that Prue Ramsay was pregnant before she was married—the illness being connected with "childbirth," not "child-bearing" or "pregnancy." Given this very literal reading, the virgin scornful of her purity seems to suggest that Prue engaged in sexual intercourse before her marriage, careless of onlookers. Whether or not this is what happened to Stella at Bognor, it does seem that Woolf felt herself partially responsible for Stella's death. But, incapable of even talking about such a horrifying prospect, she kept it to herself and referred to it only through fiction.

Instead of working through the traumatic effects of her mother's death, Woolf experienced another, perhaps even more devastating, trauma in Stella's death, and she might have considered herself par-tially responsible and felt immensely guilty, especially since she was freer without Stella to superintend her.

The record of that eventful year, 1897, begins to peter out after Stella's death. The family's visit to Painswick, the redecoration of Woolf's room at Hyde Park Gate, Woolf's attendance at King's College, her reading, her writing "a great work" (9 Aug.) are all recorded. But the effect of Stella's death upon Woolf and upon the household is the predominant topic in the sparse and spare entries in the latter part of the year. After Stella's death, Woolf seems to have repressed much. On 9 August, for example, she recorded—as she often did after Stella's death—that she had forgotten to write down what had happened and that she had therefore *"Forgot what happened."*

This poor diary is in a very bad way, but, strange though it may seem, the time is always so filled up here, that I get very little time for diarising—even if I wished to, which I dont having taken a great dislike to the whole process.

Woolf's last entry for the year, made at the beginning of 1898, concludes with the following words:

Here is life given us each alike, & we must do our best with it. Our hand in the sword hilt—& an unuttered fervent vow!

The End of 1897

These were brave, courageous, defiant, and hopeful words for the young Virginia Woolf to utter at the beginning of 1898, considering the events she had lived through in the previous year, and considering that elsewhere in her diary she recorded that "Life is a hard business— one needs a rhinoceros skin—& that one has not got!" (16 Oct.). She had navigated a precarious time in her life without giving up the notion of herself as an active, energetic human being. For 1897 had been a difficult year for Woolf—a year of enormous growth and profound change. Yet her vision of herself was in part an embattled one. She saw herself as a woman warrior, like Joan of Arc in her commitment to the cause of living her life, and possibly even killing, or dying, for her beliefs. One thing was certain: for Virginia Woolf, life was going to be a very sacred, very important, very dangerous battle—a battle she would continue to fight with all the courage she could muster. And, as the 1897 diary indicates, the courage this woman could muster was considerable.

Virginia and her mother, Julia Stephen, in 1884.

Virginia, in an undated photograph from the photo album of her half-sister, Stella Duckworth.

Virginia's sister, Vanessa Stephen (Bell), in an undated photograph from the same album.

Stella Duckworth, Virginia's half-sister and primary caregiver after Julia's death.

Julia Stephen and Stella Duckworth, Julia's daughter from her first marriage to Herbert Duckworth, who died in 1870.

Virginia's mother and father, Julia and Leslie Stephen, reading, at their summer home, Talland House, in St. Ives, ca. 1892. Virginia is in the background.

Leslie and Julia and, left
to right, Thoby Stephen,
Adrian Stephen, Stella
Duckworth, Vanessa, and
Virginia, ca. 1894–95.

Another family photo-
graph, taken at about
the same time. This one
includes both George
and Gerald Duckworth,
and excludes Stella.
Front row: Adrian,
Julia, Leslie. *Back row:*
George Duckworth,
Virginia, Thoby,
Vanessa, and
Gerald Duckworth.

Vanessa, Stella, and Virginia.

Virginia and her half-brother, George Duckworth.

George Duckworth.

The family after Julia's death, 1895.

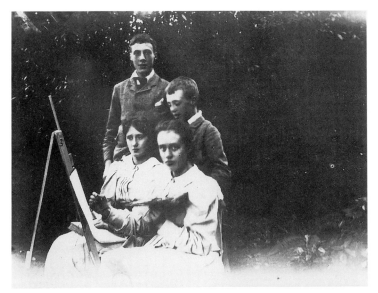

Vanessa, at her easel, with Virginia, Adrian, and Thoby.

Nursery Tea by Vanessa Bell (1912), painted after the birth of her two sons, Julian and Quentin.

The Nursery by Vanessa Bell (1930–32), a painting she likened to Virginia's effort to depict childhood in *The Waves*.

George Duckworth, Stella Duckworth, and Jack Hills, Stella's husband-to-be. They were married in 1897.

Virginia and her father,
Leslie Stephen, ca. 1903,
a year before his death.

Virginia with Violet
Dickinson, in 1902. Violet
cared for her during Virginia's
illness after Leslie's death.
Virginia described Violet
in her 1907 story, "The
Magic Garden."

Chapter Eight

AS MISS JAN SAYS

On Sunday, January 1897, just before her fifteenth birthday, Virginia Stephen, an angular, ungainly adolescent, picked up her favorite pen (and she was passionate about pens), the one with the thin sharp nib that bit into the paper as it crossed over it (but without leaving ink trails—a trait that was unforgivable in nibs). And she picked up her diary, a tiny brown leather one, trimmed with gilt, which had a lock and a key, a diary a little larger than the palm of your hand.[1] And she headed for an empty corner of the teeming Stephen family house in Hyde Park Gate in London, where she could have some solitude away from the peering, penetrating, evaluating eyes of servants and family, all of whom were always on the lookout for some sign of deviance, some sign of anxiety in this girl who had been, since her mother's death in 1893, given to rages and depressions. She wrote a diary entry in which she described how she and Vanessa and Adrian had started to record the happenings of their days in diaries. It was one of the first things that she had written since her mother's death.

After the news items in the *Hyde Park Gate News*, which had reported on the illness that her mother, Julia Stephen, had eventually died from, Virginia wrote almost nothing for two long years, the silent years.[2] In a later memoir she describes what she refers to as her first breakdown, and discussed why she had been silent for all that time.[3] It began after her mother's death, the period during which George Duckworth began to sexually molest her. Although she began to keep a diary in 1896, she quickly abandoned it. Her 1897 diary was her first successful attempt to break the silence that she herself believed was an outcome of her sexual abuse. After her mother's death, "a dark cloud settled over us; we seemed to sit all together cooped up, sad, solemn, unreal, under a haze of heavy emotion. It seemed impossible to break through."[4]

As an older woman, Woolf ascribed this time of silence to the rage and abuse that were caused by George's assaults. She was silent because she was terrified; she was silent because she was furious; she was terrified and furious because she had been abused. She couldn't speak to people and she spent hours alone in her room reading. She was furious at her father, no doubt, for not protecting her, and for being preoccupied with Stella and with his own sorrow; and she was furious at George. She wrote that the "desire" to write left her for two years.[5]

We also know from her memoirs that Virginia had been medicated and this might have exacerbated or indeed even caused the feelings of lethargy and depression which she refers to when she describes how the desire to write left her. It is important that her father (and Stella, whom he used as his agent) and their doctors turned her rage into lethargy: rather than inquiring into the causes of her rage, they wanted it to go away, and they used medicine to squelch her anger. Like so many other young Victorian women, she had been medicated to stop her from behaving in a way that was not socially acceptable,[6] which really meant that she was sedated to stop her from having an appropriate response to sexual assault. The sedation to stop her rages also killed her ambition, her energy, her desire to write.

A finger had indeed been laid on her lips. She was not only silent, she had been silenced, perhaps to protect George, surely to stop her noise, to stop her talk, to stop her telling her family that something was wrong. They taught her that she was crazy. She learned her lesson well: these feelings stayed with her all the days of her life. And her biographers have continued to portray her as mad, rather than as having been treated as if she were mad.

The value of her adolescent diaries is that in reading them one can break through the myth about Virginia's illness. For her silence lasted only for a short time. Through language, through her diary, Virginia rebuilt her life, rebuilt her psyche, through all the days of 1897, painstakingly, slowly, one day at a time. To help her with this process, she created a fictional persona whom she called Miss Jan, who appears in the first diary entry and who reappears throughout the year.

In her first diary entry, she tells how she was riding her new bicycle for the first time. And we see Miss Jan for the first time. In her entry, rather than saying that she herself is irritated because of how uncomfortable the new bicycle is, she describes how uncomfortable it is for Miss Jan.

During this year, it was far easier for her to record what Miss Jan said than it was for her to deal directly with the feelings that she herself was having. In the Stephen family, her feelings were suspect, her response to her mother's death had been labeled insane, and physicians had been called in to treat her. It is no wonder that, at fifteen, she used a fictive mouthpiece to explore sensation. Indeed, during this year, if Virginia has something very difficult to say, particularly about her feelings, she very often says it in the voice of Miss Jan. Through Miss Jan she gathered courage and often allowed herself to test her own response—in a hand that was so spidery and difficult to read that its illegibility offered its own protection from prying eyes.

In an 1897 essay, the voice of Miss Jan allowed the adolescent Virginia Stephen to explore some ideas she had about the existence of a god, thoughts of a theological nature that were, in the household of her agnostic father, tantamount to heresy. Through Miss Jan, and perhaps even because of Miss Jan, she was able to establish her own intellectual identity.

By the end of 1897, she had written not only her diary, but also at least three historical essays, an essay upon the Christian religion, which I shall describe later in this chapter, a "speculative essay called 'A History of Women,'" and a history of her own family, "all very longwinded and Elizabethan in style."[7] So far as we know, there was no fiction. And in 1899, at seventeen, she was still at it, keeping a journal during a trip the family took to Warboys, writing self-contained essays, practicing her style, describing nature, and trying to call attention to her feelings of abandonment with a little piece she called "Terrible Tragedy in a Duckpond," which she wrote as an imaginative news story. It can best be thought of as her adolescent counterpart to the short novel she wrote at ten, A *Cockney's Farming Experiences* and *The Experiences of a Pater-familias.*

In keeping a daily entry diary, she was beginning a task that many other Victorian children had been encouraged to undertake, in part because of the discipline it provided. But Virginia soon learned that, for her, keeping a daily entry diary was a very special asset. For one thing, as she described it at the end of her life, writing things down gives them a heightened significance. Keeping a diary teaches you to live differently, to slow the ongoing rush of experience, to appreciate detail, to "stay the moment." As she wrote in the penultimate entry of her last diary, describing her habit of "diarising" in relation to the dinner that she was about to cook: "Haddock & sausage meat. I think it is true that one gains a certain hold on sausage & haddock by writing them down."[8]

Keeping a diary was a way that Woolf learned to respect herself, to teach herself that her life had significance, and to give her life significance. Keeping a diary was her way of making a place for herself in time, in history, even if history had ordinarily deprived women of a place in its pages, even if history had usually recorded only the lives of "great" men.

It is especially significant, I think, that Virginia began her lifelong habit of keeping a diary during 1897, the year when her father and the physicians decided that she was not well enough to have lessons or to attend school. (This was the reason they gave, although she might have questioned why Thoby, whose behavior was far more problematic than hers, was allowed to go to school.) Here she was, the only one of the Stephens keeping a private record of her life—the others had abandoned their diaries soon after they had begun—when she was the only one of the Stephens not being trained to do anything, when she had been told, in essence, that she was not worthy enough or well enough to be educated to become anything special. Keeping a diary was an act which defied the judgments of worthlessness that had been made of her.

For a girl like Virginia, one of the outcomes of a history of sexual abuse, keeping a diary was the beginning of a lifelong process of self-actualization, of self-verification, of breaking the silence, even if the diaries themselves sometimes made her feel ashamed.[9] She was brave enough to endure the shame; she was brave enough to keep them.

Writing a diary and saving it was an act of faith and an act of optimism, for it implies that Virginia believed that it had worth and that it might serve some future purpose. Woolf herself later in her life thought that she would one day use the "deluge of words I've let loose"[10] to write her own life, a task which she had begun, but which she did not live to complete. Keeping the diaries which she had written was her way of shaping how she or someone else would write her life. She did not destroy them, nor did she destroy the beginnings of her autobiography (which she began at the end of her life), that landmark document in the history of sexual abuse—one of the few records that we have, until more recent attempts, to analyze her own psyche in relationship to what had been done to her. She dipped into these diaries while she was writing the beginning of her autobiography. They served to remind her of what she had been through.

Writing her diary was the first and most defiant act of her adolescence, but she did it in a socially acceptable way. For in its most radical manifestation, a diary is a potential historical time bomb: it lies in waiting until it explodes misapprehensions about the past, misconceptions about the role of women or other outsider groups in history, misrepresentations about how a particular life was lived.[11] Her diaries are no exception and her reference to them as a "deluge" which she "let loose" itself suggests that she was aware of this potential: her early diaries force the reader to examine the commonly held view that, during her adolescence, Virginia was insane; they show the reader what her literary apprenticeship was like, and how difficult yet exhilarating it was for someone with no formal education to train herself, with very little help from anyone, to become one of the most important writers of our time.

On 1 February 1897, a few days after her fifteenth birthday, Woolf made an entry in which she described how Vanessa had gone to a drawing lesson; how she and her father had gone out for one of their customary walks; how Stella and she had gone to the doctor for some new medicine, but had forgotten to ask the doctor if Virginia could continue her studies. The entry continues and it describes the plan that was brewing in the Stephen household, that Virginia should accompany Stella and her fiancé on their trip to Eastbourne. It is an extremely important entry, because it clearly indicates the power structure of the family, and the family dynamics within the Stephen household:

> A terrible idea started that Stella and I should take lodgings at Eastbourne or some such place, where Jack is going next week—Impossible to be alone with those two creatures, yet if I do not go, Stella will not, and Jack particularly wishes her to—The question is, whether Nessa will be allowed to come too—If so it would be better—but goodness knows how we shall come out of this *quandary* as Vanessa calls it. . . .[12]

Later on the page, she records that she has been in a temper all day, and that she has been making life difficult for Stella and Vanessa, but that she could not protest "*too* strongly against going." Here was one Victorian adolescent who believed that her rights were being violated by the family's treating her as a person who could be told what to do.

Carol Gilligan, in her controversial and widely acclaimed book *In a Different Voice: Psychological Theory and Women's Development*, has argued that "the secrets of the female adolescent pertain to the silencing of her own voice, a silencing enforced by the wish not to hurt others but also by the fear that, in speaking, her voice will not be heard."[13]

Virginia Woolf's diary entry, and indeed her entire diary, calls this finding into question. For it demonstrates the tremendous energy that the society exerted in taming dissidence, in quelling disturbance, and in silencing the voices of girls like Woolf. This silencing was not easily accomplished; nor were girls like Virginia complicitous in the eradication of their own wills. A tremendous amount of force and coercion was used to turn girls into the acquiescent, caring creatures that Gilligan describes as normative.[14]

In Virginia's case, her behavior was being controlled against the backdrop of what had been done to Laura. Rather than demonstrating how girls develop an "ethic of care," as Gilligan argues, Woolf's diary shows how, if girls want to survive, they had better pretend to develop an ethic of care, or else their very existence is at risk. Although a young woman's awareness of others' feelings is valuable in its own right, it is important that Woolf's diary documents how this awareness might develop.

Woolf's diary entry offers a moment-by-moment record of the process whereby a young woman in the process of finding her own voice had learned that she had to silence herself, apparently in the interest of others, but really for her own survival. It is a major piece of evidence in rebuttal of Gilligan's theory for it shows how one must take into account the realities of a young girl's existence in a patriarchal society in which her powerlessness is based upon her gender and a society which can use the most brutal, as well as the most subtle, forms of coercion to create what is deemed acceptable behavior for women. The entry demonstrates how a young woman, *precisely because* she knows that her authentic voice will not be heard and heeded, appears to subvert her own wishes and desires, and appears to convert them, instead, into a desire to please others. But she is doing it to save her own skin; to keep herself from being medicated, at the very least; to keep herself from being sent away from the family. Hovering over every moment of Virginia's life, once she began to show her anger, was the prospect of receiving the same treatment that Laura had received. The implied threat is apparent in an entry that Leslie made in his *Mausoleum Book* for 10 April 1897. He wrote: "Virginia has been out of sorts, nervous and overgrown too; I hope that a rest will bring her round." Bring her round to what? And what if a rest (short for "rest cure," a cessation of activities, milk, rest, and medication) didn't? Then what?

We can see how clearly the fifteen-year-old Virginia recognized her own mind and her own feelings: she knew that she did not want to go to Bognor because it was "impossible to be alone with those two creatures." She understands her own feelings, but she puts them aside, ostensibly in the interests of someone else: "yet if I do not go, Stella will not." At fifteen, we see Woolf forced into developing what Gilligan refers to as "an awareness of the connection between people" which "gives rise to a recognition of responsibility for one another, a perception of the need for response."[15]

What is significant, in Woolf's case, and I suspect in the case of many girls, is that this "awareness of the connection between people" develops in part as a defensive strategy. She states that she will act on the basis of caring about how Stella feels, and do what she does not want to do, because no one will act on the basis of how *she* feels, and they will not allow *her* to act on the basis of how she feels. She has already paid the price for showing them how she feels; she can't do it if she is to survive; they will medicate her, and she will be given a "rest" to "bring her round."

One must surely question, in this context, whether girls like Virginia really act from "a recognition of responsibility for one another" or whether they use the language of empathy to mask the fact that they have been coerced into putting aside self-interest as an appropriate motive for action.

But Virginia recognizes that Stella, because she too is a woman, is doing exactly what she is doing—putting aside her own wishes in the interests of someone else: "yet if I do not go, Stella will not, and Jack particularly wishes her to." In fact, with what we know about Stella's own training for submissiveness, we know that Stella rarely, if ever, did anything to please herself. So Stella will be no ally, yet Virginia aligns her own powerlessness with Stella's: she is being initiated into a community of women who substitute companionship for autonomy. But it is not something that is done by choice; rather it is a creative way of dealing with a role that has not been chosen.

Although Woolf knows that she is really powerless to choose what she wants to do, she states that it is her concern for Stella's wishes that prompts her to reconsider whether she will go to Bognor. This is extremely important, for we see how "empathy" makes its appearance. In Gilligan's words, we see how empathy is "built into their [girls'] primary definition of self."[16] In Woolf's case, empathy is not so much "built into" the young girl's definition of self as it is coerced.

The trip to Bognor was one of major importance, with damaging long-range consequences for Woolf's psychic development, as we have seen. Woolf was being used as a chaperone for Stella just before her marriage to Jack Hills, and she didn't want to be held responsible for their conduct. Leslie Stephen was repeating what he and Julia had done when J. K. Stephen was assaulting their home in his frantic and furious quest for Stella some years before—he was asking Virginia to once again be responsible for Stella, as the children, in 1890, had been made to tell J. K. that Stella was not at home.

Woolf's diary indicates that she was not at all naive. She knew that she might be scapegoated by the family if anything went wrong at

Bognor, and she also knew what might go wrong at Bognor. She had been exposed, through J. K. Stephen, and through her own experience, to men who could not control their lust. Her protests against not wanting to go were not the protests of an overwrought, irrational young woman, but, instead, those of one who was extraordinarily aware that she could only lose if she were forced to be responsible for Stella and Jack.

According to Gilligan, "the qualities deemed necessary for adulthood"—"the capacity for autonomous thinking, clear decision-making, and responsible action—are those associated with masculinity and considered undesirable attributes of the feminine self."[17] What becomes abundantly clear as one reads through Woolf's 1897 diary is how they tried to train those traits out of the young Virginia. Woolf could think clearly and make decisions and act responsibly but she was forced into acting *against* the independent assessment that she had made about what it was good for her to do. She was forced into doing something that she knew would damage her.

Woolf, knowing that *her* authentic feelings will not be heeded, knowing that a display of her real feelings is dangerous, reacts, appropriately, with anger: "I have been in a dreadful temper all day long." But as soon as she describes her rage, she dissociates herself from it—"I have been in a dreadful temper all day long, poor creature." She stops being Virginia when she has these feelings and she becomes a poor creature. Rather than "owning" her own feelings, she has learned to disconnect herself from them and the pity that she expresses is not for herself, but for the poor creature. She learns to disconnect herself from knowing her feelings and being able to act upon them. She learns to do the exact opposite of what is commonly defined as a criterion of mental health—a connection with and knowledge of one's feelings.

She is continually having to remind herself that anger is not appropriate in a young woman. She has it; but she squelches it. Gilligan suggests that this is a developmental task that is accomplished by women, once and for all, during adolescence. Virginia's diary suggests that girls and women are continually trying to act in ways that are appropriate to their feelings; and that they are continually shown that they will not be permitted to do so. Being coerced into adopting an ethic of care requires continual surveillance and self-control; it is not easily accomplished. She has her anger but she behaves as a young lady is expected to behave. She learns to put the wishes of others, particularly men, before her own.

And so Jack, a man, will get his way after all. And we see how Woolf converts her knowledge of her own powerlessness into a choice that she is making to control herself to please someone else. And then, at the end of the entry, we hear from her fictional self: "Poor Miss Jan is bewildered" as any person would be who was forced to squelch their unwillingness to do something, and repress their own anger, to convert a feeling of powerlessness into a concern for someone else's happiness. But she expresses her bewilderment in the voice of her fictional, rather than her actual self.

Through the persona of Miss Jan, Woolf maintains a private self whom she allows to express her feelings. Virginia Stephen used the cover of Miss Jan to express emotions that, in the Stephen household, it might have been difficult or dangerous for her to express overtly— disapproval of other people's behavior, for example, of her brother Adrian's buying a luggage carrier for his bicycle which she has Miss Jan describe as extravagant behavior. But she also used the voice of Miss Jan to chastise herself, to express, for example, self-deprecation about how she liked the pantomime Alladin because it was more accessible to her than a play written for adults; embarrassment (in an entry where she describes losing her composure when she dropped an umbrella, and talked nonsense). She uses Miss Jan to express simple discomfort (how the seat of her new bicycle was uncomfortable); boredom (how she had a horrible time at a tea at which dances were discussed, in which Miss Jan did not take much interest); self-censorship (Miss Jan cannot bring herself to enter the remarks of a group of schoolboys she saw); even extreme joy (how Jan was jubilant).[18] But the voice of Miss Jan disappears entirely from these pages after 2 May 1897 before her stepsister, Stella Duckworth Hills died, and Woolf describes many of the complex emotions dredged up as a result of Stella's death in her own voice.

What does seem clear, however, is that the voice of Miss Jan, and indeed the whole process of writing, helped Woolf to carve out an identity separate from the rest of the family. And there is extremely important evidence for the fact that the creation of Miss Jan helped Woolf achieve individuation and intellectual independence.

On 5 February 1897, Virginia Stephen entered into her diary the fact that she was writing a work called "The Eternal Miss Jan." On 28 April, she wrote, in response to a family crisis, that everything was as dismal as it could be, and how difficult it was to live in this world. She then labeled this response—that it was difficult to live in this world—a Miss Janism. And on 9 August, while she was away on a trip after Stella's death, she wrote that she had very little time for writing in her diary, but that her great work (probably "The Eternal Miss Jan") was proceeding, and that it had received Vanessa's approval.

In December 1929, when she was in the process of writing *The Waves*, Woolf made a diary entry which clarifies what "The Eternal Miss Jan," the "great work" which preoccupied her for much of 1897, was about:

> It was the Elizabethan prose writers I loved first & most wildly, stirred by Hakluyt, which father lugged home for me—I think of it with some sentiment—father tramping over the Library with his little girl sitting at H[yde] P[ark] G[ate] in mind. He must have been 65; I 15 or 16, then; & why I dont know, but I became enraptured, though not exactly interested, but the sight of the large yellow page entranced me. I used to read it & dream of those obscure adventurers, & no doubt practised their style in my copy books. *I was then writing a long picturesque essay upon the Christian religion, I think; called Religio Laici, I believe, proving that man has need of a God; but the God was described in process of change*; & I also wrote a history of Women; & a history of my own family—all very longwinded & El[izabe]than in style. [19]

Woolf's writing an essay "proving that man has need of a God" was an immensely significant act in 1897, because in it she described views that were the exact opposite of those of her father, whose famous work *An Agnostic's Apology and Other Essays* (1893) criticized those who attempt to describe the nature of God. In 1897, Woolf was doing exactly that—describing the nature of a God, and man's (or her own) need for a God. Her writing this discourse about the existence of God was an act of independent thinking in the household of a man who believed "that the ancient secret is secret still; that man knows nothing of the Infinite and Absolute; and that, knowing nothing, he had better not be dogmatic about his ignorance."[20] Woolf was, very privately and very quietly, challenging her father's system of belief and erecting a value system that she apparently needed at the time.

Believing in a mystical view of the world was, for her, a defiant act, an act of individuation, of establishing an identity as profoundly different from her father's as she could. Stephen's belief in staunch rationalism in the face of the death of his wife is quoted by his biographer Noel Annan:

> Shortly after the death of his first wife and with a heart laden with sorrow, he wrote, "Standing by an open grave, and moved by all the most solemn sentiments of our nature, we all, I think—I can only speak for myself with certainty—must feel that the Psalmist takes his sorrow like a man, and as we, with whatever difference of dialect, should wish to take our own sorrows; while the Apostle is desperately trying to shirk the inevitable and at best resembles the weak comforters who try to cover up the terrible reality under a veil of well-meant fiction. I would rather face the inevitable with open eyes."[21]

I would rather face the inevitable with open eyes; this was Sir Leslie Stephen's public account of his response to death and his avowed belief that it is effeminate to use religion to support oneself in a time of crisis. His private response was quite different, however.[22] We know from his own testimony, and from that of his daughter, that he insisted upon the sympathy of his children and his wife's children, that he acted out his own grief and his sorrow and his loss, even as he abandoned them in their grief, or even insisted that they be stoic in the face of their loss. As Woolf herself put it: "there were dreadful meal-times when . . . he gave himself up to the passion which seemed to burn within him, and groaned aloud or protested again and again his wish to die."[23] His children were denied the right to grieve which their own father permitted himself. More importantly, they completely lost him to his grief, so they had no adult presence to help them deal with their profound loss. Because of this prior history of Leslie's behavior and

Woolf's experience after the death of her mother, it is easy to see why Woolf, at age fifteen, would write an essay about man's need for a God which rebutted her own father's system of belief.[24]

There are glimpses in this diary of this private self, this Miss Jan, who believed in God or who had need of a God and who was composing a theological essay about the existence of God. On Sunday 2 May, for example, we learn from Woolf's diary that her father was lecturing on Pascal at the Kensington Town Hall, and his daughter, Virginia, was in the audience. She criticizes his performance by saying that the lecture was too deep, not only for the audience, but also that it was too logical and difficult for someone as ignorant as Miss Jan to follow. She also states that her father wasn't as good a speaker as he usually was.

What an agnostic like Sir Leslie would say publicly about Pascal's skepticism, about his "wager" that if God does not exist, the skeptic loses nothing by believing in him, but that if he does, the skeptic gains, we can only guess at. But we *do* know what Sir Leslie Stephen wrote about Pascal. Although Stephen appreciated Pascal's position, he seriously criticized it:

> I see that Pascal's morality becomes distorted; that in the division between grace and nature some innocent and some admirable qualities have got to the wrong side; that Pascal becomes a morbid ascetic, torturing himself to death, hating innocent diversion because it has the great merit of distracting the mind from melancholy brooding, looking upon natural passions as simply bad . . . . The devotion of a man to an ideal which, however imperfect, is neither base, sensual, nor antisocial, which implies a passionate devotion to some of the higher impulses of our nature, has so great a claim upon our reverence that we can forgive, and even love, Pascal. We cannot follow him without treason to our highest interests.[25]

It is ironic that certain features of the behavior Stephen ascribes to Pascal, he himself manifested—torturing himself to death, melancholy brooding. We can ascertain that in 1897, according to Virginia Woolf's own testimony, her beliefs were closer to those of Pascal than they were to those of her father; according to her father, her beliefs were "treason" to her own interests. It is easy to see why she referred to herself in the entry in which she describes her father's lecture on Pascal as the ignorant Miss Jan. For, according to her father, "no intelligent being had any right to continue to believe."[26]

But her description of herself as Miss Jan takes on even greater significance because Pascal was a Jansenist. The Jansenist confronted the issue of the extent to which human beings were in fact free agents, free to control their own destinies, in a very different way from the theological position that they opposed—the Counter-Reformation— and differently from Leslie Stephen's agnostic position. The Jansenist argued that human beings were simply not as free as the Counter-Reformation claimed they were; the Jansenist acknowledged that human destiny was arbitrary, and not the product of a certain human being making responsible choices about her or his own destiny. The Jansenist also argued that human beings were fundamentally depraved and that human nature was corrupt, especially by lust.

Because her own life had been rendered difficult by events over which she had no control, because she had been victimized by the uncontrollable sexual desires of her half brothers, it is easy to see why a doctrine like Jansenism might have had its appeal for her. In the 1897 diary, Woolf very often articulates pessimistic attitudes about the nature of the world (which she refers to as Miss Janisms) such as this one, in her 16 October entry: "Life is a hard business—one needs a rhinoceros skin—& that one has not got!"

In reality, Woolf's world had been a dismal one, and difficult to live in, and no amount of rationalist argument from her father about how that state of the world could be improved would convince her in 1897 that his views were correct. If any system of belief could help her through her very difficult times, it was not her father's agnosticism, which made him difficult to live with; rather, she would conceptualize, for herself, a God that she had need of. She would confront the dismal nature of life directly, rather than using a lens which misrepresented, which distorted reality as she had perceived it.

This was crucial. For in 1897, using Miss Jan, she refused to lie to herself about the nature of her life and of her experience. She did not live in a fantasy world. She was brave enough to say that she had suffered. In 1897, she probably understood what many adolescents understand about their parents and their elders: the difference between her father's stated system of belief and his actions; she probably knew in her own heart, although she was probably smart enough to keep it to herself, that she was living with a hypocrite, with a man who needed his illusions, even if she was bold enough to be able to challenge her own, and she probably knew that none of his public professed views would be of much help to her.

It is clear that she retained a mystical strain, which separated her from her father and from all of the extreme rationalists in her life, throughout her life, although it is likely that she did not share this strain with any but kindred spirits. In August 1929, when she was writing *The Waves*, for example, she shared the mystical side of herself with Vita Sackville-West, who would undergo her own religious conversion:

> These headaches leave one like sand which a wave has uncovered—I believe they have a mystic purpose. Indeed, I'm not sure that there isnt some religious cause at the back of them—I see my own worthlessness and failure so clearly; and lie gazing into the depths of the misery of human life; and then one gets up and everything begins again and its all covered over.[27]

"I see my own worthlessness and failure so clearly"—it is worth noting that Woolf's mysticism, both in 1897 and in 1929, was hydra-headed. Part of her mysticism was a way she set herself apart from her father and his system of belief, part of it allowed her to accomplish the act of identifying her own ideas about the way the world functioned. But there was another side to "The Eternal Miss Jan," a more pessimistic side to her discoursing on man's (and her own) need for a God. And that side was connected to her own "worthlessness and failure" which allowed her, at the same time, to understand "the depths of misery of human life" in general.

Although she understood that the circumstances of the life that she had led had caused her to have bad feelings, she had nonetheless internalized these feelings of worthlessness and failure. First, the integrity of her own being had been violated by Gerald Duckworth; then there was George; then a finger had been laid upon her lips after her mother's death. Ultimately, however, Virginia came to believe that the entire notion of God was replete with difficulty, for she told Ethel Smyth that Hyde Park Gate preachers reminded her of her cousins' attempts to convert her in her youth: she "thinks of their God as a rapist: 'He's got a finger in my mind.'"[28]

The paradox of Virginia Woolf's 1897 diary is that, although she was documenting how the expression of her authentic feelings were silenced, the diary itself is a victory because, through its use, Virginia wrested herself free from the silence which had shackled her since her mother's death.

Her next journal, the one that she kept in 1899, on a trip to War-boys, is very different. It is the journal of a writer in training. It signi-fies the success of Virginia's use of Miss Jan to help her begin to write. In the Warboys journal, there is no Miss Jan, but there is a great deal of experimentation with the use of voice, and with the sense of an audience.[29]

Quentin Bell's published description of this diary is misleading and has led at least one critic to argue that the diary depicts Woolf in the throes of insanity. Gayatri Spivak argues that the section "Time Passes" in *To the Lighthouse* "narrates the production of a discourse of madness within this autobiographical roman a clef."[30] She uses, as evidence to support her reading—that the autobiographical nature of the novel is rooted in Woolf's madness—the following description of the Warboys 1899 journal provided by Quentin Bell in his biography of Virginia Woolf. Spivak writes, quoting Bell, who, in turn, quotes Woolf:

> One is invited to interpret the curious surface of writing of Virginia Stephen's 1899 diary as a desecration of the right use of reason. It was written in "a minute, spidery, often virtually illegible hand, which she made more difficult to read by gluing her pages on to or between Dr. Isaac Watts's *Logick/or/the right use of Reason/with a variety of rules to guard against error in the affairs of religion and human life as well as in the sciences.* . . . Virginia bought this in St. Ives for its binding and its format: 'Any other book, almost, would have been too sacred to undergo the desecration that I planned.'"[31]

But the Warboys journal is not mad at all. It is an extremely lucid series of essays and writing exercises that Woolf felt impelled, at the end of the summer, to paste into Dr. Watts's book that she purchased because she liked the binding—she did not even know what the title was when she bought the book and she says so in the journal. What eludes both Bell and Spivak is that Virginia Stephen did not write this diary for the eye of either her biographer or her critic, so that to use as evidence for madness the fact that the diary is difficult to read is to miss the point completely and to misunderstand, as well, why the adolescent Virginia glued up her diary within the pages of Dr. Watts's book.

Here she was, having had her behavior scrutinized ever since she was thirteen, having been medicated, subjected to rest cures, having had her lessons curbed. Would anyone under those circumstances be foolish enough to write anything down without having a way of hiding it? Her 1897 diary had a lock and a key and was virtually illegible; she took her Warboys journal and pasted it into the pages of a book. It seems obvious that she did not want anyone in her family to be able to read her writing; it was for her eyes only; it was private; it was her own property.

What *does* require exploration is why Virginia Stephen had to go through such lengths to hide her writing exercises which are largely descriptions of nature, sunsets, places that she had seen, the history of Ramsey, a market town that was nearby, the impression that the fens made upon her, her first dinner with a curate. (There is, however, one wonderful passage exploring a water party with what she describes as a "terrible oppressive gathering of Stephens," which is biting and sarcastic, and which is right on the mark about the oddities that she perceived in the Stephen family character. It probably would have gotten her into trouble with her father because, in one sense, she was using their traits to describe his: how any ordinary person would be "ground to pulp" after just a week with them.)

Here is an entry in the Warboys journal:

the edge of this . . . [cloud] glistened with fire—vivid & glowing in the east like some sword of judgment or vengeance—& yet the intensity of its light melted & faded as it touched the gray sky behind so that there was no clearly defined outline. This one observation that I have made from my observation of many sunsets—that no shape of cloud has one line that is the least sharp or hard—nowhere can you draw a straight line with your pencil & say "this line goes so" Everything is done by different shades and degrees of light—melting & mixing infinitely—Well may an Artist despair![32]

Evidence of Woolf's insanity? Hardly. But the use of the simile of the sword of judgment or vengeance for describing the edge of a cloud is significant, and worth pondering, especially in light of Virginia's 1897 religious essay and in light of what we know about her anger. Is the sword of vengeance a representation of her righteous anger, a belief, encoded into a description of nature, that her half brothers will pay for what they have done? Does the sword of judgment signify that she had internalized a sense of guilt because she had been molested, or is she herself judging the behavior of others? No one can know for sure, but the essential aspects of this simile which depicts something menacing just beneath the surface of something beautiful recurs in all of Woolf's mature work and, in fact, synopsizes her view of the world.

At the end of another entry, one for 12 August, Woolf explores the notion that all art is imitation of a greater truth that exists in the universe. This entry is a sophisticated exploration of a Platonic conception of art, and a discourse on the limits of language and the superiority of music to describe universal truths. As early as 1899 Woolf was thinking about the nature of art, about the relationship between art and life, and she was exploring a mimetic definition of literature that she was to repeat in her maturity, and that was fundamentally different from, say, that of Clive Bell. This essay underpins the creative work that she produced in her maturity. As a writer she was forever alert to the significance of what she was doing; she was not content to create without thinking about the political, social, and artistic contexts in which she was creating, and which, in turn, were affected by her work.

According to the Woolf scholar Madeline Moore, the act of writing "completed autonomy for Woolf."[33] Many years later, when Virginia Woolf was writing *The Waves*, in the holograph of that novel, she distinguishes the children from one another by the way in which they go about the act of writing:

They sat in rows, yawning or writing very laboriously, for already, though that might have seemed impossible, they had their minds, their characters. There was, for instance, one most solemn child. He never dipped his pen without deliberation; often hesitating half an hour perhaps. But when he wrote the letters were firm & clear. Compare him with that moody fitful little girl. She swayed at her task, as if she despaired of ever getting it done; & then suddenly made a dart & wrote something very fast; & then there was a boy who gaped at the page; & rolled in his seat & rumbled his hair. And the eel like boy; so fastidious so agile. One after another they dipped their pens.[34]

Writing, in the holograph of *The Waves*, becomes the way in which the youngsters define themselves; it is also the way in which they construct a reality outside of themselves which they communicate to each other, so that each of them first creates their perceptions of what the world is like, then objectifies those perceptions in the act of writing them down, and then tests their perceptions through sharing their writing with other human beings. Although writing begins as an intensely private act, it ends as a public one—as a "great conspiracy of civilized people."[35]

The entries in Woolf's Warboys journal verify that the act of writing "completed autonomy for Woolf." The act of writing also connected her with reality, as it does for the children in the holograph of *The Waves*, and as her 1897 diary did for her. In many entries Woolf described that writing established a sense of connection with her own experience, a connection that she apparently did not feel as intensely unless she wrote down her thoughts. But in 1899, she was mature enough to be both conscious of the process and to be able to write about it. On 6 August 1899, for example, she wrote that it was necessary to write down her impressions of the moment, because they would pass quickly.

By 1899 we see her taking pleasure in the act of writing in and of itself, which is a necessary prerequisite if one is to become a mature writer. She loved to write for the sheer joy of passing pen across paper, and often described the effect of this nib, or that one, how this ink performed in comparison with another, whether or not her handwriting pleased her. She described the texture of paper and how she bound her pages together. If anything happened to one of her pens, she recorded it, and she speculated about the causes for its new (and bad) habit of leaving ink trails: usually someone (in most cases, a servant) had been using it, or had dropped it. On 7 August 1899, for example, she describes how her joy in writing is lost when her pen does not perform as it should, but, rather than describing herself as unable to perform the act of writing, she describes her pen as if it is, in fact, unwell. She developed very special relationships with her pens, with the tools of her trade, as so many professional writers do. One that her mother had owned was a special favorite.

At an important point in her 1899 journal, in her entry for 13 August, she supposes that she is writing for a generalized reader, which forces her to write for an audience other than herself, other than her family, and she describes that process as an act which is similar to putting on fancy clothes, of dressing up. Although it is likely that she had imagined such a reader for her 1897 essays, this is the first direct evidence that we have for that important step in becoming a writer: to imagine an audience beyond the limits of your own imagination, beyond the people you know. It is evidence of Woolf's growing maturity, of her developing the idea that she must write for others, that she must satisfy someone beyond the self, someone other than the family. We see her entering that great conspiracy of civilized people.

Often, in the diaries, she is delighted with herself and with her intellect; she is self-conscious, as so many young people are, about having discovered that she can think, and she describes the fact that mental activity is so important to her, that it is *the* activity that keeps her going. Because much of the 1897 diary was filled with self-doubt, it is significant that by seventeen Virginia could at times be self-satisfied, and it is important that her sense of satisfaction was intimately linked to her sense that she had a good mind.

The image that she uses to describe her thinking process is fascinating: she compares it to the function of the paddle of a steamship. Thinking is what makes her go on, just as the steamship paddle enables the ship to move through the water. Because so many of her images of self-destruction incorporate water, this entry for 7 August is an extremely important entry, for it provides a valuable insight into the conceptual process whereby Woolf dealt with her suicidal thoughts.

In one of the most important images in this journal, in her 7 August entry, Virginia compares herself to a Norseman on a long voyage, whose ship has become frozen in ice. His voyage seemingly has been halted; his prospects for survival appear to be nonexistent; it looks as if he is going to freeze to death and die. He is all alone, solely responsible for his own survival. Yet the ice within which the ship is stuck is itself drifting toward home. And, on board the ship, the Norseman has everything that he needs to survive. As Virginia phrases it, there are worse solitudes than being stuck in polar ice; and, anyway, the energy that is generated from the mind at work is sufficient to break through the ice, to force a way through to the sea and, eventually, to land.

This passage demonstrates, like no other, that at seventeen, Virginia recognized that she had been immobilized in the frozen waste of a Victorian female adolescence, immobilized and isolated and threatened by her sexual abuse. Her image of being alone in a frozen wasteland, alone responsible for whether she makes it to shore or whether she freezes to death, captures precisely the total aloneness, the complete solitude, the precariousness of the life of the incest survivor. She is, in fact, alone; if she survives, it is due to her own pluck and courage. No family member, no compatriot, no father, no mother is available in this image (nor in the image of drowning in the duckpond, which Virginia also takes up in the Warboys journal). Those who write the script of the success of Woolf's life as if it were due to the loving attention of a devoted father, eager to instruct his daughter in the niceties of thought, do not take into account that Virginia had been forced to endure the ultimate betrayal of family life: no one had rescued her from abuse.

But the most significant feature of this image, to me, is that at seventeen, Virginia believed herself to be fully capable of rescuing herself, if only she could have patience enough to wait out the situation in which she was living. Her belief in the power of the future to rescue her is illustrated in this image; if you can't count on anyone to save you, and if you yourself are powerless to effect change at the moment, then, in order to survive, you must put your faith in the fact that time will bring change. This image suggests that Virginia believed that she herself had the patience and the resources to rescue herself; she believed that she could break free using her belief in her own mental powers. Yet it also shows that she understood that her safety would not be immediate, and that she would be completely responsible if she survived.

This is a mature and completely appropriate assessment of the situation in which she found herself. She was no romantic; she understood her own situation. Her metaphor shows that she saw herself in a very perilous position—as perilous and as dangerous as a Norse adventurer. She could starve to death; she could drown; she could freeze to death.

It is important to pause for a moment to examine the symbolic nature of these possibilities. Virginia had, in fact, been starved; she had been cut off from the closeness of parental care from the first moments of her life. When, during the worst of times, she refused to eat, she was doing to herself what had, in fact, been done to her before. As Alice Miller has learned, symptoms are a form of communication. To starve yourself means that someone has starved you. Virginia's feelings were also frozen—she knew that if she showed rage, anger, nervousness, she would be medicated into submission. Moreover, cutting off feeling is one way of handling sexual abuse; the results, however, are deadening.

The image of the threat of death by drowning has a long Stephen family history. When Leslie Stephen spoke of his wife Julia's situation as a young widow, before their marriage, he quoted her as saying, "I was only 24 when it all seemed a shipwreck, and I knew that I had to live on and on. . . . And so I got deadened." When Leslie described Julia's charitable works, he wrote of how she "had saved a life from the deep waters." When he describes how Julia's emotions were choked off, he quotes her use of the nautical metaphor, that she felt "a gulf between us." He writes how Julia was "like a person reviving from drowning," how she herself sometimes felt "that she must let herself sink." After their marriage, he described the self-imposed isolation of their household as "a secluded little backwater."[36] After their mother's death, Leslie would tell Vanessa that they were "shooting Niagara"[37] if they overspent.

Virginia read her father's descriptions of her mother in 1904, when she was helping Fred Maitland with his biography of Leslie. And she herself later used the same image in an early memoir to describe her mother's death as a kind of drowning: "she sank," Virginia wrote around 1907, "like an exhausted swimmer, deeper and deeper in the water."[38]

But at seventeen, so far as we know, she hadn't yet read her father's words, so it is clear that she had already picked up the language of drowning from the family to mean both a release from the burdens of life and what happens if life becomes overwhelming. Virginia herself did not create images of drowning to describe the burdens of life; it was an image that both her parents used, certainly in conversation. When Woolf describes that she is threatened with drowning, she is using an image that she learned; she is using the image most often used in relationship to her mother.

Implicit in the image used in relationship to Julia Stephen is the fact that she can do nothing to save herself: she simply sinks; she drowns. Virginia's use of the image in 1899 both binds her to her mother (and her mother's fate) but also separates her from her mother. For Virginia provides herself with a boat (a form of protection), a mind (which provides the potential for release), and a storehold of books (which provide the information which potentiate her survival). She is like her mother, but her chances are better. In one sense, Virginia uses an identification with the male Norse adventurer to separate herself from her mother's fate: she becomes the Norse adventurer and takes on the threat but also the excitement of his self-imposed task.

The Warboys journal contains another important extract which treats the image of death by drowning. It is entitled "Extract from the Huntingdonshire Gazette. TERRIBLE TRAGEDY IN A DUCK-POND."[39] The extract describes how a boat capsizes in the water while three young people (including Virginia) were taking a moonlight ride on the pond behind the house where they were staying, a boat which had been outfitted with chairs and rugs to render the ride more enjoyable. The extract might have been drawn from an incident which had, in fact, occurred during the holiday at Warboys. Virginia wrote two versions of the "Terrible Tragedy"—this one, and one which she copied and changed in 1904 and sent to Emma Vaughan, who is named in the piece as one of the riders in the boat, together with Virginia and her brother Adrian. But the details that Virginia used and the pattern of figurative imagery that she established indicate that she was reporting something of more than passing significance, especially because, elsewhere in her journal, she had also written about the threat of drowning.

The extract is written from the point of view of a newspaper reporter; yet Virginia herself was one of the people whom she describes as nearly drowning. She is both the victim of near tragedy and the one who reports the terrible tragedy in the duckpond. This duality of vision is an important feature of the piece which details feelings of abandonment, a certain knowledge that in a time of terrible tragedy, no one, including her father, will come to her rescue. It repeats the images of the potential of death by drowning which she had explored earlier in the Warboys journal and it associates the threat of drowning with the Duckworths, through a repetition of duck imagery throughout the extract.

The duckpond was covered by "duckweed" which became "the green shroud" of those young people who drowned there.

The expedition was undertaken for pleasure, and the sounds of "merrymaking" were heard from the shore. But the pleasure of the boat ride soon turned into near tragedy when the boat capsizes. Whether the three will survive depends upon the fact that the only people capable of hearing their cries for help were in the kitchen.

The reporter describes her unwillingness to detail the scene. She describes how an "incautious" movement on the part of one of the riders caused the boat to "capsize with deadly swiftness and sureness": "The angry waters of the duckpond rose in their wrath to swallow their prey." The last thoughts of those who were drowning may have been tinged with "majestic serenity. We know not if their end was promptly consummated, or if terrible shrieks and agonised struggles for air preceded the merciful rest that soon was theirs."

The reporter describes the drowning as if it in fact happened; Virginia is imagining her own death by drowning, and she is reporting it as if it had occurred. The ambivalence of the imagery is striking: although the drowning is a tragedy, although the waters are angry and swallow their prey, the thoughts of the drowned are serene; the drowning itself becomes transmuted into a merciful rest.

One way of looking at this extract is to see it as a dress rehearsal for what Woolf would do to herself in 1941, when she filled her pockets with rocks and walked into the River Ouse; it is also an enactment of her identification with her mother. It also predicts, however, what will happen to her if no one comes to her rescue and allows her to continue to be subjected to abuse.

For the reporter ascribes the drowning to the fact that they were "alone, untended, unsoothed, with no spectator but the silver moon, with no eye to weep, no hand to caress." Virginia ascribes the tragedy to having been left alone, having been left uncared for. She uses another word, "disorder," to describe what has happened to them—it is the disorder in the family that has threatened their well-being.

The person that she names here as directly responsible for her condition is her father. He is the one who should have protected her, but who has not. So far as I know, this is the only place in all of Woolf's writings on the history of her emotional life where she associates her father's behavior with her incestuous experience. In later memoirs, she suggested that her father's rages had damaged both her and her sister Vanessa, although it is suggested in these memoirs that she had come to the realization that the elders were in some way or another responsible for the organization of their household, and that if George and Gerald were abusing Virginia and Vanessa it was, in part, because the household was organized in a way that made that possible.

She does not see her tragedy as singular; it is a collective tragedy, a family tragedy, and she includes her brother Adrian as a family member who suffers a similar fate, as indeed, Adrian suffered from a lifelong depression.

Also significant is that they are saved by the chance arrival of two siblings, of Vanessa and Thoby. It is they who notice the absence of several members of the family.

At this point in the narrative something extremely important happens; here it becomes likely that the ducks and the duckweed and the drowning on duckweed are meant to be ambiguous yet to point the finger at one of the Duckworths. The narrator reports that Vanessa and Thoby notice that *four* members of the family are missing: but the narrator has only named Emma Vaughan, Virginia, and Adrian. The fourth person is unnamed; the only family members unaccounted for are Gerald and George Duckworth, and, given the repetition of the word "duck" in the "Terrible Tragedy," it seems clear that one of the two of them was there, if not in fact, then surely in effect. If Gerald or George were in the boat, then Virginia's description of the punt capsizing because of an incautious movement is important; the "angry waters of the duck pond" rising in their "wrath to swallow their prey" are important; the victims "shrouded" in duckweed, which she refers to as "slimatica," are important.

When Virginia wrote to Emma Vaughan, after their holiday was over, she told her that she was sending her a copy of the "Terrible Tragedy," and she said this: "Do you see? You must read my work carefully—not missing my peculiar words."[40] This letter makes it clear that Virginia was trying to communicate something of more than passing importance to Emma and that she was telling her reader where to look for meaning—look at the peculiar words, the words that seem out of place, out of context.

The revisions which Virginia made to her text, especially for Emma, are significant. She adds even more "ducks" and "duckweed" to the original text. She describes herself as "One of the Drowned"; she says that she was "one moment dry & vigorous, then thrown from the warmth & animation of life to the cold jaws of a sudden & unthought of death." The reason for her death by drowning is that she is shrouded in green weed, in "duckweed," in "slimatica." The green carpet of duckweed has "closed over its prey"; but although the surface of the pond seemed unruffled, below it, however, someone was dying. A human body "rested in its maw," a human body became entombed in mud and clay on the bottom of the pond.

In an important syntactic shift, she writes that one of the party has drowned "on duckweed," but, before drowning, she has experienced "craven fear." To hammer the message home, she tells Emma that her hair and body are covered with duckweed. Throughout, she has taken the last syllable of her half brother's name—"worth"—and converted it to its opposite—"weed." In referring to them as "duckweed," she is indicating that they are noxious growths; duckweed, moreover, interferes with the normal process of growth. But a word must be said about Virginia's portrait of herself as "drowning" on duckweed.

In his notes to his edition of *Pointz Hall*, an earlier version of Woolf's novel *Between the Acts*, Mitchell Leaska, the volume's editor, has called attention to the importance of a seemingly innocuous line which appears in the text, "Swallow, my sister, O sister swallow." He identifies it as the opening line of Swinburne's "Itylus," and he suggests that the word "swallow" might be read as "an imperative form of the verb," which would introduce "considerable irony into this already sexually charged . . . allusion."[41] Women who have been sexually abused often refer to their feelings of being smothered, of not being able to breathe. In many cases these images become connected to having been forced into oral sex.

We have no way of knowing what George or Gerald forced Virginia to do; but it might be no coincidence that Virginia's images of drowning, of choking on duckweed, correspond precisely to the kinds of accounts of sexual violation that are being written about now but which surely would have been impossible to directly record then.

That she felt herself "drowning" as a result of her brothers' incestuous attacks is clear from this text (she uses precisely that word in the autobiography she wrote late in her life). Her death by drowning cannot be separated from what had happened to her. It is equally significant that in 1899 she tried to communicate this to Emma Vaughan, in the only way she knew how—by writing about it, by pointing the finger of accusation again and again to the "ducks" in the family. She said, in effect, to Emma, help me, I'm drowning.

She tried to tell Emma twice. Once in 1899, she sent her "Terrible Tragedy" to Emma. She sent it again in 1904, when she was twenty-two, the year in which she tried to kill herself by throwing herself out of a window. This was the year of her father's death. After her father's death, she describes her profound loss, her love for him, her missing him. But she also describes the fact that, after her father's death, she felt even more unprotected than she had been before: she wrote how George "never lets one alone a moment."[42]

The prospect for Virginia must have been terrifying. Her father was dead. And she was going to move into a household with George. There would now be nothing stopping him, absolutely no barrier to his approaching her. She wrote to Violet Dickinson: "I begin to dread our joint household, but it cant be helped."[43] It seems clear that Virginia's mental breakdown and her suicide attempt following her father's death were a response to the renewed threat that George posed. She describes the household as "that whirlpool."[44]

During the year after her father's death, Virginia lost her home. She was sent out of the house, probably to protect her, and she lived through what she called her "homeless vagrant days,"[45] trying to recuperate at Violet Dickinson's home and at her aunt's home in Cambridge. Like so many victims of incest, *Virginia* was the one who was sent out of the house, who had to suffer the loss of family in addition to the trauma of abuse.

In 1904, she used the manuscript of her "Terrible Tragedy" to try to communicate to Emma the cause for her suicide attempt. She told her how the "punt disaster" and its manuscript "had stuck to me" through all those years of neglect; she told Emma that she had copied it out in "the largest and boldest hand—so that even your toad-dark eyes may read."[46]

But whether or not Emma did anything to help, Virginia herself was helped by her own writing. By the end of 1904, she began to write professionally. She had to. She states very clearly in a letter that her inheritance did not cover the costs that had been incurred during her illness: "it would be a great relief to know that I could make a few pence in this way—as our passbooks came last night, and they are greatly overdrawn. It is the result of this idiotic illness."[47] When she began writing, she wrote to pay her debts; but writing, her own writing, had in fact saved her life.

Virginia had protected the original manuscript of "Terrible Tragedy" from the prying eyes of her family in 1899 by pasting it between the pages of the book that she bought for the purpose. No more eloquent gesture could have been made. She wrote her coherent and cogent analysis of the threat that had been posed to her safety in "Terrible Tragedy." She knew that with all its ducks and slime and duckweed, the manuscript had to be secreted. She tried to get an audience by sending it to Emma. That seems not to have worked in 1899.

But she found it in 1904, pried open the pages, saw her own words, read them, and the words that she had written in 1899 helped her, I think, in 1904. I think they helped her understand, again, that there was a real cause for her illness. She copied it, in her largest hand, hoping that Emma would not continue to deny the evidence on the page. And she mailed it off.

These adolescent diaries and journals record the difficult yet exhilarating process through which Woolf created herself as an adolescent, and as a writer. What is striking is the energy with which the young Virginia Stephen tried, against immense odds, and with amazing success, considering those odds, to become a writer, an independent thinker, a person apart. One is a firsthand witness to a truly remarkable portrait of a very courageous young woman; one is a firsthand witness to how Virginia Stephen used the persona of Miss Jan in the process through which she turned herself into the mature and distinguished critic, novelist, biographer, and social historian, whom we now celebrate as Virginia Woolf. Although there is much within these journals that attests to the suffering which she endured, these journals are also the testimony and the process of survival and so must take their place among those other documents which record the triumph of the spirit and of the human will. In fact, these journals attest to the fact that writing helped save Virginia Woolf's life.

Chapter Nine

CHANGING LIVES

In the course of her career, Virginia Woolf returned, again and again, to an exploration of adolescence, a time in the life cycle that she believed to be especially important. She created a score of adolescents in her novels—there are ten fully realized portraits of adolescents in *The Years* alone, for example, seven in *The Waves*. Her interest in adolescence lasted throughout her career. There are glimpses into the adolescence of Rachel Vinrace and her fiancé, Terence Hewet in *The Voyage Out*; we get to see Katharine Hilbery and Ralph Denham in *Night and Day* in their adolescence; there are the memorable portraits of Jacob Archer and his friends in *Jacob's Room*; Elizabeth Dalloway, Mrs. Dalloway's daughter; Cam and James Ramsay in *To the Lighthouse* (two of the most complex and significant of her fictional adolescent portraits); we see each of the characters in *The Waves* as adolescents—Susan, Rhoda, Jinny, Neville, Bernard, Louis, and Percival; in the beginning of *The Years*, Milly and Delia Pargiter are in their teens, and throughout that novel we get glimpses of the changes that have occurred in the lives of young people, as the years progress, and the new possibilities for the descendants of the original family are described; in *Between the Acts*, William Dodge shares the humiliation of his school days with Mrs. Swithin, telling her how his head was held under dirty water by some other boys, and how this humiliation has influenced the rest of his life. These young people recall scenes from childhood to explain to themselves the reasons for their feelings and behavior as young adults.

In many of her fictions, Woolf's adult characters return, in memory, to especially significant moments that define what their youth was like, so that a great deal more fictional time is devoted to the subject of adolescence than even the number of portraits of adolescents would suggest: Mrs. Dalloway, for example, spends much time thinking about the most important moment in her life, when, as a young woman, Sally Seton kissed her on the lips; in *The Years*, Eleanor Pargiter, as an old woman, often thinks about herself as a young woman, sitting in the parlor or waving her brother off to school. Several of these characters feel as if they are living in two time periods simultaneously because their memories of the past are so vivid. As Rose Pargiter puts it so aptly in *The Years*, "she had the odd feeling of being two people at the same time" (169). Just as Woolf's elder characters think back to their past, so too do Woolf's adolescent characters think back to their childhood, so that a nearly constant feature of Woolf's fiction is that there are at least two time frames being presented: the present and the past. A great challenge for many of Woolf's characters is to connect the present with the past, the past with the present, to assess the changes that time has effected, both in themselves and in others, and to determine to what extent "changing lives" is possible, as Eleanor Pargiter puts it (211).

In *The Voyage Out* she briefly sketches the difference between the carefully circumscribed, lonely adolescence of her heroine, Rachel Vinrace, in contrast to the wealth of experience that her fiancé, Terence Hewet, had while he was at university.[1] In *Night and Day*, Woolf explores how the growth of her heroine, Katharine Hilbery, is stultified during adolescence because she comes from a famous family, obsessed with their past.[2] She has been taught, largely by her mother, that it will be impossible for her to achieve anything that can match the brilliance, fame, and renown of her grandfather; her mother encourages Katharine to bury herself alive in the room which contains the manuscripts of this famous ancestor, which is referred to as a "grotto in a cave" (15), helping her mother write his biography. Woolf charts the extent to which, during adolescence and even earlier, Katharine's labor is exploited in the family: she is the one who runs the household: "from her childhood even," she was "put in charge of household affairs. . . . Ordering meals, directing servants, paying bills" became Katharine's responsibility. This permitted her father to go about his work untrammeled; it permitted her mother to work with her father's manuscripts unimpeded. Woolf describes a classic case of role reversal when she depicts how necessary it was for Katharine, as a young woman, "to counsel and help and generally sustain her mother" who was "beautifully adapted for life in another planet." Woolf sees Katharine's life as typical of many young women who are forced into caretaking roles for their parents: Katharine "was a member of a very great profession which has, as yet, no title and very little recognition" (44). Katharine must wait until night time to indulge in her passion for mathematics.

In *Night and Day*, Woolf also describes the adolescence of two members of the working class—Ralph Denham and his sister Joan. Ralph is determined to win his way in the world; he has spent his young life making plans; he sees his life as "stages in a prolonged campaign" (27) to get ahead. Katharine realizes that though she is the daughter of a privileged family, and Ralph comes from a poor one, she and Ralph, in effect, belong to the same class, because neither can do what they want or go where they want. This, and the fact that Ralph challenges Katharine to begin seeing things for herself and to separate herself from the past, contribute to her decision to marry him and enlarge the likelihood that she will eventually be able to do her own significant work.

In *Jacob's Room*, as Alex Zwerdling has so astutely observed, the "growth from adolescence to young manhood" of Jacob Archer "takes place against the relentless ticking of a time bomb" of World War I; the novel describes the raising of young men as "the preparation of cannon fodder."[3] Woolf's exploration of Jacob's adolescence indicates the extent to which he acts out a "preordained, mechanical program."[4] The supreme irony of this antiwar novel is that the very same training that would have assured him of success sends him off to war. In *Jacob's Room*, Woolf criticizes an educational structure that trains its men rather than educating them. She believed that war would not end until the educational system changed. Woolf also explores the life of Clara Durrant, who, as Kathleen Dobie has observed, has been brought up to live a life which consists of "an endless round of parties, tied to a teapot, busily arranging her own 'doom'"—"that of courtship and marriage."[5] *Jacob's Room* is superb social criticism which charts the disastrous outcome of how young men and young women are trained.

In *Mrs. Dalloway*, Woolf provides glimpses into Mrs. Dalloway's adolescence, and into the adolescent experiences of Peter Walsh, Sally Seton, Septimus Smith, and his wife Rezia. Indeed, Mrs. Dalloway spends the greater part of her day thinking about her adolescence, a time when life had much more significance for her.[6] She is, quite clearly, depressed, and she is feeling a rift between herself and her daughter Elizabeth, whom she imagines as not caring for her. She reads Elizabeth's preoccupation with self as a rejection of her, and imagines that Elizabeth is in love with her tutor Miss Kilman, which may or may not be true. But Mrs. Dalloway soon remembers that, as a young woman, she had been in love with Sally Seton, and that "the most exquisite moment of her whole life" was when Sally Seton "kissed her on the lips" (53).

The remainder of this chapter will provide close readings of selected works which illustrate particular aspects of Woolf's ideas about the adolescent experience: "The Journal of Mistress Joan Martyn," which she wrote in 1906, and which explores the relationship between historical forces and the treatment of young women in families; *To the Lighthouse*, which examines the conflicting feelings of Cam and James Ramsay toward their father; *The Years*, which describes the difference in the lives of the Pargiter daughters and sons in late Victorian England; a series of letters which Woolf wrote to *The New Statesman* which articulate her ideas on the education of young women; *Flush*, which describes Elizabeth Barrett Browning's life through the device of a mock-biography of her dog Flush; and *Three Guineas*, which analyzes the relationship between child rearing, education, war, and fascism.

In 1906, Virginia Woolf created her first fully realized story about the life of a young woman that she did not publish in her lifetime, "The Journal of Mistress Joan Martyn."[7] It is about a historian called Rosamond Merridew's discovery of Joan Martyn's journal describing the life of a young woman in fifteenth-century England. In this effort, Woolf located the reasons for women's oppression in a social structure, the land tenure system. Rosamond Merridew has devoted her life to uncovering women's lost history. Rosamond's persistence is rewarded when she finds a journal kept by Mistress Joan Martyn in the fifteenth century at a manor house that she stumbles upon in her travels through Norfolk.[8]

Joan's journal records her life's passage through the seasons of one year, ending with her impending marriage to a neighboring landowner and her untimely death. Her story describes the depth of her love for her mother, who rules the family during her father's frequent journeys; her pride in her father's position and her fondness for him, and his pride in her accomplishments; her joy in being able to record her thoughts in writing during a time when women were not usually taught how; her relationship with her brother Jeremy, who has far more freedom than she because he is a boy, who acts as her protector when the two embark upon their short journeys outside the stout gates of their home.

In one sense, this first fictional effort seems to be an idyll of family life, although there are important undercurrents which suggest that Joan, despite her surface bravura, might harbor some deep-seated, though unrecognized, suicidal impulses and that she begins to realize that her home is in itself not the fortress that it seemed. In this story, although the lives of girls and women are circumscribed, they come to no violence from family members. Their fathers seem to be loving; their mothers stern yet caring; their brothers appear to protect them. The threat that exists to women seems to come from outsiders, either when women venture forth beyond their homes, or when enemies break through the barriers which have been erected to keep them at bay. In this sense, "The Journal of Mistress Joan Martyn" seems a regression from the reality of violent households that Woolf had written about when she was ten years old. And yet there are certain passages that suggest otherwise.

The life of Joan's family seems warm, close-knit, and loving. And yet its women are forced to live an insulated existence behind locked gates and thick walls that keep out the bandits and murderers who roam freely and fearlessly throughout the countryside. Joan unquestioningly accepts the strictures of the society in which she moves; she is a well-socialized young woman who understands why she must be protected, and she is "thankful that there were stout gates between me and the world," although she is impatient "sometimes, when the moon rises, over a land gleaming with frost; and I think I feel the pressure of all this free and beautiful place—all England and the sea, and the lands beyond" (18).

One day when Joan does venture beyond the stout gates, she learns why she is kept behind them and why she must soon marry. On this day, she loses her innocence and she learns of the perils in the world outside her protected environment. While she is on the heath with Jeremy and the dogs, she sees "a Sanctuary man . . . prowling out of bounds in search of food. He had robbed or murdered, or perchance he was only a debtor. Jeremy swore he saw blood on his hands: but then Jeremy is a boy and would like to defend us all with his bow and arrows" (29). Joan perceives that the unequal distribution of wealth in the social order has probably caused this man to become a threat; but she slips just as easily into believing that this victim is a murderer. Later, when she visits the cottages of peasants, she inveighs against them with statements that suggest that she has been already taught about the superiority of her own class: "These are the people we must rule; and tread under foot, and scourge them to do the only work they are fitted to do; or they will tear us to pieces with their fangs" (30). She has learned to despise those who work and toil for her; she calls them "pests"; their eyes stare at her "from the . . . bushes, and the tangles of the undergrowth" (30).

When she returns home, she feels as if she has awakened from a "nightmare to enter our own clean hall"; she ascribes her mother's premature aging and her sternness to the fact that "she always saw not far from her such sights as I had seen today" (30). It is the rampant evil of the lower classes which has made her mother old before her time.

Joan does not rail against the fact that her husband will be chosen for her and that he must be a man whose landholdings will enhance those of her father's; that her father can travel to London but that she and her mother cannot; that she cannot move outside the gates of her home alone; that she goes to bed at night frequently dreaming about the highwaymen who have carried off a woman she has known.

What Rosamond Merridew knows however, and what Joan Martyn's journal illustrates, is that to be a woman in England in the fifteenth century was to be a nonperson. And yet, paradoxically, it is the story of the ordinary woman, it is Joan Martyn's story, that *truly* illuminates what life was like. Joan is taught that the only way for a woman to be powerful within her society is for her to marry and to rule her home; she does not understand that marriage is a way to control women; she romanticizes her mother's power, and when she sees her mother knitting before the fire, she thinks that it is a "great thing to be the daughter of such a woman, and to hope that one day the same power may be mine. She rules us all" (19).

Aside from her one foray into the world, Joan learns about the world outside the stout gates of her home and about history primarily through the stories that her mother tells her, through some manuscripts that her father sends her from London, and through the songs of a traveler by the name of Richard, who sings of Tristram and Iseult. She learns how to be a woman largely from these sources, for her life is so circumscribed, yet these stories have been written by men. Her father sends her a manuscript of John Lydgate's *Temple of Glas* and perhaps, also, his *Troy Story*,[9] a poem about Helen and "the siege of Troy" (20). Joan reads about Helen, "her beauty and her suitors." She pictures what Helen must have looked like, and she thinks she must have looked "something like my mother" (20). Joan's mother is a healer and her daughter believes that she is very powerful.

Yet reading about Helen, while kept behind stout gates in Norfolk, reinforces why men needed to keep their women safely locked away during the fifteenth century. Like Helen, simply because they are women, they possess within them not only the power to heal (as Joan's mother does), but also the power to unleash the lust of men. Simply by being beautiful, they have the power to begin wars. And so they must be locked away.

Helen's story reminds Joan that even the choice of a suitor for her might bring ruin upon their house for it might cause those who have been turned down to unite against Joan's father. Joan understands the analogy between her life and that of Helen of Troy: "We in Norfolk today are much the same as we were in the days of Helen, wherever she may have lived" (20), Joan observes. She equates Helen's being carried off to Troy by Paris, and her neighbor Jane Moryson's being carried off "on the eve of her wedding only last year" (20–21). Abduction and rape are common experiences for women, with a long history that often gets misrepresented in male retellings. One of her greatest difficulties is in reconciling her family's desire for her to wed with all the frightening consequences of loving inherent in the stories she reads and hears. These stories verify her fears that love entails death; that women possess the power to unleash the lusts of men and so are feared; that marriage against their inclination is their fate; that imprisonment is their natural lot. Woolf here explores how myths and stories contribute their share to a woman's acceptance of her status as a nonperson, to a woman's learning to devalue her gender. These are the kind of stories that subliminally teach women that they are destined to be powerless.

Joan's own nights are filled with fear "when the time for bed comes" (21). Although she hopes that the stout gates will keep out the enemy, she lives in perpetual fear of being raped: "The window in my room is broken, and stuffed with straw, but gusts come in and lift the tapestry on the wall, till I think that horses and men in armour are charging down upon me. My prayer last night was, that the great gates might hold fast, and all robbers and murderers might pass us by" (21). Joan, like Virginia Woolf herself, could not sleep without the fear that she would be attacked and assaulted.

Joan cannot help transferring this terror of highwaymen to men in general. Although she lives in the age of chivalry, the poetry of her own time has nothing to do with the reality of her life as a woman and her feelings about men. The code of chivalry, Woolf understood, was the stuff of poetry and romance, not the fact of women's history.

Joan Martyn's journal, then, explores the historical and societal causes of the tension between the sexes. In Joan's journal, the fear that women have of men is rooted in a landholding system that has caused a significant portion of the male population to have no means to sustain themselves and in a society which waged war and then in its peaceful interludes allowed its unoccupied warriors to roam at large, terrorizing the countryside, or which employed them to fight in internal skirmishes. These men also vented their rage upon the daughters and wives of the landholders. Woolf was exploring the issue that the girls of the rich were not necessarily pampered and protected. She saw them as potential victims of the class system. Hence the necessity of keeping their women behind locked gates. Rape and abduction of women are seen in a societal and historical context, caused by the land-tenure system itself, as much the responsibility of the landholders as of outlaws and villains. In this sense, though Joan does not realize it, her father is responsible for her fear; the price that he is willing to pay for his wealth is having his daughter raped and abducted. Her safety and well-being are less significant than his landholdings, although on the surface he seems nice enough.

Because women were denied the right to hold land, they became their father's pawns; their arranged marriages would either ensure the friendship and alliance of neighboring estates or extend the range of their father's influence. The tension between the sexes—the inability of women to join with men in equal, loving, free, and uninhibited relationships—was caused by this system, by the unacknowledged rage and chronic fear of its women, by the vindictive violence of its outlaws, by the manipulative dominance of its landholders, and by the myths and legends which taught women that this had been their fate since time began and that they could do nothing to escape it.

Joan's marriage has been arranged for her. She has adjusted to the system, and she knows that marriage might even have its rewards in conferring a status upon her that she now does not possess. But she does not always speak bravely of marriage. She believes that marriage will force her into losing her own "clean vision which is still mine" (28). She sometimes thinks that it would be "blessed" "never to marry or grow old; but to spend one's life innocently and indifferently among the trees and rivers which alone can keep one cool and child like in the midst of the troubles of the world!" (27). On the surface this seems a desire for a simple sylvan life, for a life free from the fear of those predators which lurk behind the bushes, ready to rape and pillage. Yet it might well be that there is an embedded suicidal fantasy in this dream of staying young in the cool waters of the river. She does not want to leave her own "clean vision" to marry, and at one point promises herself: "No, I will never leave you—for a husband or a lover" (28).

Joan recounts that her marriage to Sir Amyas is not far off. She does not expect much, although he is a "good gentleman, who treats me with great courtesy, and hopes to make me happy" (39). She remains discontented because she harbors a vision of what life might have held for her in a different time. She is a visionary who wants a transformation of the social order, although, she says, "what it is that I want, I cannot tell" (40).

At some level, she begins to acknowledge that although her family may appear warm and loving, they themselves present a threat to her. There is something about the look of the earth that is foreboding: she is taken aback by "a strange new look upon the surface of the land which I know so well" (40). She uses a metaphor to explain what she means, and in doing so, suggests that her fear might instead have to do with something about her family: this sense of ominous foreboding which frightens her "hints at something; but it is gone before I know what it means. If you saw such a look upon a living face, your mother or your brother, you would feel half guilty to have surprised a secret; and you would be frightened at the same time to think that one so familiar could have something lurking within them, unknown to you" (41).

Soon Joan's father finds out about her journal. He is envious and realizes that he is too lazy for such a task. He encourages her to continue keeping it; she has learned to read and write from him. He asks her to walk with him to care for his father's tomb:

> As I walked with him, I thought of his words and of the many sheets that lie written in my oaken desk. Winter had come round again since I made my first flourish so proudly, thinking that there were few women in Norfolk who could do the like; and were it not that some such pride stayed with me I think that my writing would have ceased long before this. For, truly, there is nothing in the pale of my days that needs telling; and the record grows wearisome. And I thought as I went along in the sharp air of the winter morning, that if I ever write again it shall not be of Norfolk and myself, but of knights and ladies and of adventures in strange lands. The clouds even, which roll up from the west and advance across the sky like the likeness of Captains and of soldiery and I can scarcely cease from fashioning helmets and swords as well as fair faces and high headdresses from those waves of coloured mist. (43–44)

What Rosamond Merridew values most, the recital of the progression of a young woman's ordinary days, Joan Martyn comes to value least, largely because she compares her journal with the legends she has read

271

and heard. Literacy has brought with it its own curse: the devaluation of her own experience. Joan has been taught that her own life is not worth recording. Before she can write her romantic adventures or marry, however, she dies.

In a note that Virginia Woolf made about *To the Lighthouse*, she wrote that part of her aim in writing the novel was concerned with "how much more important divisions between people are than between countries," and that such divisions were the "source of all evil."[10] In the conclusion of *To the Lighthouse*, Woolf enacts this idea, and the division between people that is the source of all evil is what divides Mr. Ramsay from his two adolescent children, Cam and James.

In the ten years that have elapsed between the first and last section of the novel, Mrs. Ramsay has died, time has passed, and Mr. Ramsay and his remaining children—Prue has died in childbed, Andrew in the war—go back to their summer home. Mr. Ramsay will join Cam and James on a trip to the lighthouse, an excursion that was originally planned for the last time they had been there, but which had not been taken. On the trip, both Cam and James think about their childhood, especially about Mr. Ramsay's treatment of them.

The early version of the novel is especially illuminating, because the insights of the children's perceptions are clearer and more direct than in the published text. On the morning of the trip, Mr. Ramsay loses his temper, a common enough occurrence for him, which prompts Lily Briscoe to question the prevailing view of fathers as bringers of order. She notices that when Mr. Ramsay approached, "ruin approached, chaos approached" (243). She notices that Cam responds to his rage with a "beaten expression twiddling her fingers, as if she would twist whatever she held until this torture ceased" and Lily Briscoe thinks that the real tragedy in the lives of Cam and James is not that their mother and two siblings have died, but rather that their father is so abusive: "That was tragedy," Lily thinks, "Not palls and funerals, dust and the shroud. But . . . children trodden under" (244).

Cam is consumed by rage as they wait to go to the lighthouse. She feels as if both her and James's heads "were bent down like trees pressed by a remorseless gale" (244) and her rage is directly linked to her father's suppressing them, "bidding them subdue themselves once more" (266). By the time they are under way, however, Mr. Ramsay has forgotten the fact of his outburst, and he ponders his duty to make his children happy. He believes that he must see "that they grow up admiring, loving, courageous"; he must "fortify them with memories" which will "help against the battle of life" (285).

The order of the characteristics he expects from them is illuminating. First, he expects them to admire him. But he never stops to question why his children should be happy. They have lost three family members, lived through a war, and lived with him. And how can they grow up courageous when he scares them half to death with his outbursts and with his habit of intoning at frequent intervals, "We perished each alone" (267)? What he wants from them as children is not possible given the context of the distant, troubled, self-involved, violent parenting he provides. Yet he expects them, as if by magic, to become the kind of child he admires. Moreover, he will not accept the reality of Cam's and James's psychic states. He wants things to be all right; he doesn't want to accept the fact that each of his adolescent children has severe emotional problems and that they desperately need and want his affirmation of their feelings as they are, not as he would have them be.

In order to fortify Cam with memories of her past, he points out their house on the distant shore. She can't see it; she is short-sighted like her mother. This "annoyed him" (286). Cam realizes that her father is annoyed at something that she cannot control and she becomes even more miserable, "with the cloud that rested on her, of the whole burden and battle and disaster of life; and how impossible of solution" (287). She really wants to make her peace with her father, however, and she has a fantasy of her father repenting his crimes, asking her forgiveness, but she then thinks of James who forbids it.

Although James sounds as if he might be too hard on his father, his position is eminently realistic: because he refuses to forgive his father, he has at least come to the recognition that his father is not to be trusted, that he is unreliable, and that he cannot change his ways.

Cam however is different: she still has fantasies of her father changing his behavior. She is very much like him, for she believes that what she wishes will happen. She cannot accept, as James apparently can, the reality of her father's implacable nature. She is, moreover, under extreme pressure because she finds him so attractive. It is her ambivalence toward him, and the extremes of her emotions, that are so maddening: "no one attracted her more than this strange old man. . . . But what remained intolerable . . . was his . . . 'Submit to me.'" When Cam enumerates her father's lovable qualities, some are entirely understandable—his "burning energy," his beautiful hands. But one characteristic is not lovable: "his remoteness" (290). Cam finds her father's remoteness attractive because she has internalized his emotional unavailability as an *admirable* quality, the very quality that James finds reprehensible; moreover, when her father is remote is when she is safe from his violence.

When James thinks about his murderous rage toward his father, he thinks that he would not like to kill Mr. Ramsay; instead, he would like to kill "a thing that descended on him; that had perched on his shoulders and pecked at them all when they were children." James too, in his own way, is willing to let Mr. Ramsay off the hook, but in a different way from Cam. Cam "owns" her ambivalence toward her father. James, however, depicts his father as a man possessed by something that was responsible for hurting them as children. He comes to view his father as "a man haunted by a devil," (308) but unconscious that he is so haunted. He has a moment, like Cam, when he has a fantasy that his father will change. He thinks that it still might be possible for the vulture that sits on his father's shoulder to fly off and leave him.

It is consoling for James to ascribe his father's bad behavior to something that possessed him, rather than to the father himself, so that he can let go of some of the rage he feels. James understands that his rage at his father means that he has become exactly like him, and this terrifies him: "he felt more and more like that sin-haunted old man" (309).

When James thinks about why he feels fear in the presence of his father, he concludes that it is because he was forced to witness acts of abuse that his father directed toward somebody else, when he was in a perambulator, and he remembers feeling terrified and helpless. He knows that his present feelings are connected with a "terror which he had suffered at his hands years and years ago" and he remembers his father from that time as a man who "crushed people's feet, yet never knew that he was doing it" (309).

James does not precisely remember who it was that his father had brutalized: he thinks "But whose foot did he crush?" (309). He speculates that it might have been his mother, and then he remembers his mother going off and leaving him alone in the perambulator feeling terrified and impotent. But he is not sure. The memory might be blurred, and connected with some other person. He does, however, remember, that in response to her husband's violence, Mrs. Ramsay "became suddenly remote, and majestic" (313). He knows that Mrs. Ramsay did not try to put a stop to it; nor did she help James with his feelings. Mrs. Ramsay's response to her husband's violence was to withdraw, but she withdrew from her children as well.

James now understands that his feelings of terror and impotence, caused by his father's rage and abuse, were compounded by his mother's leaving him alone with these feelings. Most importantly, she never verified that his response to his father's behavior was appropriate. Indeed, he is still not quite sure it is, although he is much closer to accepting his feelings than he was as a child.

James has divided up his childhood into a period of paradise "before the fall of the world" and a time of catastrophe after. He "did really divide time into the space before catastrophe, and the space after." He invests the early time with a romantic, idyllic nostalgia: he remembers their home as being "all in confusion, yet order." But then he has a tremendously important insight. He realizes that it can never have been like that, that there was no paradisiacal time, and that, from the first, "the waggon wheel must have gone over a foot there; even then" (309). Even then there was violence and suffering. The idyllic period in his memory, he understands, is his own invention; it is the story he has told himself to lessen the pain of what he had lived through, for it is very difficult to admit the persistent presence of violence in one's life. But it is necessary that he understand this and that he mourns his loss of a period of imagined bliss.

He wishes, for a moment, that he could get his mother back just long enough to "speak the truth" with her "at last—to have done with these intolerable evasions, these lies, these subterfuges" (313). He wants an admission from her that his interpretation of his childhood is correct so that he can go forward, from his adolescence into his young adulthood, with a sense of surety about his ability to make sense of the world.

Cam, in the meantime, is dealing with precisely the same issue, the issue of her father's anger. Unlike James, Cam is not able to confront the reality of her father's anger directly. She deals with it in two ways: she denies it, and she transmutes it into a suicidal fantasy that links her with him. She sees her father's anger as slipping away, whirling away, "in that broad glittering surface" of the sea that they are gliding upon. In effect, she makes her father's anger drown in the sea. She instantly replaces her rage at her father with a positive view of herself as a person "with extraordinary capacities for feeling everything here and now—so that disagreements and quarrels scarcely mattered" (319). Although on the surface it might seem as if Cam's resolution of this matter is the more positive, it is riddled with problems. In denying her feelings about him, she gains a sense of being able to live fully in the present. This, however, is a fragile accommodation, for it depends upon her ability to bury her emotions. James understands that the disagreements and quarrels *do* matter; he might not have a powerful sense of himself, given his past, but he *is* connected to the reality of his past, and he is even now in the process of mourning his unreal vision of the idyll of his childhood. In one moment of supreme insight, however, Cam realizes the toll that repression has taken. She thinks "it was never the thing itself that she felt," that she is, in fact, not capable of living fully in the present at all, for her present is obstructed by her thoughts about "why she felt it, and what some one else thought about her feeling it" (350).

Cam desperately wants her anger to dissipate, she wants the quarrels and disagreements not to matter. Rather than looking at them squarely, she has become her mother's daughter, for she is doing precisely what Mrs. Ramsay has done in the past. She is detaching herself from her feelings and so she is able to contemplate "a future which . . . was dazzling" (320). The image indicates the superficial quality of Cam's resolution of her problem. Just as Cam cannot look into her past, she invents a glowing future for herself that is not grounded in reality.

There is another pole to Cam's mood, and it reveals the depth of her despair. Like her father, and like her mother too, she sees the world poised on the brink of destruction. Sometimes, in fantasy, she sees herself and her family as the survivors of disaster; sometimes she herself is the victim. She imagines "that they were survivors of a disaster, and all depended upon her catching fish" (319). (This image echoes that of the stranded survivor in Woolf's adolescent Warboys journal.) This image is meaningful, for it should never be the responsibility of the child to save her family, yet Cam feels that that burden rests squarely on her shoulders. On the other hand, it suggests that she feels up to the task.

It is too bad that Mr. Ramsay refuses to believe that women can think, and that he has made fun of Cam for not knowing the poles of the compass, for Cam reveals herself to be a philosopher or a historian in embryo, as she thinks of ideas that she would like to share with her father. They range from questions about how the world came into existence to questions about who was the real author of Shakespeare's plays. She thinks about these issues by imagining how her father would think about them, but she does it silently, "without asking him about anything; for that would have been impossible." Her sense of order and stability still depends upon him; she sees him, in her mind, as a person "allowing no disorder" (320), an image of Mr. Ramsay which is in direct contrast to both James's and Lily Briscoe's, who both think that, when Mr. Ramsay approached, "ruin approached, chaos approached" (243). It is likely that Cam's view is fantasy.

James understands that there is no salvation in Mr. Ramsay's vision, that "his father believed that they were all sinking in a waste of waters" (352), and he tries to disengage himself from this pessimistic view of the world by seeing it as his father's view; it need not be his own. Cam, however, is more wedded to her father's vision. In one magnificent and terrifying image, however, we know that Cam's vision is terribly bleak: she imagines herself dying, like the fish that are being reeled into the boat; she imagines herself, like them, "beating their tails up and down in a pool of water on the bottom of the boat" (354). Earlier,

Cam had thought about bringing fish to rescue her family from disaster; here she becomes the fish, drowning in air, on the bottom of the boat.

Much has been made of Mr. Ramsay's praising James's execution of a difficult sailing maneuver in the published version of the novel. According to some critics, James finally gets the affirmation he so desperately wants from his father. But to believe that one compliment can eradicate a lifetime of poor parenting is wishful thinking. The novel ends with the hope that Cam and James might be able to change their bleak view of the world. Given their history and Mr. Ramsay's attitudes, it is extremely doubtful.

The Years, too, portrays the chasm between people.[11] As the novel opens, Rose Pargiter, mother of the Pargiter clan, is on her deathbed. Eleanor Pargiter, one of the daughters in her early twenties, has been forced to assume the maternal role. It is she who sees to the orderly running of the Pargiter household, with the help of her sisters Delia and Milly, while her father, Colonel Abel Pargiter, soothes himself in the arms of his mistress, Mira. Abel Pargiter is unable to enter his wife's bedroom; he leaves the task of sitting with his dying wife to his daughters. When it is reported that his wife has a fainting fit, not only does he himself not go into his wife's bedroom; he keeps his daughters at his side as he finishes his dinner.

The Pargiter girls bear the burden of their mother's illness. Delia sees her mother's illness as a kind of cage, which she hopes she will be released from—she wishes for her mother's death, and watches her carefully for signs of further decline. During the worst of it, Delia escapes by inventing a different life for herself, a life of freedom, which she imagines as having Charles Stewart Parnell standing next to her as she speaks "in the cause of Liberty" (23). In her fantasy, she is the orator; he supports her effort. Freedom for Delia would be a life of political action in Ireland, far away from Abercorn Terrace and the stultifying drawing room of the upper middle class in 1880.

Eleanor is well aware of what she and her sisters are missing: she has observed life in the lower classes, on her trips into the slums as a Victorian do-gooder. Eleanor believes that the "poor enjoy themselves more than we do," which is part rationalization, part truth, given the squalor and the horror which Eleanor reports; yet she rightly perceives that young girls of the working class have far more freedom than she or her sisters, who are "cooped up, day after day" (32).

Except for the emotional trauma that they will no doubt endure, their mother's illness does not affect the lives of the sons in the Pargiter household: Martin carries on very much in the way that he always has; Edward, away at Oxford, hasn't even been apprised of his mother's worsening condition, so that he can go about his studies unaffected by her impending death. While his sisters sit with their mother, Edward flirts outrageously with two young men at the same time, playing them against one another, driving at least one of them fairly mad with un-requited passion. He also reads Greek, and eroticizes the figure of Antigone, standing among "the marble and the asphodel" (51), who reminds him of his cousin Kitty.

In fact, his comparison is apt, for Kitty, like Antigone, is as good as buried alive, carrying out the daily rituals incumbent upon a young woman in her position—she is the daughter of a don at Oxford and must see visitors around the Bodleian, and charm the undergraduates at tea, and her father's guests at dinner, even if, like Chuffy Andrews, they put a sweaty hand on her knee. Kitty Malone's fantasy is to go off to America; failing that, she would like to become a farmer and escape the life her mother leads. But Kitty never even has the time to do the lessons assigned by Lucy Craddock, her history teacher. Kitty is senti-mental about the life Lucy leads; Lucy Craddock thinks that young women like Kitty lead wonderful lives. Neither can see the limitations of the other's predicament.

Kitty thinks that there must be another way of organizing families, and she finds a model when she visits the Robsons. Mr. Robson has worked his way into a position at Oxford; he has not been born to it. Their household is egalitarian; their children are treated as equals. Kitty has a fantasy of kissing Jo Robson, which reminds her of how, at fifteen, she kissed a farmhand called Alf. Freedom, Kitty believes, would be possible if she changed her class.

But Kitty's mother can't understand why her adolescent daughter has become distant from her. She notices that her daughter no longer enjoys the rituals which are the very fabric of their life at the Lodge; she asks her daughter, "what is it you want to do." Mrs. Malone suggests that Kitty help her father with his work; Kitty remembers her father telling her that, like all women, "Nature did not intend you to be a scholar" (81). Mrs. Malone really does not want to hear what her daughter would like to do; she wants her daughter to be happy doing precisely what is expected of her. Mrs. Malone believes that Kitty's life is enviable, far more enviable than hers was as a young woman: Mrs. Malone remembers living in Yorkshire, wondering if that was all there was in life, wanting more; Kitty, in Oxford, in what Mrs. Malone believes to be the center of everything, wants to live in Yorkshire. But Mrs. Malone looks for the solution to Kitty's disaffection in marriage; she needs to find a man who will give her daughter "what she wants." Mrs. Malone, who has no idea what this is, seizes upon the word "scope" (83). She needs to find a husband who will give her daughter "scope."

Sara and Maggie Pargiter are cousins of the Pargiters of Abercorn Terrace, and Woolf describes their lives as young women in the 1907 section of the novel. Sara is confined to bed, for reasons that are not specified. She must follow the doctor's regimen, to lie "straight, lie still" (141). Sara's disjointed responses to her mother and her sister suggest that there is something really wrong with her, or that her speech has become disjointed as a result of the "cure" that she is undergoing, perhaps accompanied by medication. Throughout the novel, Sara is uncannily accurate in her perceptions about her condition: she is the one young woman who is unwilling to hide her anger, her feeling that she is buried alive, her perception of the world as a dung-filled cave. Perhaps she is undergoing a "cure" because she cannot or will not behave as a young lady is supposed to. After reading of Antigone's fate at the hands of Creon, for example, she immediately understands the connection with her own life, and she rearranges herself, in bed, like Antigone in her tomb. Maggie, her sister, goes to parties that are such torture, apparently, that she envies the fact that her sister is bedridden. Their mother, Lady Eugenie Pargiter holds out to her daughters the image of the fulfillment of life through love, so that both Sara and Maggie have not been educated to care for themselves: they will marry well, Lady Pargiter assumes. Sara spends her young life, as "a chrysalis wrapped round in the sharp white folds of the sheet" (144). But Eugenie Pargiter and her husband Digby die unexpectedly and Sara and Maggie are suddenly and precipitously poor, eking out a living in a shabby walkup in the wrong part of town. As young women they have been left thoroughly unprepared to fend for themselves. This is the only life they are able to lead.

Both Sara and Maggie despise family life. Both believe that families harm children: Sara believes that children should be brought up "on a desert island" far apart from the malicious influence of grownups; Maggie believes that perhaps people should stop having children. The reader never finds out what harmed Sara: her history is another of the many stories that never get finished in *The Years* so that one is forced to speculate on the causes of Sara's bleak vision. We do know that her father Digby ignored his girls when they were children. But Sara's belief that human beings are "nasty little creatures, driven by uncontrollable lusts" (189) suggests that something terrible has happened to her.

North Pargiter, too, feels much the same way: he sees the family as a "conspiracy," as "the steam roller that smooths, obliterates; rounds into identity; rolls into balls." The tragedy of family life, according to North, is that all people care about is the well-being of their own children, "their own property"—not the well-being of "other people's children," of everyone's children. This attitude is what makes war possible, North thinks: "their own flesh and blood, which they would protect with the unsheathed claws of the primeval swamp. . . . How then can we be civilised" (378).

Woolf's concern with the adolescent experience was not only contained within her novels. In her nonfiction, she was especially interested in examining the ways in which the education of girls and boys determined their characters. Woolf entered into an important public debate with Desmond MacCarthy in the pages of *The New Statesman* about the intellectual capacities of women, an issue which related to whether girls and women would be provided access to education. Several major nonfictional works were devoted to this issue, such as *A Room of One's Own* and *Three Guineas.*

If in her explorations of Victorian childhood, Virginia Woolf emphasized the common experience of suffering, emotional neglect, and isolation of both girls and boys, in her explorations of adolescence she emphasized the differences between the lives of young women and young men: young men of the upper middle class were educated in a way that prepared them for lives of power and privilege and for war, while young women were prevented from being educated, and trained instead in the submissive behavior that would fit them for a lifetime of unpaid service to men.

Never having received any formal education to speak of, she was particularly concerned with the role that education played in preventing women from becoming economically independent, and in ensuring that power and privilege remained the provenance of a few men of a certain class. Her analysis of the relationship between power and privilege and education is as sound today as it was when she wrote it; indeed, she believed that although education was thought to function as a way to pass on the best in a culture, through study and learning, its real function was to create a cadre of powerful men who unquestioningly accepted their right to rule. She observed that the possibility for a revolution in the relationship between the sexes and between the classes depended upon education; and she suggested in works like "The Leaning Tower" that the written word was a powerful instrument for social change.

Of all the children in the Stephen household, she was the one who would have profited most from a formal education; all of the young men in the family—the Duckworth boys as well as the Stephen sons—never distinguished themselves at school, and often did very poorly. Yet simply by virtue of gender they were given an education and she was deprived of one. Although it was precisely because she was self-educated that she could criticize the system, nonetheless, throughout her life, she felt that she had missed something worth having. She took it upon herself to become educated, and worked diligently to give herself precisely the kind of education that enabled her to so brilliantly critique traditional education and to write her ground-breaking novels.

Woolf publicly announced her position on the complex interrelationship between gender, upbringing, education, and accomplishment in 1920, in *The New Statesman*, in an argument which appeared under the banner "The Intellectual Status of Women." Her argument was a rebuttal of the view on the innate inferiority of women that Arnold Bennett had proclaimed in his 1920 work *Our Women*. Her friend, Desmond MacCarthy, using the pseudonym Affable Hawk, had supported in *The New Statesman* Bennett's argument, that "no amount of education and liberty of action" would alter the indisputable fact of man's natural superiority to women in matters of intellectual prowess; women demonstrated their "intellectual inferiority" because of their "desire to be dominated" by men.[12] Because they were by nature inferior, their different treatment was warranted. To educate girls was to waste one's time and one's resources.

Woolf challenged their argument by remarking that "the seventeenth century produced more remarkable women than the sixteenth, the eighteenth than the seventeenth," and so on. She attributed the advance in the increasing number of notable women to "the effects of education and liberty," which, according to her, are "scarcely to be overrated."[13] Woolf pointed out that he used as evidence of women's natural inferiority an intellectual inferiority that resulted from a lack of education and freedom.

Woolf also argued that it was difficult to accord superior intellectual status to a gender who had been responsible for the horrors of World War I, which had provided ample evidence to women "that the intellect of the male sex is steadily diminishing," but that she would consider it unwise, as yet, "to announce it as a fact."[14]

MacCarthy responded to Woolf's attack by conceding but one point, that "a small percentage of women" may be "just as clever as any clever man." Though he conceded that the condition of women's lives were not conducive to accomplishment, he stated that the fact that women could not overcome obstacles to their accomplishment proved their inferiority. In those areas of endeavor in which there were not significant barriers to women's accomplishment, such as literature, poetry, music, and painting, women still had not "attained, with the possible exception of fiction, the highest achievements reached by men."[15]

Woolf responded that nurture, not nature, governed what women could achieve. She stated that, if there were no women writers of merit, "I can conceive of no reason unless it be that there was some external restraint upon their powers."[16] Woolf's scorching rebuttal itemized the restraints imposed upon women in adolescence who wanted to become musicians or painters or writers. Was there nothing, Woolf argued, to prevent women musicians like Ethel Smyth from studying abroad? "Was there no opposition from her father?" Was the training in music provided by the well-to-do for their daughters sufficient "to fit them to become musicians?" Was there sufficient money for "paints and studios" for girls who wanted to be painters, and was there "no family reason requiring their presence at home."[17] Woolf maintained that *any* person, man *or* woman, who is oppressed, who is "stinted of education and held in subjection," will not be able to realize their intrinsic potential, not because of any natural inferiority or because of their own failure (which she recognized was to blame the victim of oppression for not having surmounted it), but because accomplishment requires not only education but also "freedom of action and experience," and these conditions have not been the "lot of women."[18]

Woolf illuminated the fact that while men of privilege spent their time in educating themselves, women were being trained to subservience. Moreover, they had brought "forth the entire population of the universe." And, Woolf stated: "This occupation has taken much time and strength."[19] Woolf raised the issue of women's lack of accomplishment and denial of education in the context of the exploitation of their unpaid labor in families. She argued that using women's unpaid labor to rear children has prevented women from having the time to advance themselves either intellectually or economically; in childhood and adolescence, girls and women are denied access to education so that they have no other means of supporting themselves but to acquiesce in becoming wives and mothers. Woolf understood that the control of women's access to education was the way in which the control of women's labor without recompense in the family was assured. She saw it as a state identical to slavery.

Woolf's major quarrel with MacCarthy's and Bennett's position was their belief that education would in no way alter the inferior quality of a young woman's mind. She believed that attitudes like this would condemn women to a state of ignorance in the future. Woolf shrewdly argued that because MacCarthy had conceded that the quality of women's minds had in fact improved somewhat, then it would be illogical for him to argue that it was possible to determine the limit of the extent to which women's minds might improve if they were given access to education, liberty of experience, freedom of movement, and the ability to openly express their differences with men. As she put it, "the fact that women have improved . . . shows that they may still improve; for I cannot see why a limit should be set to her improvement." Woolf contended that it was precisely the views of Bennett and of MacCarthy, and not the inherently inferior condition of women's minds, which had held women back. She prevailed upon MacCarthy to reconsider the extent to which the publication of his views (and others like his) contributed to women's lack of advancement, and she argued that if views like his continued to prevail "we shall remain in a condition of half-civilised barbarism" which, for her, was the way the condition of England must be described because it would mean "an eternity of dominion on the one hand and of servility on the other."[20]

Woolf's conclusion was a brilliant stroke, for she implied that one should not use the label "civilized" for any culture which insisted upon the enslavement of a majority of its people. Nor could any privileged male in the British Empire who kept his wife and daughters in a condition of subservience be regarded as civilized, "for the degradation of being a slave is only equalled by the degradation of being a master."[21]

Woolf's stunning display of rational discourse, rhetoric, wit, and style was its own best argument for the abilities she was claiming for women, and MacCarthy, at last, conceded defeat by writing that if the "freedom and education of women is impeded by the expression of my views, I shall argue no more,"[22] which was tantamount to agreeing with Woolf's argument that the advancement of women had, for generations, been impeded by views such as those expressed by himself and Bennett.

Perhaps the most important aspect of *Flush*, Woolf's mock-biography of Elizabeth Barrett Browning's dog, is the fact that in 1842, when the work begins, Flush, a male puppy who has been accorded the rights and privileges of males in general, must learn, by becoming Elizabeth

Barrett's dog, the differences between what being female and male really mean.[23] Although Wimpole Street where Elizabeth Barrett lives is supposed to stand for civilization, what Flush experiences there is the condition of enforced incarceration, a condition in which the daughters of the privileged lived out their lives.

Written from Flush's point of view, the big joke at the beginning of the work, which provides Woolf with her most vital argument against how young women were treated, is the fact that a young male dog has greater freedom, greater access to experience, and is treated better than a young woman of the privileged class. As a puppy, Flush had "enjoyed with all the vivacity of his temperament most of the pleasures and some of the licences natural to his youth and sex" (19). But when he joins the Barrett household and becomes Elizabeth's dog, Flush begins to live the life which English girls live.

Elizabeth's room is described as a tomb in which she is buried alive: "Miss Barrett's bedroom . . . must by all account have been dark." But it is not the darkness (in contrast to the bright light of the fields upon which he scampered) that upsets Flush the most, but the smell of the room, which could only be compared with a "crypt, crusted with fungus, slimy with mould, exuding sour smells of decay and antiquity" (27). And the implication—that Elizabeth Barrett, and young women of her class—are buried alive is perfectly obvious.

Elizabeth Barrett, buried alive, has adjusted to her enforced captivity by becoming an invalid who rarely moves at all. Barrett's invalidism is described as an adaptive response to the barbarous condition of her own captivity. Woolf's splendid trope is that young women are treated like dogs: "There was a likeness between them. As they gazed at each other each felt: Here am I—. . . Broken asunder, yet made in the same mould, could it be that each completed what was dormant in the other? She might have been—all that; and he—But no" (31).

Flush too begins to spend time in "nothing but the bedroom" (35). The only way that Elizabeth Barrett and Flush are permitted to leave the house is to go shopping. On another day, Elizabeth "ventured upon an even more daring exploit—she had herself drawn up Wimpole Street in a bath-chair." Flush responds to the excursion with terror, a brilliant analogue for Elizabeth's agoraphobia, the natural result of her entrapment within the home and being taught that being out-side is dangerous: "he was dazed by the passage of human bodies. Petticoats swished at his head; trousers brushed his flanks; sometimes a wheel whizzed an inch from his nose." Flush responds with a full-fledged anxiety attack: "the wind of destruction roared in his ears and fanned the feathers of his paws as a van passed. Then he plunged in terror" (37).

Now unused to freedom, Flush responds to even this limited amount with a feeling of gratitude for his chain: "Mercifully the chain tugged at his collar; Miss Barrett held him tight, or he would have rushed to destruction" (37). Flush has already become the well-socialized young woman, who has been taught that her boundaries are made for her own good, and for her own protection. His natural high spirits have been broken. It hasn't taken very long at all.

Woolf's point is clear. If you treated a boy the way you treat a girl, then men too would be fearful, timid, prone to illness, and anxiety, unable to make their own way in the world without protection. Up-bringing and not natural proclivity explain behavior and character. Now that his life is like that of a girl, all "his natural instincts were thwarted and contradicted." When as a male puppy, the year before, the autumn winds blew in Berkshire, "he had run in wild scampering across the stubble" (41); now, as a feminized young dog, "at the sound of the ivy tapping on the pane," Flush becomes afraid, and a servant is asked "to see to the fastenings of the window" (41).

Although Flush hears sounds from the street, none meant "free-dom, or action, or exercise" (42). The life of Elizabeth is a death-in-life: "long hours went by . . . with nothing to mark them but the sound of steps passing on the stairs; . . . and the sound of the postman knocking" (47).

The life that Woolf describes for young women in *Flush* is equiva-lent to that described in M. V. Hughes's memoir, *A London Child of the 1870s*. As Hughes describes it, as a girl, she would write into her diary " 'Nothing peculia [*sic*] happened to-day.' Such is the entry again and again in my first diary."[24] Hughes recalls that the events in her life were so few "I was driven to record even the fact of going to bed" (30). Even when she did venture outside, "My outside amusements were purely pale reflections of what the boys [her brothers] told me about theirs." As a girl, Hughes was never taken to "anything more exciting than a picture gallery, not even to a pantomime at Christmas." Although she lived in London, she never went "to the Tower, or the Crystal Palace or Madame Tussaud's" (30), even though her brothers went, and frequently. Her father's belief, expressed as a slogan, was that "boys should go everywhere and know everything, and that a girl should stay at home and know nothing" (33). Once when she cried because she wanted something, she was severely reproved and then received a whipping because "it is as bad for a girl to cry for what she wants as for a boy to plant a blow." Although she was permitted to cry "a very little" if she was hurt, "never, never must I cry just to get something" (32).

As Hughes so well phrased it, "Victorian times are supposed to have been so settled and happy and care-free, but my recollections hardly tally with this rosy picture" (82). As Hughes rewrites the myth of girl-hood in Victorian England, so, too, does Woolf in *Flush*, using the device of writing a dog's life to write the life of a young woman. Flush demonstrates that one *learns* to behave like a girl. And how does one learn? As Flush has learned: "To resign, to control, to suppress, the most violent instincts of his nature—that was the prime lesson of the bedroom school, and it was one of such portentous difficulty that many scholars have learnt Greek with less" (42).

When Woolf tried to examine the reasons why this "bedroom school" for girls existed, why this condition of captivity existed, she rejected out of hand those theories which postulated that there was something inherent in the nature of girls which necessitated their protection, that insisted that they be denied access to the outside world. Woolf instead located the source of the incarceration of girls and young women in the need of fathers to keep their daughters to themselves, in the power which fathers had over their daughters.

In *Three Guineas*, Woolf refers to Mr. Barrett—in addition to other fathers—as she attempts to explore the reasons why young women were not permitted freedom. It is a brilliant and a profound argument, for in one bold stroke, Woolf turns the entire preoccupation with *wom-*

en's nature upside down; she redirects the reader's attention to the behavior of *fathers*.

She decides to subject the behavior of the Victorian father, and
fathers in general, to scrutiny. Using the largely male discipline of
psychology for her own political ends, she appropriates two terms, "infantile" and "fixation," and combines them into the term "infantile
fixation," using it in a wonderful, ingenious way as a term which de-
fines how fathers obsessively fixate their attention on the behavior of
their children, most often their daughters, watching their every move,
scrutinizing their behavior, controlling every detail of their existence,
preventing their freedom. "Now," she writes, "there are so many cases
of infantile fixation . . . in Victorian biography that we scarcely know
which to choose"; the "case of Mr. Barrett . . . is, perhaps the most
famous" (130). She enumerates the details of his behavior toward his
children to make the point that it is truly pathological, although representative of the extreme of a tendency in Victorian paternal behavior.
He would not allow his children to do anything that remotely smacked
of independence. They must obey him in all things. He would not
allow them to marry, which forced Elizabeth to elope, and her father
never forgave this transgression of his law.

In using the jargon word "case" to describe the behavior of Elizabeth Barrett's father, Woolf is making her position clear. Although Victorian psychology was obsessed with defining women's behavior in case
history after case history, the real "cases," the genuine examples of
psychopathology, could be found in the study of Victorian fathers. As
Woolf puts it, "We shall agree that Mr. Barrett's emotions were strong
in the extreme; and their strength makes it obvious that they had their
origin in some dark place below the level of conscious thought" (130).
The origin of the behavior, therefore, is decidedly *not* rational, although the Victorian male prided himself on his rational behavior.
She enumerates other, less well-known "cases," in a discourse which
mocks Freud, as she explores the "infantile fixation": the case of Rev-
erend Patrick Brontë, who, like Mr. Barrett, could not bear the idea of
his daughter's attachment to another man; the case of Mr. Jex-Blake,
who would not permit his daughter to be paid for the tutoring she did:
" 'to be *paid* for the work would be to alter the thing *completely*, and

would lower you sadly in the eyes of almost everybody'" (131). Woolf concludes that these men wanted to keep their daughters in their power and they acted in irrational ways because they could not control their own behavior. Thus, they persistently acted out because of their infantile fixation.

Woolf completely redefines the Oedipus complex for her readers.[25] She suggests that the Oedipus complex is a convenient fiction to mask the psychopathology of Victorian fathers. If there was anyone out of control in the Victorian family, it was the Victorian father, for he acted on the impulse of subterranean drives without examining his behavior. Rather than being treated for his condition, however, Woolf observes that "the infantile fixation was protected by society" (135).

Woolf explains the behavior of fathers in language traditionally reserved for girls and women and for female case histories. It was a powerful and deliciously subversive comparison, for if there was any being that the Victorian male did not want to be identified with, it was a woman. Mr. Barrett's emotions were "strong in the extreme"; they had their origin "in some dark place below the level of conscious thought"; Mr. Jex-Blake, like Mr. Barrett, acts on the basis of "a very strong emotion" (131).

The separate and different treatment of young women and young men in Victorian households was supported by treatises on the innate nature of sexual difference, such as that of Patrick Geddes, who in *The Evolution of Sex* (1899) argued that sexual differences arose from a basic difference in cell metabolism in girls and boys: at the cellular level, "maleness was characterized by the tendency to dissipate energy, femaleness by the capacity to store or build up energy."[26] Biology was destiny; boys took on the characteristics of their flagellate sperm and were active, knowledge seeking, inquisitive, outgoing; girls took on the characteristics of the quiescent, well-nourished ovum and were passive, intuitive, content, inactive. "What was decided among prehistoric *Protozoa*," Geddes maintained, "can not be annulled by act of parliament."[27]

Woolf completely reverses the commonly held truisms about Victorian female and male behavior: in her tongue-in-cheek but deadly serious descriptions, it is the Victorian fathers who are possessed by paroxysms of uncontrollable feeling, who moan, and cry, and shout. They are, to a man, hysterical. And their daughters, in their attempts to wrest some small measure of freedom from their fathers, are depicted by Woolf as displaying extreme self-control, keen analysis, and providing one rational, cool, carefully considered analytical argument after another.

Woolf argues that had any of these fathers treated an animal the way they treated their daughters, the society would have protected the animal—indeed legislative impetus for measures to curb cruelty to animals in England predated that for measures to curb cruelty to children.

In "The Leaning Tower," a paper that was read to the Worker's Educational Association in Brighton in May 1940, Woolf argued that all women, whatever their supposed class, had more in common with the poor than they did with men of their own class. She posed the same question in relationship to class that she had posed in relationship to gender in her previous works and asked "is there any connection between . . . material prosperity and . . . intellectual creativeness? Did one lead to the other?"[28] She answered that there was. She argued that it was commonly accepted that there was a natural and necessary division between the classes that corresponded to a kind of divine scheme, that the privileged were privileged because they deserved to be; and the poor were poor because they deserved to be; that the privileged were educated because they were superior and that the uneducated were not educated because they were incapable of deriving any benefit from education. Woolf understood, instead, that education was used to maintain a hierarchical class structure. As she put it, "England has crammed a small aristocratic class with Latin and Greek and logic and metaphysics and mathematics" and "has left the other class, the immense class to which almost all of us must belong, to pick up what we can" (152).

This statement identified the reality that women were in a different class from their fathers and husbands, and that they shared important problems with the working class, the problem of not having equal access to education, for example. But Woolf believed that once women and the working class had been taught how to read, that critical reading and the production of literature had the radical potential for changing society. She believed that education had been denied women and the poor to subvert them, to control them, to make them dependent upon men of privilege, and to extort unpaid or poorly paid labor from them. But Woolf believed that education could be used as a vehicle for reversing that.

Woolf believed, moreover, that change had to be forced by outsiders, for it is impossible to criticize a "society whole-heartedly while you continue to profit by that society" (141). Woolf isolated the reason why universal literacy has such radical potential for a society, and why literacy becomes such a carefully controlled skill in hierarchical societies. She invited the workers to whom she lectured to use their ability to read, not as a way to amuse themselves, but as a way to empower themselves.

Any work of literature written by a member of an oppressed group will be written in order to form a connection with other oppressed peoples, to be "down on the ground with the mass of human kind" (147). This was a radical possibility, for if an alliance could be forged of all oppressed people, then the structure which enslaved them would be forced to change. First and foremost, such literature would demonstrate what the nature of oppression has been, what it has felt like, that it has been systematic, and how it has been maintained. She understood that the only people capable of understanding and evaluating oppression are the oppressed themselves.

She labeled this new school of writers "the leaning tower school," a school of "auto-analysis after the suppression of the 19th century." For Woolf, there existed a link between personality and historical circumstance. She believed that it would be necessary for the oppressed to understand that their experience was not unique, that it was shared by others, that it was part of a historical pattern of oppression.

Woolf provides yet another analysis of the condition of female adolescence in Victorian England in her memoir, "The tea table was the centre of Victorian family life." The image that she develops of her room, the old night nursery, as the center of her life in adolescence, is "my own cocoon." The image of the cocoon to describe the development of girls in adolescence contrasts dramatically with the education provided for the boys in the family, which occurred outside the home.

Woolf's confinement to her room, to the old night nursery, under-scores how her treatment was infantalizing. An implicit comparison is made between the confinement of her life in the cocoon and the tem-porary freedom of an eagle which escaped from London Zoo, and which she describes as soaring over the rooftops of London. Just as the eagle has been caged, so too is she caged, and she uses the word "cage" to refer to her home. Just as visitors go to the zoo to see the eagle, so too do all the members of the household and even her teachers come to see her in the confines of her room. And the life that she experi-ences in adolescence is lived at a remove, at a distance, not directly, through the closely wound filaments of the cocoon which she tries to penetrate to understand what is going on in the world.

In an attempt to get close to the outside world, she puts her bed by the window, so that she can experience the sounds of the city. Some-times she hears dance music; sometimes the clatter of the sounds from the horse-drawn carriages in the mews near her home. Once she thought she heard an old man obscenely raving, but she can't go out-side at night to check on the accuracy of her own perceptions, and she depends upon her brothers to tell her that the sound that she heard was only a cat.

The image of the cocoon says much about the way Woolf viewed the treatment of adolescent girls in Victorian England. Girls were held in a state of suspended animation in the cocoon of the Victorian fam-ily, immobilized, frozen, unable to experience life directly but forced to see it through the thick web of protection which surrounded them. Girls were not given the experiences that boys had, as difficult as those experiences may have been. They were treated as pupae, and any changes that did occur were a result of the natural growth process, rather than through the young woman's active acquisition of knowl-edge. Perhaps Woolf knew, that the word "pupa," used for the nonfeed-ing, immobile transformation state between the larva and the imago, is derived from the Latin word for girl.

Three Guineas is Virginia Woolf's most comprehensive analysis of the impact of the difference which education makes in the lives of young women and young men. This work is also an inquiry into the origins of militarism, into what Woolf refers to as the "habit" of fighting, which has "always been the man's habit, not the woman's."[29] And Woolf's big question is whether that "habit" is based upon male instincts, or whether that habit is learned. To argue that men wage war because they are instinctively belligerent would be to argue that it is impossible to stop war. But when Woolf's imaginary correspondent in *Three Guineas* writes for a contribution to a fund to stop war, she thinks about how, in the profoundest sense, this might happen, and she concludes that the education of young men teaches them about their superiority to their sisters and to the lower class. It is this very training in their own superiority that inculcates in them the necessity of competition and the subjugation of their sisters and other subject peoples and that leads, inevitably, to war. It is a subtle and a profound argument, and one of the most thorough-going analyses of the overlooked disastrous effects of privileging one gender over another.

If war is to be stopped, then the distinctions between young women and young men, and between the privileged classes and the other classes, must be erased: "for educated men to emphasize their superiority over other people, either in birth or intellect . . . are acts that rouse competition and jealousy—emotions which . . . have their share in encouraging a disposition towards war" (21). To stop war, a new educational system must be put into place.

Woolf describes how the different processes of educating young men and young women are designed to create a gulf between brother and sister that becomes so great that it is impossible to communicate across it. To demonstrate her point, she creates a fictional young woman, called Mary Kingsley, and points out to her imaginary male audience (who has written asking her for a contribution in the cause of peace) the differences in her education from that received by her brother. Speaking in the persona of Mary Kingsley, she remarks that "being allowed to learn German was *all* the paid-for education I ever had. Two thousand pounds was spent on my brother's" (4).

Woolf states the impact of what she refers to as "Arthur's Education Fund," that "voracious receptacle," (4) on the lives of his sisters, and she points out that young women are expected to do without in order for their brothers to be educated; in fact, not only "did their education . . . go into it, but many . . . luxuries . . . which are, after all, an essential part of education—travel, society, solitude, a lodging apart from the family house" (5). It is not only that young men are privileged; it is also that because young men are privileged, young women are underprivileged.

And so it should come as no surprise that the bastions of higher learning, like Oxford and Cambridge, Woolf argues, do not look the same to young women as they do to young men. To young women, places like Oxford simply mean "petticoats with holes," and the "boat train starting for abroad" (5) without her on, the cost of her passage being paid, of course, into Arthur's Education Fund.

In thinking about the educational system that can be put in place to stop war, Woolf looks at the history of the university in England, and concludes that "the great majority of men who have ruled England . . . have received a university education" (24). She describes the attempts by young women to secure an education equal in quality to that of their brothers, and she describes how, at one point, young women at Newnham College who passed examinations petitioned for the right to "advertise the fact" by "putting letters after their names" to indicate the degree they had earned, just like their brothers. The result of that effort, which Woolf describes, was that the proposal "met with the most determined opposition." The issue aroused such interest that a great number of men turned out to vote to defeat the proposal by a "crushing majority." Woolf describes the behavior of the young male undergraduates after the result was announced: "A large band . . . proceeded to Newnham and damaged the bronze gates which had been put up as a memorial to Miss Clough, the first Principal" (29). She chronicles, as well, what she refers to as the "battle of Harley Street" (66), the battle on the part of women to open up the profession of physician to women.

Woolf states that these facts prove that "the finest education in the world, does not teach people to hate force, but to use it" (29). Education, moreover, does not teach young men "generosity and magnanimity" as is commonly supposed; rather, education makes these young men even more eager than ever to fight to "keep their possessions" and their male privilege in their own hands and in their own class, so that they will use not only direct force, "but much subtler methods . . . when they are asked to share them," and "are not force and possessiveness very closely connected with war?" (30). In her biography of Roger Fry, Woolf describes Fry's belief that he had gained little from his public school, Clifton, except a lifelong dislike for public school ideals which he found reprehensible: he especially abhorred "all those Imperialistic and patriotic emotions"[30] which the boys were expected to adopt.

But she also points out in *Three Guineas* that if the daughters of educated men are given the same education that educated men have received for centuries, then "are we not forcing her to think not about education but about war?—not how she can learn, but how she can fight in order that she may win the same advantages as her brothers" (31).

Woolf set forth the ideals that should govern any education for young women and young men that would reduce the risk of war or eliminate it entirely: what should most certainly *not* be taught were "the arts of dominating other people; not the arts of ruling, of killing, of acquiring land and capital." Rather, what should be taught are "the arts of human intercourse; the art of understanding other people's lives and minds, and the little arts of talk, of dress, of cookery that are allied with them" (34), what Woolf believed to be the arts of civilization; any "art or science that encourages war" (36–37) would, of course, be abolished.

She called this college "the cheap college" (34), and so convinced was she that traditional education contributed to war and to the subjugation of women and the other classes, that she stated that the old colleges should be set on fire, they should be left to blaze, for "we have done with this 'education'" (36). In the cheap college, one would dissuade young people from specializing; one should teach them instead to combine different areas of knowledge. Teachers should not be drawn only from the rank of "the good thinkers," there should be teachers drawn from the rank of "the good livers." And these teachers should eschew the lecture, for lecturing to students is just another way of enforcing silence, of asserting superiority. In the cheap college students could work together and enable one another, for "competition would be abolished" (34).

Woolf stated that the best way to abolish war would be to give a great deal of money to the establishment of colleges with such ideals for "the daughters of educated men." One of the functions of this education, of course, would be to prepare these daughters of educated men to earn their own living; that was the only way that Woolf saw that the subjugation of young women in the homes of their fathers would be stopped. The "education of the private house" (37) consisted mostly of enforced incarceration, of young girls not being allowed, for various reasons, to even venture out of doors. The education of the private house prepared her for one profession only: marriage. And it was "with a view to marriage that she tinkled on the piano, but was not allowed to join an orchestra" (38). But no one should be educated to desire extreme wealth; extreme wealth, Woolf thought, was a trap that would keep young women and young men from being able to participate in important activities, like knowing their children, "friendship, travel or art" (70). The professions as they were now organized, Woolf believed, insisted upon an incarceration no less virulent than that of the private house; the one "shuts us up like slaves in a harem; the other forces us to circle . . . round . . . the sacred tree, of property" (74).

She insisted that if young women were to prevent themselves from becoming enslaved by the pursuit of wealth, they would have to embrace the ideals of "poverty, chastity, derision, and . . . lack of rights and privileges," but that they could combine them with "some wealth, some knowledge, and some service to real loyalties" (79). In that way, if young women educated themselves, they would not become the clones of ambitious men.

In illuminating those subtle ways in which rank and privilege have been kept within the hands of educated men and kept out of the hands of their sisters, Woolf chronicles the impact that enforced poverty has had upon young women. She describes how women's colleges are "unbelievably and shamefully poor" (30). She wonders why women, as a class, are "so terribly poor" (41); she observes that in 1934, earning £250 a year was quite an achievement "even for a highly qualified woman with years of experience" (44). She described the difference in salaries between women and men; she wrote that the only explanation can be that "Miss" before a name "transmits sex; and sex may carry with it an aroma"; the "discrepancy is due to atmosphere" which is really misogyny; it is one of the "most powerful . . . of the enemies which the daughters of educated men have to fight" (52).

In *A Room of One's Own* Woolf had painted a composite portrait of the kind of men who subjugated their daughters or who believed that young women cannot be educated. She goes to the British Museum and discovers "the enormous body of masculine opinion . . . that [says] nothing could be expected of women intellectually."[31] She tries to account for the fact that such a view has been accepted by so many men, but not by all men, and she notices a similarity among the men who believe that girls and women are inherently inferior.

In one category of misogynists, there is Woolf's creation, Professor von X, engaged in writing his monumental work entitled *The Mental, Moral, and Physical Inferiority of the Female Sex* (31). In her rage at him, she sees him as "a faggot burning on the top of Hampstead Heath" (32). Professor von X, in writing his work, has an expression on his face as if "he were killing some noxious insect." But "even when he had killed it that did not satisfy him; he must go on killing it" (31). And then, there is Mr. Oscar Browning, "a great figure in Cambridge at one time," who believes that "the best woman was intellectually the inferior of the worst man." Woolf describes the kind of young man that Browning believes is the superior to any woman—the stable boy who waits for Browning's favors in his rooms at Cambridge: the boy is lying on the sofa, "a mere skeleton, his cheeks were cavernous and sallow, his teeth were black, and he did not appear to have the full use of his limbs." "That's Arthur," Browning remarks, "a dear boy really and most high-minded" (55).

Profound misogyny, like Professor von X's and Oscar Browning's, is so virulent that its intent is not merely to victimize women, but to exterminate them. Woolf believed such men possessed this murderous impulse, about which they might be unaware, for nothing else could account for the treatment of women throughout history. Woolf asks, "Why were they angry?" "He seemed to control everything. Yet he was angry" (34).

Woolf points out that the male supremacist attitudes of the homosexuals of the ruling class and the intelligentsia resembled the male supremacist attitude of another category of men: fascists and dictators. Consider Mussolini, who insisted "upon the inferiority of women" (36); consider Napoleon, who believed that girls and women were incapable of being educated. By pointing out that military dictators and fascists are invariably misogynists, Woolf suggests that *all* men who believe in the inferiority of women must have something of the fascist about them.

All misogynists are united by what Woolf refers to, parodying the language of psychoanalysis, as "that very interesting and obscure masculine complex" which is a "deep-seated desire, not so much that *she* shall be inferior as that *he* shall be superior" (57). This masculine complex consists of a passion for dominance which does not limit itself to the desire to dominate the women in one's family; it is "the instinct for possession" which Woolf likens to "harboring in their breasts an eagle, a vulture, for ever tearing the liver out and plucking at the lungs." (A variation of the same image appears in *To the Lighthouse*, in the description of Mr. Ramsay.) This instinct "drives them to desire other people's fields and goods perpetually; to make frontiers and flags; battleships and poison gas; to offer up their own lives and their children's lives" (38).

In *Three Guineas*, Woolf referred to these men as dictators in embryo. They were dictators, because they believed that they had the right "to dictate to other human beings how they shall live; what they shall do." Woolf believed that the dictator was alive and well and flourishing, not only abroad, in Italy or in Germany, but "in the heart of England." She believed that it was necessary for everyone to "crush him in our own country" (53), to stop the dictatorial rule of men over women, before women should be asked to stop dictatorship abroad. And so it should come as no surprise to men that women should have a different set of loyalties. Having been enslaved in their own country, one should not expect women to be patriotic. "As a woman," Woolf wrote, "I want no country. As a woman my country is the whole world" (109).[32]

When Woolf described the changes that were brewing in England, she described how the concealed force of dictatorial fathers was being challenged by another force, the force of women who were trying "not to break the laws, but to find the law." This force, which she sees as a force of "tremendous power," began, in the nineteenth century, to challenge the despotism of the father's rule; this power "forced open the doors of the private house" (138). Every woman who did this, Woolf believed, had taken on a task equivalent to that of Antigone in challenging Creon, for the voice of the dictator, Woolf believed, was not a new voice, "but a very old cry": it is the voice of Creon saying, "They must be women, and not range at large." In burying Antigone alive in a tomb, however, Creon had brought "ruin on his house" (141).

Woolf's anthem in *Three Guineas*, which she sounds at the end of the work, is the theme that runs through her explorations of the lives of adolescent women throughout her career. It is that "the public and the private worlds are inseparably connected; . . . the tyrannies and servilities of the one are the tyrannies and servilities of the other" (142).

Virginia Woolf was a significant, if often overlooked, contributor to both the history and the philosophy of education, with significant ideas about pedagogy and curriculum. Her exploration of the impact of education upon development was central to her exploration of the adolescent experience and her ideas about how the lives of girls and women could be changed. Because she related the education of boys and men to the development of imperialism, her ideas about education chart a course for how war could be averted which had nothing to do with bans and treaties. For Woolf understood that the impulse to war is rooted in the most early training which boys receive in the superiority of their own gender. If the lives of girls are to change, if the lives of the poor are to change, if war is to be averted, then misogyny (which is fundamentally a claim to superiority) must cease. Education was a key feature for Woolf in changing lives, indeed, in changing the very nature of life on this planet.

EPILOGUE

Throughout the years of Virginia Woolf's apprenticeship as a writer, while she was experimenting with form and trying to find her own voice and subject matter, she continued to live with the daily, insidious reality of sexual abuse. She called these years her "Greek slave" years, the years in which both she and her sister Vanessa were subjected to satisfying the sexual, emotional, and social needs of the men in the family. Nonetheless, during these years, Virginia Woolf carved out some space in her days to write. And from the first, she wrote about the effect of sexual abuse and the experiences of young women in a society which degraded them.

It cannot have been easy for her. She would be taken out into society by George Duckworth. Once home, she would go up into her room to undress, wondering if it were really possible that on the next day she would have time to get to her Greek or to her writing. But she would not be able to forget it. Just as she was falling asleep, the door would open; "treading gingerly, someone entered." It was George Duckworth. "Don't be frightened," he would whisper, as "he flung himself on my bed, and took me in his arms." And this would go on, with George flinging "himself on my bed, cuddling and kissing and otherwise embracing me," even as her father was in bed, with cancer, dying in the same house.[1]

After a night like this, and there were many nights like this, she would get up the next morning and, finally, pick up her pen to work on an essay, a diary entry, or a story. Her subject matter would very often be the experiences that she herself had lived through. And she no doubt wondered about how to convert her experiences into art. She

recognized that the very fabric of society insisted upon a human intercourse that was superficial. She knew that behind the social masks that
ordinary people wore, there were private sorrows, though to look at
them, one would never guess it. She understood that "it is not part of
the game to go deep: that might be dangerous."[2] Her dilemma as a
writer was that if she went deep it would indeed be dangerous, for the
experiences that she needed to transcribe into art were those of a childhood violated, of a young womanhood fairly ruined by the experiences
she had lived through and by her culture's devaluation of her gender.
There was no way for her to write her experiences without writing
works which would indict either directly or by implication the members of her family and society in general. She learned, quickly, that a
male audience would have trouble with her explicit denunciations of
the prevailing social order: when she sent her brother-in-law Clive Bell
some chapters of her first novel, he objected to what she had to say,
and she responded to his "objection" that her "prejudice against men"
made her "didactic."[3] Sometimes she retreated from the task, and
wrote from what she described as a "bloodless point of view," hoping
to find a respite in writing works that were located in a "vague and
dream like world, without love, or heart, or passion, or sex."[4] But not
for long.

At some point she understood that it would be difficult to tell the
truth about her experiences. But she did it nonetheless. As she stated
while writing her first published novel, *The Voyage Out*, a "painstaking
woman who wishes to treat of life as she finds it, and to give voice to
some of the perplexities of her sex, in plain English, has no chance at
all."[5] Yet, in her work, she carved out a way to tell her story, as we
have seen, and that of other childhood victims of abuse and neglect.

Virginia Woolf did not complete a major work of fiction until after
Leslie Stephen's death in 1904, and until she and Vanessa established
a household of their own in Bloomsbury. Her life became difficult as
she struggled to grapple with the aftermath of her father's death. She
fell victim to despair and depression and then attempted suicide. She
had felt more alone than ever, more unprotected than ever from that
life which had seemed "tangled and matted with emotion." Part of the
problem was surely her feelings of guilt about her father's death, for

her "passionate affection" for him had alternated with "passionate hatred." But most of the problem was caused by what she described as
the "emotions and complications"[6] of her family history.

Like many other victims of sexual abuse, she was sent out of her
home to recover, and so lost her father, her sanity, and her home in
rapid succession. She had nearly taken her own life. Her sister Vanessa, who had also endured her own share of sexual abuse, took
charge after Leslie's death and, at some point, told Dr. Savage about
what George had been up to. Dr. Savage confronted George, who
explained his behavior as intending to "comfort" her "for the fatal illness of my father."[7] At last, the long ordeal which had begun when
she was six years old was over, although she lived with the effects of
sexual abuse for the rest of her life.

During this time, Virginia Woolf was cared for by Violet Dickinson
who, quite literally, saved her life by offering her maternal care and
protection, and a respite from the abuse that she had lived with up to
this time. Although she had been forced to leave her home, in the
long run it was not a bad thing. She recuperated with Violet, and
Vanessa dismantled the family home at 22 Hyde Park Gate: she "had
sold; she had burnt; she had sorted; she had torn up." They would be
living in Bloomsbury; the "family which had seemed equally wedged
together had broken apart too"[8]—George had married and Gerald was
living on his own, so that, upon her recovery, the debilitating, daily
contact with the Duckworths was over.[9] Her Quaker aunt Caroline
Emelia Stephen was also important to Virginia Woolf at this time, as
Jane Marcus has described in her essay, "The Niece of a Nun." Virginia stayed part of the time with Caroline and she wrote of her aunt's
home as being "an ideal retreat for me."[10]

When Woolf described her time with Violet Dickinson in a work
that she wrote after her recovery, "The Magic Garden,"[11] she described
an idyllic world without men, where peace, freedom, joy, sisterhood,
and sensuality reigned. There were "gigantic women" reclining on
lounges, helping themselves to "strawberries and cream as though they
looked upon a vision of a jocund world" (282). There were women like
flowers whose voices "chimed like petals floating and kissing in the air"
(283). What made this "tranquil scene" possible was the fact that Vi-

olet's "listless eye" would grow "attentive" (285) if anything threatened this tranquility.

In this idyllic portrait, Woolf describes what life might be like if girls had women to care for them who truly valued their own gender. The major reason why Violet could behave in this woman-identified way is that she was "alone and had therefore no reason to veil her discontent." She had no husband who claimed attention, and so she could be herself, which meant that she could express displeasure when she felt it. The tranquility in Violet's garden, where you "could hear if you listened, either the kiss of the air or the chatter of insects" was in stark contrast to the "violent emotions"[12] which had surrounded Virginia Woolf in her own home. With Violet there to protect her, there was not "one yelp or discord" (285). And under Violet's watchful eye, even the fauns, which were so threatening if not controlled, were nothing to worry about. In Violet's garden, rather than ravishing and raping, they were innocuous creatures, given to simple, harmless pleasures. In Violet's garden, it was possible to run happily naked without shame or fear.

Inside Violet Dickinson's home, Virginia Woolf learned some precious lessons. As Virginia herself put it, "Violets cottage stood for a symbol of many things" (290). One was that not every household was filled with violence and sexual abuse, and that the protection of young women was indeed possible, although she had the insight to understand that Violet was protective because Violet was independent. Another was that Violet preferred "to build her own house" with her own hands "to living in [a] house built for you by others" (286), which symbolized to Woolf that it was indeed possible to think about the kind of psychic space you yourself wanted to inhabit, which meant that it was necessary to reject those patterns of behavior erected by others. This meant asking detailed questions about the very structure of the system; it meant taking nothing for granted; as Violet asked questions about drainage and plumbing, so too would Woolf have to ask her own questions about the edifice that she inhabited. "This," she wrote, "was the beginning of revolution"—finding out how the houses of the fathers were built, upon what foundations they were erected. Violet taught her that no one could find out these things for her; nor could she trust any of the old answers; like Violet, she had to find out for herself, for "no one could tell her how the drains were managed, for no one remembered that there were drains" (287).

Finally, Violet insisted that Woolf take herself seriously as a writer, that she convert her private diaries, essays, and fragments into published works. In Violet's house, "the talk played freely on the most interesting and instructive of subjects; modern English prose; how it is written by women; and then, for the sake of example how it is written by one woman; its beauties, possibilities aims and just to round the picture—defects" (291).

And so Virginia Woolf began.

Throughout her life, as we have seen, Virginia Woolf consistently examined the betrayal of the child's right to protection within the family. Her life's work—her memoirs and autobiography, her novels, her essays and biographies—is an invaluable missing link in the history of incest, abuse, and the effects of family violence.

But we must not forget that in 1892 a terrified ten-year-old girl by the name of Virginia Stephen first picked up her pen to write a portrait of the world as seen through the eyes of an abused child. And from that time forward throughout her lifetime she never stopped examining why and how the abuse had happened, and what it had meant to her, and what it must have meant to others. Contemporary writers may be able to write more graphically. But Virginia Woolf's life's work stands among the most insightful testimonies we have. She could not ever forget what had happened to her. She could never forget the betrayal of her childhood innocence and the consequences, which lasted a lifetime. Nor should we.

Notes

In these notes, the reader will find the titles of all books quoted; the subtitles, and all publishing information are to be found in the Select Bibliography. In the case of essays, only the major title is listed; the journal or book in which the essay appears can be found in the Select Bibliography.

References to Virginia Woolf's letters are listed according to the volume and letter number from the published collected letters (e.g., *Letters* 1:3). References to Virginia Woolf's diaries are listed according to the date of the entry and published volume number (e.g., 27 November 1939, *Diary* 5). If there is more than one quotation within a paragraph from a specified source, I have annotated only the last quotation; the reader should assume that unannotated quotes preceding are from the same source. Wherever possible, I have put page references to works cited often in parentheses in the text. Virginia Woolf's name as author has been abbreviated as "VW" throughout.

PREFACE

1. I explore that identification in "A Portrait of the *Puttana* as a Middle-Aged Woolf Scholar."

2. See Louise A. DeSalvo, *Virginia Woolf's First Voyage*; "*Melymbrosia*" by Virginia Woolf, *An Early Version of The Voyage Out*; "Lighting the Cave"; *The Letters of Vita Sackville-West to Virginia Woolf*, with Mitchell A. Leaska; "1897: Virginia Woolf at Fifteen."

3. Louise A. DeSalvo, "'To Make Her Mutton at Sixteen.'"

4. VW, *Mrs. Dalloway*, p. 3.

5. See, esp., Judith Lewis Herman, with Lisa Hirschman, *Father-Daughter Incest*; Florence Rush, *The Best-Kept Secret*; Diana E. H. Russell, *The Secret Trauma*.

6. Alice Miller, *Thou Shalt Not Be Aware*; *The Drama of the Gifted Child*; and *For Your Own Good*.

INTRODUCTION

1. VW, *To the Lighthouse*, p. 95; "A Sketch of the Past," p. 67.

2. Lyndall Gordon, *Virginia Woolf*, p. 16; Lloyd de Mause, ed., *The History of Childhood*, pp. 4–6. For the ways in which incestuous households are organized, however, see, e.g., Judith Lewis Herman, with Lisa Hirschman, *Father-Daughter Incest*; Florence Rush, *The Best-Kept Secret*. For abuse within the family, see Arthur Brittan and Mary Maynard, *Sexism, Racism and Oppression*. For Victorian households, see Carol Dyhouse, *Girls Growing Up in Late Victorian and Edwardian England*; Marilyn French, *Beyond Power*; Deborah Gorham, *The Victorian Girl and the Feminine Ideal*; Stephen Kern, "Explosive Intimacy," pp. 437–62; Steven Marcus, *The Other Victorians*; Steven Mintz, *A Prison of Expectations*; Ronald Pearsall, *The Worm in the Bud*; Martha Vicinus, ed., *Suffer and Be Still*; Martha Vicinus, ed., *A Widening Sphere*.

3. Quentin Bell, *Virginia Woolf*, 1:43. Subsequent references to Bell's argument are in parentheses in the text.

4. Jean O. Love, *Virginia Woolf*, p. 195. Subsequent references are in parentheses in the text.

5. Phyllis Rose, *Woman of Letters*, p. ix. Subsequent references are in parentheses in the text.

6. Roger Poole, *The Unknown Virginia Woolf*, p. 32. Subsequent references are in parentheses in the text.

7. Stephen Trombley, *'All That Summer She Was Mad,'* p. 297. Subsequent references are in parentheses in the text.

8. Gordon, *Virginia Woolf*, p. 119. Subsequent references are in parentheses in the text.

9. Louise Armstrong, *Kiss Daddy Goodnight*, p. 18.

10. Ellen Bass and Louise Thornton, eds., *I Never Told Anyone*, p. 18.

11. Alice Miller, *Thou Shalt Not Be Aware*, p. 320. For responses to incest, see Elaine Hilberman Carmen, Patricia Perri Rieker, and Trudy Mills, "Victims of Violence and Psychiatric Illness"; Denise J. Gelinas, "The Persisting Negative Effects of Incest." For the helping professions' reluctance to connect neurotic symptoms with incest, see Roland Summit, "Beyond Belief: The Reluctant Discovery of Incest." Subsequent references to Miller's *Thou Shalt Not Be Aware* are in parentheses in the text.

12. Sigmund Freud, quoted by Miller, in *Thou Shalt Not Be Aware*, p. 117. It is important to note that Karin Stephen, VW's sister-in-law, held a strictly Freudian view toward neurosis. She wrote in *The Wish to Fall Ill* that the "driving force behind neurotic symptoms is always a *wish*," p. 55.

13. Sigmund Freud, quoted by Herman, in *Father-Daughter Incest*, p. 10.

14. Diana E. H. Russell, *The Secret Trauma*, p. 5.

15. Herman, *Father-Daughter Incest*, pp. 9, 10.

16. Russell, *The Secret Trauma*, p. 5.

17. Rush, *The Best-Kept Secret*, p. 56.

18. Walter E. Houghton, *The Victorian Frame of Mind*. See also, Alice Miller, *For Your Own Good*; de Mause, ed., *The History of Childhood*; Anthony S. Wohl, "Sex and the Single Room"; Russell, *The Secret Trauma*, p. 102; Edwin McDowell, "Reagan's Son Tells of Abuse as a Youth by Man at Camp," p. 8.

19. Judith Lewis Herman, in *Father-Daughter Incest* states: "To be sexually exploited by a known and trusted adult is a central and formative experience in the lives of countless women" (p. 7).

Different studies report different statistics, but one of the most compelling and far reaching is that of Diana E. H. Russell. Based upon a probability sample, Russell described her "shocking findings," that one in six of the 930 women whom she studied had been incestuously abused before the age of eighteen; one in eight, before the age of fourteen—4.5 percent were abused by their fathers. These are higher figures for the incidence of incest than have ever before been reported (see Russell, *The Secret Trauma*, for these statistics). This finding suggests that girls are often being abused when they are powerless, more vulnerable, and most likely to have it be a determinant factor in their personality development, when their bodies will most likely be harmed by penetration and manipulation.

Moreover, she discovered that a staggering 38 percent of the women she studied reported at least one experience of sexual abuse before eighteen; 28 percent, before fourteen. In addition, Russell discovered that more than half of all abused women were abused repeatedly. Moreover, a great proportion of the women who reported sexual abuse indicated that it had lasted over a long period of time. In a significant number of instances, incest survivors reported being abused by more than one family member; in one-third of the cases, survivors reported that their abuser had also abused another relative (227). Regardless of how young, a majority of the survivors used "an assertive strategy to try to stop the sexual abuse from continuing or escalating" (126). Yet sexual abuse early in life increases the risk of sexual abuse later in life. And the silence that supposedly surrounds sexual abuse might not be as prevalent as was previously believed: more women reported that they had told someone of the abuse than reported that they had not told anyone. Statistics for the prevalence of incest are also provided in Gelinas, "The Persisting Negative Effects of Incest."

Alfred Kinsey and his associates, in their famous report on female sexuality, (1953), indicated that from one fifth to one third of all women reported that they had had a childhood sexual encounter with an adult male (Herman, *Father-Daughter Incest*, p. 12). Kinsey, however, minimized the impact of his findings: although 80 percent of these women reported having been traumatized by the incidents, Kinsey stated that they *"should not be"* (Herman, p. 16).

An article by Jane Brody in the *New York Times* ("Therapists Seek Causes of Child Molesting," pp. C1, C12) cited several statistics. The Sex Information and

Educational Council of the United States reported that from 20 to 40 percent of all girls between the ages of four and thirteen will be sexually victimized by an adult known to her, and that they will usually react negatively and fearfully to the experience. Parents United estimates that one out of four girls and one out of seven boys will be victims of sexual abuse and that 75 percent of sexual abusers are family members. A national poll by the *Los Angeles Times* in 1985 indicated that 10.9 million to 17.6 million American men have sexually abused a child. In a survey of 795 undergraduates at six New England colleges, 19 percent of the women and 9 percent of the men reported having been sexually abused before the age of 18. Among women attending a mental health clinic, 44 percent report having been sexually abused.

20. Herman, *Father-Daughter Incest*, p. 56. Subsequent references to Herman are in parentheses in the text.

21. Russell, *The Secret Trauma*, pp. 13–14.

22. Ibid., p. 279. Subsequent references to Russell's discussion of the effect of incest are in parentheses in the text.

23. Bass and Thornton, eds., *I Never Told Anyone*, p. 13; Russell, *The Secret Trauma*, p. 190. See also Gelinas, "The Persisting Negative Effects of Incest."

24. Herman, *Father-Daughter Incest*, p. 125.

25. Armstrong, *Kiss Daddy Goodnight*, p. 24. Subsequent references to survivors' statements are in parentheses in the text. For sleep disturbances in Woolf, see Love, *Virginia Woolf*, p. 216.

26. Woolf uses this image in a very early draft of *The Voyage Out*. See "Melymbrosia," p. 263.

27. Armstrong, *Kiss Daddy Goodnight*, p. 259. I analyze VW's "looking-glass complex" in "A Daughter Remembers."

28. VW, "A Sketch of the Past," p. 69.

29. Armstrong, *Kiss Daddy Goodnight*, p. 259.

30. They are now in the Berg Collection.

31. The phrase is Alice Miller's, and is taken from the earlier title for her *The Drama of the Gifted Child* which was originally published as *Prisoners of Childhood*.

32. VW, *Three Guineas*, p. 9.

33. Miller, *The Drama of the Gifted Child; For Your Own Good; Thou Shalt Not Be Aware.*

34. VW, "Am I a Snob?," p. 204.

35. See VW, "'Anon' and 'The Reader': Virginia Woolf's Last Essays," ed. by Brenda R. Silver, p. 395.

36. Armstrong, *Kiss Daddy Goodnight*, p. 7; Roland Summit, "Beyond Belief"; Louise Armstrong, "The Cradle of Sexual Politics."

37. VW, "Anon" and "The Reader," p. 403.

CHAPTER 1: LAURA, "HER LADYSHIP OF THE LAKE"

1. Phyllis Rose, *Woman of Letters*: "Virginia presents her childhood as radiantly happy, merry, lively, filled with people, and the center of it all was Julia," p. 12; Quentin Bell, *Virginia Woolf* (in reference to St. Ives): "It was the happiest time of a happy childhood," 1:25; Jeanne Schulkind, "Editor's Note" to "Reminiscences," in *Moments of Being*, speaks of "the vitality, affection and security which distinguished life in the Stephen family," p. 26; Lyndall Gordon, *Virginia Woolf*: "she was bathed in protective love," p. 16.

2. This is the view presented in Bell, *Virginia Woolf*; Gordon, *Virginia Woolf*; Noel Annan, *Leslie Stephen*; Frances Spalding, *Vanessa Bell*. Jean O. Love in *Virginia Woolf* paints a very different picture.

3. See, e.g., Schulkind's interpretation in *Moments of Being*, pp. 26–27. This is also the view taken by Bell in *Virginia Woolf* and Gordon in *Virginia Woolf*. According to Rose, *Woman of Letters*, when Julia died, "a palpable black pall seemed to settle over the family," p. 12.

4. VW, "A Sketch of the Past," p. 79.

5. VW, "Reminiscences," p. 30.

6. The fullest account of the difference between what London and St. Ives meant for Virginia Woolf is provided in Susan Merrill Squier, *Virginia Woolf and London*. See also Schulkind, introduction to *Moments of Being*, p. 31.

7. See Virginia Woolf's account of the episode in "A Sketch of the Past," p. 69.

8. VW, "Reminiscences," p. 44. For accounts of Virginia's infancy, see Bell, *Virginia Woolf*, and Love, *Virginia Woolf*.

9. I am indebted to the background provided by the following sources: Philippe Aries, *Centuries of Childhood*, trans. by Robert Baldick; Arthur Brittan and Mary Maynard, *Sexism, Racism, and Oppression*; Joan N. Burstyn, *Victorian Education and the Ideal of Womanhood*; Phyllis Chesler, *Women and Madness*; Louise J. Despert, *The Emotionally Disturbed Child—Then and Now*; Andrea Dworkin, *Woman Hating*; Carol Dyhouse, *Girls Growing Up in Late Victorian and Edwardian England*; Sandra M. Gilbert and Susan Gubar, *The Madwoman in the Attic*; Daniel Goleman, "Child Development Theory Stresses Small Moments," pp. C1, C3; Daniel Goleman, "Parental Influence: New Subtleties Found," pp. C1, C3; Deborah Gorham, *The Victorian Girl and the Feminine Ideal*; Mary S. Hartman, "Child-Abuse and Self-Abuse"; Stephen Kern, "Explosive Intimacy," pp. 437–62; E. Milling Kinard, *Emotional Development in Physically Abused Children*; R. D. Laing, *The Politics of the Family and Other Essays*; Jane Lewis, *Women in England 1870–1950*; "Life's First Feelings," *Nova*, Public Broadcasting System, 11 February 1986; Theresa McBride, "'As the Twig Is Bent'"; Alice Miller, *For Your Own Good*; Steven Mintz, *A Prison of Expecta-*

tions; Leon Shaskolsky Sheleff, *Generations Apart;* Elaine Showalter, *The Female Malady.*

10. Bell, *Virginia Woolf,* 1:24, 35. Stella is referred to quite frequently as "the Cow" in the 1897 Diary. For Stella as "the Old Cow," see Love, *Virginia Woolf,* p. 145.

11. The fullest published account of Julia's life is provided in Sir Leslie Stephen, *Mausoleum Book.* Unpublished letters illuminating her life are currently being prepared for publication by John Bicknell.

12. See Carol Christ, "Victorian Masculinity and the Angel in the House"; Virginia Woolf's account of her mother's overwork is recorded in "Old Bloomsbury," p. 182, e.g.; Carroll Smith-Rosenberg, *Disorderly Conduct.* See Bell, *Virginia Woolf,* 1:20.

13. See, e.g., Mary R. Chappell, "The Value of an Orderly Nursery"; "The Happiness of Children"; M. V. Hughes, *A London Child of the 1870s;* M. V. Hughes, *A London Girl of the 1880s;* A. Y. K., "Punishing vs. Training"; M. V. Shea, "'Spare the Rod and Spoil the Child'"; H. Stuart Rowe, "Fear in the Discipline of Children."

14. See Carol Dyhouse, *Girls Growing Up in Late Victorian and Edwardian England,* and Deborah Gorham, *The Victorian Girl and the Feminine Ideal.*

15. See Nora Archibald Smith, "The Child of Passionate Temper."

16. The history of this battle is graphically described in Leslie Stephen's letters to Julia Stephen, dated 4 January 1882 and following. I am indebted to John Bicknell for calling my attention to certain of these letters and for sending me extracts from his edition of these letters, in progress.

17. Letter from Leslie Stephen to Julia Stephen, 4 February 1882; Martine Stemerick, "Virginia's Early Education," p. 9.

18. Letter from Leslie Stephen to Julia Stephen, 9 April 1882. Letter from John Bicknell to me, 28 April 1987.

19. Gorham, in *The Victorian Girl and the Feminine Ideal,* states that "Victorian children were orphaned or half-orphaned more frequently than in the twentieth century, and it appears that often the parent, step-parent or guardian wanted to be rid of the child," p. 23. She describes the development of the boarding school in this connection. Peter Laslett, in *Family Life and Illicit Love in Earlier Generations,* has observed that stepchildren were at greater psychological risk than children living with their widowed mothers and fathers, p. 165. Hartman, in "Child-Abuse and Self-Abuse," also describes the plight of these children.

20. Leslie Stephen to Julia Stephen, 29 September and 10 October 1882. In his attitudes to Laura, Leslie was not alone. Peter Gay, in *The Bourgeois Experience,* vol. 1, *Education of the Senses,* describes how parents and educators still spoke calmly of "breaking the will of children," p. 428. Barbara J. Harris, in

"Recent Work on the History of the Family," has remarked that breaking the will of children was a common practice in evangelical circles, and that parents went about it with a determination "worthy of seventeenth-century Puritans," p. 169; Hartman, in "Child-Abuse and Self-Abuse," has stated that various forms of child-rearing employed the "systematic torture" of children, p. 221.

21. Lloyd de Mause, in "The Evolution of Childhood," has remarked that an ambivalence over beating children sometimes led to shutting children up as an alternative punishment, p. 43.

22. Leslie Stephen to Julia Stephen, 29 September 1882; 10 October 1882.

23. See, e.g., Leslie Stephen to Julia Stephen, 30 July 1882; 10 October 1882. According to Annan, in *Leslie Stephen*, however, it was Julia who was responsible for instituting "even stricter" forms of discipline, p. 122.

24. Leslie Stephen to Julia Stephen, 4 September 1882.

25. Leslie Stephen to Julia Stephen, 10 November 1882.

26. See Leslie Stephen to Julia Stephen, 10 October 1882; 10 November 1882; 11 December 1882.

27. Leslie Stephen to Julia Stephen, 10 October 1882.

28. Leslie Stephen to Julia Stephen, 10 November 1882.

29. This is a difficult fact to uncover, because of the way it is presented. Bell, *Virginia Woolf*, puts it this way: "Laura, Minny's child, lived apart until she was sent to a 'Home' and eventually to an asylum in York," 1:22. Virginia Woolf, in her memoir, "A Sketch of the Past," refers to "Laura, an idiot, yet living with us," p. 83. Woolf describes herself as being seven or eight at the time, when Laura was still living with them, so that Laura would have been nineteen or twenty at the time. Annan, in *Leslie Stephen*, states: Laura "eventually had to be cared for in a special part of the house," p. 113.

30. Schulkind, introduction to *Moments of Being*, p. 12.

31. Leslie Stephen to Julia Stephen, 10 November 1882.

32. The stories appear in Julia Stephen, *Stories for Children, Essays for Adults*, ed. by Diane F. Gillespie and Elizabeth Steele. Martine Stemerick was the first scholar to realize their significance. See her "Virginia Woolf and Julia Stephen." They have since been described very differently than the analysis which I present here by Zwerdling in *Virginia Woolf and the Real World*. Annan in *Leslie Stephen* describes them as "tales of the disappointments restless, rebellious children suffer who try to escape from the routine of the nursery," p. 103.

33. Julia Stephen, "The Mysterious Voice," p. 89. All other page references are supplied within parentheses in the text.

34. Spalding, *Vanessa Bell*, p. 12. There is some discrepancy between this and Virginia's own account in "A Sketch of the Past," p. 83, and Leslie Stephen's account in the *Mausoleum Book*. Spalding does not give the evidence for her statements regarding when Laura was moved out of the household. We do know from Woolf's 1897 diary that Laura was living close enough for Stella to make

regular visits. Leslie Stephen in *Mausoleum Book*, on 10 April 1897 states: "My poor Laura was settled with Dr. Corner at Brook House, Southgate, on 14th January [1897]. We had heard some complaints of Red Hill, where he had been physician, and upon his setting up this establishment thought it best to place her there," p. 103. According to Leslie Stephen's account, written in 1895, the "trouble culminated about 1882. . . . We afterwards tried governesses at home, and then a governess in the country, but at last she was sent to Eastwood, where she has had a very serious illness," p. 92.

35. Annan, *Leslie Stephen*, p. 122. Martine Stemerick first made this point, as Annan's note indicates.

36. Annan, *Leslie Stephen*, p. 122.

37. Leslie Stephen to Julia Stephen, 4 January 1887.

38. Love, in *Virginia Woolf*, says Laura was "tragically psychotic from an early age," p. 70; Gordon, in *Virginia Woolf*, refers to her as "disturbed," p. 24.

39. The Children Act of 1908 represented forty years of work on the part of the National Society for the Prevention of Cruelty to Children to call attention to the deliberate starvation, systematic beating, sexual assault, physical assault, deliberate cruelty, incestuous assault, infant and child murder of a significant number of the nation's children. Interest in brutality toward animals preceded interest in brutality towards children. See the account provided in George Behlmer, *Child Abuse and Moral Reform in England, 1870–1908*.

40. Stephen, *Mausoleum Book*, pp. 44, 91.

41. Leslie Stephen to Julia Stephen, 24 March 1884.

42. Love, *Virginia Woolf*, pp. 162, 167. Winifred Gerin's *Anne Thackeray Ritchie* provides the following view: "Her poor father [Leslie] had to admit that she had never yet learned to read, though he had taken her in hand himself; and by comparison with his clever stepchildren, he could not overlook the fact that she was increasingly inarticulate," p. 195. I am grateful to Carol MacKay for pointing out this quotation.

43. Leslie Stephen to Julia Stephen, 4 February 1882; 4 February 1882 (second letter of the day); 10 September 1882; 4 September 1882; 29 September 1882; 10 October 1882; 29 September 1882.

44. Love, *Virginia Woolf*, p. 161.

45. See Hartman, "Child-Abuse and Self-Abuse."

46. Sander L. Gilman, *Difference and Pathology*, p. 205.

47. Hartman, "Child-Abuse and Self-Abuse," p. 241.

48. Gilman, *Difference and Pathology*, p. 40.

49. Love, *Sources of Madness and Art*, p. 161.

50. De Mause, "The Evolution of Childhood," p. 48. The list of child-rearing attitudes that are responsible for severe neurosis in adulthood are listed in Alice Miller, *For Your Own Good*. They are precisely those attitudes present in a "typical" Victorian upbringing; see pp. 59–60. See also Despert, *The Emotionally Disturbed Child—Then and Now*, p. 159.

51. Steven Mintz, A *Prison of Expectations*, p. 31. There is a significant body of literature to support this. One excellent source which allows one to see Laura's symptoms as having been caused by her upbringing is Despert, *The Emotionally Disturbed Child—Then and Now*. De Mause, "The Evolution of Childhood," p. 49, points out that "children in the past were actually retarded physically as a result of their poor care." This occurred among the well-to-do as well as the poor.

52. Stephen, *Mausoleum Book*, p. 43.

53. Love, *Virginia Woolf*, p. 162.

54. Arthur Brittan and Mary Maynard, *Sexism, Racism and Oppression*, p. 79. For the care that would have been necessary for Laura to overcome her grief, see "Children and Death," pamphlet from National Funeral Directors Association Library of Publications: "Children are people. They react to traumatic situations with emotional overtones as disbelief, bodily distress, anger, guilt, anxiety and panic—just as adults do"; " 'Bottled up' grief may later find a release in more serious problems"; "Adults must take great care not to work out their own grief experience through the child." There is no evidence that Leslie ever grieved with his children; rather, his children were expected to be a source of comfort to him.

55. Annan, *Leslie Stephen*, p. 122; Stemerick, "Virginia's Early Education," pp. 3–4, p. 8.

56. Gerin, *Anne Thackeray Ritchie*, p. 239, p. 246. I am grateful to Carol MacKay for pointing this out. VW, "A Sketch of the Past," p. 91.

57. Laslett, *Family Life and Illicit Love in Earlier Generations*, p. 162. Laslett describes the "deplorable effects on our children" of parental deprivation which he believes has remained constant through time: according to his estimates, one-third of all children, for one reason or another, are "parentally deprived," p. 170.

58. Despert, *The Emotionally Disturbed Child—Then and Now*, p. 157. According to Despert, emotional disturbances in children are always caused by anxiety, by the deprivation of "emotional interchange," p. 159. See also Miller, *For Your Own Good*.

59. Priscilla Robertson, "Home As a Nest," p. 419. The tendency to send away children is documented in Gorham, *The Victorian Girl and the Feminine Ideal*, pp. 22–23.

60. Annan, *Leslie Stephen*, pp. 15–16.

61. See E. Milling Kinard, *Emotional Development in Physically Abused Children*, p. 13. Kinard also points out that "battering parents tend to have poor self-concepts and low self-esteem," p. 12. This is evident in Leslie Stephen's statements about himself, in his *Mausoleum Book*, where he describes, on more than one occasion, his "inferiority," p. 92.

62. Annan, *Leslie Stephen*, pp. 16–17.

63. Ibid., p. 18.

64. Ibid., p. 21.

65. Interview with Patricia Rosen. See John Addington Symonds, *The Memoirs of John Addington Symonds*, ed. by Phyllis Grosskurth; also James Fitzjames Stephen, introduction to *Liberty, Equality, Fraternity*, p. 4.

66. Elizabeth Stoneman, unpublished paper on *To the Lighthouse*.

67. De Mause, *The History of Childhood*, p. 32. See Laslett, *Family Life and Illicit Love in Earlier Generations*, p. 35; Leonore Davidoff, "Class and Gender in Victorian England," p. 94; Deborah Gorham, "The 'Maiden Tribute of Modern Babylon' Re-Examined," p. 378.

68. Davidoff, "Class and Gender in Victorian England," p. 94.

69. Alice Miller, *Thou Shalt Not Be Aware*, p. 257.

70. Davidoff, "Class and Gender in Victorian England," p. 93; Robertson, "Home as a Nest," p. 424.

71. Annan, *Leslie Stephen*, p. 122.

72. Kinard, *Emotional Development in Physically Abused Children*.

73. I am grateful to Jane Marcus and to Katherine Hogan for alerting me to this possibility.

74. VW, *Letters* 2:1204.

75. Gorham, *The Victorian Girl and the Feminine Ideal*, p. 46; Gilman, *Difference and Pathology*, pp. 43, 48; VW, *Letters*, 5:2887. In "Old Bloomsbury," VW juxtaposes the report of her abuse with information about Laura.

76. Gerin, *Anne Thackeray Ritchie*, p. 259. I am grateful to Carol MacKay for pointing this out. VW, "A Sketch of the Past," p. 92.

77. VW, *Letters*, 1:199 (italics added).

78. Bell, *Virginia Woolf*, 1:51, quoting Virginia Woolf to Vita Sackville-West, 19 February 1929. See VW, *Moments of Being*, p. 112, regarding her reading.

79. Stephen, *Mausoleum Book*, p. 19. See Jane Marcus, "Liberty, Sorority, Misogyny," for a brilliant analysis of the Stephen family.

80. Annan, *Leslie Stephen*, p. 122. Annan, like many of Woolf's biographers, describes the effects of violence and its origin in a way that suggests that they simply exist, rather than that they have a cause: "Madness," he writes, "hovered in the air," p. 113. See also Bell, *Virginia Woolf*: "madness walked the streets"; "there was madness in the home; Laura," 1:35. Laura is *never* referred to as "mad" in any contemporary account. See Gilbert and Gubar, *The Madwoman in the Attic*. Given the fact of Laura, the reasons for Virginia Woolf's often-remarked-upon criticism of anger in relationship to Charlotte Brontë's *Jane Eyre* in *A Room of One's Own* should be clear: Jane Eyre and the madwoman in the attic closely resembled the conditions of Woolf's own childhood. Laura's outbursts and anger must have been used as the partial cause or justification for her treatment in the household. It is no wonder, then, that Woolf retained a lifelong terror of her own anger. See Sara Ruddick, "New Combinations."

81. This information is provided in a footnote in Bell, *Virginia Woolf*, 1:22. Annan, however, states that Laura died in 1946, at the age of 76, p. 371.

82. Leslie Stephen to Julia Stephen, 8 October 1883.

83. Stephen, *Mausoleum Book*, p. 109. See Chesler, *Women and Madness*, p. 116, who states that if the same behavior is manifested by men and women, it will be perceived as pathological in women.

84. This bizarre story is told in Stephen, *Mausoleum Book*, p. 84.

85. Annan, *Leslie Stephen*, p. 117. Annan refers to letters from G. T. Worsley to Julia Stephen, 6 and 20 March, 4 April 1894, quoted in Martine Stemerick, "Virginia Woolf and Julia Stephen," unpublished dissertation. Stemerick documented the vastly different treatment accorded girls and boys in the Stephen household.

86. Kinard, *Emotional Development in Physically Abused Children*; Jean Renvoize, *Incest*.

87. VW, *Letters*, 1:199; 2:1178, 1197, 1204; 5:2887. In her memoir, "Old Bloomsbury," Woolf wrote of how "Laura had been finally incarcerated with a doctor in an asylum," p. 184, in a context which suggests that this event occurred after Leslie Stephen's death.

88. VW, 1897 Diary.

89. VW, "Old Bloomsbury," p. 182.

90. Bell, *Virginia Woolf*, 1:35.

91. See Vida D. Scudder, *Le Morte D'Arthur of Sir Thomas Malory*, p. 126.

92. Ibid., p. 196.

93. Ibid., p. 127.

CHAPTER 2: STELLA, "THE OLD COW"

1. Frances Spalding, *Vanessa Bell*, p. 20.

2. Ibid.

3. Leslie Stephen, *Mausoleum Book*, p. 59.

4. VW, "A Sketch of the Past," p. 90.

5. Jean O. Love, *Virginia Woolf*, p. 95.

6. Ibid., p. 173.

7. VW, *Moments of Being*, p. 42; Stephen, *Mausoleum Book*, pp. 42, 59.

8. Julia Margaret Cameron, *Victorian Photographs of Famous Men and Fair Women*, plate 30. There is a question about the date of this photograph. Stella appears to be older than the date of the photograph would indicate. It perhaps is an error.

9. An account of Julia's life can be found in Sir Leslie Stephen, *Mausoleum Book*, but her life is also described in Leslie Stephen's letters, a selection of which are being prepared for publication by John Bicknell, and in introductions to her *Stories for Children, Essays for Adults*. See also Love, *Virginia Woolf*.

10. See Denise J. Gelinas, "The Persisting Negative Effects of Incest."

11. Noel Annan, *Leslie Stephen*, p. 121; Stephen, *Mausoleum Book*, p. 59.

12. VW, "Reminiscences," p. 42.

13. Spalding, *Vanessa Bell*, p. 7; VW, *Moments of Being*, p. 92. See Mark Spilka's analysis of this in *Virginia Woolf's Quarrel with Grieving*.

14. Vanessa Bell to Virginia Woolf, [24? July 1910].

15. Letter from Leslie Stephen to Julia Stephen, dated "12/11/1882."

16. Philippe Ariès, *Centuries of Childhood*, p. 332.

17. In November 1939, when money was scarce, Woolf wrote of her "legacy," "Stella's settlement money," which, upon the death of Jack Hills, reverted to the Stephen children. VW, entry for 27 November 1939, *Diary 5*.

18. Love, *Virginia Woolf*, p. 145.

19. Ibid., p. 176.

20. Ibid.

21. Spalding, *Vanessa Bell*, p. 8.

22. Martine Stemerick, "The Madonna's Clay Feet," pp. 2–4.

23. Ibid., pp. 5, 10.

24. Ibid., p. 13.

25. See Judith Lewis Herman, *Father-Daughter Incest*.

26. Annan, *Leslie Stephen*, p. 114.

27. See Jane Marcus, "Liberty, Sorority, Misogyny."

28. Ibid., pp. 72–73.

29. VW, "A Sketch of the Past," pp. 98, 99.

30. Steven Marcus, *The Other Victorians*, p. 177.

31. VW, "A Sketch of the Past," p. 98.

32. Ibid.

33. Leslie Stephen, *The Life of Sir James Fitzjames Stephen*, p. 475.

34. Ibid., p. 408.

35. Ibid., p. 472.

36. Ibid., p. 474. There are other versions of this incident. Quentin Bell, in *Virginia Woolf*, 1:35, states that "The nature of the accident is not certainly known; in the Stephen family it was said that he was struck by some projection from a moving train." According to Annan, in *Leslie Stephen*, p. 114, however, "When visiting friends near Felixstowe he was hit on the head by one of the sails of a windmill which worked a pump." All versions attribute J. K.'s madness to this blow on the head but the widely divergent explanations seem to suggest that it was only after J. K. began to manifest symptoms of erratic behavior that the cause was sought in an event that had occurred; this would then absolve J. K. of any responsibility for his actions. The poetry that he was writing at the time, although profoundly hateful of women and expressive of murderous impulses, is extremely lucid. The only illogical writings that I have come across is a letter to Stella that I cite later in this chapter.

37. Stephen, *The Life of Sir James Fitzjames Stephen*, p. 475.

38. VW, "A Sketch of the Past," p. 98.

39. Annan, *Leslie Stephen*, p. 114.

40. Stephen, *Mausoleum Book*, p. 78.

41. Bell, *Virginia Woolf*, 1:36.

42. Annan, *Leslie Stephen*, p. 114.

43. Stephen, *Mausoleum Book*, p. 78.

44. Annan, *Leslie Stephen*, p. 114.

45. Stephen, *Mausoleum Book*, p. 78.

46. Ibid.; see also Leonore Davidoff, "Class and Gender in Victorian England," pp. 87–141, p. 91.

47. Annan, *Leslie Stephen*, p. 114.

48. Stephen, *Mausoleum Book*, pp. 78, 114.

49. Ibid., p. 78.

50. Michael Harrison, *Clarence*, p. 109.

51. Quoted in ibid., pp. 114–15.

52. Quoted in ibid., p. 168.

53. Marcus, "Liberty, Sorority, Misogyny," p. 61.

54. Quoted in Harrison, pp. 169–70.

55. Stephen, *The Life of Sir James Fitzjames Stephen*, pp. 470, 476.

56. Annan, *Leslie Stephen*, p. 114. Annan refers to the poems as "dazzling parodies."

57. Harrison, *Clarence*, p. 156.

58. J. K. Stephen to Stella Duckworth Hills, 25 October 1890.

59. Bell, *Virginia Woolf*, 1:36.

60. Bell, ibid., puts it this way: "the most difficult and painful thing about his insanity was that it led him to desire Stella and violently to pursue her."

61. *Catalogue of Books from the Library of Leonard and Virginia Woolf*. She owned a copy signed "J. K. S." dated Cambridge, July 1891.

62. J. K. S[tephen]., *Lapsus Calami*, pp. 38, 39, 30. I am grateful to the reference librarians at Fairleigh Dickinson University for locating and borrowing a copy of these poems.

63. Coral Lansbury, "Gynaecology, Pornography, and the Antivivisection Movement," p. 421.

64. Stephen, *Lapsus Calami*, p. 39.

65. Lansbury, "Gynaecology, Pornography, and the Antivivisection Movement."

66. Stephen, *Lapsus Calami*, pp. 39–40.

67. Letter from J. K. Stephen to Stella Duckworth Hills, 25 October 1890.

68. Lansbury, "Gynaecology, Pornography, and the Antivivisection Movement," p. 423.

69. Judith R. Walkowitz, "Jack the Ripper and the Myth of Male Violence," pp. 543–44.

70. Ibid., pp. 545–46.

71. Ibid., p. 563.
72. Ibid., p. 566.
73. Ibid., p. 567.
74. Spalding, *Vanessa Bell*, p. 23.
75. Ibid., p. 20.
76. Annan, *Leslie Stephen*, p. 116.
77. Herman, *Father-Daughter Incest*, pp. 1–2; VW, "A Sketch of the Past," pp. 145–46; VW, "Reminiscences," pp. 44–45.
78. Stephen, *Mausoleum Book*, p. 97; Spalding, *Vanessa Bell*, p. 20.
79. VW, "A Sketch of the Past," p. 94.
80. Love, *Virginia Woolf*, p. 186.
81. VW, "Reminiscences," p. 41.
82. Leslie Stephen, *Swift*, p. 131.
83. Ibid., p. 1. For example, Stephen remarked that Swift, who was a walker, had he lived in "more civilized times," "might have been a mountaineer," p. 27, like Leslie himself was.
84. Ibid., p. 136. Virginia Woolf did not agree, although she had obviously read her father's biography. In an essay on Swift, "Swift's 'Journal to Stella,'" in *The Second Common Reader*, she disagreed with her father's view and wrote "the woman he [Swift] had chosen was no insipid slave," p. 62.
85. Stephen, *Swift*, p. 140.
86. Spalding, *Vanessa Bell*, p. 21.
87. Stephen, *Mausoleum Book*, p. 101.
88. Annan, *Leslie Stephen*, p. 116.
89. Ibid.
90. Stephen, *Mausoleum Book*, p. 77.
91. Ibid., p. 78.
92. VW, "Reminiscences," pp. 42–43.
93. Stephen, *Mausoleum Book*, p. 77.
94. Spalding, *Vanessa Bell*, p. 21.
95. Stephen, *Mausoleum Book*, p. 103.
96. VW, "A Sketch of the Past," p. 102.
97. Spalding, *Vanessa Bell*, p. 21; VW, "A Sketch of the Past," p. 103.
98. VW, "Reminiscences," pp. 40, 50.
99. VW, "A Sketch of the Past," p. 101.
100. VW, entry for 27 June 1925, *Diary 3*.
101. Quoted in Louise A. DeSalvo, "1897," p. 101. Love in *Virginia Woolf* cites two letters from Violet Dickinson to Vanessa Bell, p. 193; Phyllis Rose, in *Woman of Letters*, has remarked that, with the emphasis on premarital purity, the wedding night may have been a "barbaric trial," p. 57.
102. VW, "A Sketch of the Past," p. 104.
103. VW, entry for 9 January 1939, *Diary 5*.

104. Stephen, *Mausoleum Book,* p. 103.

105. Virginia Stephen [Woolf], 1897 Diary. Entries regarding Stella's illness can be found on 28, 29, 30 April; 1, 2, 3 May; 3, 5, 6, 7, 8, 9, 10, 12, 21, 24, 25, 30 June; 3, 12, 13, 15, 16, 17, 18 July. The 19 July entry tells of Stella's death.

There is some confusion concerning the cause of Stella's illness and death. No cause of death was noted. Annan in *Leslie Stephen,* p. 116, writes, "Stella fell ill with appendicitis; and when that summer she became pregnant, the doctors decided to operate. She died the next day." Spalding in *Vanessa Bell* tells it differently. She describes Stella's April illness as being diagnosed as "gastro-enteritis"; her "condition grew suddenly critical and peritonitis was suspected" (22). There are a number of causes of peritonitis, but one of them is pelvic imflammatory disease. It seems unclear whether appendicitis was diagnosed at the outset, as Virginia Woolf indicates in *Moments of Being,* or developed later. No contemporary account that I have found describes why Stella was operated upon; the two contemporary accounts that exist both call the disease peritonitis from the outset.

106. Spalding, *Vanessa Bell,* p. 22.

107. Entry for 19 July 1897, Virginia Stephen [Woolf], 1897 Diary.

108. VW, 9 January 1939, *Diary 5.*

109. VW, 22 August 1922, *Diary 2.*

110. VW, "A Sketch of the Past," p. 98.

111. VW, *Letters* 1:3; entry for 30 March 1897, 1897 Diary.

112. VW, *Letters* 1:5.

113. VW, *Letters* 1:6.

114. In her 1897 Diary, Woolf records how her gift from her father for that year had been a gift to him. VW, 18 May 1920, *Diary 2.*

115. VW, *Letters* 2:730.

116. VW, "A Sketch of the Past," p. 97. Woolf calls it her mother's "laughing" nickname for Stella. But hostility, I believe, was concealed in that nickname, especially given Julia's treatment of Stella.

117. VW, 23 July 1918, *Diary 1.*

118. VW, *Letters* 1:57.

119. VW, *Letters* 1:188.

120. VW, *Moments of Being,* pp. 59, 141.

121. VW, *Letters* 1:98.

122. VW, "A Sketch of the Past," p. 141.

123. VW, 9 January 1939, *Diary 5.*

124. VW, "A Sketch of the Past," p. 141.

125. Ibid.

126. Annan, *Leslie Stephen,* p. 121.

127. VW, *Letters* 1:109.

128. VW, 9 January 1939, *Diary 5.*

129. VW, 6 October 1940, *Diary 5*.
130. VW, "Reminiscences," pp. 41–42.
131. Ibid., p. 42.
132. Ibid., p. 43.
133. Although Herman has argued in *Father-Daughter Incest* that a strong relationship with one's mother is a deterrent to incestuous exploitation, Diana E. H. Russell in *The Secret Trauma* has stated: "What does it say about male behavior and sexuality if young girls are unsafe in their own houses with their own relatives . . . ? It is the opportunistic, exploitative, and destructive behavior of the offending males that is the problem, as well as their gross lack of responsibility in the very relationships in which responsibility should be a primary feature," p. 384.
134. VW, "Reminiscences," p. 45.
135. The word is Virginia Woolf's. She used it in reference to her father's behavior after Stella's death in his treatment of Vanessa: "he was quite prepared to take Vanessa for his next victim." "Reminiscences," p. 57.
136. Ibid., p. 45, and "A Sketch of the Past," p. 94.
137. VW, "A Sketch of the Past," p. 137.

CHAPTER 3: VANESSA, "THE SAINT"

1. Vanessa Bell to Virginia Woolf, [6 August 1907].
2. VW, *Letters* 1:333.
3. VW, *Letters* 1:406.
4. VW, *Letters* 1:406.
5. VW, *Moments of Being*, p. 143.
6. Ibid., pp. 28–29.
7. Ibid., pp. 28–31.
8. VW, *Letters* 1:328; *Letters* 1:309.
9. VW, *Moments of Being*, p. 57.
10. Ibid., p. 58.
11. Ibid.
12. Vanessa Bell to Virginia Woolf, 20 April [1908].
13. See Jane Marcus, "Liberty, Sorority, Misogyny."
14. VW, *Moments of Being*, p. 106.
15. Ibid., pp. 170–71.
16. Virginia Stephen [Woolf], Hyde Park Gate Diary, 1897. See Frances Spalding, *Vanessa Bell*.
17. VW, *Moments of Being*, p. 171.
18. VW, *Letters* 1:29, e.g.
19. VW, *Moments of Being*, p. 171.
20. Vanessa Bell to Virginia Woolf, 8 September [1904].

21. VW, *Letters* 5:2887.

22. VW, *Moments of Being*, p. 156.

23. Leslie Stephen, *Swift*, quoted in Spalding, *Vanessa Bell*, p. 214.

24. Stephen, *Swift*, p. 129.

25. Spalding, *Vanessa Bell*, p. 23.

26. Virginia Woolf discusses this history in her memoir, "Old Bloomsbury," pp. 181–201.

27. Spalding, *Vanessa Bell*, p. 40.

28. VW, *Moments of Being*, p. 56.

29. Spalding, *Vanessa Bell*, p. 40.

30. VW, *Moments of Being*, p. 145.

31. Ibid., p. 56.

32. Ibid., p. 116.

33. Spalding, *Vanessa Bell*, p. 108.

34. VW, *Moments of Being*, p. 144.

35. For two very different interpretations of this relationship see Angelica Garnett, *Deceived with Kindness*, and Spalding, *Vanessa Bell*.

36. Spalding, *Vanessa Bell*, p. 255.

37. Spalding, *Vanessa Bell*, p. 140.

38. See, e.g., Diana E. H. Russell, *The Secret Trauma*, for a discussion of the tendency to repeat the pattern in the family; see also Judith Lewis Herman, *Father-Daughter Incest*, for an illuminating discussion in this regard; see also the general discussion in the introduction in this book.

39. Spalding, *Vanessa Bell*, p. 347.

40. Ibid., p. 172.

41. See Russell, *The Secret Trauma*.

42. Spalding, *Vanessa Bell*, p. 170.

43. Ibid., p. 337.

44. Stephen, *Swift*, p. 131.

45. Spalding, *Vanessa Bell*, pp. 336–37.

46. Vanessa Bell to Virginia Woolf, [3 August 1907]. She also speaks of writing her biography in other letters written on 30 July, 2 August, 6 August 1907.

47. Vanessa Bell to Virginia Woolf, [13 August 1907].

48. Vanessa Bell to Virginia Woolf, 1 August [1907].

49. The painting is reproduced between pp. 272 and 273 in Spalding, *Vanessa Bell* and in this volume.

50. Ibid., p. 105.

51. Ibid., p. 121.

52. Vanessa Bell to Virginia Woolf, 17 August 1913.

53. Angelica Garnett records her dream in *Deceived with Kindness*, p. 59. VW, *Letters* 1:574.

54. Spalding, *Vanessa Bell*, pp. 217–19.

55. Ibid., p. 251. It is reproduced between pp. 272 and 273.

56. Ibid., pp. 251–52.

57. Spalding, *Vanessa Bell*, p. 250, gives a far different interpretation; she sees the painting as a nostalgic evocation of childhood, with the mother empowering her child to be independent. It is reproduced in this volume.

58. Ibid., p. 250.

59. Ibid., p. 313.

60. "Life's First Feelings," *Nova*, Public Broadcasting System, 11 February 1986; Daniel Goleman, "Child Development Theory Stresses Small Moments," pp. C1, C3.

61. Spalding, *Vanessa Bell*, p. xv.

62. Ibid., p. 289.

63. Ibid., p. 253.

64. Ibid., p. 272.

65. Ibid., p. 288.

66. Leslie Stephen quoted in Jean O. Love, *Virginia Woolf*, p. 149.

67. VW, 28 March 1929, *Diary* 3.

68. Angelica Garnett, quoted in Spalding, *Vanessa Bell*, p. 313.

69. Vanessa Bell, in a letter to Virginia Woolf, quoted in Spalding, *Vanessa Bell*, p. 316.

70. Virginia Woolf, quoted in Spalding, *Vanessa Bell*, p. 363.

71. Leonard Woolf, quoted in Spalding, *Vanessa Bell*, pp. 336–37.

72. Spalding, *Vanessa Bell*, p. 97.

73. Angelica Garnett, quoted in Spalding, *Vanessa Bell*, pp. 336–37.

74. Clive Bell, quoted in Spalding, *Vanessa Bell*, p. 51.

75. Spalding, *Vanessa Bell*, p. 71.

76. See Russell, *The Secret Trauma*, and the general discussion in the introduction above.

77. VW in a letter to Vanessa Bell, "I see Quentin will inspire me to illicit passion—which he won't return," *Letters* 2:1070; "I shall rape Angelica one of these days," *Letters* 3:1894.

78. Virginia Stephen [Woolf], 1897 Diary.

79. Spalding, *Vanessa Bell*, p. 26.

80. VW, *Moments of Being*, p. 84.

81. Vanessa Bell to Virginia Woolf, 8 September [1904].

82. Love, *Virginia Woolf*, p. 200.

83. See Jean Renvoize, *Incest*.

84. Spalding, *Vanessa Bell*, p. 13.

85. Vanessa Bell to Virginia Woolf, [2 June 1912].

86. Ibid., 13 April [1905].

87. Spalding, *Vanessa Bell*, p. 62.

88. Vanessa Bell to Virginia Woolf, 19 August [1912].

89. Ibid., 2 September [1912].

90. Ibid., 17 July [1910].

91. Ibid., [5 July 1910].

92. Garnett, *Deceived with Kindness*, p. 7. Subsequent references are in parentheses in the text.

93. Leon Edel, *Bloomsbury*, p. 273. Garnett, *Deceived with Kindness*, p. 7. Subsequent references to Garnett are in parentheses in the text.

94. VW, *Letters* 2:1004.

95. Spalding, *Vanessa Bell*, p. 179.

96. Ibid., p. 208.

97. VW, *Letters* 6:3657.

98. Spalding, *Vanessa Bell*, p. 177.

99. See the pictures on p. 82, e.g.

CHAPTER 4: A DAUGHTER REMEMBERS

1. VW, "A Sketch of the Past," p. 64.

2. VW, 20 May 1938, *Diary* 5.

3. VW, *Letters* 6:3443.

4. VW, 29 January 1939; 2 December 1939, *Diary* 5; *Letters* 6:3678.

5. VW, 11 February 1940, *Diary* 5: "The idea struck me that the Leaning Tower school is the school of auto-analysis after the suppression of the 19th Century." See her essay, "The Leaning Tower."

6. VW, 15 April 1939, *Diary* 5.

7. VW, *Letters* 2:1178.

8. See Ellen Bass and Louise Thornton, *I Never Told Anyone*.

9. VW, "A Sketch of the Past," p. 64.

10. Ibid. Subsequent references are in parentheses in the text. For another reading of these memories, see Susan Merrill Squier, *Virginia Woolf and London*, pp. 15 ff.

11. She uses a variation on this first memory in her first novel, *The Voyage Out*, during the death scene of her character Rachel Vinrace. She uses every element of the first memory, the sound of the waves breaking, the blind, the acorn being dragged across the floor, but she writes it in a way that overtly expresses the sense of terrible danger implicit in her first memory: "Rachel went to bed; she lay in the dark. . . . Turning her eyes to the window, she was not reassured by what she saw there." And then, "The movement of the blind as it filled with air and blew slowly out, drawing the chord with a little trailing sound along the floor, seemed to her terrifying, as if it were the movement of an animal in the room." (VW, *The Voyage Out*, p. 328.)

12. VW, *Letters* 5:2915.

13. See Alice Miller, *The Drama of the Gifted Child*.

14. VW, *Melymbrosia*, p. 263.

15. VW, *Letters* 5:2335.

16. VW, "22 Hyde Park Gate," p. 170.

17. Noel Annan, *Leslie Stephen*, p. 65.

18. "Breaking the Silence," Public Broadcasting System, 11 August 1987.

19. Leslie Stephen to Charles Eliot Norton, 20 April 1888; I am grateful to John Bicknell for providing a transcription of this letter. I am grateful to Mary Devery for describing to me her nursing experience with such cases in the early part of this century.

20. Quentin Bell, *Virginia Woolf*, 1:25.

21. VW, "A Sketch of the Past," p. 69. Italics have been added.

22. See Deborah Gorham, *The Victorian Girl and the Feminine Ideal*. Virginia Woolf states this idea precisely in an early draft of *To the Lighthouse*, which I discuss in chap. 9 below.

23. Robert Fliess, *Erogeneity and Libido*, p. xvii.

24. "Breaking the Silence."

25. VW, "22 Hyde Park Gate," p. 183.

26. See Alice Miller, *Thou Shalt Not Be Aware*, pp. 125–27.

27. VW, 11 June 1936, *Diary* 5.

28. VW, *Letters* 3:1489.

29. VW, 1 April 1936, *Diary* 5.

30. VW, 21 June 1936, *Diary* 5.

31. VW, 2 March 1937, *Diary* 5.

32. VW, 1 March 1937, *Diary* 5.

33. VW, 15 September 1926, *Diary* 3.

34. VW, *Letters* 4:2201.

35. VW, *Moments of Being*, p. 169.

36. VW, *Letters* 1:225.

37. VW, *Letters* 4:2341.

38. Denise J. Gelinas, "The Persisting Negative Effects of Incest."

39. See Phyllis Rose, *Parallel Lives*, p. 56; Ronald Pearsall, *The Worm in the Bud*, pp. 97, 145–46. I should like to thank Susan Shapiro for bringing the latter to my attention.

40. See, e.g., Mitchell A. Leaska's discussion in *The Novels of Virginia Woolf*, pp. 56–57. See my discussion of *The Voyage Out* in "In the Beginning There Was the Nursery."

41. Julia Stephen, *Notes from Sickrooms*, p. 49.

42. Bell, *Virginia Woolf*, 1:39.

43. Leslie Stephen, *Mausoleum Book*, p. 65.

44. VW, *Moments of Being*, p. 39. Stephen, *Mausoleum Book*, p. 57.

45. Stephen, Mausoleum Book, p. 57.

46. Ibid., pp. 96–97.

47. VW, 23 November 1926, *Diary* 3.

48. See, e.g., the family photograph reproduced on the cover of the *Bulletin of The New York Public Library*, Virginia Woolf Issue, Winter 1977.

49. Annan, *Leslie Stephen*, p. 45; see also, Leslie Stephen to Julia Stephen, 6–15 June 1890, 29 January 1893; Bell, *Virginia Woolf*, 1:39.

50. Annan, *Leslie Stephen*, p. 135.

51. Daniel Goleman, "Child Development Theory Stresses Small Moments," pp. C1, C2.

52. Leslie Stephen, *James Fitzjames Stephen*.

53. Annan, *Leslie Stephen*, p. 117.

54. Bell, *Virginia Woolf*, 1:18.

55. Leslie Stephen to Julia Stephen, 9 April 1882.

56. See, e.g., Mary Chappell, "The Value of an Orderly Nursery."

57. VW, *Letters* 4:2179.

58. Bell, *Virginia Woolf*, 1:22, 24.

59. See Alice Miller's analysis in *For Your Own Good*.

60. Annan, *Leslie Stephen*, p. 109.

61. Bell, *Virginia Woolf*, 1:20.

62. VW, *Letters* 3:1760.

63. See the discussions of Julia throughout Leslie Stephen's *Mausoleum Book*.

64. See Mark Spilka, *Virginia Woolf's Quarrel with Grieving*.

65. VW, 25 April 1940, *Diary* 5.

66. VW, "Professions for Women," p. 59.

67. VW, *Letters* 6:3678.

68. VW, *Letters* 4:2194.

69. Blanche Wiesen Cook, "'Women Alone Stir My Imagination.'"

70. For a discussion of Virginia Woolf's valorization of chastity, see Jane Marcus, *Virginia Woolf and the Languages of Patriarchy*, pp. 115 ff.

71. "Breaking the Silence."

72. Stephen, *Mausoleum Book*, p. 84.

73. The silencing that Woolf refers to might be understood in the context of the fact that incest began to be scrutinized, and legislation was being considered, which was in fact enacted in 1908, making "incest punishable by imprisonment up to seven years and not less than three." The definition of incest included relationships with grandparents, parents, and siblings, but not stepchildren (Anthony H. Wohl, "Sex and the Single Room," p. 210).

74. VW, *Moments of Being*, p. 182.

75. The quotations appear in *Moments of Being*, pp. 45, 58. She expressed her interest in the British Sex Society in an entry for 21 January 1918, *Diary* 1.

76. VW, *Moments of Being*, p. 177.

77. VW, *Letters* 2:1218.

78. VW, 1 May 1934, *Diary 4*.

79. Ibid.

80. See the several examples of abuse that Virginia Woolf described near the end of her life in her novel *Between the Acts*. It is important to note that she was creating these fictional instances of abuse and writing of abuse in the lives of real women at about the same time that she was exploring the impact of abuse on her own psyche.

81. VW, 31 May 1929, *Diary 3*.

82. VW, *Letters* 1:576.

83. VW, *Letters* 3:1562.

84. See the editors' note, *Letters* 3, p. 198.

85. Vita Sackville-West, [Diary of a journey to France with Virginia Woolf].

86. VW, *Letters* 4:2245.

87. VW, *Letters* 4:2246.

88. VW, *Letters* 4:2268, 2277.

89. VW, *Letters* 4:2335.

90. VW, *Letters* 4:2341.

91. VW, *Letters* 6:3153.

92. See Marcus, *Virginia Woolf and the Languages of Patriarchy*; Martine Stemerick, "Virginia Woolf and Julia Stephen."

93. Stephen Kern, "Explosive Intimacy," pp. 454–56.

94. Florence Rush, *The Best-Kept Secret*, p. 58.

95. VW, 1 November 1937, *Diary 5*.

96. VW, "A Sketch of the Past," pp. 184, 93, 116, 79.

97. Ibid., p. 111.

98. Madeline Moore, *The Short Season between Two Silences*, p. 16.

99. VW, 23 November 1940, 18 September 1940, 22 October 1940, *Diary 5*.

100. Alex Zwerdling, *Virginia Woolf and the Real World*, p. 289.

101. VW, 20 June 1940, *Diary 5*.

102. VW, 26 January 1940, *Diary 5*. Her first attempt was made during this week. See Appendix A, *Letters 6*.

103. VW, 27 June 1940, *Diary 5*.

104. VW, *Moments of Being*, p. 166; 18 March 1918, *Diary 1*; *Letters* 3:1717; 22 February 1930, *Diary 3*; 22 February 1930, *Diary 3*.

105. VW, *Moments of Being*, p. 124.

106. VW, 26 July 1940, *Diary 5*.

107. VW, 11 September 1940, *Diary 5*.

108. VW, 22 September 1940, *Diary 5*.

109. VW, *Letters* 6:3705.

110. Woolf, *Letters* 6:3710.

111. Woolf, 26 January 1941, *Diary 5*.

112. Note 1, *Letters* 6, p. 432.
113. Woolf, *Letters* 6:3702.
114. Woolf, *Letters* 6:3705.
115. VW, *Letters* 6:3710.
116. VW, 8 March 1941, *Diary* 5.
117. VW, *Letters* 4:2072.

CHAPTER 5: IN THE HOUSE OF THE PATERFAMILIAS

1. References to the works will be in parentheses in the text.
2. It was issued regularly through December 1892; after a hiatus it was taken up again in 1895, the year of Julia Stephen's death. See Quentin Bell, *Virginia Woolf*, 1:28.
3. Lyndall Gordon, in *Virginia Woolf*, calls it "an uproarious serial about a henpecked but aspiring cockney, his bungling efforts at farming, and a comic power struggle between him and his wife," p. 16.
4. Martine Stemerick, a brilliant biographer of Woolf's early years, none-theless sees the period before Julia's death in these romantic terms in "Virginia Woolf and Julia Stephen," p. 6.
5. The photograph is to be found in Leslie Stephen, *Mausoleum Book*, facing p. 90.
6. VW, *Letters* 2:1172.
7. See Meredith Skura, *The Literary Use of the Psychoanalytic Process*.
8. Keith Odom, "Caught in the Brontës' Web of Childhood," pp. 1–2.
9. Noel Annan, *Leslie Stephen*, p. 110.
10. Leslie Stephen to Julia Stephen, 25 January 1891.
11. Ibid., 27 January 1891; see also, Stephen, *Mausoleum Book*, p. 89.
12. Annan, *Leslie Stephen*, p. 86.
13. Bell, *Virginia Woolf*, 1:38–39. Quoted in Mitchell A. Leaska, *The Novels of Virginia Woolf*, p. 228.
14. Stephen, *Mausoleum Book*, p. 87.
15. Annan, *Leslie Stephen*, p. 110.
16. Stephen, *Mausoleum Book*, p. 89.
17. Bell, *Virginia Woolf*, 1:38.
18. See the letters from Leslie Stephen to Julia Stephen, written during this year.
19. Stephen, *Mausoleum Book*, p. 74.
20. Leslie Stephen to Julia Stephen, 31 July 1893; Bell, *Virginia Woolf*, 1:189.
21. Vanessa Bell, *Notes on Virginia's Childhood*, unpaginated.
22. Ibid.; Bell, *Virginia Woolf*, 1:29.

23. *Hyde Park Gate News*, 18 January 1892, quoted in Bell, *Virginia Woolf*, 1:29.

24. *Hyde Park Gate News*, 12 September 1892, quoted in Bell, *Virginia Woolf*, 1:32.

25. *Hyde Park Gate News*, 4 March 1895, quoted in Bell, *Virginia Woolf*, 1:37.

26. VW, *Moments of Being*, p. 95.

27. Bell, *Notes on Virginia's Childhood*.

28. Bell, *Virginia Woolf*, 1:29–30.

29. See Linda Schierse Leonard, *The Wounded Woman*.

30. *Hyde Park Gate News*, 6 June 1892, quoted in Bell, *Virginia Woolf*, 1:30.

31. Bell, *Notes on Virginia's Childhood*.

32. Ibid.

33. Leslie Stephen to Julia Stephen, 29 July 1893.

34. Ibid., 3 August 1893.

35. VW, 23 February 1897, 1897 Diary.

36. Ellen Ross, "'Fierce Questions and Taunts,'" pp. 576–77.

37. Sally Mitchell, "Sentiment and Suffering," p. 45.

38. Priscilla Robertson, "Home as a Nest," p. 417.

39. Leslie Stephen to Julia Stephen, 26 January 1893.

40. Ibid., 29 January 1893.

41. Ibid., 1 February 1893.

42. Leslie Stephen to Charles Eliot Norton, 20 April 1888. I am grateful to John Bicknell for sending me a transcription of this letter.

43. The insight is Jane Lilienfeld's. She has suggested that Mrs. Jackson's lifelong illness might have resulted from an addiction to drugs like sleeping draughts and chloral, which were freely given her for minor complaints.

44. VW, Monks House Papers, MH/A.5d, pp. 36–37.

45. Annan, *Leslie Stephen*, p. 73.

46. VW, *Moments of Being*, p. 99.

47. I would like to thank John Bicknell for this information.

48. VW, *Moments of Being*, p. 99.

49. Daniel Goleman, "In Memory, People Re-create Their Lives To Suit Their Images of the Present," pp. C1, C2.

50. See Jane Marcus, *Virginia Woolf and the Languages of the Patriarchy*, p. 86. In one sense, this story can be thought of as an elegy for Laura.

51. Mary S. Hartman, "Child-Abuse and Self-Abuse: Two Victorian Cases," p. 377.

52. See Jane Lewis, *Women in England: 1870–1950*.

53. Ibid.

54. "Breaking the Silence," Public Broadcasting System.

55. Alice Miller, *Thou Shalt Not Be Aware*, p. 198.

56. Mary Ann Clawson, "Early Modern Fraternalism and the Patriarchal Family," p. 372.

57. Ibid., p. 387.

58. Leslie Stephen to Julia Stephen, "4/ii/1893."

59. VW, *Letters* 4:2414, to Vita Sackville-West: "Here's my half brother on pigs (the 3rd copy he's sent me)."

60. VW, 1 May 1934, *Diary* 4.

CHAPTER 6: "IN THE BEGINNING THERE WAS THE NURSERY"

1. Subsequent references to the novel are in parentheses in the text.

2. Subsequent references to the novel are in parentheses in the text. See my *Virginia Woolf's First Voyage.*

3. On the condition of nursemaids, see Peter Laslett, *Family Life and Illicit Love in Earlier Generations*; Jane Lewis, *Women in England 1870–1950*; Deborah Gorham, *The Victorian Girl and the Feminine Ideal*; and Priscilla Robertson, "Home as a Nest," e.g.

4. On the severity of fathers, see Arthur Brittan and Mary Maynard, *Sexism, Racism, and Oppression*; Steven Mintz, *A Prison of Expectations*, e.g.

5. Subsequent references to the novel are in parentheses in the text. For illuminating discussions of the novel, see Kathleen Dobie, "This is the Room that Class Built"; Alex Zwerdling, *Virginia Woolf and the Real World.*

6. See, e.g., Ruth Sidel, *Women and Children Last*; Kathleen Walsh D'Arcy, unpublished paper on *Jacob's Room.*

7. For an analysis of this scene, see Mitchell A. Leaska, *The Novels of Virginia Woolf*, p. 84.

8. Kathleen Walsh D'Arcy, unpublished paper on *Jacob's Room.*

9. See Zwerdling, *Virginia Woolf and the Real World.*

10. On Virginia Woolf and pacifism, see Jane Marcus, *Virginia Woolf and the Languages of the Patriarchy*, pp. 131–32.

11. D'Arcy, unpublished paper.

12. VW, 14 May 1925, *Diary* 3.

13. Subsequent page references are in parentheses in the text. See Mitchell A. Leaska, *Virginia Woolf's Lighthouse*; Jane Lilienfeld, "Where the Spear Plants Grew"; Beverly Ann Schlack, "Fathers in General."

14. VW, *To the Lighthouse: The original holograph draft*, p. 71. Because the earlier version of the novel is far more direct about the condition of childhood than the published text, many of the examples used here are drawn from the earlier version. Subsequent references to the holograph version are in parentheses in the text, with an "h" following the page to distinguish it from the citations to the published text. Thus "(71h)" refers to the holograph version, "(71)" to the published text.

15. Elizabeth Stoneman, unpublished paper.

16. Deirdre Roshkill, unpublished paper.
17. See Elizabeth Abel, "Cam the Wicked."
18. If this is autobiographical, it is extremely significant. See "A Daughter Remembers."
19. See the discussion in "A Daughter Remembers."
20. VW, *The Waves, The two holograph drafts*. This discussion is based upon the earlier version. As in the case of *To the Lighthouse*, the analysis of childhood is more direct.
21. VW, 28 May 1929, *Diary* 3.
22. VW, 23 June 1929, *Diary* 3.
23. VW, *The Waves, The two holograph drafts*, p. I/1 verso.
24. VW, *Letters* 4, p. 395, note 1.
25. VW, *The Waves, the two holograph drafts, p.* I/62.
26. VW, *The Waves, The two holograph drafts*, p. I/45. Further references in these notes will simply list the draft number followed by a slash followed by the page reference: "I/45."
27. I/62.
28. I/11.
29. I/7.
30. I/7.
31. I/6.
32. I/42.
33. I/42.
34. I/43.
35. I/32.
36. I/134.
37. I/24.
38. I/85.
39. I/134.
40. I/32.
41. I/33.
42. D'Arcy, unpublished paper.
43. Ibid.
44. I/34.
45. I/35.
46. I/78.
47. I/79–80.
48. I/i44.
49. I/74.
50. I/75.
51. I/74.
52. I/64.
53. I/71.

54. I/67.

55. I/71.

56. I/14.

57. I/14.

58. I/32.

59. I/251.

60. I/134.

61. Mitchell A. Leaska, introduction, to Virginia Woolf, *The Pargiters*, p. xv.

62. VW, 10 November 1932, *Diary 4*.

63. Subsequent references to the published novel are in parentheses in the text.

64. VW, *The Pargiters*, p. 28. Subsequent references to *The Pargiters* in the notes will simply note the page number. See Grace Radin, *Virginia Woolf's The Years*; Marcus, *Virginia Woolf and the Languages of the Patriarchy*.

65. P. 36. For a discussion of "street love," see Susan Merrill Squier, *Virginia Woolf and London*, pp. 142–53, 169–70.

66. Pp. 36–37. For the significance of crocodiles, see "A Daughter Remembers."

67. Pp. 40–41.

68. P. 41.

69. P. 42.

70. Pp. 42–43.

71. Pp. 43, 45.

72. Pp. 46–47.

73. For a discussion of the interchapters, see Mitchell A. Leaska, Introduction to *The Pargiters*; Radin, *Virginia Woolf's The Years*.

74. P. 50.

75. P. 48.

76. Pp. 50–51.

77. Pp. 54–55.

78. *Three Guineas*, p. 9; subsequent references to *Three Guineas* are in parentheses in the text.

79. See Marcus, *Virginia Woolf and the Languages of the Patriarchy*, pp. 78–79. For an illuminating discussion, see Berenice A. Carroll, "'To Crush Him in Our Own Country.'"

80. John Stuart Mill, *The Subjugation of Women*.

81. See Kate Millett, "The Debate over Women."

82. Judith Lewis Herman, *Father-Daughter Incest*, p. 110.

83. Ibid., p. 73.

84. Susan Merrill Squier first discussed the significance of this essay. See *Virginia Woolf and London*, pp. 182–86.

85. VW, "Thoughts on Peace in an Air Raid," p. 245.

86. Ibid.

87. VW, 16 December 1935, *Diary 4*. Page references to *Roger Fry* are in parentheses in the text.

88. On the austerity of such an upbringing, see Walter E. Houghton, *The Victorian Frame of Mind*; Robertson, "Home as a Nest," p. 415.

89. Fry's experience was far from idiosyncratic. Priscilla Robertson, in "Home as a Nest," reports that nineteenth-century parents often tried to break the will and the spirit of their children. At five years of age, a child by the name of Augustus Howe was "shut up in his room for two days on bread and water explicitly to break his spirit," p. 415.

90. See, e.g., Phyllis Grosskurth, ed., *The Memoirs of John Addington Symonds*; William L. Langer, Foreword to Lloyd de Mause, ed., *The History of Childhood*, writes that sending a child to a boarding school at such a young age really amounts to "institutionalized abandonments," p. 32.

91. Mary S. Hartman, in "Child-Abuse and Self-Abuse," describes the controversy in the *Englishwoman's Domestic Magazine* in 1870 regarding corporal punishment for girls. A "Lady Principal" writes to explain the "correct" procedure of whipping, "and she does so in minute detail, even to descriptions of how the tunic of the victim should be tucked up and under the lower part of the stays to facilitate the process" (240). Other letters "discuss the merits of rods of varying woods and thicknesses, leather 'tawes,' and other devices" (240). Many women described memories of beatings, also "citing fond memories" of those who beat them severely (240).

92. VW, 21 November 1934, *Diary 4*.

93. Woolf had toyed with the idea of using the experimental device of writing Fry's biography in the first person: "it should be told in the first person.—Would that do as a form for Roger?" VW, 3 November 1936, *Diary 5*.

94. See the discussion of biography in Alice Miller, *Thou Shalt Not Be Aware*, pp. 330–31. She did not, however, tell the truth about Fry's love affair with her sister Vanessa Bell. My remarks refer to her refusal to cover up the condition of his childhood.

95. See E. Milling Kinard, *Emotional Development in Physically Abused Children*.

96. VW, 23 August 1938, *Diary 5*.

97. VW, 22 March 1938, *Diary 5*.

98. See Philippe Ariès, *Centuries of Childhood*, p. 313. See Grosskurth, *The Memoirs of John Addington Symonds*; Hartman, "Child-Abuse and Self-Abuse."

99. VW, 13 April 1938, *Diary 5*. Page references are in parentheses in the text.

100. See Mitchell A. Leaska's Introduction to *Pointz Hall*.

101. VW, *Pointz Hall*, p. 374. Subsequent references in these notes will simply list the page number.

102. P. 375.

103. P. 559.

104. P. 560.

105. See the Notes to *Pointz Hall* provided by Mitchell A. Leaska.

106. P. 190.

107. P. 220.

108. P. 231.

109. P. 233.

110. See Leon Shaskolsky Sheleff, *Generations Apart*.

111. For an illuminating analysis of Oedipus, from the child's point of view, see Miller *Thou Shalt Not Be Aware*, pp. 145 ff.

112. An early version is different from the published text. It reads: "Unfaithful all day, as they had been, the children, even the thought of the children . . . renewed their marriage" (184). But, in a later version, the thought of their children renews "their hostility" (187).

CHAPTER 7: 1897: VIRGINIA WOOLF AT FIFTEEN

1. Quentin Bell, *Virginia Woolf*, 1:44.

2. VW, "Reminiscences," p. 44.

3. Ibid., p. 45.

4. Ibid.

5. VW, "A Sketch of the Past," p. 94.

6. Martine Stemerick, "The Madonna's Clay Feet," and "Virginia Woolf and Julia Stephen."

7. VW, *Letters* 1:2.

8. VW, 1 January 1898, 1897 diary.

9. These events are recorded in the following entries: stays, 1 April; Stella's marriage, 10 April; Stella's death, 19 July; Woolf's illness, 23 January, 9 May, passim; writing desk, 20 January; fifty volumes, passim; Lockhart, 26 January through 21 February; *Fawcett*, 23 August; *Notes*, 23 May; King's, 16 October; writing the moment down, 6 July; Queen Victoria, 22 June; *Mariana*, 22 February; *Hamlet*, 12 October; *As You Like It*, 2 March; *Faust*, 2 June; zoo, 7 and 12 January; Kensington Gardens, 31 January; Battersea Park, 3 January; Round Pond, 25 January; Serpentine, 17 January; National Gallery, 6 January; National Portrait Gallery, 19 January, 11 March; Carlyle's House, 29 January; ice skating, 28 January; bicycle riding, 8 February.

10. VW, "A Sketch of the Past," p. 116.

11. Ibid., p. 136.

12. Bell, *Virginia Woolf*, 1:44.

13. Stella Duckworth, 1896 Diary.

14. 15 February; 2 March 1897; 1897 Diary.

15. VW, "The tea table was the centre of Victorian family life."

16. See Stephen Trombley, *"All That Summer She Was Mad."*

17. 7 July, 1897 Diary.

18. 28 January, 1897 Diary. See Mrs. Leslie Stephen, *Notes from Sick Rooms.*

19. 25 February, 1897 Diary; Violet Dickinson to Vanessa Bell, quoted in Jean O. Love, *Virginia Woolf,* p. 193; Bell, *Virginia Woolf,* 1:39; Leslie Stephen, *Mausoleum Book.*

20. See Elaine Showalter, *The Female Malady.*

21. Vanessa, 2 March; 16 April; 24 April; 10 June; 16 June; passim. Adrian and Thoby, 6 January; 11 April; Stephen, *Mausoleum Book,* 10 April 1897; Father, 21 January; letter from Leslie Stephen to Stella Duckworth Hills, 10 April 1897; Frederic William Maitland, *The Life and Letters of Leslie Stephen;* Noel Annan, *Leslie Stephen;* Stella, 3 January through 10 April. Her half brothers, passim; 18 November.

22. 4 June, 1897 Diary. Diary entries cited within the text will be by day and month (although VW herself used 7/4 to indicate 4 July).

23. Maitland, *The Life and Letters of Leslie Stephen,* pp. 27–28.

24. Daniel Goleman, "Child Development Theory Stresses Small Moments."

25. Stephen, *Mausoleum Book,* 10 April 1897 entry. See "Laura, 'Her Ladyship of the Lake.'"

26. See "A Daughter Remembers."

27. See "Stella, 'The Old Cow.'"

28. These events are recorded on 1 July, 7 and 8 April, and 18 April.

29. The diary entries after Stella's illness indicate the extent to which new responsibilities were delegated to Woolf.

30. She uses the word in reference to how Vanessa was treated after Stella's death.

31. Woolf's entry for such an important event is curious. She records it in an offhand manner as if to soften the blow of her father's refusal. It is possible that the entry demonstrates her detachment, her denial, or her depression.

32. P. 102. I should like to thank Mitchell A. Leaska for describing these passages to me, from Anna Battista's transcription, even before the reprinting of Julia Stephen's pamphlet. It can also be found in Julia Stephen, *Stories for Children, Essays for Adults.*

33. VW, *Moments of Being,* p. 116.

34. Stephen, *Mausoleum Book,* p. xxviii.

35. VW, *Moments of Being,* p. 86.

36. For a discussion of the effects of adolescent reading upon development, see Louise M. Rosenblatt, *Literature as Exploration.*

37. See B. J. Kirkpatrick, *A Bibliography of Virginia Woolf;* Beverly Ann Schlack, *Continuing Presences.*

38. VW, holograph draft of *"The Antiquary,"* in holograph notebook, "Essays, 1924." On a manuscript page numbered 167 by the Berg Collection, Woolf dated an essay "52 Tavistock Sq., Oct. 5th." On page 187 of the notebook she began a draft of the essay entitled *"The Antiquary."* By my calculations, based upon the possibility that Woolf began a new page each day, she might have started the essay on or about 16 October 1924.

39. VW, 17 October 1924, *Diary* 2.

40. That Mr. Ramsay was the prototype for the antiquary is recorded in John Gibson Lockhart, *Memoirs of the Life of Sir Walter Scott.*

41. VW, *To the Lighthouse*, p. 176.

42. Ibid., pp. 179–80.

43. Sir Walter Scott, *The Antiquary*, p. 64.

44. Ibid., p. 83. Woolf's essay on *The Antiquary* has been reprinted as part of the essay, "Sir Walter Scott."

45. VW, *To the Lighthouse*, pp. 304–305.

46. Ibid., p. 253.

47. Ibid., pp. 283–84.

48. See Sonya Rudikoff, "How Many Lovers Had Virginia Woolf?"

49. VW, "Essays, 1924." To my knowledge, the editors and the readers of the *New Republic* did not catch the misreading; nor have any Woolf scholars or critics. I have read the "Letters" to the *New Republic* in the months following the publication of the essay on 3 December 1924, and none was published regarding Woolf's misreading.

50. Leslie Stephen, *Mausoleum Book*, xxvi.

51. VW, *Moments of Being*, p. 55.

52. Ibid., pp. 142–55.

53. Love, *Virginia Woolf*, p. 193. Love cites two 1942 letters from Violet Dickinson to Vanessa Bell.

54. Stella Duckworth in her 1896 diary was meticulous in recording her and Vanessa's and Virginia's menstrual cycles. The record continues into 1897. The last occurrence recorded for Stella was on 28 January 1897. There is no record for February, March, or April. In May she records the recurrence of Virginia's and Vanessa's cycles, but not hers, indicating that she was pregnant by that date. Whether Stella never menstruated after January 1897 can, of course, not be determined. That the record exists, however, suggests that this might be so and that Woolf therefore might have had reason to fancy that Stella became pregnant on the trip to Bognor, which occurred in February.

55. VW, *To the Lighthouse*, pp. 98–99.

CHAPTER 8: AS MISS JAN SAYS

1. The diary is now in the Berg Collection. I should like to thank Jane Marcus, Melissa Hield, the Department of English, Women's Studies, College

of Liberal Arts, and the Humanities Research Center of the University of Texas at Austin for inviting me to participate in their celebration of "Bloomsbury in Texas." A portion of this chapter was read at that celebration.

2. Martine Stemerick, "Virginia Woolf and Julia Stephen"; her 1897 Diary refers to the fact that she had kept a diary briefly in 1896 (which has not survived, to my knowledge). See the discussion of the *Hyde Park Gate News* in chap. 5.

3. See VW, "A Sketch of the Past."

4. VW, *Moments of Being*, p. 93.

5. VW, Monks House Papers, MH/A5c.

6. See Stephen Trombley, *"All That Summer She Was Mad"*; Elaine Showalter, *The Female Malady*.

7. Stemerick, "Virginia Woolf and Julia Stephen." VW, 8 December 1929, *Diary* 3.

8. VW, 8 March 1941, *Diary* 5.

9. VW, 15 January 1941, *Diary* 5.

10. See entry for 17 August 1938: "what my intention is in writing these continual diaries. Not publication . . . a memoir of my own life? Perhaps," *Diary* 5.

11. See Annette Kolodny, *The Land Before Her*.

12. 1 February, 1897 Diary.

13. Carol Gilligan, *In a Different Voice*.

14. In an earlier version of this chapter, "As 'Miss Jan Says,'" the view I presented was very different. I revised my view in response to criticism raised at the Hunter College Women's Studies Seminar, particularly in response to the objections of my colleague, Professor Joan Tronto, to whom I am grateful.

15. Gilligan, *In a Different Voice*, p. 30. Gilligan demonstrates this development by discussing the response of an eleven-year-old girl.

16. Gilligan, quoting Nancy Chodorow, *In a Different Voice*, p. 8.

17. Gilligan, *In a Different Voice*, p. 17.

18. The Miss Jan entries appear on the following dates in the 1897 Diary: 3, 4, 5 January; 11, 15, 19 February; 20, 28 April; 2 May. To my knowledge, Miss Jan does not appear after Sunday 2 May. This means that Miss Jan as a figure does not appear in this diary after the death of Stella Duckworth.

19. VW, 8 December 1929, *Diary* 3.

20. Leslie Stephen, "'An Agnostics Apology' and Other Essays," p. 41. Quoted in Noel Annan, *Leslie Stephen*, p. 173.

21. Ibid., p. 175.

22. See Mark Spilka, *Virginia Woolf's Quarrel with Grieving*. For Leslie Stephen's account, see *Mausoleum Book*.

23. VW, *Moments of Being*, pp. 40–41.

24. I should like to thank Jane Marcus for helping me clarify these issues. For an analysis of the impact of the life and works of Virginia Woolf's aunt Car-

oline Emelia Stephen, a great Quaker theologian, upon her work, see Jane Marcus, "The Niece of a Nun."

25. Leslie Stephen quoted in Annan, *Leslie Stephen*, p. 195.

26. Annan, *Leslie Stephen*, p. 191. The words are Annan's summarizing Stephen's position. Virginia Woolf owned several volumes of Pascal's works. See *Catalogue of Books from the Library of Leonard and Virginia Woolf.*

27. VW, *Letters* 4:2056.

28. Jane Marcus, "Liberty, Sorority, Misogyny," p. 70.

29. See, e.g., Loren S. Barritt and Barry M. Kroll, "Some Implications of Cognitive-Developmental Psychology for Research in Composing."

30. Gayatri C. Spivak, "Unmaking and Making in *To the Lighthouse*." I refer to Spivak's essay because it demonstrates the critical errors one can make if one does not examine Woolf's diaries themselves. This section of this chapter was first presented as a response to Blanche Wiesen Cook's paper, "Biographer and Subject," presented at the Columbia Women's Studies Seminar.

31. Spivak, "Unmaking and Making in *To the Lighthouse*," p. 316. Bell, *Virginia Woolf*, 1:65.

32. Quoted in Bell, *Virginia Woolf*, 1:65. An extremely interesting entry which discusses the mimetic function of art is that of 12 August 1899, which means that Woolf was thinking through this as an issue well before her contact with Clive Bell.

33. Madeline Moore, *The Short Season between Two Silences*, p. 12.

34. VW, *The Waves, the Two Holograph Drafts*, I/3. I have reproduced the sense of the passage.

35. Ibid., I/16.

36. Leslie Stephen, *Mausoleum Book*, pp. 40, 41, 53, 56–57, 62.

37. VW, *Moments of Being*, p. 144.

38. Ibid., p. 39.

39. Another version exists in Monks House Papers, University of Sussex England. According to the catalogue, it was written in 1899 and copied in 1904 for Emma Vaughan. It is MH/a.10, "A Terrible Tragedy in a Duckpond: a Note of Correction and Addition to the above. by one of the Drowned." It appears in *The Virginia Woolf Manuscripts from the Monks House Papers at the University of Sussex.*

40. VW, *Letters* 1:27.

41. Mitchell A. Leaska, ed., *Pointz Hall*, p. 220.

42. VW, *Letters* 1:170.

43. Ibid.

44. VW, *Letters* 1:84.

45. VW, *Letters* 1:187.

46. Ibid.

47. VW, *Letters* 1:191.

CHAPTER 9: CHANGING LIVES

1. See Louise A. DeSalvo, *Virginia Woolf's First Voyage.*

2. For superb readings of *Night and Day*, see Susan Merrill Squier, *Virginia Woolf and London*; Jane Marcus, *Virginia Woolf and the Languages of the Patriarchy*; Mitchell A. Leaska, *The Novels of Virginia Woolf.*

3. Alex Zwerdling, *Virginia Woolf and the Real World*, p. 65.

4. Ibid., p. 74.

5. Kathleen Dobie, "This is the Room that Class Built," p. 201.

6. See the discussion of *Mrs. Dalloway* in Leaska, *The Novels of Virginia Woolf.*

7. VW, "The Journal of Mistress Joan Martyn," ed. by Susan M. Squier and Louise A. DeSalvo. Page numbers in parentheses refer to Woolf's page numbers, which are indicated in this edition.

8. VW, *Letters* 1:282.

9. There is some confusion about the text sent Jane by her father. The manuscript reads that her father sent her "The Towe Palace of Glass, by Mr. John Lydgate," with Towe cancelled. But, immediately after that, the description of the poem as recounting Helen's story is presented. Woolf is certainly referring to the *Temple of Glas*, although she seems to have forgotten the exact title, but she might have transposed the subject of the *Troy Story* with the title of *Temple*. There is a brief reference to Helen of Troy in *Temple of Glas*, and this may have been the reason for the confusion.

10. VW, *To the Lighthouse, The original holograph draft*, p. 12. Further references are to this edition and are in parentheses in the text. See Jane Lilienfeld, "'The Deceptiveness of Beauty,'" "Where the Spear Plants Grew"; Elizabeth Abel, "Cam the Wicked."

11. VW, *The Years*. Page references are in parentheses in the text.

12. VW, *Letters* 2, Appendix III, p. 339.

13. VW, *Letters* 2, Appendix III, p. 339.

14. Ibid.

15. VW, *Letters* 2, Appendix III, p. 340.

16. Ibid.

17. VW, *Letters* 2, Appendix III, p. 341.

18. Ibid.

19. VW, *Letters* 2, Appendix III, p. 342.

20. Ibid.

21. Ibid.

22. Ibid.

23. VW, *Flush*, p. 24. For excellent discussions of *Flush*, see Squier, *Virginia Woolf and London*; Lola L. Szladits, "The Life, Character and Opinions of Flush the Spaniel."

24. P. 30. Subsequent page references in this discussion are in parentheses in the text.

25. Susan Gubar, "The Birth of the Artist as Heroine," p. 49.

26. Jill Conway, "Stereotypes of Femininity in a Theory of Sexual Evolution," p. 143.

27. Conway, quoting Geddes, p. 146.

28. Page references to "The Leaning Tower" are in parentheses in the text.

29. VW, *Three Guineas*, p. 6. Subsequent page references are in parentheses in the text.

30. VW, *Roger Fry*, p. 38.

31. VW, *A Room of One's Own*, p. 56. See Marcus, *Virginia Woolf and the Languages of the Patriarchy*.

32. See Berenice A. Carroll, "'To Crush Him in Our Own Country.'"

EPILOGUE

1. VW, *Moments of Being*, pp. 177, 182.

2. VW, Hyde Park Gate Diary, p. 14.

3. VW, *Letters* 1:471.

4. VW, *Letters* 1:272.

5. VW, *Letters* 1:469.

6. VW, *Moments of Being*, p. 183.

7. Ibid., p. 182.

8. Ibid., p. 184.

9. Ibid.

10. Jane Marcus, "The Niece of a Nun," p. 122.

11. VW, "Friendships Gallery," ed. by Ellen Hawkes. Subsequent page references are in parentheses in the text.

12. VW, *Moments of Being*, p. 183.

Select Bibliography

In the case of articles in books, publication data can be found in the entry for the book.

Abel, Elizabeth. "'Cam the Wicked': Woolf's Portrait of the Artist as her Father's Daughter." In *Virginia Woolf and Bloomsbury*, ed. by Jane Marcus, pp. 170–94.
———. "Narrative Structure(s) and Female Development: The Case of *Mrs. Dalloway.*" In *The Voyage In*, ed. by Elizabeth Abel et al., pp. 161–85.
Abel, Elizabeth, Marianne Hirsch, and Elizabeth Langland, eds. *The Voyage In: Fictions of Female Development*. Hanover, N.H.: University Press of New England, 1983.
Annan, Noel. *Leslie Stephen: The Godless Victorian*. Chicago and London: University of Chicago Press, 1984, 1986.
———. *Leslie Stephen: His Thought and Character in Relationship to His Time*. Cambridge, Mass.: Harvard University Press, 1952.
Apter, T. E. "Self-Defence and Self-Knowledge: The Function of Vanity and Friendship in Virginia Woolf." In *Virginia Woolf*, ed. by Eric Warner, pp. 83–98.
Ariès, Philippe. *Centuries of Childhood: A Social History of Family Life*. Trans. by Robert Baldick. New York: Alfred A. Knopf, 1962.
Armstrong, Louise. *Kiss Daddy Goodnight: A Speak-Out on Incest*. New York: Pocket Books, 1978.
———. "The Cradle of Sexual Politics: Incest." In Martha Kirkpatrick, *Women's Sexual Experience*, pp. 109–25.
Ascher, Carol, Louise DeSalvo, and Sara Ruddick, eds. *Between Women: Biographers, Novelists, Teachers and Artists Write about Their Work on Women*. Boston: Beacon Press, 1984.
Auerbach, Nina. *Communities of Women: An Idea in Fiction*. Cambridge, Mass.: Harvard University Press, 1978.
———. *Woman and the Demon: The Life of a Victorian Myth*. Cambridge, Mass.: Harvard University Press, 1982.

Bailey, Peter. "'A Mingled Mass of Perfectly Legitimate Pleasures': The Victorian Middle Class and the Problem of Leisure." *Victorian Studies* 21 (Autumn 1977): 7–28.

Barickman, Richard, Susan MacDonald, and Myra Stark. *Corrupt Relations: Dickens, Thackeray, Trollope, Collins, and the Victorian Sexual System.* New York: Columbia University Press, 1982.

Barritt, Loren S., and Barry M. Kroll. "Some Implications of Cognitive-Developmental Psychology for Research in Composing." In *Research on Composing: Points of Departure,* ed. by Charles R. Cooper and Lee Odell.

Bass, Ellen, and Louise Thornton, eds. *I Never Told Anyone: Writings by Women Survivors of Child Sexual Abuse.* New York: Harper & Row, 1983.

Bayley, John. "Diminishment of Consciousness: A Paradox in the Art of Virginia Woolf." In *Virginia Woolf: A Centenary Perspective,* ed. by Eric Warner, pp. 69–82.

Bazin, Nancy Topping. *Virginia Woolf and the Androgynous Vision.* New Brunswick, N.J.: Rutgers University Press, 1973.

Behlmer, George. *Child Abuse and Moral Reform in England, 1870–1908.* Stanford: Stanford University Press, 1982.

Beja, Morris. *Epiphany in the Modern Novel.* Seattle: University of Washington Press, 1971.

Bell, Clive. *Old Friends: Personal Recollections.* London: Chatto & Windus, 1956.

Bell, Quentin. "The Biographer, the Critic, and the Lighthouse." In *Ariel* 2 (January 1971): 94–100.

———. "Of Sound or Unsound Mind." Review of '*All That Summer She Was Mad*': *Virginia Woolf and Her Doctors,* by Stephen Trombley. *The Observer,* 15 November 1981, 27.

———. *Virginia Woolf: A Biography.* 2 vols. New York: Harcourt Brace Jovanovich, 1972.

Bell, Vanessa. 371 letters to Virginia Woolf, 8 September [1904] through [13 March 1940]. The Henry W. and Albert A. Berg Collection of English and American Literature of the New York Public Library, Astor, Lenox and Tilden Foundations.

———. *Notes on Virginia's Childhood: A Memoir.* Ed. by Richard F. Schaubeck, Jr. New York: Frank Hallman, 1974. (Published in an edition of 300 numbered copies; printed by Andrew Hoyem in San Francisco).

———. *Vanessa Bell's Family Album.* Compiled by Quentin Bell and Angelica Garnett. London: Jill Norman & Hobhouse Ltd., 1981.

Bennett, Paula. *My Life/A Loaded Gun: Female Creativity and Feminist Poetics.* Boston: Beacon Press, 1986.

Bernikow, Louise. *Among Women.* London: Harper Colophon, 1980.

Berry, Maxine Metzner. "The Case of Virginia Woolf: A Psycho-biographical Investigation of Her 'Madness.'" Unpublished paper.

Bicknell, John. "Mr Ramsay was Young Once." In *Virginia Woolf and Blooms-bury*, ed. by Jane Marcus, pp. 52–67.

Black, Naomi. "Virginia Woolf and the Women's Movement." In *Virginia Woolf*, ed. by Jane Marcus, pp. 180–97.

Blackstone, Bernard. *Virginia Woolf: A Commentary*. New York: Harcourt Brace Jovanovich, n.d.

"Breaking the Silence." Public Broadcasting System, 11 August 1987.

Brewster, Dorothy. *Virginia Woolf*. New York: New York University Press, 1962.

Bridenthal, Renate, and Claudia Koonz, eds. *Becoming Visible: Women in European History*. Boston: Houghton Mifflin, 1977.

Brittan, Arthur, and Mary Maynard. *Sexism, Racism and Oppression*. Oxford: Basil Blackwell, 1984.

Brody, Jane E. "Therapists Seek Causes of Child Molesting: Problem Found Far More Widespread than Had Been Thought." *New York Times*, 13 January 1987, science section, pp. C1, C12.

Brownstein, Rachel M. *Becoming a Heroine: Reading about Women in Novels*. New York: Penguin Books, 1984. First published by Viking Press, 1982.

Burroughs, Peter. "The Human Cost of Imperial Defence in the Early Victorian Age." *Victorian Studies* 24 (Autumn 1980): 7–32.

Burstyn, Joan N. *Victorian Education and the Ideal of Womanhood*. London: Croom Helm, 1980; Totowa, N.J.: Barnes & Noble, 1980.

Caine, Barbara. Review of *Victorian Education and the Ideal of Womanhood*, by Joan N. Burstyn. *Victorian Studies* 25 (Autumn 1981): 107–108.

Cameron, Julia Margaret. *Victorian Photographs of Famous Men & Fair Women*, with Introductions by Virginia Woolf and Roger Fry. Expanded and revised edition by Tristram Powell. Boston: David R. Godine, 1973. First published in 1926.

Carmen, Elaine Hilberman, Patricia Perry Rieker, and Trudy Mills. "Victims of Violence and Psychiatric Illness." *American Journal of Psychiatry* 141 (March 1984): 378–83.

Carroll, Berenice A. "'To Crush Him In Our Own Country': The Political Thought of Virginia Woolf." *Feminist Studies* 4 (February 1978): 99–131.

Catalogue of Books from the Library of Leonard and Virginia Woolf, taken from Monks House, Rodmell, Sussex, and 24 Victoria Square, London, and now in the possession of Washington State University, Pullman. Brighton, England: Holleyman & Treacher, 1975.

Chappell, Mary R. "The Value of an Orderly Nursery." *The Outlook* (14 December 1895), pp. 1021–22.

Chesler, Phyllis. *Women and Madness*. Garden City, N.Y.: Doubleday, 1972.

Chesney, Kellow. *The Anti-Society: An Account of the Victorian Underworld*. Boston: Gambit, 1970.

"Children and Death." Pamphlet from National Funeral Directors Association Library of Publications, 135 West Wells Street, Milwaukee, Wis., n.d.

Select Bibliography

Chodorow, Nancy. *The Reproduction of Mothering.* Berkeley: University of California Press, 1978.

Christ, Carol. "Victorian Masculinity and the Angel in the House." In *A Widening Sphere,* ed. by Martha Vicinus, pp. 146–62.

Clawson, Mary Ann. "Early Modern Fraternalism and the Patriarchal Family." *Feminist Studies* (Summer 1980), pp. 372–88.

Comstock, Margaret. "The Loudspeaker and the Human Voice: Politics and the Form of *The Years.*" *Bulletin of The New York Public Library* 80 (Winter 1977): 252–75.

Conway, Jill. "Stereotypes of Femininity in a Theory of Sexual Evolution." In *Suffer and Be Still,* ed. by Martha Vicinus, pp. 140–54.

Cook, Blanche Wiesen. "'Women Alone Stir My Imagination': Lesbianism and the Cultural Tradition." *Signs* 4 (Summer 1979): 718–39.

Cooper, Charles R., and Lee Odell, eds. *Research on Composing: Points of Departure.* Urbana, Ill.: National Council of Teachers of English, 1978.

Cory, Donald Webster, and R. E. L. Masters, eds. *Violation of Taboo: Incest in the Great Literature of the Past and Present.* New York: Julian Press, 1963.

Cott, Nancy F. "Passionlessness: An Interpretation of Victorian Sexual Ideology, 1790–1850." *Signs* 4 (Winter 1978): 219–36.

Daly, Mary. *Beyond God the Father: Toward a Philosophy of Women's Liberation.* Boston: Beacon Press, 1973.

———. *Gyn/Ecology: The Metaethics of Radical Feminism.* Boston: Beacon Press, 1978.

D'Arcy, Kathleen Walsh. Unpublished paper on *Jacob's Room.*

———. Unpublished paper on *To the Lighthouse.*

Daugherty, Beth Rigel. "'There she sat': The Power of the Feminist Imagination in *To the Lighthouse.*" *Otterbein Miscellany* 20 (Fall 1986): 1–16.

Davidoff, Leonore. "Class and Gender in Victorian England: The Diaries of Arthur J. Munby and Hannah Culliwick." *Feminist Studies* 5 (Spring 1979): 87–141.

de Mause, Lloyd. "The Evolution of Childhood." In *The History of Childhood,* ed. by Lloyd de Mause, pp. 1–73.

———, ed. *The History of Childhood.* New York: Psychohistory Press, 1974.

DeSalvo, Louise A. "As 'Miss Jan Says': Virginia Woolf's Early Journals." In *Virginia Woolf and Bloomsbury,* ed. by Jane Marcus, pp. 96–124.

———. "Bloomsbury Born and Bred." Review of *Deceived with Kindness,* by Angelica Garnett. *Women's Review of Books* 2 (August 1985): 3–4.

———. "1897: Virginia Woolf at Fifteen." In *Virginia Woolf,* ed. by Jane Marcus, pp. 78–108.

———. "Lighting the Cave: The Relationship between Vita Sackville-West and Virginia Woolf." *Signs* 8 (1982): 195–214.

———. "A Portrait of the Puttana as a Middle-Aged Woolf Scholar." In *Between Women,* ed. by Carol Ascher et al., pp. 35–54.

————. "Shakespeare's *Other* Sister." In *New Feminist Essays on Virginia Woolf,* ed. by Jane Marcus, pp. 61–81.

————. "'To Make Her Mutton at Sixteen': Rape, Incest and Child Abuse in Djuna Barnes' *The Antiphon.*" Unpublished paper.

————. *Virginia Woolf's First Voyage: A Novel in the Making.* Totowa, N.J.: Rowman & Littlefield, 1980; London: Macmillan, 1980.

————. "Virginia Woolf's Politics and Her Mystical Vision." *Tulsa Studies in Women's Literature* 4 (Fall 1985): 281–90.

————, ed. *"Melymbrosia" by Virginia Woolf: An Early Version of The Voyage Out.* New York: The New York Public Library, Astor, Lenox and Tilden Foundations, 1982.

DeSalvo, Louise, and Mitchell A. Leaska, eds. *The Letters of Vita Sackville-West to Virginia Woolf.* New York: William Morrow, 1985; London: Hutchinson, 1985.

Despert, J. Louise. *The Emotionally Disturbed Child—Then and Now.* New York: Vantage Press, 1965.

DiBattista, Maria. *"To the Lighthouse:* Virginia Woolf's Winter's Tale." In *Virginia Woolf,* ed. by Ralph Freedman, pp. 161–88.

Dinnerstein, Dorothy. *The Mermaid and the Minotaur: Sexual Arrangements and Human Malaise.* New York: Harper & Row, 1976.

Dobie, Kathleen. "This is the Room that Class Built: The Structures of Sex and Class in *Jacob's Room.*" In *Virginia Woolf and Bloomsbury,* ed. by Jane Marcus, pp. 195–207.

Douglas, Ann. *The Feminization of American Culture.* New York: Alfred A. Knopf, 1978.

Duckworth, Stella. 1896 Diary. The Henry W. and Albert A. Berg Collection of English and American Literature of the New York Public Library, Astor, Lenox and Tilden Foundations.

Dunae, Patrick A. "Boys' Literature and the Idea of Empire, 1870–1914." *Victorian Literature* 24 (Autumn 1980): 105–21.

————. "Penny Dreadfuls: Late Nineteenth-Century Boys' Literature and Crime." *Victorian Studies* 22 (Winter 1979): 133–50.

Dworkin, Andrea. *Woman Hating.* New York: E. P. Dutton, 1974.

Dyhouse, Carol. *Girls Growing Up in Late Victorian and Edwardian England.* London: Routledge & Kegan Paul, 1981.

Edel, Leon. *Bloomsbury: A House of Lions.* New York: Avon Books, 1979, 1980.

Ehrenreich, Barbara, and Deirdre English. *Complaints and Disorders: The Sexual Politics of Sickness.* Old Westbury, N.Y.: Feminist Press, 1973.

————. *For Her Own Good: 150 Years of the Experts' Advice to Women.* Garden City, N.Y.: Anchor Books, 1979.

Ellmann, Mary. *Thinking about Women.* New York: Harcourt, Brace & World, 1968.

Epstein, Barbara. "Family, Sexual Morality, and Popular Movements in Turn-of-the-Century America." In *Powers of Desire*, ed. by Ann Snitow et al., pp. 117–30.

Fassler, Barbara. "Theories of Homosexuality as Sources of Bloomsbury's Androgyny." *Signs* 5 (1979): 237–51.

Feinstein, Sherman C. "Why They Were Afraid of Virginia Woolf: Perspectives on Juvenile Manic-Depressive Illness." *Adolescent Psychiatry, Developmental and Clinical Studies* 3 (1980): 332–43.

Fetterley, Judith. *The Resisting Reader: A Feminist Approach to American Fiction*. Bloomington: Indiana University Press, 1978.

Firestone, Shulamith. *The Dialectic of Sex: The Case for Feminist Revolution* New York: William Morrow, 1970.

Fliess, Robert. *Erogeneity and Libido: Addenda to the Theory of the Psychosexual Development of the Human*. New York: International Universities Press, 1956.

Forster, Edward Morgan. *Virginia Woolf*. New York: Harcourt Brace, 1942.

Foucault, Michel. *The History of Sexuality*. Vol. 1, *An Introduction*. Trans. by Robert Hurley. New York: Vintage Books, 1980.

Fox, Alice. "Virginia Liked Elizabeth." In *Virginia Woolf: A Feminist Slant*, ed. by Jane Marcus, pp. 37–51.

———. "Virginia Woolf at Work: The Elizabethan *Voyage Out*." *Bulletin of Research in the Humanities* 84 (Spring 1981): 65–84.

Freedman, Ralph., ed. *Virginia Woolf: Revaluation and Continuity*. Berkeley: University of California Press, 1980.

French, Marilyn. *Beyond Power: On Women, Men, and Morals*. New York: Summit Books, 1985.

Freud, Sigmund. *The Origins of Psycho-Analysis: Letters to Wilhelm Fliess, Drafts and Notes: 1887–1902*. Ed. by Marie Bonaparte, Anna Freud, and Ernst Kris; authorized translation by Eric Mosbacher and James Strachey; Introduction by Ernst Kris. New York: Basic Books, 1954.

Fry, Roger Eliot. 2 letters to Leonard Sidney Woolf. The Henry W. and Albert A. Berg Collection of English and American Literature of the New York Public Library, Astor, Lenox and Tilden Foundations.

———. Manuscript extracts by Virginia Woolf from Roger Fry's correspondence, unsigned and undated, 4 pages. Extracts dated 2 March 1906–14 February 1910. The Henry W. and Albert A. Berg Collection of English and American Literature of the New York Public Library, Astor, Lenox and Tilden Foundations.

Gadd, David. *The Loving Friends: A Portrait of Bloomsbury*. New York: Harcourt Brace Jovanovich, 1974.

Gallop, Jane. *The Daughter's Seduction: Feminism and Psychoanalysis*. Ithaca, N.Y.: Cornell University Press, 1982.

Garnett, Angelica. *Deceived with Kindness: A Bloomsbury Childhood*. New York: Harcourt Brace Jovanovich, 1985.

Garnett, Henrietta. *Family Skeletons.* New York: Alfred A. Knopf, 1987.

Gay, Peter. *The Bourgeois Experience, Victoria to Freud.* Vol. 1, *Education of the Senses.* New York: Oxford University Press, 1984. Vol. 2, *The Tender Passion.* New York: Oxford University Press, 1986.

Gelinas, Denise J. "The Persisting Negative Effects of Incest." *Psychiatry* 46 (November 1983): 312–33.

Gerin, Winifred. *Anne Thackeray Ritchie: A Biography.* Oxford: Oxford University Press, 1985.

Gilbert, Sandra M. "Woman's Sentence, Man's Sentencing: Linguistic Fantasies in Woolf and Joyce." In *Virginia Woolf and Bloomsbury,* ed. by Jane Marcus, pp. 208–24.

Gilbert, Sandra M., and Susan Gubar. *The Madwoman in the Attic: The Woman Writer and the Nineteenth-Century Literary Imagination.* New Haven: Yale University Press, 1979.

Gillespie, Diane Filby. "Political Aesthetics: Virginia Woolf and Dorothy Richardson." In *Virginia Woolf,* ed. by Jane Marcus, pp. 132–52.

Gilligan, Carol. *In a Different Voice: Psychological Theory and Women's Development.* Cambridge, Mass.: Harvard University Press, 1982.

Gillis, John R. *For Better, For Worse: British Marriages, 1600 to the Present.* New York: Oxford University Press, 1985.

Gilman, Sander L. *Difference and Pathology: Stereotypes of Sexuality, Race, and Madness.* Ithaca, N.Y.: Cornell University Press, 1985.

Glendinning, Victoria. *Vita: A Biography of Vita Sackville-West.* New York: Alfred A. Knopf, 1983.

Goleman, Daniel. "Child Development Theory Stresses Small Moments." *New York Times,* 21 October 1986, science section, pp. C1, C3.

———. "Depression Tied to Some Excesses in Youth." *New York Times,* 9 September 1986, science section, pp. C1, C2.

———. "In Memory, People Re-create Their Lives to Suit Their Images of the Present." *New York Times,* 23 June 1987, science section, pp. C1, C2.

———. "Parental Influence: New Subtleties Found." *New York Times,* 29 July 1986, science section, pp. C1, C3.

———. "Research Affirms Power of Positive Thinking." *New York Times,* 3 February 1987, science section, pp. C1, C5.

Gordon, Linda, and Ellen DuBois. "Seeking Ecstasy on the Battlefield: Danger and Pleasure in Nineteenth-Century Feminist Sexual Thought." *Feminist Studies* 9 (Spring 1983): 7–25.

Gordon, Lyndall. *Virginia Woolf: A Writer's Life.* New York: W. W. Norton, 1984.

———. "A Writer's Life." In *Virginia Woolf: A Centenary Perspective,* ed. by Eric Warner, pp. 56–68.

Gorham, Deborah. "The 'Maiden Tribute of Modern Babylon' Re-Examined:

Child Prostitution and the Idea of Childhood in Late-Victorian England."
Victorian Studies 21(3): 353–79.

———. *The Victorian Girl and the Feminine Ideal.* Bloomington: Indiana University Press, 1982.

Gornick, Vivian, and Barbara K. Moran, eds. *Woman in Sexist Society: Studies in Power and Powerlessness.* New York: Basic Books, 1971.

Green, Martin. *Children of the Sun.* New York: Basic Books, 1976.

Gregor, Ian. "Virginia Woolf and Her Reader." In *Virginia Woolf,* ed. by Eric Warner, pp. 41–55.

Grosskurth, Phyllis. *Leslie Stephen.* Published for the British Council and the National Book League by Longmans, Green & Co., London, 1968.

———, ed. *The Memoirs of John Addington Symonds.* Chicago: University of Chicago Press, 1984.

Gubar, Susan. "The Birth of the Artist as Heroine: (Re)production, the *Kunstlerroman* Tradition, and the Fiction of Katherine Mansfield." In *The Representation of Women in Fiction,* ed. by Carolyn G. Heilbrun and Margaret Higonnet, pp. 19–59.

Guiguet, Jean. *Virginia Woolf and Her Works.* Trans. by Jean Stewart. New York: Harcourt, Brace & World, 1965.

Haller, Evelyn. "Isis Unveiled: Virginia Woolf's Use of Egyptian Myth." In *Virginia Woolf,* ed. by Jane Marcus, pp. 109–31.

"The Happiness of Children." *Spectator,* 5 March 1892, pp. 331–32.

Harris, Barbara J. "Recent Work on the History of the Family: A Review Article." *Feminist Studies* 3 (Spring/Summer 1976): 159–72.

Harrison, Jane Ellen. *Ancient Art and Ritual.* New York: Greenwood Press, 1969.

———. *Prolegomena to the Study of Greek Religion.* New York: Meridian Books, 1959. First published in 1903.

Harrison, Michael. *Clarence, The Life of H. R. H. the Duke of Clarence and Avondale (1864–1892).* London: W. H. Allen, 1972.

Hartman, Mary S. "Child-Abuse and Self-Abuse: Two Victorian Cases." *History of Childhood Quarterly, The Journal of Psychohistory* 2 (Fall 1974): 221–48.

Haule, James M. "'Le Temps Passe' and the Original Typescript: An Early Version of the 'Time Passes' Section of *To the Lighthouse.*" *Twentieth Century Literature: A Scholarly and Critical Journal* 29 (Fall 1983): 267–311.

———. "Virginia Woolf." *Contemporary Literature* 23 (Winter 1982): 100–104.

Haule, James M., and Philip H. Smith, Jr. *A Concordance to Between the Acts by Virginia Woolf.* Oxford: Oxford Microform Publications, 1982.

———. *A Concordance to Mrs. Dalloway by Virginia Woolf.* Oxford: Oxford Microform Publications, 1985.

———. *A Concordance to Night and Day by Virginia Woolf.* Oxford: Oxford Microform Publications, 1986.

——. *A Concordance to Orlando by Virginia Woolf.* Oxford: Oxford Microform Publications, 1985.

——. *A Concordance to To the Lighthouse by Virginia Woolf.* Oxford: Oxford Microform Publications, 1983.

——. *A Concordance to The Voyage Out by Virginia Woolf.* Ann Arbor: UMI, 1987.

——. *A Concordance to The Waves by Virginia Woolf.* Oxford: Oxford Microform Publications, 1981.

——. *A Concordance to The Years by Virginia Woolf.* Oxford: Oxford Microform Publications, 1984.

Hawkes, Ellen. "Woolf's 'Magical Garden of Women.'" In *New Feminist Essays on Virginia Woolf,* ed. by Jane Marcus, pp. 31–60.

Heilbrun, Carolyn G. *Toward a Recognition of Androgyny.* New York: Alfred A. Knopf, 1973.

——. "Virginia Woolf in Her Fifties." In *Virginia Woolf,* ed. by Jane Marcus, pp. 236–53.

Heilbrun, Carolyn G., and Margaret R. Higonnet, eds. *The Representation of Women in Fiction: Selected Papers from the English Institute, 1981.* New Series, no. 7. Baltimore: Johns Hopkins University Press, 1983.

Henke, Suzette A. "*Mrs Dalloway*: the Communion of Saints." In *New Feminist Essays on Virginia Woolf,* ed. by Jane Marcus, pp. 125–47.

Herman, Judith Lewis, with Lisa Hirschman. *Father-Daughter Incest.* Cambridge, Mass.: Harvard University Press, 1981.

Higonnet, Margaret R. "Introduction." In *Representation of Women in Fiction,* ed. by Carolyn G. Heilbrun and Margaret R. Higonnet, pp. xiii–xxii.

Himmelfarb, Gertrude. *Marriage and Morals among the Victorians.* New York: Alfred A. Knopf, 1986.

Hirsch, Marianne. "Spiritual *Bildung*: The Beautiful Soul as Paradigm." In *The Voyage In,* ed. by Elizabeth Abel et al., pp. 23–48.

Holroyd, Michael. *Lytton Strachey and the Bloomsbury Group: His Work Their Influence.* Middlesex, Eng.: Penguin Books, 1971.

——, ed. *Lytton Strachey by Himself: A Self-Portrait.* New York: Holt, Rinehart & Winston, 1971.

Houghton, Walter E. *The Victorian Frame of Mind, 1830–1870.* New Haven: Published for Wellesley College by Yale University Press, 1957.

——. "Victorian Periodical Literature and the Articulate Classes." *Victorian Studies* 22 (Summer 1979): 389–412.

Hughes, M. V. *A London Child of the 1870s.* Oxford: Oxford University Press, 1934, 1977.

——. *A London Girl of the 1880s.* Oxford: Oxford University Press, 1946, 1978.

————. A *London Home in the 1890s*. Oxford: Oxford University Press, 1946, 1969.

Hussey, Mark. *The Singing of the Real World: The Philosophy of Virginia Woolf's Fiction*. Columbus: Ohio State University Press, 1986.

Ingram, Angela. "'The Sacred Edifices': Virginia Woolf and Some of the Sons of Culture." In *Virginia Woolf and Bloomsbury*, ed. by Jane Marcus, pp. 125–45.

Janeway, Elizabeth. "'Who Is Sylvia?' On the Loss of Sexual Paradigms." *Signs* 5 (Summer 1980): 573–89.

Jensen, Emily. "Clarissa Dalloway's Respectable Suicide." In *Virginia Woolf*, ed. by Jane Marcus, pp. 162–79.

Johnson, Manly. *Virginia Woolf*. New York: Frederick Ungar, 1973.

Johnston, Judith L. "The Remediable Flaw: Revisioning Cultural History in *Between the Acts*." In *Virginia Woolf and Bloomsbury*, ed. by Jane Marcus, pp. 253–77.

K., A. Y. "Punishing vs. Training." *Outlook* 48 (5 August 1893): 266.

Kaplan, Marion. "Interview: Mothers in the Fatherland." With Claudia Koonz. *New Directions for Women* (May/June 1987), p. 3.

Kelley, Mary. *Private Woman, Public Stage: Literary Domesticity in Nineteenth-Century America*. New York: Oxford University Press, 1984.

Kempton, Grace C. "Nervous Children and How to Help Them." *Outlook* 48 (4 November 1893): 807–8.

Kenney, Susan M. "Two Endings: Virginia Woolf's Suicide and *Between the Acts*." *University of Toronto Quarterly*, vol. 44 (Summer 1975).

Kenney, Susan M., and Edwin J. Kenney, Jr. "Virginia Woolf and the Art of Madness." *Massachusetts Review* (Spring 1982):161–85.

Kern, Stephen. "Explosive Intimacy: Psychodynamics of the Victorian Family." *History of Childhood Quarterly, The Journal of Psychohistory* 1 (Winter 1974): 437–62.

Kiell, Norman. *The Adolescent through Fiction: A Psychological Approach*. New York: International Universities Press, 1959.

Kinard, E. Milling. *Emotional Development in Physically Abused Children: A Study of Self-Concept and Aggression*. Palo Alto, Calif.: R & E Research Associates, 1978.

Kirkpatrick, B. J. *A Bibliography of Virginia Woolf*. 3d ed. Oxford: Clarendon Press, 1980.

Kirkpatrick, Martha. *Women's Sexual Experience: Explorations of the Dark Continent*. New York: Plenum Press, 1982.

Kolodny, Annette. *The Land before Her: Fantasy and Experience of the American Frontiers, 1630–1860*. Chapel Hill: University of North Carolina Press, 1984.

Koonz, Claudia. *Mothers in the Fatherland: Women, the Family and Nazi Politics*. New York: St. Martin's Press, 1987.

Kunzle, David. "Dress Reform as Antifeminism: A Response to Helene E. Roberts's 'The Exquisite Slave: The Role of Clothes in the Making of the Victorian Woman.'" *Signs* 2 (Spring 1977): 570–79.

Laing, R. D. *The Politics of the Family and Other Essays*. New York: Pantheon Books, 1969, 1971.

Lansbury, Coral. "Gynaecology, Pornography, and the Antivivisection Movement." *Victorian Studies* 28 (3): 413–37.

Laslett, Peter. *Family Life and Illicit Love in Earlier Generations: Essays in Historical Sociology*. New York: Cambridge University Press, 1977.

Leaska, Mitchell A. *The Novels of Virginia Woolf: From Beginning to End*. New York: John Jay Press, 1977.

———. *Virginia Woolf's Lighthouse: A Study in Critical Method*. London: Hogarth Press, 1970.

———, ed. *Pointz Hall: The Earlier and Later Typescripts of Between the Acts*, by Virginia Woolf, with an Introduction, Annotations, and an Afterword. New York: University Publications, 1983.

Lee, Hermione. "A Burning Glass: Reflection in Virginia Woolf." In *Virginia Woolf*, ed. by Eric Warner, pp. 12–27.

Lehmann, John. *Virginia Woolf and Her World*. London: Thames & Hudson, 1975.

Leonard, Linda Schierse. *The Wounded Woman: Healing the Father-Daughter Relationship*. Boston: Shambhala, 1982, 1983.

Lesser, Simon O. *Fiction and the Unconscious*. Boston: Beacon Press, 1957.

Lewis, Jane. *Women in England, 1870–1950: Sexual Divisions and Social Change*. Bloomington: Indiana University Press, 1984.

Lewis, Thomas S. W. "Virginia Woolf's Sense of the Past." Unpublished paper.

———, ed. *Virginia Woolf: A Collection of Criticism*. New York: McGraw-Hill, 1975.

"Life's First Feelings." *Nova*, Public Broadcasting System. 11 February 1986. Transcript available from WGBH Transcripts, 125 Western Avenue, Boston, Mass. 02134.

Lilienfeld, Jane. "'The Deceptiveness of Beauty': Mother Love and Mother Hate in *To the Lighthouse*." *Twentieth Century Literature* 23 (October 1977): 345–76.

———. "Where the Spear Plants Grew: the Ramsays' Marriage in *To the Lighthouse*." In *New Feminist Essays on Virginia Woolf*, ed. by Jane Marcus, pp. 148–69.

Little, Judy. *Comedy and the Woman Writer: Woolf, Spark, and Feminism*. Lincoln: University of Nebraska Press, 1983.

———. "*Jacob's Room* as Comedy: Woolf's Parodic *Bildungsroman*." In *New Feminist Essays on Virginia Woolf*, ed. by Jane Marcus, pp. 105–24.

Livy. *The History of Early Rome*. Trans. by Aubrey de Selincourt. Norwalk, Conn.: Easton Press, 1978.

Lockhart, John Gibson. *Memoirs of the Life of Sir Walter Scott*. New York: Houghton Mifflin, 1901.

Love, Jean O. *Virginia Woolf: Sources of Madness and Art*. Berkeley: University of California Press, 1977.

———. *Worlds in Consciousness: Mythopoetic Thought in the Novels of Virginia Woolf*. Berkeley: University of California Press, 1970.

Lydgate, John. *Lydgate's Temple of Glas*. Ed. by J. Schick. London: Oxford University Press, 1891.

Macaulay, Thomas Babington. *Lays of Ancient Rome*. London: Richard Edward King, n.d.

MacKay, Coral Hanbery. "The Thackeray Connection: Virginia Woolf's Aunt Anny." In *Virginia Woolf and Bloomsbury*, ed. by Jane Marcus, pp. 68–95.

Maitland, Frederic William. *The Life and Letters of Leslie Stephen*. London: Duckworth, 1906.

McLaren, Angus. "Abortion in England, 1890–1914." *Victorian Studies*, vol. 20 (Summer 1977).

McLaughlin, Ann L. "An Uneasy Sisterhood: Virginia Woolf and Katherine Mansfield." In *Virginia Woolf*, ed. by Jane Marcus, pp. 152–61.

Malory, Sir Thomas Malory. *Le Morte D'Arthur*. 2 vols. Ed. by Janet Cowen, with an Introduction by John Lawlor. Middlesex, Eng.: Penguin Books, 1962.

Marcus, Jane. "Art and Anger." *Feminist Studies* 4 (February 1978): 69–98.

———. "Enchanted Organs, Magic Bells: *Night and Day* as Comic Opera." In *Virginia Woolf*, ed. by Ralph Freedman, pp. 97–122.

———. "Liberty, Sorority, Misogyny." In *Representation of Women in Fiction*, ed. by Carolyn G. Heilbrun and Margaret R. Higonnet, pp. 60–97.

———. "The Niece of a Nun: Virginia Woolf, Caroline Stephen, and the Cloistered Imagination." In *Virginia Woolf: A Feminist Slant*, ed by Jane Marcus, pp. 7–36.

———. "'No More Horses': Virginia Woolf on Art and Propaganda." *Women's Studies* 4 (1977): 286–87.

———. "Pargeting 'The Pargiters': Notes of an Apprentice Plasterer." *Bulletin of the New York Public Library* (Spring 1977), pp. 416–35.

———. "Ruminations." *Women's Review of Books* 3 (March 1986): 7–8.

———. "'Taking the Bull by the Udders': Sexual Difference in Virginia Woolf—A Conspiracy Theory." In *Virginia Woolf and Bloomsbury*, ed. by Jane Marcus, pp. 146–69.

———. "Thinking Back through Our Mothers." In *New Feminist Essays on Virginia Woolf*, ed. by Jane Marcus, pp. 1–30.

———. *Virginia Woolf and the Languages of the Patriarchy*. Bloomington: Indiana University Press, 1987.

———. "*The Years* as Greek Drama, Domestic Novel, and Gotterdammerung." *Bulletin of the New York Public Library* 80 (Winter 1977): 276–301.

———, ed. *New Feminist Essays on Virginia Woolf*. London: Macmillan, 1981.

————, ed. *Virginia Woolf and Bloomsbury: A Centenary Celebration*. London: Macmillan Press, 1987.

————, ed. *Virginia Woolf: A Feminist Slant*. Lincoln: University of Nebraska Press, 1983.

Marcus, Steven. *The Other Victorians: A Study of Sexuality and Pornography in Mid-Nineteenth-Century England*. New York: Basic Books, 1964.

Martin, Wendy. "Seduced and Abandoned in the New World: The Image of Woman in American Fiction." In *Woman in Sexist Society*, ed. by Vivian Gornick and Barbara K. Moran, pp. 226–39.

Masson, Jeffrey Moussaieff. *The Assault on Truth: Freud's Suppression of the Seduction Theory*. New York: Farrar, Straus & Giroux, 1984.

May, Clifford D. "Behind a Rise in Sexual-Abuse Reports." *New York Times*, (2 March 1986), p. 8E.

May, Keith M. *Characters of Women in Narrative Literature*. New York: St. Martin's Press, 1981.

Maze, J. R. "Classical Female Oedipal Themes in *To the Lighthouse*." *International Review of Psycho-Analysis* 8 (1981): 155–71.

————. "Virginia Woolf: Ideas of Marriage and Death in *The Voyage Out*." *International Review of Psycho-Analysis* 10, pt. 1 (1983): 95–103.

McBride, Theresa. "'As the Twig Is Bent': The Victorian Nanny." In *The Victorian Family*, ed. by Anthony H. Wohl, pp. 44–58.

McConnell-Ginet, Sally, Ruth Borker, and Nelly Furman, eds. *Women and Language in Literature and Society*. New York: Praeger, 1980.

McLaurin, Allen. "Consciousness and Group Consciousness in Virginia Woolf." In *Virginia Woolf*, ed. by Eric Warner, pp. 28–40.

Meredith, George. *Love in the Valley*. In *Poems*. New York: Charles Scribner's Sons, 1908.

Mill, John Stuart. *The Subjection of Women* (1869). In *Essays on Sex Equality*, by John Stuart Mill and Harriet Taylor Mill, ed. and with an Introductory Essay by Alice S. Rossi. Chicago: University of Chicago Press, 1970.

Miller, Alice. *The Drama of the Gifted Child*. Trans. by Ruth Ward. New York: Basic Books, 1979. Originally published as *Prisoners of Childhood*.

————. *For Your Own Good: Hidden Cruelty in Child-Rearing and the Roots of Violence*. Trans. by Hildegarde Hannum and Hunter Hannum. New York: Farrar, Straus & Giroux, 1983, 1984.

————. *Thou Shalt Not Be Aware: Society's Betrayal of the Child*. Trans. by Hildegarde Hannum and Hunter Hannum. New York: Farrar, Straus & Giroux, 1984.

Miller, J. Hillis. *Fiction and Repetition: Seven English Novels*. Cambridge, Mass.: Harvard University Press, 1982.

Miller, John Hawkins. "'Temple and Sewer': Childbirth, Prudery and Victoria Regina." In *The Victorian Family*, ed. by Anthony S. Wohl, pp. 23–43.

Millett, Kate. *Sexual Politics*. Garden City, N.Y.: Doubleday, 1970.

Mintz, Steven. *A Prison of Expectations: The Family in Victorian Culture.* New York: New York University Press, 1985.

Mitchell, Juliet. *Psychoanalysis and Feminism.* New York: Vintage Books, 1974, 1975.

Mitchell, Sally. "Sentiment and Suffering: Women's Recreational Reading in the 1860s." *Victorian Studies* 21 (Autumn 1977): 29–45.

Moore, Madeline. *The Short Season between Two Silences: The Political and the Mystical in the Works of Virginia Woolf.* Boston: Allen & Unwin, 1984.

———. "Some Female Versions of Pastoral: *The Voyage Out* and Matriarchal Mythologies." In *New Feminist Essays on Virginia Woolf,* ed. by Jane Marcus, pp. 82–104.

Naremore, James. *The World without a Self: Virginia Woolf and the Novel.* New Haven: Yale University Press, 1973.

Nathan, Monique. *Virginia Woolf.* Paris: Editions du Seuil, 1956.

Newton, Judith Lowder. Review of *Communities of Women: An Idea in Fiction,* by Nina Auerbach, and *The Dilemma of the Talented Heroine: A Study in Nineteenth Century Fiction,* by Susan Siefert. *Victorian Studies* 23 (Autumn 1979): 130–32.

Noble, Joan Russell, ed. *Recollections of Virginia Woolf.* New York: William Morrow, 1972.

Novak, Jane. *The Razor Edge of Balance: A Study of Virginia Woolf.* Coral Gables, Fla.: University of Miami Press, 1975.

Odom, Keith. "Caught in the Brontës' Web of Childhood." *Brontë Newsletter* 5 (1986): 1–2.

Osborne, John Morton. Review of *The Healthy Body and Victorian Culture,* by Bruce Haley. *Victorian Studies* 23 (Autumn 1979): 134–35.

O'Shea, M. V. "'Spare the Rod and Spoil the Child.'" *Outlook* 58 (8 January 1898): 128–30.

Pearsall, Ronald. *The Worm in the Bud: The World of Victorian Sexuality.* Middlesex, Eng.: Penguin Books, 1969.

Perry, Ruth. *Women, Letters, and the Novel.* New York: AMS Press, 1980.

Pippett, Aileen. *The Moth and the Star: A Biography of Virginia Woolf.* Boston: Little, Brown, 1955.

Pleck, Elizabeth. "Feminist Response to 'Crimes against Women,' 1868–1896." *Signs,* Special Issue: Women and Violence, 8 (Spring 1983): 451–70.

Poole, Roger. *The Unknown Virginia Woolf.* Cambridge: Cambridge University Press, 1978.

Pope, Barbara Corrado. "Angels in the Devil's Workshop: Leisured and Charitable Women in Nineteenth-Century England and France." In *Becoming Visible,* ed. by Renate Bridenthal and Claudia Koonz, pp. 296–324.

Poovey, Mary. "'Scenes of an Indelicate Character': The Medical 'Treatment' of

Victorian Women." Working Paper no. 3. University of Wisconsin–Milwaukee, Center for Twentieth Century Studies, Fall 1985.

Radin, Grace. *Virginia Woolf's The Years: The Evolution of a Novel*. Knoxville: University of Tennessee Press, 1981.

Renvoize, Jean. *Incest: A Family Pattern*. London: Routledge & Kegan Paul, 1982.

Restuccia, Frances L. "'Untying the Mother Tongue': Female Difference in Virginia Woolf's *A Room of One's Own*." *Tulsa Studies in Women's Literature* 4 (Fall 1985): 253–64.

Rich, Adrienne. "Compulsory Heterosexuality and Lesbian Existence." In *Powers of Desire*, ed. by Ann Snitow et al., pp. 177–205.

———. *Of Woman Born: Motherhood as Experience and Institution*. New York: Bantam Books, 1977.

Richter, Harvena. *Virginia Woolf: The Inward Voyage*. Princeton: Princeton University Press, 1970.

Roberts, David. "The Paterfamilias of the Victorian Governing Classes." In *The Victorian Family*, ed. by Anthony S. Wohl, pp. 59–81.

Roberts, Helene E. "The Exquisite Slave: The Role of Clothes in the Making of the Victorian Woman." *Signs* 2 (Spring 1977): 554–69.

Robertson, Priscilla. "Home as a Nest: Middle Class Childhood in Nineteenth-Century Europe." In *The History of Childhood*, ed. by Lloyd de Mause, pp. 407–31.

Roe, Jill. "Modernisation and Sexism: Recent Writings on Victorian Women. *Victorian Studies* 20 (Winter 1977): 179–92.

Rose, Phyllis. *Parallel Lives: Five Victorian Marriages*. New York: Vintage Books, 1984.

———. *Woman of Letters: A Life of Virginia Woolf*. New York: Oxford University Press, 1978.

Rosenbaum, S. P., ed. *The Bloomsbury Group*. Toronto: University of Toronto Press, 1975.

Rosenberg, Rosalind. "In Search of Woman's Nature, 1850–1920." *Feminist Studies* 3 (Fall 1975): 141–54.

Rosenblatt, Louise M. *Literature as Exploration*. New York: Noble & Noble, 1938, 1968.

Rosenman, Ellen Bayuk. *The Invisible Presence: Virginia Woolf and the Mother-Daughter Relationship*. Baton Rouge: Louisiana State University Press, 1986.

Roshkill, Deirdre. Unpublished paper on *To the Lighthouse*, 1987.

Rosowski, Susan J. "The Novel of Awakening." In *The Voyage In*, ed. by Elizabeth Abel et al., pp. 49–68.

Ross, Ellen. "'Fierce Questions and Taunts': Married Life in Working-Class London, 1870–1914." *Feminist Studies* 8 (Fall 1982): 575–602.

Ross, Ellen, and Rayna Rapp. "Sex and Society: A Research Note from Social

History and Anthropology." In *Powers of Desire*, ed. by Ann Snitow et al., pp. 51–73.

Rowe, Stuart H. "Fear in the Discipline of Children." *Outlook* 60 (24 September 1898): 234–36.

Rubinstein, David. "Cycling in the 1890s." *Victorian Studies* 21 (Autumn 1977): 47–71.

Ruddick, Sara. "New Combinations: Learning from Virginia Woolf." In *Between Women*, ed. by Carol Ascher et al., pp. 137–60.

———. "Private Brother, Public World." In *New Feminist Essays on Virginia Woolf*, ed. by Jane Marcus, pp. 185–215.

Rudikoff, Sonya. "How Many Lovers Had Virginia Woolf." *Hudson Review* 34 (Winter 1979/80): 540–65.

Rumblelow, Donald. *The Complete Jack the Ripper*. London and New York: W. H. Allen and New York Graphic Society, 1975.

Rush, Florence. *The Best-Kept Secret: Sexual Abuse of Children*. New York: McGraw-Hill, 1980.

Russell, Diana E. H. *The Secret Trauma: Incest in the Lives of Girls and Women*. New York: Basic Books, 1986.

Sackville-West, Victoria Mary [Vita]. Diary of a journey to France with Virginia Woolf in 1928. The Henry W. and Albert A. Berg Collection of English and American Literature, the New York Public Library, Astor, Lenox and Tilden Foundations.

———. Extracts from her diaries, Harold Nicolson's diaries, and Vita's letters to Harold and his replies, concerning Virginia Woolf, made in 1976 by Nigel Nicolson. Copy of a typescript provided by Nigel Nicolson to the author.

———. *The Letters of Vita Sackville-West to Virginia Woolf*. Ed. by Louise DeSalvo and Mitchell A. Leaska. New York: William Morrow, 1985.

Schlack, Beverly Ann. *Continuing Presences: Virginia Woolf's Use of Literary Allusion*. University Park: Pennsylvania State University Press, 1979.

———. "Fathers in General: The Patriarchy in Virginia Woolf's Fiction." In *Virginia Woolf*, ed. by Jane Marcus, pp. 55–77.

Scott, Sir Walter. *The Antiquary*. New York: A. L. Burt, n.d.

Scudder, Vida D. *Le Morte D'Arthur of Sir Thomas Malory and Its Sources*. New York: E. P. Dutton, 1917.

Sears, Sallie. "Theater of War: Virginia Woolf's *Between the Acts*." In *Virginia Woolf*, ed. by Jane Marcus, pp. 212–35.

Shanley, Mary Lyndon. "'One Must Ride Behind': Married Women's Rights and the Divorce Act of 1857." *Victorian Studies* 25 (Spring 1982): 355–76.

Sheleff, Leon Shaskolsky. *Generations Apart: Adult Hostility to Youth*. New York: McGraw-Hill, 1981.

Showalter, Elaine. "Critical Cross-Dressing: Male Feminists and the Woman of the Year." *Raritan* (Fall 1983), pp. 130–49.

————. "Family Secrets and Domestic Subversion: Rebellion in the Novels of the 1860s." In *The Victorian Family*, ed. by Anthony S. Wohl, pp. 101–16.

————. *The Female Malady: Women, Madness, and English Culture, 1830–1980.* New York: Pantheon Books, 1985.

————. *A Literature of Their Own: British Women Novelists from Brontë to Lessing.* Princeton: Princeton University Press, 1977.

Sidel, Ruth. *Women and Children Last: The Plight of Poor Women in Affluent America.* New York: Viking, 1986.

Silver, Brenda. "*Three Guineas* Before and After: Further Answers to Correspondents." In *Virginia Woolf*, ed. by Jane Marcus, pp. 254–76.

————. *Virginia Woolf's Reading Notebooks.* Princeton: Princeton University Press, 1983.

————, ed. "'Anon' and 'The Reader': Virginia Woolf's Last Essays." Ed. with an Introduction and Commentary. *Twentieth Century Literature* 25, Virginia Woolf Issue (Fall/Winter 1979): 356–441.

Skura, Meredith Anne. *The Literary Use of the Psychoanalytic Process.* New Haven: Yale University Press, 1981.

Smith, Catherine F. "*Three Guineas*: Virginia Woolf's Prophecy." In *Virginia Woolf and Bloomsbury*, ed. by Jane Marcus, pp. 225–41.

Smith, Nora Archibald. "The Child of Passionate Temper." *Outlook* 51 (16 March 1895): 429–30.

Smith-Rosenberg, Carroll. *Disorderly Conduct: Visions of Gender in Victorian America.* New York: Alfred A. Knopf, 1985.

Snitow, Ann, Christine Stansell, and Sharon Thompson, eds. *Powers of Desire: The Politics of Sexuality.* New York: Monthly Review Press, 1983.

Spacks, Patricia Meyer. *The Adolescent Idea: Myths of Youth and the Adult Imagination.* New York: Basic Books, 1981.

Spalding, Frances. *Vanessa Bell.* New Haven: Ticknor & Fields, 1983.

Spater, George, and Ian Parsons. *A Marriage of True Minds: An Intimate Portrait of Leonard and Virginia Woolf.* New York: Harcourt Brace Jovanovich, 1977.

Spilka, Mark. *Virginia Woolf's Quarrel with Grieving.* Lincoln: University of Nebraska Press, 1980.

Spivak, Gayatri C. "Unmaking and Making in *To the Lighthouse*." In *Women and Language in Literature and Society*, ed. by Sally McConnell-Ginet et al., pp. 310–27.

Sprague, Claire, ed. *Virginia Woolf: A Collection of Critical Essays.* Englewood Cliffs: Prentice-Hall, 1971.

Squier, Susan. "Mirroring and Mothering: Reflections on the Mirror Encounter in Virginia Woolf's Works." *Twentieth Century Literature* 27 (Fall 1981): 272–88.

————. "The Politics of City Space in *The Years*: Street Love, Pillar Boxes and

Bridges." In *New Feminist Essays on Virginia Woolf*, ed. by Jane Marcus, pp. 216–37.

————. "A Track of Our Own: Typescript Drafts of *The Years*." In *Virginia Woolf*, ed. by Jane Marcus, pp. 198–211.

Squier, Susan Merrill. *Virginia Woolf and London: The Sexual Politics of the City*. Chapel Hill: University of North Carolina Press, 1985.

Stemerick, Martine. "The Madonna's Clay Feet: Julia Stephen's Anti-Egalitarian Ideals." Unpublished paper.

————. "Virginia's Early Education." Unpublished paper.

————. "Virginia Woolf and Julia Stephen: The Distaff Side of History." Unpublished paper.

Stephen, Adrian. *The "Dreadnought" Hoax*. London: Hogarth Press, 1936.

————. 64 letters to Vanessa Stephen [Bell]. 20 May [1915?]–11 June 1947. The Henry W. and Albert A. Berg Collection of English and American Literature of the New York Public Library, Astor, Lenox and Tilden Foundations.

————. 5 letters to Virginia Woolf. 15 June [1910]–14 September 1910. The Henry W. and Albert A. Berg Collection of English and American Literature of the New York Public Library, Astor, Lenox and Tilden Foundations.

S[tephen]., J[ames]. K[enneth]. *Lapsus Calami*. Cambridge: Macmillan & Bowes, 1891.

Stephen, J[ames]. K[enneth]. Letters to Stella Duckworth. The Henry W. and Albert A. Berg Collection of English and American Literature of the New York Public Library, Astor, Lenox and Tilden Foundations.

Stephen, Julia. "The Mysterious Voice." In *Stories for Children, Essays for Adults*, by Julia Stephen, ed. by Diane Gillespie and Elizabeth Steele.

————. *Notes from Sick Rooms*. Introduction by Constance Hunting. Orono, Maine: Puckerbrush Press, 1980. Reprint of London edition of 1883.

————. *Stories for Children, Essays for Adults: The Unpublished Writings of Julia Stephen*. Ed. by Diane Gillespie and Elizabeth Steele. Syracuse, N.Y.: Syracuse University Press, 1987.

Stephen, Karin. *The Wish to Fall Ill: A Study of Psychoanalysis and Medicine*. Cambridge: Cambridge University Press, 1960.

Stephen, Sir Leslie. 442 letters to Julia Stephen, [before 31 March 1877?] to 16 April 1895. The Henry W. and Albert A. Berg Collection of English and American Literature of the New York Public Library, Astor, Lenox and Tilden Foundations.

————. *The Life of Henry Fawcett*. London: Smith, Elder, 1885.

————. *The Life of Sir James Fitzjames Stephen*. New York: G. P. Putnam's Sons; London: Smith, Elder, 1895.

————. *Sir Leslie Stephen's Mausoleum Book*. Introduction by Alan Bell. Oxford: Clarendon Press, 1977.

————. *Swift*. London: Macmillan, 1882. Republished, Detroit: Gale Research Company, 1968.

Stoneman, Elizabeth. Unpublished paper on *To the Lighthouse*, 1987.

Strachey, Julia, and Frances Partridge. *Julia: A Portrait of Julia Strachey by Herself and Frances Partridge*. Boston: Little, Brown, 1983.

Summit, Roland. "Beyond Belief: The Reluctant Discovery of Incest." In *Women's Sexual Experience*, ed. by Martha Kirkpatrick, pp. 127–50.

Symonds, John Addington. *The Memoirs of John Addington Symonds*. Ed. by Phyllis Grosskurth. Chicago: University of Chicago Press, 1984.

Szasz, Thomas S. *The Myth of Mental Illness: Foundations of a Theory of Personal Conduct*. Rev. ed. New York: Harper & Row, 1974.

Szladits, Lola L. "The Life, Character and Opinions of Flush the Spaniel." *Bulletin of the New York Public Library* 74 (April 1970): 211–18.

Taylor, Karen J. "Venereal Disease in Nineteenth-Century Children." *Journal of Psychohistory* 12 (Spring 1985): 431–63.

Temple, Ruth Z. "Never Say 'I': *To the Lighthouse* as Vision and Confession." In *Virginia Woolf*, ed. by Claire Sprague, pp. 90–100.

Thomas, J. M. Letters to Violet Dickinson, 14 September [1913] and 9 April 1915. The Henry W. and Albert A. Berg Collection of English and American Literature of the New York Public Library, Astor, Lenox and Tilden Foundations.

Transue, Pamela J. *Virginia Woolf and the Politics of Style*. Albany: State University of New York Press, 1986.

Trautmann, Joanne. *The Jessamy Brides: The Friendship of Virginia Woolf and V. Sackville-West*. University Park: Pennsylvania State University, 1973.

Trombley, Stephen. *'All that Summer She was Mad': Virginia Woolf and Her Doctors*. London: Junction Books, 1981.

Tufte, Virginia, and Barbara Meyerhoff, eds. *Changing Images of the Family*. New Haven: Yale University Press, 1979.

Vicinus, Martha. "Sexuality and Power: A Review of Current Work in the History of Sexuality." *Feminist Studies* 8 (Spring 1982): 133–56.

———, ed. *Suffer and Be Still: Women in the Victorian Age*. Bloomington: Indiana University Press, 1972.

———, ed. A *Widening Sphere: Changing Roles of Victorian Women*. Bloomington: Indiana University Press, 1977.

Walkowitz, Judith R. "Jack the Ripper and the Myth of Male Violence." *Feminist Studies* 8 (Fall 1982): 542–74.

———. "Male Vice and Female Virtue: Feminism and the Politics of Prostitution in Nineteenth-Century Britain." In *Powers of Desire*, ed. by Ann Snitow et al., pp. 419–38.

———. *Prostitution and Victorian Society: Women, Class and the State*. Cambridge: Cambridge University Press, 1980.

———. "Science, Feminism, and Romance: The Men and Women's Club, 1885–1889." *History Workshop* 21 (Spring 1986): 37–59.

Wallace, Marjorie. *The Silent Twins*. New York: Prentice Hall, 1986.

Warner, Eric, ed. *Virginia Woolf: A Centenary Perspective.* New York: St. Martin's Press, 1984.

Warren, Joyce W. *The American Narcissus: Individualism and Women in Nineteenth-Century American Fiction.* New Brunswick, N.J.: Rutgers University Press, 1984.

Weeks, Jeffrey. *Sex, Politics and Society: The Regulation of Sexuality since 1800.* London: Longman, 1981.

Welter, Barbara. *Dimity Convictions: The American Woman in the Nineteenth Century.* Athens: Ohio State University Press, 1976.

White, Barbara A. *Growing Up Female: Adolescent Girlhood in American Fiction.* Westport, Conn.: Greenwood Press, 1985.

Wohl, Anthony S. "Sex and the Single Room: Incest among the Victorian Working Classes." In *The Victorian Family,* ed. by Anthony S. Wohl, pp. 197–216.

———, ed. *The Victorian Family: Structure and Stresses.* New York: St. Martin's Press, 1978.

Wolf, Ernest S., and Ina Wolf. "We Perished Each Alone: A Psychoanalytical Commentary on Virginia Woolf's *To the Lighthouse.*" *International Review of Psycho-Analysis* 6 (1979): 37–47.

Woolf, Leonard. *Beginning Again: An Autobiography of the Years 1911 to 1918.* New York: Harcourt Brace Jovanovich, 1963.

———. *Downhill All the Way: An Autobiography of the Years 1919 to 1939.* New York: Harcourt, Brace & World, 1967.

Woolf, Virginia. "Am I a Snob?" In *Moments of Being,* pp. 203–20.

———. "'Anon' and 'The Reader': Virginia Woolf's Last Essays." Ed., Introduction, and Commentary by Brenda R. Silver. *Twentieth Century Literature* 25, Virginia Woolf Issue (Fall/Winter 1979): 356–441.

———. "'The Antiquary.'" Holograph draft, in "Essays, 1924." The Henry W. and Albert A. Berg Collection of English and American Literature of the New York Public Library, Astor, Lenox and Tilden Foundations.

———. "'Aurora Leigh.'" In *The Second Common Reader.* New York: Harcourt, Brace & World, 1932, 1960.

———. [Autobiographical fragment, "The tea table was the centre of Victorian family life . . . ,"]. The fragment was probably written in October 1940. The Henry W. and Albert A. Berg Collection of the New York Public Library, Astor, Lenox and Tilden Foundations.

———. *Between the Acts.* New York: Harcourt Brace Jovanovich, 1969. Originally published London: Hogarth Press, 1941.

———. *The Captain's Death Bed and Other Essays.* New York: Harcourt Brace Jovanovich, 1950.

———. Christmas, 1904–31 May 1905. The Henry W. and Albert A. Berg Collection of English and American Literature of the New York Public Library, Astor, Lenox and Tilden Foundations.

———. *A Cockney's Farming Experiences* and *The Experiences of a Pater-*

familias. Ed., Introduction by Suzanne Henig. San Diego: San Diego State University Press, 1972.

———. *The Common Reader: First Series*. New York: Harcourt, Brace & World, 1925, 1953.

———. *Contemporary Writers*. Preface by Jean Guiguet. New York: Harcourt, Brace & World, 1965.

———. *The Death of the Moth and Other Essays*. New York: Harcourt Brace Jovanovich, 1942, 1970.

———. Diary. April 1906–1–14 August 1908. The Henry W. and Albert A. Berg Collection of English and American Literature of the New York Public Library, Astor, Lenox and Tilden Foundations.

———. Diary. Cornwall. 1905. The Henry W. and Albert A. Berg Collection of English and American Literature of the New York Public Library, Astor, Lenox and Tilden Foundations.

———. *The Diary of Virginia Woolf*. Ed. by Anne Olivier Bell. Vol. 1, 1915–1919. New York: Harcourt Brace Jovanovich, 1976.

———. *The Diary of Virginia Woolf*. Ed. by Anne Olivier Bell, assisted by Andrew McNeillie. Vol. 2, 1920–1924. New York: Harcourt Brace Jovanovich, 1978.

———. *The Diary of Virginia Woolf*. Ed. by Anne Olivier Bell, assisted by Andrew McNeillie. Vol. 3, 1925–1930. New York: Harcourt Brace Jovanovich, 1980.

———. *The Diary of Virginia Woolf*. Ed. by Anne Olivier Bell, assisted by Andrew McNeillie. Vol. 4, 1931–1935. New York: Harcourt Brace Jovanovich, 1982.

———. *The Diary of Virginia Woolf*. Ed. by Anne Olivier Bell, assisted by Andrew McNeillie. Vol. 5, 1936–1941. New York: Harcourt Brace Jovanovich, 1984.

———. "The Duchess and the Jeweller." In *A Haunted House and Other Stories*, pp. 94–102.

———. 1897 Diary. The Henry W. and Albert A. Berg Collection of English and American Literature of the New York Public Library, Astor, Lenox and Tilden Foundations.

———. "Ellen Terry." In *The Moment and Other Essays*, pp. 205–12.

———. "Essays, 1924." The Henry W. and Albert A. Berg Collection of English and American Literature of the New York Public Library, Astor, Lenox and Tilden Foundations.

———. *Flush: A Biography*. New York: Harcourt Brace Jovanovich, 1933, 1961.

———. *Freshwater: A Comedy*. Ed. by Lucio P. Ruotolo. New York: Harcourt Brace Jovanovich, 1976.

———. "Friendships Gallery." Ed. by Ellen Hawkes *Twentieth Century Literature* 25 (Fall/Winter 1979): 273–302.

———. "Gas at Abbotsford." In *The Moment and Other Essays*, pp. 56–62.

————. Greece/Italy Diary. 14 September [1906]–25 April 1909. Original in the British Library. Typescript carbon copy in the Henry W. and Albert A. Berg Collection of English and American Literature of the New York Public Library, Astor, Lenox and Tilden Foundations.

————. *Granite and Rainbow.* New York: Harcourt Brace Jovanovich, 1958.

————. *A Haunted House and Other Stories.* New York: Harcourt, Brace & World, 1921, 1944.

————. "'Haworth': November, 1904." Holograph of essay, unsigned and undated, 6 pages. The Henry W. and Albert A. Berg Collection of English and American Literature of the New York Public Library.

————. "The Humane Art." In *The Death of the Moth and Other Essays,* pp. 58–63.

————. Hyde Park Gate Diary. 1903? The Henry W. and Albert A. Berg Collection of English and American Literature of the New York Public Library, Astor, Lenox and Tilden Foundations.

————. "The Journal of Mistress Joan Martyn." Ed. by Susan M. Squier and Louise A. DeSalvo. *Twentieth Century Literature* 25 (Fall/Winter 1979): 240–69.

————. "Julia Margaret Cameron." In *Victorian Photographs of Famous Men & Fair Women,* by Julia Margaret Cameron, pp. 13–19.

————. "Lappin and Lapinova." In *A Haunted House and Other Stories,* pp. 68–78.

————. "The Leaning Tower." In *The Moment and Other Essays,* pp. 128–54.

————. "The Legacy." In *A Haunted House and Other Stories,* pp. 126–35.

————. "Leslie Stephen." In *The Captain's Death Bed and Other Essays,* pp. 69–75.

————. *The Letters of Virginia Woolf.* Vol. 1, 1888–1912. (Virginia Stephen). Ed. by Nigel Nicolson and Joanne Trautmann. New York: Harcourt Brace Jovanovich, 1975. Originally published in England as *The Flight of the Mind.*

————. *The Letters of Virginia Woolf.* Vol. 2, 1912–1922. Ed. by Nigel Nicolson and Joanne Trautmann. New York: Harcourt Brace Jovanovich, 1976. Originally published in England as *The Question of Things Happening.*

————. *The Letters of Virginia Woolf.* Vol. 3, 1923–1928. Ed. by Nigel Nicolson and Joanne Trautmann. New York: Harcourt Brace Jovanovich, 1977. Originally published in England as *A Change of Perspective.*

————. *The Letters of Virginia Woolf.* Vol. 4, 1929–1931. Ed. by Nigel Nicolson and Joanne Trautmann. New York: Harcourt Brace Jovanovich, 1978. Originally published in England as *A Reflection of the Other Person.*

————. *The Letters of Virginia Woolf.* Vol. 5, 1932–1935. Ed. by Nigel Nicolson and Joanne Trautmann. New York: Harcourt Brace Jovanovich, 1979. Originally published in England as *The Sickle Side of the Moon.*

————. *The Letters of Virginia Woolf.* Vol. 6, 1936–1941. Ed. by Nigel Nicolson and Joanne Trautmann. New York: Harcourt Brace Jovanovich, 1980. Originally published in England as *Leave the Letters Till We're Dead*.

———. "Lewis Carroll." In *The Moment and Other Essays*, pp. 81–83.

———. *The London Scene*. New York: Random House, 1975.

———. MH/A.26, Monks House Papers. The Virginia Woolf Manuscripts from the Monks House Papers at the University of Sussex. Brighton, England: Harvester Press Microform Publications, 1985.

———. *The Moment and Other Essays*. New York: Harcourt Brace Jovanovich, 1948.

———. *Moments of Being: Unpublished Autobiographical Writings*. Ed., Introduction, and Notes by Jeanne Schulkind. 2d ed. New York: Harcourt Brace Jovanovich, 1985.

———. *Mrs. Dalloway*. New York: Harcourt, Brace, 1925.

———. "Mrs. Thrale." In *The Moment and Other Essays*, pp. 50–55.

———. "The New Biography." In *Granite and Rainbow*, pp. 149–55.

———. *Night and Day*. New York: Harcourt Brace Jovanovich, 1920, 1948.

———. "Old Bloomsbury." In *Moments of Being*, pp. 179–202.

———. *The Pargiters: The Novel-Essay Portion of The Years*. Ed., Introduction by Mitchell A. Leaska. New York: New York Public Library and Readex Books, 1977.

———. *Pointz Hall: The Earlier and Later Typescripts of Between the Acts*. Ed., Introduction, Annotations, and an Afterword by Mitchell A. Leaska. New York: University Publications, 1983.

———. "Professions for Women." In *Death of the Moth and Other Essays*. New York: Harcourt Brace Jovanovich, 1942, 1970.

———. "Reminiscences." In *Moments of Being*, pp. 25–60.

———. *Roger Fry: A Biography*. New York: Harcourt Brace Jovanovich, 1940, 1968.

———. *A Room of One's Own*. New York: Harcourt, Brace & World, 1957.

———. "'A Room with a View.'" Review of *A Room with a View*, by E. M. Forster. In *Contemporary Writers*.

———. "Sara Coleridge." *The Death of the Moth and Other Essays*, pp. 111–18.

———. "The Searchlight." In *A Haunted House and Other Stories*, pp. 120–25.

———. *The Second Common Reader*. New York: Harcourt, Brace & World, 1932, 1960.

———. "Sir Walter Scott." In *The Moment and Other Essays*, pp. 56–78.

———. "A Sketch of the Past." In *Moments of Being*, pp. 61–160.

———. "Swift's 'Journal to Stella.'" In *The Second Common Reader*, pp. 58–67.

———. "The tea table was the centre of Victorian family life." The Henry W. and Albert A. Berg Collection of English and American Literature of the New York Public Library, Astor, Lenox and Tilden Foundations.

———. "A Terrible Tragedy in a Duckpond: a Note of Correction and Addition to the Above. by One of the Drowned." MH/A10. The Virginia Woolf Manuscripts from the Monks House Papers at the University of Sussex. Brighton, England: Harvester Press Microform Publications, 1985.

————. *To the Lighthouse.* New York: Harcourt, Brace, 1927.

————. *To the Lighthouse: The original holograph draft.* Ed. by Susan Dick. Toronto: University of Toronto Press, 1982.

————. "Thoughts on Peace in an Air Raid." In *The Death of the Moth and Other Essays,* pp. 243–48.

————. *Three Guineas.* New York: Harcourt, Brace & World, 1938, 1966.

————. "22 Hyde Park Gate." In *Moments of Being,* pp. 162–78.

————. *The Virginia Woolf Manuscripts from the Monks House Papers at the University of Sussex.* Brighton, England: Harvester Press Microform Publications, 1985.

————. Warboys Summer Holidays 1899. The Henry W. and Albert A. Berg Collection of English and American Literature of the New York Public Library, Astor, Lenox and Tilden Foundations.

————. *The Waves.* New York: Harcourt, Brace & World, 1923, 1950.

————. *The Waves: The two holograph drafts.* Ed. by J. W. Graham. Toronto: University of Toronto Press, in association with the University of Western Ontario, 1976.

————. *The Years.* New York: Harcourt, Brace & World, 1937, 1965.

Zwerdling, Alex. *Virginia Woolf and the Real World.* Berkeley: University of California Press, 1986.

Index